The Engaging Reader

The Engaging Reader

Third Edition

Anne Mills King
Prince George's Community College

Allyn and Bacon
Boston   London   Toronto   Sydney   Tokyo   Singapore

Vice President: Eben W. Ludlow
Editorial Assistant: Morgan Lance
Manufacturing Buyer: Megan Cochran
Marketing Manager: Lisa Kimball
Editorial-Production Service: Electronic Publishing Services Inc.
Cover Administrator: Linda Knowles

WordPerfect Version 6.1 Reference Manual (pages 188–193), © 1994
Novell, Inc. All Rights Reserved. Used with Permission.

Acknowledgments appear on pages 397-401, which constitute an exten-
sion of the copyright page.

Library of Congress Cataloging-in-Publication Data
The engaging reader / [edited by] Anne Mills King. — 3rd ed.
    p. cm.
  Includes index.
  ISBN 0-205-17423-X
  1. College readers. 2. English language—Rhetoric. I. King,
Anne Mills.
PE1417.E47 1995
808'.0427—dc20   95-34846
                                               CIP

Printed in the United States of America
10 9 8 7 6 5 4 3 2 1   99 98 97 96 95

Contents

Part Two

THE ORDINARY WORLD: OTHER PEOPLE AND PLACES   **65**

Part Three
DIVERSITY: VARIETIES OF SELF   113

Part Four

HERITAGE: DIVERSITY OF CULTURE 173

Part Five
CONTROVERSIES   217

1. Poverty

2. Preservation

3. Civil Rights

4. A Dilemma: The Right to Die

Part Six

RISKS: TAKING CHANCES   281

Rhetorical Contents

Aimed at instructors who would like to have a guide to the rhetorical categories of the selections in *The Engaging Reader*, the following contents indicate the principal strategy in each selection's composition. Some selections fit under more than one category; hardly any writer deliberately sets out to compose purely in one style.

Narration

Description

Classification

Illustration/Example

Process

Argumentation

Some selections belong in genres of writing:

Autobiography

Letters

Diaries, Journals

Legends

Orations, Informal Talk

Interviews

Book and Play Reviews

Poems

Public Documents

Writing and Media

Preface:
To The Instructor

The third edition of *The Engaging Reader*, like the first two, is a multi-cultural reader designed for "nontraditional" students, who have now become the norm in both community and four-year colleges. Included in this group are students whose "cultural literacy" is minimal, not by choice, but because their education has been spotty: unmotivated eighteen-year-olds, extremely motivated older, working students, returning women, recent immigrants, military personnel, seniors, upwardly mobile inner-city minorities, and honors students getting ready to transfer to the university. These students need empowerment, not what Louisa May Alcott called "moral pap for the young."

These new students add their own diverse perspectives to the classroom experience. *The Engaging Reader* intends to use today's classroom diversity to the fullest, thus benefitting both the new students and the traditional college-age students. You have in front of you a book that engages developmental or regular composition students in a journey from passivity to connectedness in their reading and writing.

Beginning with the first edition, I developed a reader arranged by themes because themes generate curiosity and often interest students in reading selections on their own. I found that students in beginning composition classes invariably learn to write rather sterile but perfectly organized themes—about nothing. Yet their own lives were full of interest and excitement. Out there in their world, in the newspaper and magazine fiction, sports articles, and editorials; in diaries, letters and advertisements, in speeches and public documents, and on television and in electoral campaigns, appear samples of the fascinating, even controversial matter they can read with involvement and interest and respond to with verve and style. *The Engaging Reader* offers all these types of selections in addition to essays.

Many of the selections in *The Engaging Reader* fit into this scheme as models for students to follow in becoming more aware of both themselves and of the society surrounding them. Their minds need to be stretched by challenging reading and their writing style enlivened by some exciting assignments. The Vocabulary sections ("Engaging the Text") are a special help, especially for international students and recent immigrants, to make their involvement more meaningful to them. One reviewer called it "a complete cultural indoctrination in cameo."

The text contains 71 short readings and follows a thematic organization. The Annotated Table of Contents reveals an overall pattern of progression in ways of knowing, from the self, to other people, to sharing, to creating, analyzing, and taking risks. Assignments may be given in that sequence, selecting readings at appropriate levels from within each of the six sections. Each thematic section includes readings of differing sophistication with writing assignments ranging from simple narration and description to complex argumentation and research. Thus classes of varying ability can use the text profitably, without the self-conscious feeling of being steered to an "easy reader." The Rhetorical Contents aids instructors who want examples of a particular rhetorical pattern. Since the book intends to engage readers from the start, a frequent rhetorical type is narration. Description, comparison/contrast, definition, analysis, classification, illustration, description, process, and argumentation represent ways to challenge students and open up to them diverse methods of thinking and writing in and out of academia.

The book starts with a section addressed to students on writing and reading—simple suggestions for making a book or article their own, along with a sample essay by a recent student. It includes the writing on writing of a popular mystery novelist, and an essay on keeping diaries by another well-known writer. They contain new material for active reading and encourage the use of a reading journal to make the bridge from reading to writing.

Reading Selections

Selections run the gamut from advice on writing a friendly letter by a well known author to advertisements, newspaper and magazine editorials on current subjects, and new material on the process of writing. A large proportion of the writings are by women, African Americans, Hispanic Americans, Native Americans, and other minority writers, expressing views from contentment to rage.

Reading selections aim for entertainment as well as usefulness. They represent a mixture of writing types: letters, speeches, and textbook excerpts. To represent fiction, the book contains short selections from longer works of fiction. It also offers a book review, a play review, feature articles, travel articles, and interviews. "How To" articles appear also, as well as editorials. Something loosely called a "report" or "reportage"—a factual account without editorializing—shows in several selections. Selections from word processing manuals and a piece on the Internet develop new ways of writing and communicating. A legend, several poems, and two important public documents that provide some weighty meat for discussion round out the material.

The subjects covered branch through all kinds of human endeavor from sport to civil rights. Headnotes introduce the authors and set each piece in context. Following each selection, exercises in using, defining, and analyzing unfamiliar words ("Engaging the Text") add to vocabulary and start the writing process. Then questions for discussion, for journal writing, or for peer group activities ("Engaging the Reader") involve both the individual student and peer writing groups and reinforce reading comprehension. Suggestions for paragraph- and essay-length pieces ("The Engaged Writer") also accompany selections. Information on ways to use journal-writing and peer-group techniques appears in the *Instructors' Manual*, along with a bibliography on writing.

Paired and Clustered Selections

Though many selections provide unusual and different views of the same topics and are cross-referenced outside of the thematic arrangement, some planned pairs or focus groups of selections give different perspectives on the same theme. To pique students' interest and elicit committed, involved writing, these range from different personal world views to scientific analyses.

Writer's Guide

In addition, the final section in the text, "Writer's Guide," has been augmented to increase the focus on the connections between reading and writing. It provides eleven sections of helpful "survival skill" information on writing. The topics covered are:

Writing a Summary of What You Read
"How to Write a Personal Letter" by Garrison Keillor, with a student letter modelled on his advice.
Writing a Letter to the Editor
Looking Up Words in a Dictionary
Finding a Topic to Write On (including a new search strategy and a list of topics from "The Engaged Writer" sections of the book)
"How to Start" by Robert Pirsig
Getting Started
How to use E-Mail, CD-Rom, and Internet to Improve Your Writing (with samples from instruction manuals)
Backing Up What You Say (including a sample documented essay)
A Guide for Composition Revision
Concluding; How to End What You Write

These sections, cross-referenced throughout the text, provide help for the student as well as possible class assignments. They need not be assigned in sequence; in fact, they may be referred to from any point in the book.

New To This Edition

The idea of paired selections from earlier editions has been expanded to gather definite clusters of three or four related selections that can be assigned together, giving varied perspectives on issues like homelessness and poverty, race relations and civil rights, the preservation of the human environment, and the process of writing. This last emphasis on writing has been strengthened by additional materials in the introduction, where the writing process is examined, and in the Writers' Guide, where writing and communicating with computers adds new dimensions to the writing and composing process.

Genres of writing have also benefited by revision: interviews, technical manuals, student work, and diaries have been augmented and strengthened. The portion of the Writers' Guide on library research has been completely revised because of the new on-line research tools available, and the dictionary exercises have also benefited from thorough revision. A new section: HERITAGE: DIVERSITY OF CULTURE, replaces the former section on WORK, and gathers together from other sections of the book selections on some of the diverse cultures that make up the world, such as music, midwives, and the clashing of cultures that often results in wars and the suffering of innocents.

In "Controversies," grouped writing selections show various postures toward the controversial issues of mercy killing, historic and ecological preservation, the homeless and welfare, and civil rights. Finally, in the section entitled "Risks," two Declarations of Rights, from the U.S. Constitution and the Seneca Falls Resolutions, differ markedly. More student writing gives models to follow. The Instructors' Manual accompanying *The Engaging Reader* gives further examples of paired and clustered selections and offers ways to use them in the classroom.

The thematic organization from self to making connections and taking risks continues in this edition, as well as the feminist, multicultural consciousness evident in earlier editions. The book still considers the students in your classes today as experienced, knowledgeable people who know that they need work on reading and writing, but who expect to be treated with dignity and with some recognition of the rich and varied lives they have already led.

The Engaging Reader, therefore, can stand as the main component of a writing course, along with a simple, basic handbook. I hope that teaching and learning from the Third Edition will be a pleasant experience for you and your student writers.

Acknowledgments

I particularly want to credit the expertise and enthusiasm of my former editor at Macmillan, Barbara Heinssen. Now that Eben Ludlow has taken over my book, I am still in good hands. He and Morgan Lance of Allyn & Bacon have shepherded this edition with ease and style. Colleagues at Prince George's Community College who shared their knowledge with me during the book's history give "faculty" a good name: Susan Roth, Margaret Warner, Marianne Rough, and John Bartles from the Library; Diana Hacker, Mary Brown, and Mary Stevenson, my colleagues in English; and former colleagues and present friends Chris McMahon, Joyce Magnotto, and Sandra Kurtinitis, who shared the early growing pains of this book.

Without the constructive criticism of readers, a textbook might exist in a vacuum. Those reviewers whose suggestions resulted in positive contributions to this edition are Stephanie A. Bertoni, Butte College, and Shirley Sawdon, South Puget Sound Community College. Many students from my own classes and from colleges around the country also encouraged this new edition with perceptive comments. Colleen Quinn gave the final expert touch to the production of this edition. I'm grateful to all these people for their continued support for *The Engaging Reader.*

A. M. K.

Introduction

The Joys of Reading and Writing

As you grew to adulthood, you ceased being passive and dependent, and you developed connections with others. Your horizons expanded with knowledge of the diversity of other people and eye-opening experiences of school and work. Finally, as a thinking adult, you make choices in <u>controversial matters</u> and take risks as a result of those choices. Awareness of different points of view will produce <u>depth</u> of vision—the way two eyes do. That is what this book offers: different ways of looking at objects and ideas to give an in-depth view of the world.

The following section and those in the "Writer's Guide" in the back of the book address you directly. These sections give you practical advice on basic reading and writing tools and provide help for problems you may encounter as you read this book and work through the exercises. The "Writer's Guide" sections are cross-referenced throughout the book so you can turn to them whenever you need help. They are designed to aid you as you turn from reading, responding, and discussing to writing essays, papers, reports, essay examinations, and reports on research. You will need to consult a basic handbook to answer questions on grammar, spelling, syntax, and ways to quote and use material. You should also invest in a <u>good collegiate dictionary</u>. Your instructor may either assign or recommend these. You probably use a computer at work, at home, or at school. Investigate the tools (Speller, Grammar Checker) that can help you as you write using word processor software.

Reading Anything

British novelist, essayist, and feminist Virginia Woolf (1882–1941) gave a talk to college students called "How Should One Read a Book?" She insisted that the title of her talk was a question, not an answer. She thought, instead, that "the only advice, indeed, that one person can give another about reading is to take no advice, to follow your own instincts, to use your own reason, to come to your own conclusions" (*Collected Essays*, vol. 2: 1). Following her own advice, she said, allowed her to make a few suggestions about reading books. She felt strongly that a reader must be free to read and judge and value books.

This is the spirit in which I offer this collection, with hopes that you will read and enjoy. But—how is one to read a book—or even a single article?

You approach library shelves laden with all sorts of reading: fiction, biography, how-to articles, argument, philosophy. How can you choose what to read and then absorb all those words?

I recall getting a library card in a foreign country and finding a couple of favorite authors to read. By the end of this reading sprint, formal study appeared on the track, and other authors and other subjects pushed the two friendly writers out of sight for a while. But I never forgot them. They taught me this: read what you like and find fascinating; follow a familiar name and grow from there. In reading a paragraph, ignore the unfriendly words, the words you don't know, and try to figure out the sense of the story or argument, skimming the first time around just for sense. Then go back, underline unfamiliar words, pick out some to look up in the dictionary. You don't have to look up every word at once; you can come back later. Don't be afraid to "occupy the book . . . stomp around in it" as Anatole Broyard wrote in the *New York Times* (April 10, 1988). (Turn to "Looking Up Words in a Dictionary.")

Whatever you read, you will need boldness and imagination. Do not hesitate to jump after a new idea. Do not think that you have to understand everything before you leap. The first stage in reading is simply to get started. Learn to make friends with characters, to satisfy your curiosity about their lives and their dreams by reading on to the end. But don't read only to become familiar with a specific writer or character. Read to stretch and exercise your own imagination. There is nothing wrong with stopping now and then, either, looking out of the window, dreaming a little, making a cup of coffee, jotting a note—and then going back refreshed, perhaps with more insight than before.

Why read? There are some useful reasons: to get information, to pass a course, to "keep up" with the news. But somehow, as Virginia Woolf says, some occupations "are good in themselves, and some pleasures . . . are final." Reading is one. So make some of these essays your own, as Andrew Cain did with his reading in "Scribbling," the article that follows.

ANDREW CAIN

Scribbling

This short newspaper article follows the ideas discussed in the preceding section, "Reading Anything," by proposing a method of "scribbling" your way through a book. Making a book your own can add dimensions to reading. It can transform reading into a hobby and encourage self-expression. In addition, scribbling provides creative and dynamic ways to enjoy reading. Try Andrew Cain's method as you read this book.

Cain's article appeared in a small Shenandoah Valley weekly paper. Good writing can crop up everywhere: in mass-market magazines, scholarly journals, and in small-town papers. It also can be found in advertisements such as Garrison Keillor's "How to Write a Personal Letter" in Writer's Guide.

So tell me, have you scribbled any good books lately?   1

Book scribbling, I should explain, is its own art form, a hybrid   2 of two other pleasurable pastimes—reading and writing.

I became a scribbler in college, where an English professor   3 urged us to buy books and read with pen in hand. Using this technique, he said, you can make notes in the margins, <u>underline for emphasis</u> or react (!) to interesting passages.

The other night I spent some time legitimizing my bookshelf by   4 leafing through the dustiest volumes. In a number of tiresome textbooks I came across some revealing reactions.

5   In a Sociology book, "People, Power, Change," I apparently took issue with a so-called expert's explanation for social unrest in the 1960's:

6   "According to Feuren," the text says, "student activists take out their parental hatred on parental surrogates such as university administrators, by mounting political protests based on their irrational psychological motivations."

7   In the margin I wrote, "C'mon buddy, give me a break."

8   In a course on English literature I had procrastinated to the point where I had to review an entire syllabus of material in one night. I didn't get very far.

9   After wading through the musty musings of Thomas De Quincey for two hours I had littered passages with notations such as, "vain S.O.B.", "who cares?" and "What a Jerk!"

10   Other college assignments gave way to midnight sarcasm.

11   Midway through Shakespeare's epic romance, *Antony and Cleopatra*, a messenger brings Cleo bad tidings. The queen is not pleased.

12   "Horrible villain!" Cleo cries, "I'll spurne thine eyes like balls before me. I'll unhair thy head: Thou shalt be whipped with wire and stewed in brine . . ."

13   Underneath her ravings I wrote, "I think she's mad."

14   Some of the markings become future bookmarks, riveting attention to memorable passages.

15   Tattered Fitzgerald and Hemingway paperbacks are dotted by simple salutes, stars and exclamation points indicative of great stuff.

16   Jotting things down also helps you slog through puzzling paragraphs.

17   William Faulkner's *Absalom, Absalom!* for example, is a wonderful book, but for the first 100 pages I had no idea what was going on. On page 143 I guess I got frustrated as the author went off on his umpteenth tangent.

18   "What is this garbage?" I wrote. "Who is she talking to? Stick to the story!"

19   One of the great things about fiction is that it forces us to use our imaginations. We take part in the creative process by visualizing people and their predicaments, transforming characteristics into characters.

Later in Faulkner's *Absalom* we meet Rosa Coldfield, a proud, 20 embittered spinster, recalling the one love of her life.

"A certain segment of rotten mud walked into my life," she 21 says. "He spoke that which to me was never heard before and shall never be heard again, and walked out. That was all."

Beside the quote I envisioned Rosa with two words, "Bette 22 Davis."

As Lance Morrow of *Time* magazine explained in a recent essay, 23 bookshelves are sacred ground, where the ordinary is made fascinating and heroes come alive.

"Our books are ourselves, our characters, our insulation against 24 those who would take away our books," Morrow wrote.

"There on that wall, Ahab storms. Hamlet mulls. Keats looks 25 into Chapman, who looks at Homer, who looks at Keats. All this happens on a bookshelf continually, while you are walking the dog, or pouting or asleep."

Up on West Main Street there's a billboard from the Virginia 26 Education Association. "Reap the Joys of Life," it says. "Read."

I think I'll scribble through a book this weekend, that is, if I can 27 find a pen.

Engaging the Text

1. Cain, recently a student, does part of his outlining on some pretty pretentious words, some "musty musings" (9) that annoy him. What does he mean by "musty musings"? Does he add to the effect he wants to give the reader by using alliteration (repeating consonants at the beginning of the words)?
2. Cain uses compound words from the same root: visualizing (19) and envisioned (22). What is the root of these two words and how does it apply to the meanings of the words?
3. He also uses words with the same suffix, such as legitimizing (4) and visualizing (19), and irrational and psychological (6). Find other words in this selection that end in -izing and -al and use them in sentences.
4. Cain gives many examples and illustrations to back up what he says. List some of them.
5. Cain quotes from his textbooks and from *Time* magazine to support his points. He introduces each quotation by a statement

of his own. Make a list of these signal phrases for your own use when you quote another writer in a future paper.

Engaging the Reader

1. How did the author discover what he had written in some of his college textbooks?
[9 → 2. What does Cain find useful about this activity?
reminder how of

The Engaged Writer

1. Try brainstorming as if you were a casting director for a film of one of your favorite novels or stories. Assign a part to an actor as Cain does the part of Rosa in Faulkner's *Absalom, Absalom!* Justify your choice.
2. Write an essay around a gerund (participle used as a noun) like "scribbling." Some possibilities are walking, swimming, doodling, lounging, or jogging, or use another gerund (verb + -*ing*).

To Be a Writer

Often you read to discover the main idea of a piece. The annotated table of contents for *The Engaging Reader* describes the main idea of each selection in a sentence or two. Look at some of these and see if the short summary makes you want to read the story. As you read a selection, underline the main idea with two lines; the ideas that support it, or seem less important, with one line. When you reread, you will find the main ideas automatically emphasized. This method, in addition, is extremely useful for studying for a test.

However, you don't read just to study for a test or to pick out ideas. You read to write. Your pencil or keyboard should be just as busy as your hand turning the page. The bridge from active reading to active writing is not wide, but it is there. Some of us just can't get that first idea out of our head, through our hand, and onto the paper. We hear about "writer's block" a lot, but we don't hear about many of the simple ways of getting over that imaginary block.

Some of these ways are purely mechanical, such as underlining. Others, too, are simple and include recording your ideas on a tape recorder and then transcribing them to paper to be edited later. Once you make the connection among eye and ear and hand, you have something on paper that can be edited carefully later on.

The most important part of writing is to have an idea, something to say; the next is being able to organize your ideas coherently. Finally, essential but less important, come the punctuation, spelling, and other easily fixable errors and glitches. Some people act as if the order of importance were reversed. Not so; if you have something to say and care a lot about saying it, your paper will fall into place.

Another technique for getting that first draft on paper is "mind-mapping." On a sheet of paper draw a circle to indicate your main idea. Then cluster balloons around it and write the supporting ideas in those balloons, with connecting lines between them and your main idea. Be loose—don't hesitate to change if something else comes up (there are always erasers). Then, when you start writing, you will have a map of the sections of your paper in front of you.

Other ways to move from being a reader to being a writer involve groups: peer writing groups or editing and critiquing groups. Your classmates, acting as your audience, can be very fair in helping you write. Another technique is to work on your own. A journal is possibly the most useful way to practice writing. Here you might keep a log of your reading, record your random thoughts or ideas, talk to yourself, talk to your journal, work over ideas that come to your mind. People who use word processing often find that method liberating if they have previously found writing difficult. The way ideas flow out onto that screen, the simple way they can be edited, corrected, moved around, or even wiped out completely, often unblocks the most blocked writer.

Reading and writing are interconnected. The "scribbles" you put in your book or on the photocopy of the article are all pieces of writing, just waiting to be strung into a coherent essay or paper. Be sure you can find those sources again. It also helps to take notes in your notebook or journal, on cards, or on your computer. When you do this, write down on each note the page number where you found the material and a short title or author's name to identify the item. Otherwise you will forget where you found it. Many a good point has been left out of a paper because the author couldn't find the reference again. On your computer, name your files so you can find them again.

Quote material exactly as it appears in your source and put it in quotation marks. If you merely summarize, put it all in your own words. Even a few words taken directly from the source need to be set off with quotation marks, or else you risk what is called *plagiarism*. If a note does not have quotation marks, your instructor will assume that you are the author of the statement, so make sure that you are.

All of these suggestions are paths you can take to become a writer (you are one already, though you may not know it!). Editing and correcting errors is the last stage in writing, not the first. It is the stage at which you toss away the obstructions to the path you have constructed by your "scribbling" so that you have a clear way ahead.

Engaging the Text

You will notice in some of the readings in *The Engaging Reader* and elsewhere that articles and essays use an informal language and vocabulary. Others are more like the formal academic essays you may be asked to write in this or other courses. It is helpful to be able to recognize these various levels of speaking and writing and to use them appropriately in your own writing.

For example, with your friends and family you might use slangy speech or writing. Garrison Keillor in his article on "How to Write a Personal Letter" urges you to do just that. He tells you not to worry about sentences, but just to talk on paper. On the other hand, if you were writing a formal report for your boss or a speech for a presentation, you would use a more structured form. You would start with an introduction that stated your main idea and what you were going to use to support it. Then you would follow with body paragraphs that develop those supports. You would end with a conclusion that wrapped it together with both logic and conviction. In that paper you would use a clear but slightly formal vocabulary. Slang terms such as "kids" and "guys," for example, would not fit in that setting. Computer programs like Grammatik® analyze the level of vocabulary and help you establish the right tone (see section from the Grammatik handbook in the Writer's Guide).

On the other hand, sometimes your instructor will ask you to "brainstorm" (orally) or "freewrite" (on paper). In this case, you will write very informally, "off the cuff." Later you may take an idea you thought up this way and develop it into a formal essay.

Engaging the Reader

The most important stages of going from reading to writing, then, are to consolidate, to compare, and to put ideas together. This is the hardest part of preparing to write. It is easy to learn to summarize the main ideas, but harder to make them your own by comparing them with something you've experienced or thought. As you grow intellectually, you first relate only to yourself. Then you emerge from yourself enough to accept ideas from others. Another breakthrough occurs when you begin to question these ideas and to connect one idea with another apparently unrelated one. Finally, you begin to construct ideas on your own.

The human mind works in strange ways. It acts at times like a determined mountain climber, a Jeff Lowe ("On the Edge"). It plugs along on a plateau for some time, apparently taking little in, then suddenly all is upset. A sharp climb, a leap up the precipice, and new ideas rush in. Chaos ensues, but the mind finally reaches a new plateau. As you go about your life, bits of your reading will come back to you, will fall into place, and will release their hidden meanings like a refreshing drink of water to the hiker. The climbs are exhilarating, but so is the plateau where ideas come together. The arrangement of readings and writing suggestions in *The Engaging Reader* follows this growth pattern to lead you from the self to the world and its diversity, and in the end to confront controversy and to take risks.

The Engaged Writer

As you read and discuss the selections in *The Engaging Reader,* your instructor may assign various types of writing from those listed under "The Engaged Writer" heading after each selection. The writing process for these exercises reveals itself in some of the models throughout the book. In this section, the process of writing was compared to mountain climbing—you often feel out of breath, develop aches and pains, and get lost along the way. Finally, though, you get to the top and into the sunlight, with a great view in front of you. *The Engaging Reader* could be your trail map, marking the trees and coding the slopes as you write, revise, write again, and revise again.

In class or on your own as you prewrite, you may do some informal, off-the-cuff, journal-type writing, as Andrew Cain did in the well-titled "Scribbling." Writing informally in a journal, revising little, Cain still showed some organization of his thoughts around a theme or topic: a way to start turning scribbling into composing.

In the next selection, Ray Bradbury, a successful writer, gives examples of stories he felt impelled to write and gives advice on how to move from scribbling to a final paper. He tells us to care passionately about an idea, and then to try it out, first hesitantly, then strongly. In paragraph 12 he warns us that one day we will construct, the next day destroy what we've written. This is the process of writing—like mountain climbing, it is painful, frustrating, but rewarding in the end.

Here's a list of some models in this book to help you on your way as a writer. Look them up as you are assigned writing in each style.

Freewriting, journal writing

Andrew Cain, "Scribbling"
From this simple, easy, laid-back kind of writing, you can jump to more involved styles. But it is good practice. If you were going to be a musician, you would practice every day. This is what you are doing with your journal.

Personal writing: a friendly letter

Garrison Keillor, "How to Write a Personal Letter"
This first jump is easy if you think about your audience—your friend. In a journal you are writing to an audience of one: yourself. In a letter you've expanded that audience outward to a friend who really wants to hear from you.

Argument and thesis: an editorial and letters to the editor

Roger Rosenblatt, "The Quality of Mercy Killing," and letters to the editor responding to this magazine editorial
Add thesis, as Pirsig suggests, to a strongly held argument, as Bradbury advises, and your letter turns into a persuasive essay aimed at a larger audience—the general public.

Sample documented paper: an essay based on letters to the editor of a newspaper

Maribel Etudiante, "Funding Our Heritage" in "Backing Up What You Say"

In this argumentative writing, you want to mention, then logically demolish the argument on one side, at the same time making the audience agree with your side. You look briefly at the opposition, then marshal your strongest points for your side. Make sure the reader knows your stand on the issue clearly.

The Rhetorical Contents lists the readings in *The Engaging Reader* as models for many other kinds of papers you may be asked to write in this class or another. Check these lists for examples of each rhetorical type.

From Reading to Writing

Both reading and writing define our lives. Now, at the end of the twentieth century, we feel that the ability to read parallels the ability to write. In the past, only an elite class could read or write, and society valued only certain kinds of writing: essays, poetry of an elevating nature, sermons, classic authors. The kinds of writing that ordinary people did, such as the letters of pioneer Elinore Pruitt Stewart ("The Arrival at Burnt Fork and Filing a Claim"), were dismissed as light stuff, done by women, not serious. Today we value that writing as part of genuine American history, as we do the slave narratives and the diaries and letters of great and ordinary Americans. The feelings of writer Ray Bradbury about creative writing show the intimate connection between reading and writing.

RAY BRADBURY

The Impulse to Write

Science fiction writer Ray Bradbury has written hundreds of exciting, dynamic stories. In this article he shares his enthusiasm for fiction writing with some advice that applies to all kinds of writing from first draft through almost-finished product to revision. Have something to say, feel passionately about it, and writing will become an impulse you can't stifle!

1   If you are writing without zest, without gusto, without love, without fun, you are only half a writer. . . . For the first thing a writer should be is—excited. He should be a thing of fevers and enthusiasms. Without such vigor, he might as well be out picking peaches or digging ditches. God knows it'd be better for his health.

2   How long has it been since you wrote a story where your real love or your real hatred somehow got onto the paper? When was the last time you dared release a cherished prejudice so it slammed the page like a lightning bolt? What are the best things and the worst things in your life, and when are you going to get around to whispering or shouting them?

3   Wouldn't it be wonderful, for instance, to throw down a copy of *Harper's Bazaar* you happened to be leafing through at the dentist's, and leap to your typewriter and ride off with hilarious anger, attacking their silly and sometimes shocking snobbishness? I did just that a few years back. I came across an issue where the *Bazaar* photographers, with their perverted sense of equality once again utilized natives in a Puerto Rican back-street as props in front of which their starved-looking mannikins postured for the benefit of yet more emaciated half-women in the best salons in the country. The photographs so enraged me I ran, did not walk, to my machine and wrote "Sun and Shadow," the story of an old Puerto Rican who ruins the *Bazaar* photographer's afternoon by sneaking into each picture and dropping his pants.

4   I dare say there are a few of you who would like to have done this job. I had the fun of doing it; the cleansing after-effects of the hoot, the holler, and the great horselaugh. Probably the editors at the *Bazaar* never heard. But a lot of readers did and cried, "Go it, *Bazaar;* go it, Bradbury!" I claim no victory. But there was blood on my gloves when I hung them up.

5   When was the last time you did a story like that, out of pure indignation?

6   When was the last time you were stopped by the police in your neighborhood because you like to walk, and perhaps think, at night? It happened to me just often enough that, irritated, I wrote "The Pedestrian," a story of a time, fifty years from now, when a

man is arrested and taken off for clinical study because he insists on looking at un-televised reality, and breathing un-air-conditioned air.

Irritations and angers aside, what about loves? What do you 7 love most in the world? The big and little things, I mean. A trolley car, a pair of tennis shoes? These, at one time when we were children, were invested with magic for us. During the past year I've published one story about a boy's last ride in a trolley that smells of all the thunderstorms in time, full of cool green moss-velvet seats and blue electricity, but doomed to be replaced by the more prosaic, more practical-smelling bus. Another story concerned a boy who wanted to own a pair of new tennis shoes for the power they gave him to leap rivers and houses and streets, and even bushes, sidewalks, and dogs. The shoes were to him, the surge of antelope and gazelle on African summer veldt. The energy of unleashed rivers and summer storms lay in the shoes; he had to have them more than anything else in the world.

So, simply then, here is my formula. 8

What do you want more than anything else in the world? What 9 do you love, or what do you hate?

Find a character, like yourself, who will want something or not 10 want something, with all his heart. Give him running orders. Shoot him off. Then follow as fast as you can go. The character, in his great love, or hate, will rush you through to the end of the story. The zest and gusto of his need, and there *is* zest in hate as well as in love, will fire the landscape and raise the temperature of your typewriter thirty degrees.

All of this is primarily directed to the writer who has already 11 learned his trade; that is, has put into himself enough grammatical tools and literary knowledge so he won't trip himself up when he wants to run. The advice holds good for the beginner, too, however, even though his steps may falter for purely technical reasons. Even here, passion often saves the day.

The history of each story, then, should read almost like a weath- 12 er report: Hot today, cool tomorrow. This afternoon, burn down the house. Tomorrow, pour cold critical water upon the simmering coals. Time enough to think and cut and rewrite tomorrow. But today—explode—fly apart—disintegrate! The other six or seven drafts are going to be pure torture. So why not enjoy the first draft, in the hope that your joy will seek and find others in the world who, reading your story, will catch fire, too?

13   It doesn't have to be a big fire. A small blaze, candlelight perhaps; a longing for a mechanical wonder like a trolley or an animal wonder like a pair of sneakers rabbiting the lawns of early morning. Look for the little loves, find and shape the little bitternesses. Savor them in your mouth, try them on your typewriter. . . . Ideas lie everywhere, like apples fallen and melting in the grass for lack of wayfaring strangers with an eye and a tongue for beauty whether absurd, horrific, or genteel.

The Engaged Writer

1. Freewrite, as Bradbury suggests, about the last thing that made you as mad as the ad in *Harper's Bazaar* made Bradbury.
2. Put your response to question one in a notebook that you will use as your journal during this course—and, we hope, for years to come!
3. Answer the questions Bradbury asks in paragraphs 2 and 9.

One kind of writing is the personal kind illustrated in Elinore Stewart's and Garrison Keillor's "friendly letters." Another is a cooperative type, one that groups of people write. Some of the most famous and inspiring documents were drafted and written by committees of peers: the Declaration of Independence, the Constitution, the Bible, your daily newspaper. Some or all of the following methods or techniques can help you, the writer.

Together: Peer Groups

In your classroom, your instructor may divide the class into peer groups for research (two or three students to work on a computer or a terminal in the library), for writing (to write a group paper), or for mutual help (to critique each others' papers). Note the following advice to writers and readers in group situations.

To Writers

1. It's important to remember that if the piece of writing doesn't work out, you, the writer, are still an O.K. person—just the same as if you had lost a swimming race or tennis match.

2. Writing isn't good or bad in a moral sense; it is only engaging or off-putting, effective or ineffective. It is effective if
   — It accomplishes the writer's purpose.
   — It has the intended effect on the reader.
   — You, the writer, decide whether it fulfills these two criteria based on the responses of the reader.
3. You can't be your own audience—the reader is. You need helpful readers who give responses *and* reasons for those responses, for example, "I think this is boring because you give the same example in every paragraph."
4. Both of these statements are true:
   — Your reader can't be wrong about her or his reaction.
   — You don't have to change anything you don't want to change.

To Readers

1. It is easier to make trivial suggestions, but they are the least helpful.
2. Look for the big concerns first: Does the essay have a purpose?
3. Do you like the writer's tone—does it seem real?
4. Do you want to keep on reading?
5. What do you wish the writer had said more about?
6. Use "I" statements: "I'd like to see more details about your false arrest."

Alone: Journal Writing

The opposite of peer group techniques involves the personal journal, which the student writes alone and generally for himself or herself, without depending on peer evaluation. Peer group writing develops almost a group product, with audience predominant; journal writing stands alone, the self talking to itself. The rules of journal writing, if they can be called such, are few:

1. You should be free to delete portions from any journals handed in to the instructor.
2. Your instructor should comment on your journal in writing, without much reference to grammar, spelling, or punctuation.
3. Your journal should not be a diary (a record of daily activity) but a record of thoughts that you write regularly. (The word *journal* comes from the French *jour*, which means day.) Such

thoughts can be reactions to readings or notes for papers or comments on ideas expressed in class or read in newspapers or magazines.

One way to start journal writing is to write on an assigned topic during the first ten minutes of class. Then one or two students may wish to share their ten-minute writing with the rest of the class. As is true with peer-group interaction, no comments should be made on the shared material, though you might write your comments in your own journal.

Freewriting

Here is a sample of freewriting, written in ten minutes, with no erasures.

Topic: What's the last thing that made you as mad as the ad in *Harper's Bazaar* made Bradbury?

Is this a serious assignment? I can't believe anyone would let such a wide-open topic go. What if I wrote something about my school? Or about HER—the teacher? Or about this person who sits in front of me with legs sprawled all over the place. Well, I have to write something. I hardly ever get mad enough to find the last thing—but that person who honked the horn in front of my apartment house this morning at 4:30 deserves more than ten minutes of vituperations. I kept hearing this honk—honk—honk—honk. Then it would stop, and I would think—well, the person being called has come out. I would pull the covers over my head with relief. Then it would start again—honk—honk—honk. By this time I was completely awake and I imagine that the whole building was, at least on this side, unless some of my neighbors and either deaf or drunk or stoned. I can't imagine being so insensitive as that driver of the car to think that honking, rather than going up to the door and politely and softly knocking, was the polite thing to do, to think of all the other people he was waking up. I think that would be a writing topic—common human politeness and thoughtfulness. I could have killed! I thought of pouring boiling oil out of the window, calling the police, yelling at the person (but that would identify me and we don't want reprisals). What a world! Believe it or not, nobody in my building said or did anything. We have come to be slaves of caution. Well . . . (ten minutes are up!)

GAIL GODWIN

A Diarist on Diarists

Gail Godwin is the author of many books and articles, including the novels *The Finishing School* and *The Odd Woman*. This article first appeared in the literary magazine *Antaeus*, and then was part of the Bread Loaf Anthology *Writers on Writing*, edited by Robert Pack and Jay Parini. Bread Loaf is a summer school of writing, sponsored for many years by Middlebury College. Many of today's writers got their start there, and many of them return each summer to teach others.

This inescapable duty to observe oneself: if someone else is observing me, naturally I have to observe myself too; if none observe me, I have to observe myself all the closer.

—KAFKA, NOVEMBER 9, 1921

I fall back on this journal just as some other poor devil takes to drink.

—BARBELLION

I am enamoured of my journal.

—SIR WALTER SCOTT

Diarists: that shrewdly innocent breed, those secret exhibitionists 1 and incomparable purveyors of sequential, self-conscious life: how they fascinate me and endear themselves to me by what they say and do not say. If my friends kept diaries, and if I read them, would I know them as well as I know Kafka, standing in front of his mirror, playing with his hair? And Virginia Woolf, languishing because of a snide remark made about her novels by an undergraduate. And poor Dorothy Wordsworth, trying valiantly to stick to descriptions of sunsets while losing all her teeth. And Pepys, giving a colorful account of his latest fight with his wife. And Camus, coolly observing, "Whatever does not kill me strengthens me." Or plantation owner William Byrd, "dancing his dances" and "rogering his wife" (code words for bowel movements and sexual intercourse). Or the anonymous Irish scribe driven to confide into the margin of a medieval text: "I am very cold without fire or covering . . . the robin is singing gloriously, but though its red breast is beautiful I am all alone. Oh God be gracious to my soul and grant me a better handwriting."

2   In the old days everybody kept diaries. That's how we know that "Carlyle wandered down to tea looking dusky and aggrieved at having to live in such a generation": from Caroline Fox's diary; and that Henry James "kept up a perpetual vocal search for words even when he wasn't saying anything": from his nineteen-year-old nephew's diary; and that when Liszt played, he compressed his lips, dilated his nostrils and, when the music expressed quiet rapture, "a sweet smile flitted over his features": from George Eliot's diary. People came home from their dinners and visits and wrote down what others said and how the great men looked and who wore what and who made an ass or a pig of himself ("A little swinish at dinner," the diligent Dr. Rutty wrote of himself in his eighteenth-century diary). Those who stayed home alone also documented their evenings. ("I dined by myself and read an execrably stupid novel called 'Tylney Hall.' Why do I read such stuff?" wrote Macaulay.) Even a literate body-snatcher gave an account of himself before he turned in at night: "March 16, 1812, Went to Harps got 3 Large and 1 Large Small, 1 Small & 1 Foetus, took 2 Large to St. Thomas's, 1 Large to Guy's."

3   Are there fewer diarists now? It seems so, to me, but perhaps I'm unusual in that I have not one friend who keeps a diary—or at least who admits to it. Sometimes I'll happen upon a diarist and we greet each other like lonely explorers. Last spring I discovered a fellow diarist over lunch, and what a time we had discussing the intricacies of our venture-in-common, our avocation . . . specialty . . . compulsion? We confessed eccentricities (he has a pseudonym for the self that gambles; I often reread old journals and make notes to my former selves in the margin). We examined our motives: why keep these records, year after year? What would happen if we stopped? *Could* we stop? We indulged in shop-talk; hardbound or softcover? lined or unlined? about how many pages a night? proportion of external events to internal? Did one write more on bad days than on good? More or less on quiet days? (More, we both decided.) Did we feel honor-bound to report in at night, even when exhausted—or intoxicated? Ah, it was a good lunch we had.

"I should live no more than I can record, as one should not have 4
more corn growing than one can get at. There is a waste of good
if it be not preserved." This, from Boswell, expresses the aspect of
duty that many diarists typically feel. Queen Victoria continued
her diary strictly as a duty from the age of thirteen to eighty-two.
Unfortunately, much of it reads like it. Many diaries, left by long-
forgotten owners in attic trunks, describe neither affairs of state nor
the table talk of great geniuses nor the growing pains of profound
souls. But a sense of *accountability* emanates from these old books.
("Went with Maud to Chok's for a soda. J. L. lost two heifers from
shipping disease . . . nothing of interest to record today.") Man and
woman was beholden to the *recording* of God's hours, be they interesting or not.

> No mighty deeds, just common things,
> The tasks and pleasures each day brings.
> And yet I hope that when I look
> Over the pages of this book,
> Twill be (and, if so, I'm content)
> The record of five years well spent.

This, from the title page of my mother's college diary, offers cap- 5
tured memory as incentive to daily diligence. *Nulla dies sine linea,*
it orders, and my mother obeyed, detailing in tiny handwriting, in
a variety of inks, the social and mental highlights of 1932–36. People seemed to go to the movies every day, sometimes twice in one
day. They ate a lot of spaghetti—but, of course, there was a Depression. No longer a diarist, my mother offered the little blue and gold
book to me (we had to pick the lock—she had no idea it was even
hers until we opened it). Her parents had given her the five-year
diary as a going-away present for college, and she felt she owed it
to them to write in it. I'm glad she did. How many daughters can
read—in purple ink—about the night they were conceived?

Now I'm the only practicing diarist in my family. Not one of my 6
friends keeps a diary, as I've mentioned. "To tell the truth, I've
never thought I was that interesting," says one. "I'm not a *writer*,"
says another. A third writes letters, sometimes three or four every
evening, and says this serves the purpose of a diary. Another person who is a very prolific writer has advised me to "put all that
material into stories rather than hide it in your journals. When you

feel haunted or sad, write a story about a person, not necessarily yourself, who feels haunted or sad. Because, you see, it's the feelings that are universal, not the person."

7   Art, fiction, if it is to be public, must tap the universal. A diary by its very nature is the unfolding of the private, personal story—whether that story be told from a distance (the "I" in a political diary, observing affairs of state; the "I" in the captain's log, marking latitude, longitude, and the moods of the sea) or with the subjectivity of a person whose politics and moods and sea-changes exist inside his own head. I need to write a diary, just as I need to write fiction, but the two needs come from very different sources. I write fiction because I need to organize the clutter of too many details into some meaning, because I enjoy turning something promising into something marvelous; I keep a diary because it keeps my mind fresh and open. Once the details of being me are safely stored away every night, I can get on with what isn't just me. So, as I explained to my friend, the fictional and the diary-making processes are not interchangeable. I had to keep a diary for many years before I could begin writing fiction.

Engaging the Text

1. In a reference work, such as a biographical dictionary, look up some of the people Godwin mentions who kept diaries, listed in paragraphs 1 and 2: Kafka, Virginia Woolf, Dorothy Wordsworth, Pepys, Camus, William Byrd, Caroline Fox, George Eliot, Macaulay.
2. What is a diary? How does Godwin define it, and how does she restrict the term?
3. What kinds of material do diaries contain? Why does Godwin use her mother's diary to illustrate her article?

Engaging the Reader

1. Do you keep a diary? Or do you keep a journal for a course, or to practice writing? Talk about how you organize, write, or keep your journal; compare with your classmates' experiences.
2. What is the difference, according to Godwin, between fiction and a diary?

The Engaged Writer

1. Find one of the diaries mentioned by Godwin in your library, read some of it, and write a review, appraisal, or appreciation of what you have read.
2. Find a notebook, five-year diary, or something you would enjoy writing in, and start your own diary. Since Godwin insists diaries are private, this will not be a part of your course work, yet you can mine it for ideas for later writing.

PATRICIA CORNWELL

In Cold Blood

Patricia Cornwell is the author of a successful series of novels featuring a forensic pathologist, Dr. Kay Scarpetta, who is called on to solve some grisly crimes. First an English major, then a newspaper writer, Patricia Cornwell was determined to write, and did research in morgues and police departments to develop her chosen themes. Rejected by seven publishing houses, her first novel, *Post Mortem,* was finally accepted and published and became an international bestseller. The following account of her writing process is part of a series of occasional essays in the *Washington Post Book World* by authors on subjects that concern them and their work.

I remember working on my first novel while a senior at Davidson   1
College in North Carolina. The apartment I rented that year had no heat. I often typed late at night with my winter coat on and could see my breath. That first book, blessedly, was never published and is not worth remembering. But the words of a sage, older friend I will not forget. "Writing," he said to me, "is a way of having experiences without scars."

I thought this a wonderful insight at the time. I could write   2
about any subject, even murder, and not suffer. I did not have to get close. I could sit at my desk and simply imagine the morgue. Of course I was wrong.

So now I will tell the way it really is when I sit down to write   3
novels about Kay Scarpetta, medical examiner: I am a reporter; I

am Dr. Scarpetta's feet, hands and eyes. I gather facts like shards of brilliant, bloody glass and fashion from them a window. On the other side is a dimension of life, powerful in its darkness and exhausting in its extremes. I have come to know that side profoundly well because listening to secondary accounts about the tracks that crime leaves was not and will never be enough. I must see, smell, hear and touch the evidence for myself.

4   When I first wrote crime fiction in the early '80s, the stories turned to air in my hands. I could not grasp the characters nor understand what they felt. My voice had no authority, and even after laboring to create a world, I could see it was not good. I needed more than library articles and interviews. I began working very hard for the legitimacy that would earn me passage into the places I needed to see—places I still find painful to traverse.

5   Sometimes I spent 12 hours a day in surgical scrubs, assisting forensic pathologists as they performed autopsies in a Richmond, Va. morgue. I will never forget the first time I placed my gloved hands in a chest cavity and was startled to find that the blood was cold.

6   Death becomes very real when it has been refrigerated, and no matter how many times someone may have told me that bodies in the morgue are stored this way, the reality did not grab my soul until I felt firsthand. Since those early days of research, I have camped in the shadow of violent death and befriended the troops of stalwart spirits and great minds who war against it. I am forever changed.

7   Memory for me is like one of those Civil War greenhouses sadly built of daguerreotypes instead of glass panes. If I walk into my thoughts and quietly sit, I suddenly find myself surrounded by haunting faces and harrowing tableaux. I conjure up soldiers who have run into bayonets—bodies of young people who fight believing they will never die. I see mere boys giving their last Rebel Yell, and they are not so different from last week's teenager who decided to stand up suddenly in the back of a pickup truck, not realizing it was about to go under a bridge. I remember he came to the morgue with a dented can of Old Spice deodorant in one pocket, 35 cents in the other.

8   In the greenhouse of my memories I have worn a police uniform and driven an unmarked car. I have directed traffic during Richmond summers when heat shimmered like snow in a relentless sun, and carbon monoxide fumes made me light on my feet. I

remember being ridiculed, almost run down and verbally abused for being "a cop." I remember the turgid bureaucracy of a police department that first sent me out into rush hour without training.

I have said goodbye in the morgue to a homicide detective who 9 was my friend, and stared stunned at the small hole in his chest. In these ways I have come to understand Pete Marino, the homicide detective in my books; I know he would not speak to me had I not lived in his world and done my best to learn its language.

Benton Wesley, the FBI profiler in my novels, makes demands 10 of me that are more tolerable. The FBI Academy at Quantico is the finest law enforcement facility in the world. To go there is to feel one is at Oxford University or in a monastery where doors are never locked because the people are so good. The Academy is rarefied, scholarly. Yet, ironically, the cases studied by the Investigative Support Unit concern some of the most evil people in the land: Ted Bundy, Jeffrey Dahmer, John Wayne Gacy.

The public has heard of them—these creatures who inevitably 11 find their way onto the cover of People magazine after murdering 33 victims or cannibalizing the lovers they bring home from the bar. But what I find worse is the monster no one reads about or sees on the six o'clock news. We would like to think that the ones we know are all there are.

There are other monsters—other cries that no one hears: the girl 12 jogging; the newspaper boy riding his bicycle; the old woman who lives alone; the child wandering off in the mall while his mother pays the cashier. They become statistics, case numbers, photographs passed around a conference room.

I am told my novels are different from traditional mysteries, and 13 I would agree. It would be misleading for me to claim to be an expert in such a masterful, old genre. But I have become—for reasons even I do not fully understand—a passionate student of crime. No matter how well I may do, I can never forsake the work that got me where I am—the dogged research into time of death, the slides in the lab, the slab in the morgue.

Now I am at work on my sixth Scarpetta novel. The research has 14 not changed. The new novel began on a snowy night in the subway tunnels of New York City as I stepped over syringes and crack vials. I wore a surgical mask and gloves, and rats ran over my boots. The next morning I went to the Office of the Chief Medical Examiner where a body was being autopsied, and I realized that he was the police officer who had been slain the night before. This frigid fact-gathering trip ended with a flight over New York's Potter's Field. From the air I watched prisoners burying simple pine boxes on a barren island where the dead are stacked on top of each other and many have no names.

15   I tried to sleep in that vibrating BellJet Ranger, cold air blowing on my neck. I thought about what it was I had seen that day. I felt dirty, exhausted, depressed. For more than ten years I have put myself through the same thing and wondered if I should stop—or at least, ease up.

16   I cannot. If I stop seeing, hearing, touching, there will be no story. I will be a writer with nothing to say—a violin with no music to play. The journeys I find myself taking inevitably unfold the story, and the characters who accompany me always reveal more to me with time.

Engaging the Text

1. Cornwell shows she is a fiction writer by some of the colorful language she uses: "facts like shards of brilliant, bloody glass" (3), "the stories turned to air in my hands" (4), "the reality did not grab my soul" (6), "the heat shimmered like snow in a relentless sun" (8). Pick out some more examples of this kind of language from the article.

Engaging the Reader

1. What is the thesis of Cornwell's article? Try to summarize it in a single sentence.
2. What impresses you about the way Cornwell researches material for her Dr. Kay Scarpetta novels? When you think of "research," you often think of libraries. What kinds of "libraries" does Cornwell use?

The Engaged Writer

1. As you work through the assignments in *The Engaging Reader*, start keeping a "Writing Journal," telling, as Cornwell does, how you began writing, what subjects you chose to write about, how you practiced until your writing became vivid, and where you found material to make them authentic and realistic.

2. Read one of Cornwell's novels and write a report on it for your class. Note especially if Cornwell really writes as she says she does—does she give an authentic "Writer's Journal"?
3. Cornwell's novels appear often on lists of best-sellers. For research: using the listings of "best-sellers" in several newspapers and magazines, tabulate the types of stories that make the cut, how long they stay on the lists, and what conclusions you can draw from the idea of "best-sellers."

With a Machine: Computer Assisted Writing

Today, many writers use word processors or computers with word processing software to write their papers. They can easily revise, replace words, move paragraphs around, and edit quickly and carefully. On the whole, this technology aids both you and your instructor. You should be aware that spelling checkers, word frequency programs, even grammar and punctuation programs can help you write well. Your instructor receives a more finished product, or ideally, can interact with you as the paper is processed on the machine. None of these electronic servants should be ignored either for work at home or for classroom use if the equipment exists at your college.

See the section in the Writer's Guide on using Grammatik® to check your writing for mechanical and stylistic errors.

American Library Association

Why Read?

Your first love letter.
A newspaper article
that moved you to
tears. The book that
made a difference.
Experience the power
and pleasure
of words.
Read.
American Library Association

PART

1

The Self

I celebrate myself, and sing myself,
And what I assume you shall assume,
For every atom belonging to me as good belongs to you.
I loafe and invite my soul,
I lean and loafe at my ease observing a spear of summer
  grass.
My tongue, every atom of my blood, form'd from this soil,
  this air,
Born here of parents born here from parents the same, and
  their parents the same,
I, now thirty-seven years old in perfect health begin,
Hoping to cease not till death.

Walt Whitman, the exuberant nineteenth-century poet, used himself as a representative human being. His "Song of Myself," excerpted here, celebrates the human body, a daring subject in the 1850s in America. In this poem, he progresses from writing about himself to cataloging the whole of America of his time, listing hundreds of occupations and hobbies. Whitman's long, detailed lists and conversation-like lines have influenced many writers. His philosophy also has influenced generations of Americans. The preceding selection contains only the first lines of the long "Song of Myself," which began the first edition of *Leaves of Grass* in 1855.

Whitman was certainly not the first chronicler of human life. Anthropologists place that activity very early in human affairs. As early as the end of the last Ice Age (40,000 to 100,000 years ago), people lived in extended families and had a long tradition of storytelling.

Around the fire after a hunt, a long trek across the tundras, or an escape from an enemy, men and women told stories of themselves. Most stories begin with the person who is doing the telling. Through the long, exaggerated boast of the warrior or hunter, the ever-fascinating details of childbirth, the magic of a seemingly miraculous escape, most of these tales focus on the individual's awareness of self.

Today, still, the personal account is one of the most popular forms of reading. You may glance at the headlines or browse through the editorials in the newspaper, but you read at length the personal accounts of the survivors of an airplane crash, the hostages who have finally returned home, or the partner in a political scandal. The sixteenth-century Frenchman, Michel Montaigne, said "I study myself" ("To the Reader," *Essays*). The study of self continues to be fascinating. In the first section of this book, you will find excerpts from biographies and autobiographies of people whose experiences may be like your own. Amy Tan's Chinese woman thinks about her mother while Jack McClintock writes about a freak accident. George Moore's Esther hides a pregnancy while Russell Baker, Alex Kotlowitz, and Julia Siler write about the effect of city violence on children, and Richard Rodriguez tells of his experiences as a minority student.

ROBERT GRUDIN

A Dog

Robert Grudin starts his astonishing 1992 novel with the ordinary yet extraordinary title of *BOOK* with the following one-page incident. *BOOK* itself has stories within stories, but none is more remarkable than this small sketch of one consciousness—that of a dog. We observe the dog and follow his thoughts and actions, all from the point of view of the dog; yet since the dog cannot speak, the author tells his story. The dog's master has not come home for a very dramatic reason; you will have to read the book to find out why!

1 He sat on his haunches, his breath clouding the glass on the inside of the front door, his brown eyes intent on the far corner of the lau-

rel hedge past the driveway, where he might first catch sight of his master returning. He sat completely still, postured like some Egyptian statue; yet no Egyptian artisan, ambitious to adorn Pharaoh's palace or tomb, would have condescended to depict the big black long-hair mongrel, with his rounded mastiff head, barrel chest and sashlike tail. He sat as though arrested in time, as though the hours that stiffened his muscles and wheeled his shadow clockwise on the rug were the single second before he saw his master, heard his step, felt his hand. Master of the loving hand, master of the endearing voice, master of the comforting smell, master of the heaped bowl.

His bowels ached and writhed. The need to be outside, to wander off at his master's side to the relief of some breezy alien forest or some field rich in odors of decay, oppressed him till his head pounded with the effort of restraint. His shadow slowly faded; the light grew dim. The little road outside was busy with returning cars. He rose and stretched forlornly and turned and with slow steps sought the remotest corner of the house, the broom closet behind the kitchen, to commit with infinite relief the unthinkable deed. Climbing the stairs to the darkened bathroom, he drank greedily from the toilet bowl. He came down the stairs and stood in the living room, listening. Now it was night again in the hungry house. Now neighbor dogs came by walking their people, dogs of easy familiar smells, masters who knew him and had petted him. He went to the big chair in front of the slightly opened front window and put his forepaws up on the chair's back and barked thunderously, cocking his ears as the echoes faded. He went to the front door and barked and barked, his great body shuddering with the agony of expression.

Engaging the Text

1. Grudin uses some phrases that put us into the mind of this nameless dog. A couple of these are "to commit with infinite relief the unthinkable deed" (2) and "dogs came by walking their people" (2). What do these two statements mean? How do you translate them into the human point of view?
2. Grudin uses an analogy—"Egyptian statue," and "Egyptian artisan, ambitious to adorn Pharoah's palace or tomb" to give us a picture of the dog waiting inside the front door. Can you

describe what Grudin attempts to show the reader in another way?

Engaging the Reader

1. What do you think the dog is doing in this short page? Tell the story in your own words. Then compare with the version of some of your classmates.
2. Would this story be different if the animal involved were a cat?
3. Do you want to continue reading this story? The start of any piece of writing needs to grab the reader's interest; does this one do that for you? Consider this when you start your next piece of writing.
4. How do you jump from writing about yourself to writing about someone else, as Grudin did with this dog?

The Engaged Writer

1. Compare this story about a dog with Aldo Leopold's account of a walk with his dog in "Red Lanterns" in Part 2. Look at descriptions, point of view, and realism, to start.
2. If you have a dog, write a sketch of yourself from the point of view of your dog.
3. Write a sketch like "Dog" from the point of view of another animal: a chimpanzee used for experimental purposes, the elephant in the zoo, a rare endangered species, the bird that comes to your feeder, or a member of some other species. Remember to think of it as what it is, a animal, not an animal made into a human, personified ("Mickey Mouse").

AMY TAN

Scar

Amy Tan (b. 1952) wrote her first novel, *The Joy Luck Club* (1989), about four Chinese women who began meeting in San Francisco in 1949 to play mah jong, eat dim sum, and tell stories about their pasts. When one of the women dies, her daughter takes her place in the club. This action starts a long train of remembrances of the sometimes violent lives of the women as well as their daughters. As each mother and daughter tells her story, the past is revealed. An-mei Hsu is one of the mothers. In the following selection, she remembers living with Popo (her grandmother) when she was a child. An-mei's absent mother was considered a "ghost"—a non-person—after she left the family to become the concubine of a wealthy man.

When I was a young girl in China, my grandmother told me my 1 mother was a ghost. This did not mean my mother was dead. In those days, a ghost was anything we were forbidden to talk about. So I knew Popo wanted me to forget my mother on purpose, and this is how I came to remember nothing of her. The life that I knew began in the large house in Ningpo with the cold hallways and tall stairs. This was my uncle and auntie's family house, where I lived with Popo and my little brother.

But I often heard stories of a ghost who tried to take children 2 away, especially strong-willed little girls who were disobedient. Many times Popo said aloud to all who could hear that my brother and I had fallen out of the bowels of a stupid goose, two eggs that nobody wanted, not even good enough to crack over rice porridge. She said this so that the ghosts would not steal us away. So you see, to Popo we were also very precious.

All my life, Popo scared me. I became even more scared when 3 she grew sick. This was in 1923, when I was nine years old. Popo had swollen up like an overripe squash, so full her flesh had gone soft and rotten with a bad smell. She would call me into her room with the terrible stink and tell me stories. "An-mei," she said, call-ing me by my school name. "Listen carefully." She told me stories I could not understand.

One was about a greedy girl whose belly grew fatter and fatter. 4 This girl poisoned herself after refusing to say whose child she car-ried. When the monks cut open her body, they found inside a large white winter melon.

"If you are greedy, what is inside you is what makes you always 5 hungry," said Popo.

Another time, Popo told me about a girl who refused to listen 6 to her elders. One day this bad girl shook her head so vigorously to refuse her auntie's simple request that a little white ball fell from her ear and out poured all her brains, as clear as chicken broth.

7   "Your own thoughts are so busy swimming inside that everything else gets pushed out," Popo told me.

8   Right before Popo became so sick she could no longer speak, she
pulled me close and talked to me about my mother. "Never say her
name," she warned. "To say her name is to spit on your father's
grave."

9   The only father I knew was a big painting that hung in the main
hall. He was a large, unsmiling man, unhappy to be so still on the
wall. His restless eyes followed me around the house. Even from
my room at the end of the hall, I could see my father's watching
eyes. Popo said he watched me for any signs of disrespect. So
sometimes, when I had thrown pebbles at other children at school,
or had lost a book through carelessness, I would quickly walk by
my father with a know-nothing look and hide in a corner of my
room where he could not see my face.

10   I felt our house was so unhappy, but my little brother did not
seem to think so. He rode his bicycle through the courtyard, chas-
ing chickens and other children, laughing over which ones
shrieked the loudest. Inside the quiet house, he jumped up and
down on Uncle and Auntie's best feather sofas when they were
away visiting village friends.

11   But even my brother's happiness went away. One hot summer
day when Popo was already very sick, we stood outside watching
a village funeral procession marching by our courtyard. Just as it
passed our gate, the heavy framed picture of the dead man toppled
from its stand and fell to the dusty ground. An old lady screamed
and fainted. My brother laughed and Auntie slapped him.

12   My auntie, who had a very bad temper with children, told him
he had no *shou*, no respect for ancestors or family, just like our
mother. Auntie had a tongue like hungry scissors eating silk
cloth. So when my brother gave her a sour look, Auntie said our
mother was so thoughtless she had fled north in a big hurry,
without taking the dowry furniture from her marriage to my
father, without bringing her ten pairs of silver chopsticks, without paying respect to my father's grave and those of our ancestors. When my brother accused Auntie of frightening our mother
away, Auntie shouted that our mother had married a man named
Wu Tsing who already had a wife, two concubines, and other bad
children.

And when my brother shouted that Auntie was a talking chick- 13
en without a head, she pushed my brother against the gate and
spat on his face.

"You throw strong words at me, but you are nothing," Auntie 14
said. "You are the son of a mother who has so little respect she has
become *ni,* a traitor to our ancestors. She is so beneath others that
even the devil must look down to see her."

That is when I began to understand the stories Popo taught me, 15
the lessons I had to learn for my mother. "When you lose your face,
An-mei," Popo often said, "it is like dropping your necklace down
a well. The only way you can get it back is to fall in after it."

Now I could imagine my mother, a thoughtless woman who 16
laughed and shook her head, who dipped her chopsticks many
times to eat another piece of sweet fruit, happy to be free of Popo,
her unhappy husband on the wall, and her two disobedient children. I felt unlucky that she was my mother and unlucky that she
had left us. These were the thoughts I had while hiding in the corner of my room where my father could not watch me.

I was sitting at the top of the stairs when she arrived. I knew it 17
was my mother even though I had not seen her in all my memory.
She stood just inside the doorway so that her face became a dark
shadow. She was much taller than my auntie, almost as tall as my
uncle. She looked strange, too, like the missionary ladies at our
school who were insolent and bossy in their too-tall shoes, foreign
clothes, and short hair.

My auntie quickly looked away and did not call her by name 18
or offer her tea. An old servant hurried away with a displeased
look. I tried to keep very still, but my heart felt like crickets scratch-
ing to get out of a cage. My mother must have heard, because she
looked up. And when she did, I saw my own face looking back at
me. Eyes that stayed wide open and saw too much.

In Popo's room my auntie protested, "Too late, too late," as my 19
mother approached the bed. But this did not stop my mother.

"Come back, stay here," murmured my mother to Popo. "*Nuyer* 20
is here. Your daughter is back." Popo's eyes were open, but now
her mind ran in many different directions, not staying long enough
to see anything. If Popo's mind had been clear she would have
raised her two arms and flung my mother out of the room.

21   I watched my mother, seeing her for the first time, this pretty woman with her white skin and oval face, not too round like Auntie's or sharp like Popo's. I saw that she had a long white neck, just like the goose that had laid me. That she seemed to float back and forth like a ghost, dipping cool cloths to lay on Popo's bloated face. As she peered into Popo's eyes, she clucked soft worried sounds. I watched her carefully, yet it was her voice that confused me, a familiar sound from a forgotten dream.

22   When I returned to my room later that afternoon, she was there, standing tall. And because I remember Popo told me not to speak her name, I stood there, mute. She took my hand and led me to the settee. And then she also sat down as though we had done this every day.

23   My mother began to loosen my braids and brush my hair with long sweeping strokes.

24   "An-mei, you have been a good daughter?" she asked, smiling a secret look.

25   I looked at her with my know-nothing face, but inside I was trembling. I was the girl whose belly held a colorless winter melon.

26   "An-mei, you know who I am," she said with a small scold in her voice. This time I did not look for fear my head would burst and my brains would dribble out of my ears.

27   She stopped brushing. And then I could feel her long smooth fingers rubbing and searching under my chin, finding the spot that was my smooth-neck scar. As she rubbed this spot, I became very still. It was as though she were rubbing the memory back into my skin. And then her hand dropped and she began to cry, wrapping her hands around her own neck. She cried with a wailing voice that was so sad. And then I remembered the dream with my mother's voice.

28   I was four years old. My chin was just above the dinner table, and I could see my baby brother sitting on Popo's lap, crying with an angry face. I could hear voices praising a steaming dark soup brought to the table, voices murmuring politely, "*Ching! Ching!*"— Please, eat!

29   And then the talking stopped. My uncle rose from his chair. Everyone turned to look at the door, where a tall woman stood. I was the only one who spoke.

30   "Ma," I had cried, rushing off my chair, but my auntie slapped my face and pushed me back down. Now everyone was standing

up and shouting, and I heard my mother's voice crying, "An-mei! An-mei!" Above this noise, Popo's shrill voice spoke.

"Who is this ghost? Not an honored widow. Just a number-three 31 concubine. If you take your daughter, she will become like you. No face. Never able to lift up her head."

Still my mother shouted for me to come. I remember her voice 32 so clearly now. An-mei! An-mei! I could see my mother's face across the table. Between us stood the soup pot on its heavy chimney-pot stand—rocking slowly, back and forth. And then with one shout this dark boiling soup spilled forward and fell all over my neck. It was as though everyone's anger were pouring all over me.

This was the kind of pain so terrible that a little child should 33 never remember it. But it is still in my skin's memory. I cried out loud only a little, because soon my flesh began to burst inside and out and cut off my breathing air.

I could not speak because of this terrible choking feeling. I could 34 not see because of all the tears that poured out to wash away the pain. But I could hear my mother's crying voice. Popo and Auntie were shouting. And then my mother's voice went away.

Later that night Popo's voice came to me. 35

"An-mei, listen carefully." Her voice had the same scolding 36 tone she used when I ran up and down the hallway. "An-mei, we have made your dying clothes and shoes for you. They are all white cotton."

I listened, scared. 37

"An-mei," she murmured, now more gently. "Your dying 38 clothes are very plain. They are not fancy, because you are still a child. If you die, you will have a short life and you will still owe your family a debt. Your funeral will be very small. Our mourning time for you will be very short."

And then Popo said something that was worse than the burn- 39 ing on my neck.

"Even your mother has used up her tears and left. If you do not 40 get well soon, she will forget you."

Popo was very smart. I came hurrying back from the other 41 world to find my mother.

Every night I cried so that both my eyes and my neck burned. 42 Next to my bed sat Popo. She would pour cool water over my neck from the hollowed cup of a large grapefruit. She would pour and pour until my breathing became soft and I could fall asleep. In the morning, Popo would use her sharp fingernails like tweezers and peel off the dead membranes.

43   In two years' time, my scar became pale and shiny and I had no memory of my mother. That is the way it is with a wound. The wound begins to close in on itself, to protect what is hurting so much. And once it is closed, you no longer see what is underneath, what started the pain.

Engaging the Text

1. Since this is a family remembrance, the vocabulary is simple and the narration direct. But Tan gives an authentic feeling to the story by using such sentences as "She said this so that the ghosts would not steal us away." Find some other sentences like this one and explain what they mean.
2. Though Tan uses Chinese words and phrases, she always explains them in context, so we don't need a glossary to understand them. Some of these are *shou* (12), *ni* (14), and *Ching!* (28). Find these words and tell what they mean.

Engaging the Reader

1. The last part of the story is a flashback to the event that produced the "scar" that gives the episode its title. Why is this told at the end, and why is the scar so important?
2. Reconstruct the history of this family as if it were being told by an adult present at the time, rather than through the memories of a young child.

The Engaged Writer

1. Interview an elderly member of your own family. Ask for a family story told to that person as a child. Write that story as a narrative.
2. "The Joy Luck Club" became a film in 1993. See this film. In your journal or as a short essay, write how you think the selection here played as a film. You may wish to go on from there to a critique or evaluation of the whole film.

JACK McCLINTOCK

Real Trouble Ahead

Jack McClintock, a writer living in Coconut Grove, Florida, wrote this piece in 1987 about an ordinary outdoor task that developed into what he calls an "adventure"—accidentally hitting himself on the head. This adventure led to McClintock's thinking about more serious problems. His essay reflects the fact that more and more Americans live alone.

Hitting myself on the head with a pickax changed a pleasant after- 1
noon of puttering in the yard into a revelation. Or perhaps I should say half a revelation. The blow knocked my glasses off; they haven't turned up yet, and my view of the event—and its meaning—is still unclear.

It began with the lawn. I regard the lawn as the enemy. I've 2
hated lawns since boyhood, when it was my chore to mow ours, and the only way to earn pocket money was to mow the neighbors' too. I would spend the next week resentfully watching the grass grow. Lawns make no sense.

When I bought this house nine months ago, I decided to do 3
away with nearly all the lawn. Almost every day I take out grass and install something else: trees, shrubs, ferns, deck, ground cover, flowers, pathways of cypress chips—anything but grass.

The mango tree I had ordered had not arrived that afternoon, 4
but I decided to get a head start and begin digging. Where I live in south Florida, a head start is a good idea. There is solid limestone six inches down.

It was hot. I had on shorts and a T-shirt. I wore a sun hat and 5
an old pair of glasses. I got the necessary tool from the garage. I think it is accurately called a pick mattock. The pick end of the blade—the end you use for rock—is a 10-inch spike of steel. The mattock end is wide and flattened, almost like a curved hoe.

You have to take a big swing to penetrate the turf with the mat- 6
tock. You grip the tool with both hands like an ax, raise it high over your shoulder and then bring it down with all your might. *Chop,* it goes into the detested sod. I have found this very satisfying.

7   I picked up the mattock and brought it down as hard as I could. But it never struck the ground. What hit the ground was me. I was lying on my back on the lawn, my hat in the grass beside my right foot, the mattock by my left. I looked up groggily. A mockingbird chirped merrily in the mahogany tree above me.

8   I felt blank, then dizzy, then confused; I touched my face. I was sweating a lot. I looked at my palm. No, I was bleeding a lot. I stumbled, trying to rise and my vision seemed unclear.

9   It took a few seconds to figure out what had happened. I had brought the mattock down on the clothesline. This was a well-built clothesline: steel pipes solidly set in concrete and heavy wire. I had hit the wire on the downswing and, like the string of a bow, it had flung the mattock straight back into my face, point first.

10   I yanked off my blood-soaked T-shirt and wadded it against my face, covering the right eye, and stumbled into the house to inspect the damage. I looked into the hall mirror and hesitantly moved the shirt aside. The eye was full of blood. I couldn't remember pulling the mattock point out of the eye, but knew that I must have.

11   I decided not to try to drive. And it struck me just then, trying to think what to do, staring into a bloody face that mirrored horror, that one of my worst fears had been realized.

12   I don't know how to phrase this fear exactly, because it is not entirely clear, but it goes something like this: I live alone and something happens—I get sick or hurt or poor or old—and nobody is *there*.

13   And it had just happened! And my first thought was, "It isn't so bad."

14   I called a friend, who said, "I'll be right there."

15   She arrived, took over, calmly said that she could see the skull in the bloody gap and we'd better get rolling.

16   "You're going to have a dashing scar on your brow," she said, glancing over but keeping both hands on the wheel. The sight of blood makes careful drivers.

17   Things went smoothly at the doctor's office. His quick inspection showed that, under the blood, the eye was fine; I had missed it by an inch. My vision was still bleary, but now I could see clearly enough to know why—my glasses were missing. The gash was perfectly straight and closed up neatly with only five stitches. The skull was whole.

The doctor gave me a tetanus shot. The nurse gave me a bill for 18
"Laceration Repair Face etc.," and I wrote a check. The dizziness
went away in a few hours, though I had a terrific headache that
night and a queasy stomach the next day.

What seems remarkable now are the gaps in this adventure. 19
There was the gap of consciousness—before I found myself on my
back on the lawn. There was a mundane insurance coverage gap:
I had left a job and the health insurance it provided and had not
yet established my own coverage. I suspect the doctor gave me a
break on the bill.

There was a gap between the idiotic Dagwood Bumstead com- 20
edy of incompetence I had created and the serious damage it could
have caused and didn't—the gap between what happened to me
and real trouble; I knew this was not real trouble.

And there was the gap between the daily necessary illusion of 21
safety and the truth: that sweet life can turn sour in a second.

There is, too, that matter of what I had feared. My father died 22
six months ago; my mother had been with him 24 hours a day for
all the years of heart attacks, bone cancer, kidney failure,
Alzheimer's disease. It was terrible for her, and she was enor-
mously brave. Perhaps everyone who has witnessed the aging of
loyal parents knows the anxiety I felt: When things get really bad,
will someone be there for me? Our times are not like theirs.

Home from the doctor's, I wandered into the backyard. The 23
mattock and my hat were lying where I'd left them on the lawn. I
touched the bristling stitches over my eye, smiled and said thanks
again.

Over the next few days my friend was generous and kind, 24
sometimes there and sometimes not. Sometimes it was good to be
alone, unsmothered. Others called and stopped by. I got to tell my
comical Dagwood story lots of times and began to see it as a short
movie about this ridiculous character in a funny hat who wakes up
to the mockingbird's chirp. The audience always laughed.

The problem is that real trouble exists. I didn't have to face it 25
this time; even without health insurance or a loving partner, I
didn't need anything more than was there. The scar will be
insignificant, not dashing at all.

But real trouble exists, and how many of us are equipped to 26
endure it alone? I still don't know how to think about this. And

every time I go into the backyard I search for my glasses. But they're still missing.

Engaging the Text

1. Some of the expressions McClintock uses need explanations. One is "Dagwood Bumstead," the name of a comic strip character, the husband of "Blondie." Another is *Alzheimer's disease*. In your college library, find a source for information on these two items. Record the information and the name of the source book in your journal.

2. Other words that may be unfamiliar pertain to McClintock's accident. These are tetanus (18), queasy (18), laceration (18), mundane (19), incompetence (20). Use each of them in a sentence, or use all of them in one sentence.

3. From whose point of view is the story written? What can you tell about the writer from the details in the story—for example, his life-style, his interests, his hobbies?

4. Notice how the writer places some of the details in the story. For example, he mentions his "old pair of glasses" early, then twice later on. Where are these details placed? How does the story change at each point they appear?

Engaging the Reader

1. This account is told in chronological order, except for the first paragraph. Why do you think the author summarized the whole experience in the first paragraph? *because he wants to attract reader*

2. How did the writer bring out changes in emotion during the story—from thinking of what happened as a funny experience to fear of the future? *He call a friend*

3. What are the "gaps in this adventure" the author discusses? List them.

The Engaged Writer

1. Describe a tool you use every day and how you use it—it can be one from your job, your kitchen, or your hobby. Model your description on McClintock's paragraphs about the mattock (5, 6).

2. What are the problems and fears uncovered by McClintock's seemingly simple accident?

3. McClintock thought that "one of his worst fears had been realized." What was this fear? Do you have a similar fear? Describe it, imagining it has been realized. What would you do?

4. This easy makes McClintock reflect on getting old and helpless. Discuss the treatment of elderly or handicapped people today and the problems they have with self-esteem.

GEORGE MOORE

A Kitchen Maid

Realistic writing began toward the end of the 1800s when writers began to depict real people in real situations, not knights and ladies in castles of the imagination. The growth of science and experimentation made writers aware of the importance of observation. Virginia Woolf and George Moore (1852–1933), among others, wrote novels about ordinary people and described their lives in detail, even—as in the following selection—reaching within them to describe internal sensations. In *Esther Waters* written in 1894 and from which the following selection is taken, Moore describes the feelings of a young woman at the instant she realizes she is pregnant. It is remarkable writing, because Moore, of course, never had this feeling himself. Esther is a kitchen maid on a horse farm; her lover, the footman, has deserted her to run away with one of the "young ladies" of the house.

Esther listened with an unmoved face and a heavy ache in her 1 heart. She had now not an enemy nor yet an opponent; the cause of rivalry and jealousy being removed, all were sorry for her. They recognised that she had suffered and was suffering, and seeing none but friends about her, she was led to think how happy she might have been in this beautiful house if it had not been for William. She loved her work, for she was working for those she loved. She could imagine no life happier than hers might have been. But she had sinned, and the Lord had punished her for sin, and she must bear her punishment uncomplainingly, giving Him thanks that He had imposed no heavier one upon her.

2   Such reflection was the substance of Esther's mind for three months after William's departure; and in the afternoons, about three o'clock, when her work paused, Esther's thoughts would congregate and settle on the great misfortune of her life—William's desertion.

3   It was one afternoon at the beginning of December; Mrs. Latch had gone upstairs to lie down. Esther had drawn her chair towards the fire. A broken-down race-horse, his legs bandaged from his knees to his fetlocks, had passed up the yard; he was going for walking exercise on the downs, and when the sound of his hoofs had died away Esther was quite alone. She sat on her wooden chair facing the wide kitchen window. She had advanced one foot on the iron fender; her head leaned back, rested on her hand. She did not think—her mind was lost in vague sensation of William, and it was in this death of active memory that something awoke within her, something that seemed to her like a flutter of wings; her heart seemed to drop from its socket, and she nearly fainted away, but recovering herself she stood by the kitchen table, her arms drawn back and pressed to her sides, a death-like pallor over her face, and drops of sweat on her forehead. The truth was borne in upon her; she realised in a moment part of the awful drama that awaited her, and from which nothing could free her, and which she would have to live through hour by hour. So dreadful did it seem, that she thought her brain must give way. She would have to leave Woodview. Oh, the shame of confession! Mrs. Barfield, who had been so good to her, and who thought so highly of her. Her father would not have her at home; she would be homeless in London. No hope of obtaining a situation. . . . they would send her away without a character, homeless in London, and every month her position growing more desperate. . . .

4   A sickly faintness crept up through her. The flesh had come to the relief of the spirit; and she sank upon her chair, almost unconscious, sick, it seemed, to death, and she rose from the chair wiping her forehead slowly with her apron. . . . She might be mistaken. And she hid her face in her hands, and then, falling on her knees, her arms thrown forward upon the table, she prayed for strength to walk without flinching under any cross that He had thought fit to lay upon her.

5   There was still the hope that she might be mistaken; and this hope lasted for one week, for two, but at the end of the third week

it perished, and she abandoned herself in prayer. She prayed for strength to endure with courage what she now knew she must endure, and she prayed for light to guide her in her present decision. Mrs. Barfield, however much she might pity her, could not keep her once she knew the truth, whereas none might know the truth if she did not tell it. She might remain at Woodview earning another quarter's wages; the first she had spent on boots and clothes, she second she had just been paid. If she stayed on for another quarter she would have eight pounds, and with that money, and much less time to keep herself, she might be able to pull through. But would she be able to go undetected for nearly three whole months, until her next wages came due? She must risk it.

Three months of constant fear and agonising suspense wore 6 away, and no one, not even Margaret, suspected Esther's condition. Encouraged by her success, and seeing still very little sign of change in her person, and as every penny she could earn was of vital consequence in the coming time, Esther determined to risk another month; then she would give notice and leave. Another month passed, and Esther was preparing for departure when a whisper went round, and before she could take steps to leave she was told that Mrs. Barfield wished to see her in the library. Esther turned a little pale, and the expression of her face altered; it seemed to her impossible to go before Mrs. Barfield and admit her shame. Margaret, who was standing near and saw what was passing in her mind, said—

"Pull yourself together, Esther. You know the Saint—she's not 7 a bad sort. Like all the real good ones, she is kind enough to the faults of others."

"What's this? What's the matter with Esther?" said Mrs. Latch, 8 who had not yet heard of Esther's misfortune.

"I'll tell you presently, Mrs. Latch. Go, dear, get it over." 9

Esther hurried down the passage and passed through the baize 10 door without further thought. She had then but to turn to the left and a few steps would bring her to the library door. The room was already present in her mind. She could see it. The dim light, the little green sofa, the round table covered with books, the piano at the back, the parrot in the corner, and the canaries in the window. She knocked at the door. The well-known voice said, "Come in." She turned the handle, and found herself alone with her mistress. Mrs. Barfield laid down the book she was reading, and looked up. She did not look as angry as Esther had imagined, but her voice was harder than usual.

11   "Is this true, Esther?"

12   Esther hung down her head. She could not speak at first; then she said, "Yes."

13   "I thought you were a good girl, Esther."

14   "So did I, ma'am."

15   Mrs. Barfield looked at the girl quickly, hesitated a moment, and then said—

16   "And all this time—how long is it?"

17   "Nearly seven months, ma'am."

18   "And all this time you were deceiving us."

19   "I was three months gone before I knew it myself, ma'am."

20   "Three months! Then for three months you have knelt every Sunday in prayer in this room, for twelve Sundays you sat by me learning to read, and you never said a word?"

21   A certain harshness in Mrs. Barfield's voice awakened a rebellious spirit in Esther, and a lowering expression gathered above her eyes. She said—

22   "Had I told you, you would have sent me away then and there."

Engaging the Text

1. List any words that you are unsure of and look up their meanings in your dictionary. If your dictionary does not give you enough information, refer to "Looking Up Words in a Dictionary" in the Writer's Guide section of this book.

2. From what has been said about realistic writing, can you see why there are not many unfamiliar words in this selection?

3. It seems remarkable that Moore, a man, is able to describe for the reader how Esther, a woman, feels as she experiences the first flutter of life in her unborn child. List some of the details Moore uses.

Engaging the Reader

1. What is Esther's mood at the beginning of the selection? Is she happy in her work? Why?

2. At what point did you realize that Esther was pregnant? Was it before she did herself? If so, what clues did you find in the text to tell you this? List them.

3. What is Esther's "sin"? What does her feeling about it say about her own religious upbringing?
4. What gives Esther's employer the right to sit in judgment on her?

The Engaged Writer

1. List some details from a simple, physical experience you have had: a delicious meal, a small accident (like McClintock's in the previous selection), participation in an active sport (swimming, football, hockey, etc.). Then write a description similar to Moore's of Esther's awareness of the changes in her body.
2. What is a "good person"? How do you try to be a "good" person according to your own definition?
3. Find a piece of writing that you have already done for this class as a diagnostic essay, for another class, or on the job. In your writing example, find a place where you could have added details about an inner, physical experience. Try adding those details to your writing example.
4. Compare and contrast the differences between the treatment of Esther in this story (written in 1895) and today's treatment of an unmarried mother. Esther loses her job, has to leave her baby with inadequate caregivers, and works very hard in low-paying jobs to bring up her son successfully.

RUSSELL BAKER
___

Growing Up

Russell Baker, newspaper columnist and writer of the best-seller *Growing Up* (1982), was born in 1925 and grew up during the Great Depression. His father died young, leaving Russell's mother with nothing to rely on to provide for herself or her three children. She gave the baby to a relative to raise and took the two oldest children to New Jersey, where she stayed with her brother and his wife and existed on part-time jobs. Finally, Russell's mother was able to move to Baltimore with her children to a home of their own. Their apartment was above a seedy funeral parlor. The selection, which appeared in *Growing Up*, begins there, with twelve-year-old Russell trying to help out by delivering newspapers.

1   The thrill of a new life in a home of our own in Baltimore was short-lived. The only job my mother could find was selling magazine subscriptions door-to-door. There was no salary, just commissions on her sales. There were a few weeks when she sold nothing and there was no pay. . . .

2   I was too busy trying to learn the arts of survival in a big city to realize my mother was having a hard time making ends meet. On the third or fourth day at my new school I was authoritatively beaten up by a boy named Pete. It wasn't gentleman's combat such as I'd known in Belleville, but a savage, murderous beating. The playground at that school was a small fenced yard paved with brick. Pete flattened me on my back, straddled me and pounded my head into the brick with his fists while a hundred other boys, all strangers to me, cheered him on. My nose was bloodied, my lips split, my eyes blackened, and my face swollen for days afterwards. When a teacher finally pulled him off we were both hauled to the principal, who terrified me by threatening to expel us both from school if we were ever brought before her again.

3   Pete was not chastened. When we left the principal's office under orders to go immediately to our classes, he grabbed my arm and said, "Let's go outside and finish this right now."

4   "You already won," I said.

5   "Come on, we'll go outside and finish it," he said.

6   I was horrified. He wanted to kill me and was willing to risk expulsion from school to do it. "No," I said.

7   "Anytime you want to finish it, I'll be waiting," he said.

8   We went our separate ways to different classrooms. When I walked into mine the class had already begun. The teacher, a man admired by the students for his wit, interrupted the lesson to glance at me, then turned to the class and said, "Well, if it isn't 'Battling Baker.'" The class erupted in laughter. I hated that teacher, hated the school, and, above all, hated and feared the terrible Pete.

9   After that I felt like hunted prey. I feared that Pete was stalking me, looking for an opportunity to finish me off. I adjusted my habits to avoid him. At lunchtime I never went into the schoolyard, where he could trap me, but sat inside pretending to be absorbed in unfinished homework. I learned where Pete lived and was careful never to walk within two blocks of the place. I noted the route he walked to school and worked out another for myself that would keep me off his path. Even in areas where I felt reasonably safe, I

developed the habit of knowing always who was behind me on the sidewalk and studying intersections ahead for the slightest hint of danger. Learning the same jungle moves that quarry use to avoid their predators, I was developing the reflexes necessary to survive in cities.

Soon I learned other dangers peculiar to city streets at night. At   10
my twelfth birthday my mother had got me a job delivering the *Baltimore News-Post* and *Sunday American*. The *News-Post* was an afternoon paper, but the *American* didn't come off the presses until long after midnight and had to be delivered before dawn on Sunday. Usually I set my alarm clock for two A.M. on Sundays and tiptoed out of the house to avoid waking my mother and Doris. It was always an eerie experience: streets dark and abandoned, silences so deep that I jumped in fear at the sudden screech of a cat. . . .

Outside, the bracing cold air lifted my spirits, though there was   11
nothing inspiring in the landscape. Baltimore was the dullest place to look at I'd ever seen. Miles and miles of row houses, all with red brick facades, flat rooftops, four or five marble or sandstone steps. It was a triumph of architectural monotony, illuminated at night only by dim little globes of light that came from gas street lamps. Still, it was always exciting to rip open the bundles of fresh newspapers and be the first in the neighborhood to know tomorrow's news. Lately it had been more and more about Hitler, Mussolini, Chamberlain, and Stalin. The chanceries of Europe. War in the air, and so forth, and so on.

This morning, however, there was a bloodcurdling revelation.   12
Page one was half filled with a picture of several parcels, crudely wrapped in newspapers, lying on a police-station table. The story said they were pieces of a human body which had been dissected by an insane killer and discarded in the Baltimore sewer system. I scanned the story rapidly and felt a little better to learn that all the human parts so far recovered had been found in East Baltimore, a full two miles from West Lombard Street. Police had still not found the victim's head, however, and what was worse, the insane dissector was still at large.

A few months earlier Baltimore movie theaters had shown *Night*   13
Must Fall, a terrifying film about a killer who carried his dismembered victim's head around in a hatbox. I had seen this film. So, apparently, had the reporter writing this morning's story. It was possible, the story said, that the Baltimore madman was wander-

ing the streets carrying his victim's head. The *American* was a Hearst newspaper, and I knew Hearst papers sometimes tried to make a good story better than it actually was, but at that hour of the morning, alone on the streets of southwest Baltimore, I was incapable of mustering any reassuring skepticism. Still, the newspapers had to be delivered, no question about that, and I would do it, but I didn't want to meet anybody on those abandoned streets this morning while I was getting it done.

14   With a tonnage of Sunday papers held to my hip by the web strap, I set off up the Lombard Street side of Union Square. This was the best part of the route. There was good street light, and all the customers paid their bills every Saturday. Twelve cents for six afternoon papers and a nickel for the Sunday. Seventeen cents a week. Everything was quiet on Lombard Street and around on Gilmor Street, too. Not a sound stirring, not a shadow moving.

15   Out of papers, I went back to the drop point for a second bundle. This part of the route took me to Pratt Street, where half my customers were slow payers, wanting me to carry them three or four weeks until the bill ran up to 51 or 68 cents. When I finally threatened to cut off their service, they might come up with seventeen or maybe thirty-four cents and promise to pay in full next week. The worst part of Pratt Street was that the houses were cut up into small apartments and the customers expected me to come inside buildings, climb steps, and leave papers at their doors. Often there was no hallway light, which meant groping around in the darkness on tricky staircases and maybe falling over somebody's roller skate and spilling my whole load of papers. Trying to recover fifteen or twenty Sunday papers in a pitch-black hallway was no picnic. I always walked in these places like a soldier in a mine field.

16   This morning I had no intention of going inside those houses. Delivering news of a mad dissector and the missing human head, I was in no mood to grope around on dark staircases. If I'd touched something human in there, which was possible since every once in a while I stumbled across drunks sleeping it off in unlit hallways, I might have died of fright. So I left the papers in downstairs hallways, deciding to let the customers howl next payday when most of them weren't going to pay anyhow.

17   When I went back to the drop point for the third bundle I was tired, and I sat down for a break to treat myself to the funny

papers. I knew the natural sounds of the city at this hour—the clang of a distant trolley car, the clatter of a dog rooting in a garbage can, the faint wail of fire engine sirens far away. I could detect the unfamiliar sound—and therefore the potentially dangerous sound—at considerable distances. This was what I heard now while I was looking at "The Katzenjammer Kids." It was the sound of footsteps, a man's footsteps. One man, and coming toward me from the east.

I saw his silhouette a block away, down at Calhoun Street. 18 Quickly hoisting a bundle of papers, I rammed them under the strap and set off at a right angle to his line of march. It was dark in this direction. Halfway down the block there was an alley with two outlets. If he'd seen me and followed, I could dump the papers and run. I ducked into the alley and waited. No footsteps. Peeking around the corner, I saw why. He had stopped at the intersection I'd just abandoned and seemed undecided which way to go.

When he started to walk again it was not in my direction, but towards Union Square. I'd had a good look at him while he stood under the gaslight at the corner. He was short, wore a dark overcoat with the collar turned up around his neck, and was hatless. Under the light, his hair looked silvery gray. He was not carrying a hatbox.

My imagination had got the best of me. He was probably a 19 drunk out too late, I thought. I saw drunks like that now and then on these Sunday mornings. Sometimes they bought a paper, gave me a quarter, and told me to keep the change. I'd probably missed a bonus by running away from this one. I resumed the work, feeling relaxed now that the bad moment was over. I finished the third bundle and was almost finished with the last when I turned the corner at McHenry and Stricker streets and found myself face to face with a man in a black overcoat. The collar was turned up around his neck. His hair looked silvery gray.

"Good morning," he said.   20

I was beyond speaking. I still had a few papers left to deliver 21 and, like an automaton, headed toward the houses where they belonged.

"Mind if I walk along with you?"   22

Terror made me speechless.   23

"It must be lonely with nobody to talk to," he said.   24

I shook my head. No, it wasn't lonely.   25

27   "It's cold this morning. Aren't you cold?"

28   With the combination of exertion and fear, I was sweating.

29   "I'm lonely too," he said.

30   I'd been mechanically dropping newspapers on doorsteps, and now as I dropped the last and turned from the doorway I was facing him under a good light. I'd never seen a man who looked so elegant. Certainly not in southwest Baltimore. He was from another, fancier section of town, I thought. His shoes glistened like patent leather. His overcoat seemed to have been finely tailored, as if molded to his body. The face was soft, sallow under the dim gaslight, but the eyes were piercing. The hair, I could now see, was not silver but yellow gone to gray. It was fastidiously barbered and slicked back with an unguent. I could smell a faint perfume.

31   "I've got to get home now," I said, sliding the strap off my shoulder. It was fitted with a heavy metal buckle. When doubled up so that the buckle was at the end of the loop, it made a weapon of sorts.

32   "You don't want to go home yet, it's early," he said, striding along beside me. "I know where there's a party. Would you like to go to a party?"

33   It was now around four-thirty in the morning.

34   "I'm too tired," I said.

35   "Don't you like parties? There'll be girls there."

36   "Not tonight," I said. We were getting closer to Lombard Street. I groped in my pocket for the door key.

37   "You'll like these girls," he said. "They're the kind of girls who let you do things to them."

38   I didn't believe that. Even if I had it wouldn't have tempted me to set off with him. I'd begun to have fantasies about such girls, but fantasy girls and real girls were not the same. I was scared in the presence of real girls, but I was not stupid about them. I knew that the kind of girls who let men do things to them weren't going to pass time with somebody like me at four-thirty on a Sunday morning.

39   We'd finally reached Lombard Street, just a few doors from home.

40   "Come on," he said. "I've got a nice girl for you. She likes to do things and she's fourteen years old. She knows what to do."

41   "I don't like girls," I said.

I had my key out now. With a quick bound, I was up the steps   42
and had the key in the lock, but he was just as fast, and he was up
the steps leaning against me with his hand slammed down over
the key before I could turn it. I twisted aside to free the hand that
held the web strap and swung it as hard as I could, but in such
close contact I couldn't get any momentum into the blow and the
strap whacked him harmlessly across one shoulder.

The hostility of the blow, though, cooled him a bit, and he   43
backed down two steps and studied me.

"Come on, you'll have a wonderful time," he said, speaking   44
very low now, almost whispering.

"No."   45

He took one step back toward me. I brought the strap around   46
as hard as I could and heard it slash across the side of his face and
saw him back off holding his hand to his jaw. I twisted the key in
the lock, pushed the door open, slid into safety, and slammed the
door behind me. I stood in the vestibule, soaked with perspiration,
my hands shaking violently. . . .

When I woke around noon I decided against telling my moth-   47
er, or anybody else, about the man with the silvery hair. A few days
later when the madman who dissected his victims was arrested,
the pictures of him in the *News-Post* showed a squat and shabby
longshoreman with matted black hair who had lost his temper in
a lover's quarrel and, panicked by what he had done to his love,
dismembered her with a butcher knife. For months afterwards I
spent the dark hours before Sunday dawn on guard against the
man with the silvery hair, just as I spent the daytime hours on
guard against Pete, but I never saw him again.

Engaging the Text

1. Baker is an experienced newspaper reporter. He organizes his
   story according to time. Outline the story the way Russell
   Baker tells it, indicating the times of the events.
2. Here are some of the words Baker uses to create the atmosphere of threat and violence found in these two incidents.
   Check their meanings and show how Baker uses them to create horror and suspense in his story: survive (9), authoritatively (2), chastened (3), stalking (9), predators (9), reflexes (9),

monotony (11), dissected (12), dissector (16), dismembered (13, 47), mustering (13), skepticism (13), automaton (22), sallow (30), fastidiously (30), unguent (30), momentum (42).

Engaging the Reader

1. What hints do you get in paragraph 1 from Baker's descriptions of his home and his town that the story will not be a humorous one?
2. What two dangers greet Russell in the nighttime city streets? How does he overcome them?

The Engaged Writer

1. Compare Baker's description of Baltimore with Richard Rodriguez's description of the town where he grew up.
2. Write about an important, memorable, or disturbing experience you have had and describe it as Baker does his two experiences with violence.
3. Compare Baker's experience as a new boy in school with Richard Rodriguez's ("The Achievement of Desire"), the students' in Donald Baker's "Graduation in the Mountains", or Amiri Baraka's (excerpt from *The Autobiography of LeRoi Jones*). What similarities and what differences exist among them? How do you account for the differences?
4. Tell about a frightening experience you have had; organize it chronologically. If they fit, use some of the words from exercise 2 in "Engaging the Text."

RICHARD RODRIGUEZ

The Achievement of Desire

In his autobiography, *Hunger of Memory: The Education of Richard Rodriguez,* the author tells of his journey from a working-class Mexican American family to a Ph.D. and scholarship at the British Museum, the research library in London. Along the way, he becomes troubled by his increasing alienation from his family and the values they hold. As Rodriguez prepares to speak to a class, he attempts to sort

out his conflicting emotions: shame, satisfaction, pride, and regret—
all directed toward his feelings about his "success."

I stand in the ghetto classroom—'the guest speaker'—attempting   1
to lecture on the mystery of the sounds of our words to rows of dif-
fident students. 'Don't you hear it? Listen! The music of our words.
"Summer is i-cumen in. . . ." And songs on the car radio. We need
Aretha Franklin's voice to fill plain words with music—her life.' In
the face of their empty stares, I try to create an enthusiasm. But the
girls in the back row turn to watch some boy passing outside.
There are flutters of smiles, waves. And someone's mouth elon-
gates heavy, silent words through the barrier of glass. Silent
words—the lips straining to shape each voiceless syllable: *'Meet
meee late errr.'* By the door, the instructor smiles at me, apparently
hoping that I will be able to spark some enthusiasm in the class.
But only one student seems to be listening. A girl, maybe fourteen.
In this gray room her eyes shine with ambition. She keeps nodding
and nodding at all that I say; she even takes notes. And each time
I ask a question, she jerks up and down in her desk like a mari-
onette, while her hand waves over the bowed heads of her classmates. It is myself (as a boy) I see as she faces me now (a man in
my thirties).

The boy who first entered a classroom barely able to speak Eng-   2
lish, twenty years later concluded his studies in the stately quiet
of the reading room in the British Museum. Thus with one sentence I can summarize my academic career. It will be harder to
summarize what sort of life connects the boy to the man.

With every award, each graduation from one level of education   3
to the next, people I'd meet would congratulate me. Their refrain
always the same: 'Your parents must be very proud.' Sometimes
then they'd ask me how I managed it—my 'success.' (How?) After
a while, I had several quick answers to give in reply. I'd admit, for
one thing, that I went to an excellent grammar school. (My earliest teachers, the nuns, made my success their ambition.) And my
brother and both my sisters were very good students. (They often
brought home the shiny school trophies I came to want.) And my
mother and father always encouraged me. (At every graduation
they were behind the stunning flash of the camera when I turned
to look at the crowd.)

4   As important as these factors were, however, they account inadequately for my academic advance. Nor do they suggest what an odd success I managed. For although I was a very good student, I was also a very bad student. I was a 'scholarship boy,' a certain kind of scholarship boy. Always successful, I was always unconfident. Exhilarated by my progress. Sad. I became the prized student—anxious and eager to learn. Too eager, too anxious—an imitative and unoriginal pupil. My brother and two sisters enjoyed the advantages I did, and they grew to be as successful as I, but none of them ever seemed so anxious about their schooling. A second-grade student, I was the one who came home and corrected the 'simple' grammatical mistakes of our parents. ('Two negatives make a positive.') Proudly I announced—to my family's startled silence—that a teacher had said I was losing all trace of a Spanish accent. I was oddly annoyed when I was unable to get parental help with a homework assignment. The night my father tried to help me with an arithmetic exercise, he kept reading the instructions, each time more deliberately, until I pried the textbook out of his hands, saying, 'I'll try to figure it out some more by myself.'

5   When I reached the third grade, I outgrew such behavior. I became more tactful, careful to keep separate the two very different worlds of my day. But then, with ever-increasing intensity, I devoted myself to my studies. I became bookish, puzzling to all my family. Ambition set me apart. When my brother saw me struggling home with stacks of library books, he would laugh, shouting: 'Hey, Four Eyes!' My father opened a closet one day and was startled to find me inside, reading a novel. My mother would find me reading when I was supposed to be asleep or helping around the house or playing outside. In a voice angry or worried or just curious, she'd ask: 'What do you see in your books?' It became the family's joke. When I was called and wouldn't reply, someone would say I must be hiding under my bed with a book.

6   (How did I manage my success?)

7   What I am about to say to you has taken me more than twenty years to admit: *A primary reason for my success in the classroom was that I couldn't forget that schooling was changing me and separating me from the life I enjoyed before becoming a student.* That simple realization! For years I never spoke to anyone about it. Never mentioned

a thing to my family or my teachers or classmates. From a very early age, I understood enough, just enough about my classroom experiences to keep what I knew repressed, hidden beneath layers of embarrassment. Not until my last months as a graduate student, nearly thirty years old, was it possible for me to think much about the reasons for my academic success. Only then. At the end of my schooling, I needed to determine how far I had moved from my past. The adult finally confronted, and now must publicly say, what the child shuddered from knowing and could never admit to himself or to those many faces that smiled at his every success. ('Your parents must be very proud. . . .')

Engaging the Text

1. *"Sumer is i-cumen in . . ."* is the opening line of a fourteenth-century popular song. Aretha Franklin is a contemporary singer. Rodriguez is talking about sounds and words. Does his message get through to the students he is addressing? Why or why not?
2. Throughout the excerpt, Rodriguez uses incomplete sentences, for example, in paragraph 4, "Exhilarated by my progress." He also begins many sentences with "And . . ." What effect do these sentence structures have on the reader?
3. The epithet "Four Eyes," used by Rodriguez's brother, will be understood by anyone who had to wear glasses as a child. Give some examples from your own experience of this kind of childish name-calling.

Engaging the Reader

1. Can you "summarize your academic career" in one sentence, as Rodriguez does in paragraph 2?
2. Why does Rodriguez have difficulty admitting that he has become "successful" by separating himself from the life he enjoyed with his family before becoming a student?
3. What kind of an argument do you think Rodriguez is making—does he seem to be in favor of affirmative action or against it? Does he think he "made it" on his own, or with the help of his parents, school officials, and scholarships? How does he feel about that?

The Engaged Writer

1. Start writing your own autobiography. Start with the questions: What is it like to be me? What event or events changed my life?

ALEX KOTLOWITZ

There Are No Children Here

Alex Kotlowitz writes about urban affairs and social issues for the *Wall Street Journal.* The articles he wrote about a particular family living in the run-down Chicago projects became a book called *There Are No Children Here* (1991) and won the Robert F. Kennedy journalism award. He lives in Chicago, where the following account takes place. Kotlowitz interviewed and visited the family he wrote about over a period of three years. He witnessed nearly half of the scenes he described; the rest he documented from eyewitnesses and official records of the Chicago Police Department and the Bureau of Alcohol, Tobacco, and Firearms. He became involved in the lives of Pharoah, Lafeyette, and their mother LaJoe, helping them in many ways, including using proceeds from the book to help the boys enter a private school. He says in the book's Epilogue: "I know there are people who will say that I became too involved with the family, that I broke my pact as a journalist to remain detached and objective."

1   The Children called home "Hornets" or, more frequently, "the projects" or, simply, the "jects" (pronounced *jets*). Pharoah called it "the graveyard." But they never referred to it by its full name: the Governor Henry Horner Homes.

2   Nothing here, the children would tell you, was as it should be. Lafeyette and Pharoah lived at 1920 West Washington Boulevard, even though their high-rise sat on Lake Street. Their building had no enclosed lobby; a dark tunnel cut through the middle of the building, and the wind and strangers passed freely along it. Those tenants who received public aid had their checks sent to the local currency exchange, since the building's first-floor mailboxes had all been broken into. And since darkness engulfed the building's corridors, even in the daytime, the residents always carried flash-

lights, some of which had been handed out by a local politician during her campaign.

Summer, too, was never as it should be. It had become a season 3 of duplicity.

On June 13, a couple of weeks after their peaceful afternoon on 4 the railroad tracks, Lafeyette celebrated his twelfth birthday. Under the gentle afternoon sun, yellow daisies poked through the cracks in the sidewalk as children's bright faces peered out from behind their windows. Green leaves clothed the cottonwoods, and pastel cotton shirts and shorts, which had sat for months in layaway, clothed the children. And like the fresh buds on the crabapple trees, the children's spirits blossomed with the onset of summer.

Lafeyette and his nine-year-old cousin Dede danced across the 5 worn lawn outside their building, singing the lyrics of an L. L. CoolJ rap, their small hips and spindly legs moving in rhythm. The boy and girl were on their way to a nearby shopping strip, where Lafeyette planned to buy radio headphones with $8.00 he had received as a birthday gift.

Suddenly, gunfire erupted. The frightened children fell to the 6 ground. "Hold your head down!" Lafeyette snapped, as he covered Dede's head with her pink nylon jacket. If he hadn't physically restrained her, she might have sprinted for home, a dangerous action when the gangs started warring. "Stay down," he ordered the trembling girl.

The two lay pressed to the beaten grass for half a minute, until 7 the shooting subsided. Lafeyette held Dede's hand as they cautiously crawled through the dirt toward home. When they finally made it inside, all but fifty cents of Lafeyette's birthday money had trickled from his pockets.

Lafeyette's summer opened the way it would close, with gun- 8 shots. For Lafeyette and Pharoah, these few months were to be a rickety bridge to adolescence.

If the brothers had one guidepost in their young lives these few 9 months, though, it was their mother, LaJoe. They depended on her; she depended on them. The boys would do anything for their mother.

A shy, soft-spoken woman, LaJoe was known for her warmth 10 and generosity, not only to her own children but to her children's friends. Though she received Aid to Families with Dependent Children, neighbors frequently knocked on her door to borrow a can of soup or a cup of flour. She always obliged. LaJoe had often mothered children who needed advice or comforting. Many young men and women still called her "Mom." She let so many people through her apartment, sometimes just to use the bathroom, that she hid the toilet paper in the kitchen because it had often been stolen.

11   But the neighborhood, which hungrily devoured its children, had taken its toll of LaJoe as well. In recent years, she had become more tired as she questioned her ability to raise her children here. She no longer fixed her kids' breakfasts every day—and there were times when the children had to wash their own clothes in the bathtub. Many of the adults had aged with the neighborhood, looking as worn and empty as the abandoned stores that lined the once-thriving Madison Street. By their mid-thirties many women had become grandmothers; by their mid-forties, great-grandmothers. They nurtured and cared for their boyfriends and former boyfriends and sons and grandsons and great-grandsons.

12   LaJoe, in her youth, had been stunning, her smooth, light brown complexion highlighted by an open smile. When she pulled her hair back in a ponytail, she appeared almost Asian, her almond-shaped eyes gazing out from a heart-shaped face. She had been so pretty in her mid-twenties that she briefly tried a modeling career. Now she was thirty-five, and men still whistled and smiled at her on the street. Unlike many other women her age, she hadn't put on much weight, and her high-cheek-boned face still had a sculptured look. But the confidence of her youth had left her. Her shoulders were often hunched. She occasionally awoke with dark circles under her eyes. And her smile was less frequent now.

13   LaJoe had watched and held on as the neighborhood slowly decayed, as had many urban communities like Horner over the past two decades. First, the middle-class whites fled to the suburbs. Then the middle-class blacks left for safer neighborhoods. Then businesses moved, some to the suburbs, others to the South. Over the past ten years, the city had lost a third of its manufacturing jobs, and there were few jobs left for those who lived in Henry Horner. Unemployment was officially estimated at 19 percent; unofficially, it was probably much higher. There were neighborhoods in Chicago worse off than Horner, but the demise of this particular community was often noted because it had once been among the city's wealthiest areas.

LaJoe sometimes believed that the city had all but given up here.   14
A local billboard warned NEEDLES KILL. There was a time when
such a message read DRUGS KILL.

And despite Horner's proximity—one mile—to the city's   15
booming downtown, LaJoe and her neighbors felt abandoned.
Horner sat so close to the city's business district that from the Sears
Tower observation deck tourists could have watched Lafeyette
duck gunfire on his birthday. But city residents never had reason
to pass the housing complex unless they attended a basketball or
hockey game at the Chicago Stadium, just a block away.

Exacerbating the isolation was the fact that nearly half of the   16
families in Henry Horner, including the Riverses, had no telephone. Residents also felt disconnected from one another; there
was little sense of community at Horner, and there was even less
trust. Some residents who didn't have a phone, for instance, didn't
know any others in their building who would let them use theirs.
Some neighbors wouldn't allow their children to go outside to
play. One mother moved aside her living room furniture to make
an open and safe place where her children could frolic.

But though the isolation and the physical ruin of the area's   17
stores and homes had discouraged LaJoe, it was her family that
had most let her down. Not that she could separate the two. Sometimes she blamed her children's problems on the neighborhood; at
other times, she attributed the neighborhood's decline to the
change in people, to the influx of drugs and violence.

Her three oldest children, to whom she felt she'd given every-   18
thing she could, had all disappointed her. All had dropped out of
school. All had been in jail at least once. All had been involved with
drugs. The oldest, LaShawn, a slender twenty-year-old, was so delicately featured some called her "China Doll." She worked as a
prostitute from time to time to support her drug habit. The next
oldest, nineteen-year-old Paul, named after his father, had served
time in an Indiana prison for burglary. Terence, now seventeen,
had been the most troublesome problem for LaJoe and, because of
their extraordinary closeness, her biggest disappointment. He
began selling drugs at the age of eleven and had been in and out,
usually in, trouble with the law ever since.

LaJoe also had a set of four-year-old triplets: Timothy, Tiffany,   19
and Tammie. The two girls so resembled each other that not even
their father could tell them apart.

20   All eight children had the same father, Paul, to whom LaJoe had been married for seventeen years. But the two had long ago fallen out of love. He lived at home only sporadically.

21   LaJoe wanted it to be different for Lafeyette and Pharoah, different from the way it had been for her three oldest children and different from the way it had been for her.

Engaging the Text

1. Many of the verbs and words derived from verbs used in this selection add to the picture of the Rivers family's life: sprinted (6), trickled (7), devoured (11), aged (11), abandoned (11), hunched (12), decayed (13), exacerbating (16), discouraged (17), and disappointed (18). Find these and other similar words that Kotlowitz uses. Try using such descriptive verbs in your own writing, rather than verbs such as "is" or "was."
2. The author uses paraphrased incidents and some direct quotations from the participants to enliven the story. Find some of these and describe how they are integrated smoothly into the text.
3. The names of the central characters in this study are not misspelled—that is how they are actually spelled. Can you figure out why they have such unusual spellings?

Engaging the Reader

1. This example of journalistic writing is a "case study," in which the lives and actions of the subjects are examined in detail to give the reader an unbiased picture of them. What are some of the details Kotlowitz used to make this a factual study?
2. What are some of the details Kotlowitz used to add emotional color to the story—to make us see and feel the atmosphere surrounding the Rivers family?
3. How do we learn about some of the changes that occurred in the Henry Horner Homes since the 1950s, when the boys' grandparents first moved there? Why have these changes occurred?

The Engaged Writer

1. Do you agree with the last statement in the introduction to this selection? It implies that a journalist should not become emo-

tionally involved with his or her "story." Argue for or against
Kotlowitz's statement.

2. Most of this selection deals with LaJoe Rivers, mother of eight
and resident in the Henry Horner Homes, a Chicago low-
income housing project. From the index of your local paper or
that of a city near you, find some similar articles about conditions in low-income housing and use them as the basis for
writing an article modeled on Kotlowitz's.

JULIA FLYNN SILER

Growing Up Poor—and Scared to Death

The following article is an example of a book review. This review,
which originally appeared in *Business Week*, evaluates and discusses Alex Kotlowitz's book, *There Are No Children Here: The Story
of Two Boys Growing Up in the Other America*, published in 1991. (The
previous selection in *The Engaging Reader* was excerpted from this
book.) The reviewer, in addition to a brief summary of the book,
develops an important thesis—that the author "has fashioned a
powerful work." Often a reviewer will use the assignment of a book
review to write an essay on a subject drawn from that book, and
that's what Siler has done.

On Mar. 30, a 14-year-old girl from a Chicago housing project was   1
shot in the face after arguing with a man police say stole her cig-
arettes. Her death got a brief mention in the metro section of the
Chicago Tribune two days later. The *Chicago Sun-Times* ignored it. In
a city that remains one of the nation's most segregated, black children are often victims of brutal crime. One more death is hardly
news.

That's one reason Alex Kotlowitz, a reporter in *The Wall Street*   2
Journal's Chicago bureau, wrote *There Are No Children Here*. Kotlowitz says he hoped "a book about the children would make us
all hear, that it would make us all stop and listen." To that end, he
has fashioned a powerful work. Through deeply affecting portraits
of two brothers in the Governor Henry Horner Homes on the city's

West Side, Kotlowitz makes vivid the terrors of growing up in the projects. He confronts us with the daily experience of Pharoah and Lafeyette Rivers, 9 and 11 years old at the outset, over two years.

3   Perhaps the book can help narrow the compassion gap between mainstream Americans and the inner-city poor. It certainly shows how wide that gap is. In the opening, we see Pharoah, Lafeyette, and some other boys playing in a field by some railroad tracks. It's the summer of 1987, and they're trying to catch snakes. When a train carrying mostly white commuters approaches, the boys dive for cover. One bursts into tears. All have heard that the suburbanites shoot at black kids from behind the tinted train windows, because they're trespassing on the tracks. Kotlowitz notes that commuters, equally frightened of the kids, often move away from the windows as the train passes through the city's blighted core.

4   In 1956, when the boys' maternal grandparents moved into the homes, public housing projects seemed an impressive effort to shelter the less fortunate. The complex of high rises boasted a new playground and a grass baseball diamond. Lafeyette and Pharoah's mother, LaJoe, who grew up in the building they live in, attended Girl Scout meetings and roller-skating parties in the basement. Members of the family were active in politics and were friendly with the neighborhood's white alderman. Two of them worked for city agencies.

5   Since then, there has been a terrible transformation. The boys and their family often huddle against the walls of their first-floor apartment as gangs exchange gunfire outside. LaJoe, the unemployed mother of eight, heads the family; her husband, an alcoholic and heroin addict, is often absent. Fourteen-year-olds in the projects can earn $600 in a week—more than LaJoe gets from welfare in a month—running drugs.

6   While most kids wonder what they'll be when they grow up, Lafeyette and Pharoah wonder if they'll grow up at all. LaJoe, for her part, wonders if the apartment was once used by an abortionist who flushed fetuses down the toilet, because a horrible smell issues from it. The building manager finds, instead, that the basement is full of rotting animal carcasses and human and animal excrement. Months pass before the mess is removed by workers in gas masks.

When we meet the brothers, the gang warfare is at a hot-weather 7
high. The younger one, Pharoah, "now trembled at any loud
noise," Kotlowitz writes. "While bullets tore past the living room
window, Pharoah had pleaded . . . 'M-m-m-m-mamma, make'em,
make'em stop!' As the gunfire continued, he fainted."

Sometimes Pharoah won't talk about the violence and death all 8
around. Other times, he can't, because of a worsening stutter.
When an older brother gets 10 years in prison for armed robbery,
Pharoah says: "Mama, I'm just too young to understand how life
really is." One night, LaJoe finds him crawling in the hallway, still
asleep, while automatic weapons rat-a-tat-tat outside. A few days
later, Pharoah says: "I worry about dying, dying at a young age."

Lafeyette also suffers, especially after his friend Bird Leg is shot 9
to death. At the funeral, a friend tells him: "We're gonna die one
way or the other by killing or plain out. I just wanna die plain out."
Lafeyette nods: "Me too." Soon after, a teenager he admires is
killed in a questionable shooting by an agent from the Bureau of
Alcohol, Tobacco & Firearms. Lafeyette is plagued by nightmares
and diarrhea. He tells LaJoe: "Mama, I'm real tired. . . . Anytime I
go outside, I ain't guaranteed to come back."

But the boys are also brave and resilient. During one shoot-out, 10
LaJoe must stop Lafeyette from running out to bring his brother
safely inside. Pharoah studies hard in the crowded apartment
to prepare for a spelling bee. Not only does he overcome his stutter during the bee, he places second. Kotlowitz says Pharoah
clutches childhood "with the vigor of a tiger gripping his meat."
He reads *Old Yeller*, watches cartoons, saves for video games and
candy. When the boys see their first rainbow, he chases through the
bleak neighborhood looking for a pot of gold. Lafeyette calls that
"kiddie stuff" and stays behind. But later, he wonders whether "I
could have found some real little peoples and they'd of been my
friends . . ."

Readers can't help but care about Lafeyette and Pharoah. It's not 11
surprising that Kotlowitz does, too. He has given them money for
private school, taken them on fishing trips, and bought them jeans
and sneakers. With proceeds from his book, he plans to set up a
trust fund for them. Kotlowitz could be faulted for abandoning his
objectivity. But at least, unlike most of the world outside the projects, he hasn't abandoned the boys.

Engaging the Text

1. The author uses paraphrased incidents and direct quotations from the book to discuss it. How does she integrate them smoothly into her narrative? What are some of the transitions?
2. The quotations from the book are direct: they reflect the way Lafeyette and Pharoah really speak. How does this add to the effectiveness of the story?

Engaging the Reader

1. What do we learn about the changes that occurred in the Henry Horner Homes since the 1950s, when the boys' grandparents moved there? Why have these changes occurred?
2. After reading the excerpt from the book and this book review, would you enjoy reading the whole book? Why or why not?

The Engaged Writer

1. Using a tape recorder, interview a relative who has lived a difficult or challenging life. Transcribe this interview, and form it into an organized essay with a thesis, reproducing, as well as you can, the exact words and dialect, if any, of the person you interview.
2. Do you agree with the reviewer that "Kotlowitz could be faulted for abandoning his objectivity"? Why or why not?

PART
2

The Ordinary World: Other People and Places

This section begins with the world outside us. It tells how we move out of ourselves and learn to use and relate to information from our surroundings.

Through reading, speaking, or writing, we emerge from our private self. A child learns to speak, then to read, and then to write. Writers express themselves through their choice of words and the way they put them together. A deaf person learns sign language; a hearing person learns to speak; a speaker learns to write. The outside world impinges on us, in both spoken and written form. The writer becomes more adept at using words and learns to control them choosing words that best fit the purpose of the piece of writing. Although the material in this section is still about people, these stories and articles look at other people's lives and experiences, as well as those of the narrator.

This section also suggests different ways of organizing ideas that come from outside the self and of putting them into written paragraphs or essays. The first method of organizing material involves making a simple list. Sometimes the list itself can form an essay, as when Michael Dobbs, author of "The ABCs of the U.S.A." humorously pokes fun at some of America's habits and customs, listing items alphabetically.

The next kind of organization compares and contrasts two things, two people, or two ideas. One selection does this directly, contrasting two prominent women, both named Roosevelt (Richard Cohen, "Glittering Alice and Sad Eleanor"). Two very different essays discuss traveling across America by road (William Least Heat-Moon, "South by Southeast," and Sue Hubbell, "On the Road"). Another pair (Donald P. Baker, "Graduation in the Mountains," and Amiri

Baraka, "Young") describes different high school experiences in a rural and a city school.

Still another method of organization involves definition. One essay, "Deep in Truth's Country," by C. L. Rawlins goes far beyond defining the term *wilderness* to discuss spirituality.

Compassion, delight, and humor form the basis of two more essays: one, Aldo Leopold's "Red Lanterns," is simply a reflective October walk with a dog; the other is a humorous essay on the ever-present cockroach by a busy journalist, Courtland Milloy.

MICHAEL DOBBS

The ABCs of the U.S.A.:
Americana, Seen with European Eyes

British-born, Michael Dobbs returned to the United States in 1987 after seven years in Europe as a foreign correspondent for a major newspaper. He returned with a new look at things American, which he expresses in these impressions, organized from A to Z.

1   America can be a strange experience for a foreigner. My wife and I arrived in the United States in January after seven years overseas—four in France, three in Poland. From the jumble of first impressions, we compiled an A-to-Z explanation of why America can be such a foreign country to those who arrive here from Europe.

2   I should explain at the outset that I am from Britain, but my Florida-born wife Lisa is as American as apple pie. In this alphabet, however, A does not stand for apple pie. It stands for:

3   *Ambition.* In the Old World, people are taught to hide it. An exception was Macbeth who (Shakespeare tells us) nurtured "an ambition that o'er-leaps itself and falls on the other side"—and look what happened to him. Here, it seems quite proper to announce that you are after the boss's job or want to make a million dollars by the age of 30.

4   *Breakfast.* The American habit of conducting business at breakfast has reached Europe, but I doubt that it will ever really catch

on. In France and Britain, breakfast is too much a family affair. Here, it has become part of the power game.

Credit Cards. You really can't leave home without them. It is interesting, and somewhat infuriating, to discover that bad credit is better than no credit at all: I was refused a Visa card on the grounds that I did not have a credit profile. Speaking of credit cards, we are bemused by the relatively new fad of destroying the carbons. Back in Europe, people prefer to keep their fingers clean.

Dreams. The American Dream, dented though it's been recently, is still very much alive. Dreaming great dreams is what keeps American society going—from the waitress who wants to become a car dealer to the street kid who wants to become a basketball star. Europeans dream dreams too, but don't seem to believe in them so much. See *Ambition.*

Exercise. A couple of years ago, I came to Washington in the slipstream of French President François Mitterrand. A cheer went up from the French press corps as our bus passed a fitness center—and we saw body-conscious Americans bending, stretching and leaping from side to side. America's fetish for fitness amuses—and puzzles—Europeans.

First names. In Europe, there is a natural and orderly progression from the use of last names to the use of first names. Here, it's first names at first sight. This can create confusion. I have one acquaintance who calls me Bill—and I am not quite sure how to correct him.

Gadgets. These can be addictive. It is difficult to imagine now how we survived for so long without the cruise control, the automatic ice dispenser, the microwave and the cordless telephone.

Hechinger. If I were in charge of arranging the programs of visiting delegations from communist countries, I would include a compulsory visit to Hechinger. We know Polish farmers who have to wait months to buy fencing for their livestock. Their eyes would pop out of their heads in this temple of American capitalism.

Insurance. Americans have a policy to cover every risk, both conceivable and inconceivable. So far, we have refused rental reimbursement insurance for our car, death insurance for our mortgage and supplementary title insurance for our house. It gives us a feeling of living dangerously.

Junk food. Anyone who wants to understand why Americans suffer from higher rates of cancer and arteriosclerosis only has to look at what they eat.

13   *Ketchup.* I had to come to America to discover that it can be eaten with anything—from french fries to French cheese.

14   *Lines.* American lines—beginning with the yellow line at immigration control—are the most orderly and organized in the world. The British queue, once internationally renowned, has begun to fray at the edges in recent years. *La queue Française* was never very impressive, and *la linea Italiana* is simply a mob.

15   *Money.* In Europe, money is something that everybody likes to have—but is careful not to flaunt. Unless it has been in the family for several generations, there is often an assumption that it has been acquired dishonestly. In America, the green justifies the means.

16   *No smoking.* No longer just a polite injunction in America, almost an evangelical campaign. Nobody would dare ask a Frenchman to put out his Gauloises in a restaurant.

17   *Ollie North.* What other major western democracy would allow a lieutenant colonel to make foreign policy? A hero for some, a traitor for others, Ollie (see *first names*) is a wonderful example of the American go-for-it attitude that both awes and alarms foreigners.

18   *Patriotism.* Exists everywhere, of course, but the American version is brasher, louder, and more self-conscious than the European. In Britain, it is taken for granted that a citizen or politician loves his country. Here, he is expected to prove it.

19   *Quiet.* American cities are quieter than European cities—thanks to noise controls on automobiles and the recent spate of environmental legislation. This was a major surprise for someone brought up to assume that America was a noisy place.

20   *Religion.* It's difficult, somehow, to imagine an English version of Jim and Tammy Bakker. When my parents came to visit recently, they were startled at the sight of a fire-breathing Jimmy Swaggart denouncing the Bakkers on live TV. That's not the kind of way they behave in our dear old Church of England.

21   *Sales.* Ever since arriving in Washington, we have been hurrying to take advantage of this week's unrepeatable *offer*—only to discover that it is usually repeated next week. We are just catching on that there is always an excuse for a sale.

22   *Television.* How grown-ups can watch game shows and sitcoms at 11 A.M. mystifies me—but the national habit, day or night, is contagious. I recently found myself nodding in full agreement with a professorial type who was saying that American kids watch too

much television. It was only later that I realized that I was watching him say this on television.

Ulcers. See Work.   23

Visas. Americans don't need visas to visit Britain (or most Euro-   24
pean countries, for that matter). To get my entry permit for the
United States, I had to sign a document promising that I would not
overthrow the government by force, had never been a member of
the Communist Party, and was not wanted for war crimes. I had
to provide details of my affiliation to labor unions as well as affi-
davits from four countries stating that I had no criminal record. All
this for cruise control and a cordless telephone.

Work. A leading Polish sociologist, Jan Szczepanski, once told   25
me that many Poles imagine that they will become rich simply by
emigrating to America. He tries to persuade whoever will listen
that America became a rich society through work, work and more
work. It is still true.

X-rated movies. We have them in Europe too, but not on motel   26
room TVs and not in most small towns.

Yuppies. The European counterpart remains a pale shadow of   27
the all-American original. The animal seems more driven, more
ubiquitous on this side of the Atlantic.

Zillion. What other nation would have invented a number that   28
is infinitely more than a billion? America may not always be the
best, but it is certainly the biggest.

Engaging the Text

1. This essay is full of words, obviously, though some of them
    need footnotes, such as credit profile (5) and Hechinger (10—
    a chain of home, garden, do-it-yourself superstores in the
    Washington, DC, area). Other words may need to be looked
    up: bemused (5), slipstream (7), fetish (7), arteriosclerosis (12),
    evangelical (16), brasher (18, adjective), affiliation (24), affi-
    davits (24), and ubiquitous (27). Try using some of these in a
    sensible sentence, such as "The evangelical preacher was
    brasher than the bemused victim of arteriosclerosis" or "The
    ubiquitous client of Hechinger had a fetish about signing affi-
    davits."

2. The article is full of what might be called clichés (old, over-
    worked phrases). Examples are "as American as apple pie" or

"can't leave home without it." Change these and others from the selection so that they are new and fresh, instead of stale and overworked.

Engaging the Reader

1. The stand the author is taking (the place, frame of mind, or attitude the author takes) is called *point of view*. Point of view is very important here. Explain why the author chose his subtitle.
2. Form is the other important aspect of this article. The ABC device allows the writer to make a list rather than organize the essay around a topic or theme. What is the theme of the essay, even though it is not stated as such?

The Engaged Writer

1. Choose any item in Dobbs's alphabet, and using his basic ideas, develop a paper discussing the item further. Include a topic sentence.
2. Start collecting ABCs from your favorite hobby, from the world of rock music, from the company where you work, from your college. Develop one of them into an article as Dobbs does—with seriousness mixed with humor.
3. Compare Dobbs's view of America, essentially that of a foreigner, with George and Helen Waite Papashvily's description of a first view of America in "Yes, Your Honesty."
4. If you came to America fairly recently, make your own list of American objects, ideas, or products that amazed or amused you and write a paragraph about each the way Dobbs does, or choose one of them for a longer paper.

RICHARD COHEN

Glittering Alice and Sad Eleanor

Richard Cohen writes for the *Washington Post*. He took time from commenting on national affairs to write this comparison of two important women, relatives, both now dead. These two women expressed very different attitudes toward their looks, their lives, and their occupations. Alice Roosevelt Longworth was the eldest daughter of President Theodore Roosevelt (1900–1909). She was married in the White House to Speaker of the House Nicholas Longworth. She lived a long and glamorous social life and died in 1980, the date of this article. Eleanor Roosevelt, wife of President Franklin D. Roosevelt (1932–1945), led a busy and useful life during her husband's thirteen years as president. After his death in 1945, she continued a distinguished career as diplomat, writer, and speaker. She died in 1962.

It is one of those coincidences of history that Alice Roosevelt Long- 1 worth, daughter of the grand and unforgettable Teddy and wife of the totally forgettable Nicholas, died the very same week two more books were published about her cousin, Eleanor. The two hated each other—at least Alice hated Eleanor—thinking probably that they had little in common but a family name. They had something else: They were prisoners of their looks.

Alice, of course, was radiant and pretty—daughter of a presi- 2 dent, a Washington debutante, a standard of style and grace, the one who gave the color Alice Blue to the nation as surely as her father gave his name to a certain kind of stuffed toy bear.

She married in the White House, took the speaker of the House 3 of Representatives for her husband, and stayed pretty much at the center of things Washingtonian for something like 70 years. She was, as they say, formidable.

Eleanor, on the other hand, was homely. She had a voice pitched 4 at the level of chalk on a blackboard, and the teeth of a beaver. She was awkward in both speech and manner and when she talked— when she rose to speak—the experience was both painful to her and her audience. She had a husband, but there is reason to believe that she was unloved by him. There is about Eleanor Roosevelt an aura of aching sadness, yet in her own way she, too, was formidable. She certainly endures.

It is interesting to consider how their looks—the way they 5 looked to the world—shaped these two women. It is interesting because in some ways they were so similar. They were both Roosevelts—one of the Oyster Bay branch, the other of the Hyde Park—both well-off, both of the aristocracy, and both manifestly bright.

6   Eleanor's intelligence proclaimed itself. She threw herself into causes. She spoke for people who had no spokesperson and she spoke well. She championed the poor, the black, women and other minorities. She campaigned and lectured and gave speeches and she did this with such intensity and such effect that it is not too much to say that before her death she was either a goddess or a witch to most Americans.

7   I am partial to the goddess side, thinking that the worst you can call a person is not "do-gooder" but rather "do-nothinger." That is something you could never call Eleanor Roosevelt.

8   As for Alice, she showed her intelligence in her wit. It was she who said, "The secret of eternal youth is arrested development," and who commented on Wendell Willkie after he received the presidential nomination: "He sprang from the grass roots of the country clubs of America."

9   Her most admired remark, the one about Thomas Dewey looking like the "bridegroom on a wedding cake," was not hers at all. The reason we know is that she admitted it. She borrowed it, popularized it, but did not invent it.

10   No matter. She invented enough so that Washington adored her and presidents more or less routinely elbowed themselves to her side so that they could hear what she had to say.

11   Yet with Alice, there it stopped. She was what she was, and what she was was beautiful. She did more or less what was expected of pretty girls. She was perfect just being—just being Alice and being pretty—and in the America of both her youth and her maturity there was nothing better than to be rich and pretty and well-married.

12   That she was also intelligent was almost besides the point, like the gilding on a lily. And while she later became cherished for her wit, it was not because she could use it for any purpose, but because it was like her beauty itself: something of a jewel. She was the perfect appurtenance, the one men wanted seated next to them.

13   With Eleanor, the story is different. Her looks were not her strong suit and so she had to declare herself in another way—by intellect, character, indomitability. She did this well, found causes, gave purpose to her life and left this earth with the certainty that she had mattered.

14   The conventional view is to see Eleanor as sad and Alice as glittering. To an extent, I'm sure, that's true. But in reading the obitu-

aries, in reading how Alice cruelly imitated Eleanor and mocked her good causes, you get the sense that Alice herself realized that something ironic had happened, that she had somehow become trapped by her own good looks, by her perfection, by her wit—that she had become the eternal debutante, frozen in time. Eleanor was actually doing something.

So now Eleanor and Alice are dead. One led a sad life, the other a glittering one. But one suspects that as the books came out on Eleanor, Alice realized the tables had turned. There is something sad about being an ugly duckling, but there is something sadder yet about being the belle of the ball after the music has stopped, the guests have gone home and the rest of the world has gone to work.

Engaging the Text

1. Find a synonym—a word meaning the same thing—for the following words Cohen uses in his comparison: radiant (2), debutante (2, 14), formidable (3, 4), aristocracy (5), manifestly (5), popularized (9), appurtenance (12), and indomitability (13). Then look back at the original sentence and decide whether the original word or the synonym best fits the meaning.

2. Draw a line down the center of a piece of paper. Then label one side "Alice" and the other "Eleanor." Summarize briefly what the writer says about each one, leaving enough space between each notation to form an outline of the article. How does it look? Do the arguments alternate? Or is there another pattern? You can use this pattern for a comparison/contrast essay of your own.

3. Can you guess the attitude of the writer, Richard Cohen, toward each of these women? Which one does he like better? Now pick out some words or phrases the writer chooses that show this attitude.

Engaging the Reader

1. Who are the two women who are being contrasted? Why do you think Cohen picked these two particular women?

2. What is their connection with each other and with American history?

3. How were they alike? How different?

The Engaged Writer

1. Without referring to the article, write your own character sketch of Eleanor Roosevelt.
2. Do the same for Alice Longworth.
3. Then check back to see how accurate you were.
4. Using as a guide the outline you made in question 2 under "Engaging the Text," write an essay comparing and contrasting one of the following pairs of well-known people:

   — President Clinton and President Bush
   — Queen Elizabeth and Princess Diana
   — Your math teacher and your English teacher
   — Meryl Streep and Elizabeth Taylor
   — Michael Jackson and Bruce Springsteen
   — Norman Schwartzkopf and Oliver North
   — Booker T. Washington and W. E. B. Du Bois (in Part Five: Controversies)

LOUISE ERDRICH

Most-Decorated Hero

A member of the Turtle Mountain Band of Chippewa, Louise Erdrich is a distinguished poetry and fiction writer with many awards to her credit. She wrote novels containing interlocking stories of the lives of Chippewa Indians and their relatives and neighbors: *Love Medicine* (1984), *The Beet Queen* (1986), and *Tracks* (1988). The stories follow these complex and fascinating characters from 1912 to the present, weaving back and forth in time. In *The Beet Queen*, Russell Kashpaw, wounded in the Korean War, returns to the tribal lands badly scarred. In spite of his injuries he manages to build a fishing hut on the ice but has a stroke as he fishes. In the following excerpt, a festival parade is held to crown the Beet Queen (celebrating the successful introduction of sugar beets into the area), and Russell is paraded as the "Most-Decorated Hero."

1 The orderly hoisted Russell out of his wheelchair, rolled him onto the bed, and stripped him of his thin cotton pajamas. Eli Kashpaw

sat at his kitchen table with a coffee, watching. Fleur was stationed in the shadows of the next room, supervising the orderly with stern attention. She unpacked Russell's uniform from an old cracked valise. The green wool exuded naphthalene. The orderly dressed Russell in it, moving carefully under Fleur's eye. He strained to lift Russell back into his chair. Fleur took Russell's medals from a leather case and pinned the whole bright pattern over his heart. Then she put his rifle, in a long bag of olive drab, across his lap. Russell waited for his hat to be set on at an angle, the way it was in his portrait-studio pictures.

When everything was done, he locked his hands on the arm-   2
rests. He could use his arms to push. The orderly wheeled Russell into the morning heat, across the yard of tough grass, and up a ramp into the nursing-home van. He slammed the door. The van pulled out and then it was driving the back roads. There were no windows on the sides, but there was a plastic bubble in the ceiling. Tipping his head Russell saw sky, clouds, and after a while some crisscrossing wires. After an hour of driving, they stopped. Outside the van he heard horses blowing and stamping. An amplified voice called out numbers and directions.

Suddenly his chair was yanked from behind and, in one swoop,   3
went down the ramp out of the van backward. Across the street, in a parking lot of armory trucks, he saw lines of antique cars, drivers in goggles, women under old-time parasols. A majorette was stretching her golden legs out on the ground. Legionnaires passed him, not feet away. Nobody looked at him. Finally the son of his old boss at Argus National clapped him lightly on the arm and bent over his chair.

"What a day for it," he said, and that was all.   4

The air was dry and the sun far away, veiled by clouds of dust.   5
A jeep rumbled up, hauling his float. It was the same one the American Legion always used. The orderly strained to lift Russell onto the float, then strapped him upright between raised wooden bunkers. A field of graves stretched down before him, each covered with plastic grass and red poppies. A plain white cross was planted at his feet.

Very soon, the parade would start to move. The skirted, flimsy   6
high school floats and go-cart clowns were falling into place. The announcer's high-pitched voice had gone ragged. The bands turned up, hoisted their drums and tubas.

7   The float moved.

8   Russell felt the small jolts in his face as they bounced over pot-
holes. With each lurch, the cross above the grave at his feet shook.
He sat high, hands clutching his knees, and stared above the crowd
as he passed. There were men with children on their shoulders,
girls in bright dresses. His float continued past the glass storefronts
and banks, past the bars that featured dancing girls and Happy
Nites, past the post office. The drums rattled and the plastic horns
squawked in the clown's go-cart. The noise was tiring. Russell
tried to hold his head high, to keep the fierce gaze smoking, but
his chin dropped. His eyes closed, and suddenly the noise and
people seemed far off.

9   He thought of a distant storm. Low thunderheads collided and
the air was charged with a vibrant, calm menace. Before him he
saw a large hunched woman walking slowly down a dirt road. He
started after her, and then he recognized his sister Isabel, dead
these many years. Now she was walking this road, wearing a traditional butterfly-sleeved calico dress and quilled moccasins. Her
black hair hung loose. She turned and signaled him to follow. Russell hesitated, although he felt it happening. He felt his mind
spread out like a lake. His heart slowed and numbed and seemed
to grow until it pressed against his ribs.

10   "He looks stuffed," cried a shrill woman from the curb. Russell
heard her clearly. At one time her comment would have shamed
him, but now he simply opened his eyes to the blurred scene, then
shut them down. His sister was still there, not far in front of him.
Isabel looked over her shoulder with her old grin. He saw that
she'd had a tooth knocked out.

11   "Wait for me," he called.

12   She turned and kept walking. The road was narrow. The grass
on either side flowed off forever, and the clouds pressed low. He
followed her, thinking that he might see Celestine. She might join
them. But then it occurred to him this wouldn't happen, because
this was the road that the old-time Chippewas talked about, the
four-day road, the road of death. He'd just started out.

13   I'm dead now, he thought with calm wonder.

14   At first he was sorry that it had happened in public, instead of
some private place. Then he was glad, and he was also glad to see
he hadn't lost his sense of humor even now. It struck him as so
funny that the town he'd lived in and the members of the Ameri-

can Legion were solemnly saluting a dead Indian, that he started
to shake with laughter.

The damn thing was that he laughed too hard, fell off the road, 15
opened up his eyes before he'd gone past the point of no return,
and found himself only at the end of the parade. He quickly shut
his eyes again. But the road had gone too narrow. He stumbled. No
matter how hard he called, his sister continued forward and
wouldn't double back to help.

Engaging the Text

1. Erdrich's vocabulary is descriptive and vivid. Just a few of the
   words that she uses to appeal to sight or smell are naphthalene
   (1), lurch (8), hunched (9), and quilled moccasins (9). Use each
   of these in a sentence, without looking back at the story; then
   look back and see how close you got to Erdrich's meaning.
2. Erdrich uses objects, such as the van, the parade, and the
   floats, to symbolize Russell's feelings and attitudes. What do
   you think these objects mean to Russell?
3. How does the author switch from what is actually happening
   to what is happening in Russell's mind? Show where in the
   story this switch from reality to imagination occurred.

Engaging the Reader

1. What kind of a person do you think Russell is? What kind of
   life has he lived? What is happening to him in this story?
2. What does Russell think is happening to him on the float?
3. What do you think happens to Russell after the parade?

The Engaged Writer

1. Explain what you think the title *The Beet Queen* means.
2. Explain what is meant by the last sentence of the story.
3. Compare Russell, a wounded veteran, with one of the following: William Least Heat-Moon, another Native American and
   the author of "South by Southeast" from *Blue Highways*; the
   speaker in Leslie Marmon Silko's "The Man to Send Rain
   Clouds"; or N. Scott Momaday, author of "The End of My
   Childhood."
4. None of the Native Americans listed in question 3, including
   the fictional Russell Kashpaw, can be called a "stereotype" or

over-simplified idea or image of a whole group. Explain how you feel about "stereotyping" people on the basis of a few examples or a fixed idea.

WILLIAM LEAST HEAT-MOON

South by Southeast

When William Least Heat-Moon lost his teaching job, he decided he would recapture his Native American heritage by traveling around the country in a fixed-up van. He drove on "blue highways," the small roads lined in blue on highway maps (the larger roads were red). His encounters with all sorts of people as he camped in his van and ate in small towns show the flavor of rural America through very observant eyes. He also wrote *PrairyErth* (1991), an in-depth portrait of a county in rural Kansas. The section here from his book, *Blue Highways* (1982), tells of an incident in Selma, Alabama, scene of the early civil rights marches. Heat-Moon found that things have changed very little there.

1   Martin Luther King, Jr., Drive used to be Sylvan Street. Some whites in Selma still called it Sylvan Street. It's the main route through the so-called project—a typical federally sponsored housing district—and the street the Southern Christian Leadership Conference assembled the marchers on, using the block under the high steeple of Brown's Chapel as the starting point. The first marchers walked down Sylvan (as it was then), up Water Avenue, turned left, and started across Pettus Bridge. About half a mile. At the other end of the bridge, deputies and troopers, shouting to the people they had no permit to march, forced them back to Water Street. But for once, chants and signs and feet were better weapons than anything the state could summon. Whitman, the egalitarian, said it a century before:

> I will make a song for the ears of the President, full of weapons with menacing points,
> And behind the weapons countless dissatisfied faces.

When King assembled the marchers again two weeks later, he 2
had not only a permit, he had also the protection—albeit spotty—
of federal troops called out by President Johnson, the man with the
big ears. People gathered at Brown's Chapel and walked fifty miles
to Montgomery. The two marches roused Washington as none of
the other SCLC confrontations had, and a few months later the
Congress passed the Federal Voting Rights Act.

It was dark and moonless when I started looking for Brown's 3
Chapel. I planned just to drive by, but I stopped near a big brick
church that fit the description to ask a black man if it was the
chapel. "That's it," he said. "What difference does it make?"

Without knowing it, he had asked me the question I'd come to 4
Selma to answer. "Isn't this where King started the march?"

"What they say. So who cares?" 5

I stood on the step of the van. "I'm trying to find out if things 6
have changed since the march."

"Tell you in three words. *Ain't nothin' changed.*" 7

"Let me ask another question. Could you get a drink in Mick- 8
ey's tonight?"

"Go ask me if I *want* in there, because I'll tell you they don't 9
gotta keep this man out because he don't want in."

"I hear you, but *could* you?" 10

"Minute I do it's membership time." 11

"I just went in and nobody said anything about membership." 12

"Your membership's got a way of standin' out—just like mine." 13

Several teenagers gathered around. I was the wrong color on the 14
wrong street, but no one said anything. The man talking to me was
James Walker, born and raised in the Selma project and just dis-
charged from four years in the Air Force. "Been almost ten years
to the day since King got shot," he said, "and the movement's been
dead that long. Things slippin'. Black man's losin' ground again.
My momma's afraid to talk to a white, and my grandmomma
don't care. She just worries about the kids."

"Didn't the march do anything you can see?" 15

"Say what? Last week I went to get my driver's license. Twelve- 16
thirty. Lunchtime. Sign on the door says they open again at one. I
wanted to wait inside, so I pulled on the door. Trooper comes out
and says, 'What's wrong, fool? Cain't read? Get off that door less
you want me next time comin' out shootin'.' There's your change."

17   "Where?"

18   "Ten years ago he woulda come out shootin' the first time."

19   "What happened?"

20   "Nothin', dude. This man's not stupid. I know when to shut up and I know when to talk. This man knows when he's got a chance."

21   A police car cruised by. A teenager said, "That's twice." A Buick pulled up and Walker got in. He said, "You're makin' people nervous comin' in down here. You ain't the right color, you know. Better watch your ass tonight." The car jumped forward then backed up. "If you ain't jivin' about the church, come round the basketball court in the mornin'."

22   I drove out to George Corley Wallace Community College, one of three new schools by that name in the state. Sometime after midnight, the Ghost shook a little and I woke up. It shook again. I crept to the front curtain. A man standing on the bumper played a light over the seats. Just as I opened the door, he got into a squadcar. "What's wrong?" I called out.

23   "Only checking, neighbor." He drove off quickly.

24   I closed up again and went back to bed. Checking? What the hell for?

Engaging the Text

1. Heat-Moon tells a lot of history in a low-key manner. He does not show his emotion. Is that style effective? Would more vigorous writing be as effective in giving the atmosphere of the town?

2. Heat-Moon reports conversations using dialect and slang. Pick out some of the slang words he uses. Are they the right ones for that situation?

Engaging the Reader

1. Heat-Moon refers to the events of the 1960s. If these are familiar to you, write your recollections in your journal or tell your classmates about them. Or if you prefer, recount the events of another decade, perhaps the 1970s or 1980s, as they affected your life.

2. Does Selma, Alabama, seem to you a typical southern town? Why?

3. Explain why you think the author quotes Walt Whitman in the first paragraph.
4. What is the question Heat-Moon asked of a black man? What response did he get? What evidence does Heat-Moon find that confirms this answer?

The Engaged Writer

1. Choose two real or imaginary people who speak very different forms of English. For example, an elderly immigrant and his or her American grandson; a teacher and a teenage student. Write a short conversation between them in the style of Heat-Moon's conversations with the people he meets in Selma.
2. Take one of the expository (factual, reporting) essays you have written so far, and rewrite it with as much dialogue as possible. Have your speakers themselves and the contrast between them tell your theme, rather than stating it outright as you did in the expository writing.
3. This section of Heat-Moon's book tells of an important time in recent history: the battle for civil rights in the 1960s. Take one or more of the people and events mentioned in the piece: Selma, Southern Christian Leadership Conference, Martin Luther King, Jr., Federal Voting Rights Act, George Corley Wallace (a person as well as the name of the community college where Heat-Moon parked his truck). Look them up, first in an unabridged dictionary in your college library and then in an encyclopedia. Write a report on what you find.
4. If you were around in 1964, write about your memory of that time. If not, interview an older person who was. You can start with questions like these:

> — Where were you at the time of the Freedom March on Montgomery, Alabama?
> — What did you think about it at the time?
> — Where were you when President John F. Kennedy and Reverend Martin Luther King, Jr., were assassinated?

SUE HUBBELL

On the Road: A City of the Mind

Sue Hubbell has been a trucker. More recently she delivered honey from her bee farm in a three-quarter-ton pickup to retailers around the country. She is also a writer whose articles have appeared in magazines such as the *New Yorker*. She is the author of *A Book of Bees, A Country Year, On This Hilltop*, and most recently, *Broadsides from the Other Orders: A Book of Bugs*. Her article "On the Road" appeared in *The American Scene* in *Time* magazine in 1985. Though they both involve traveling in a truck, her experiences and William Least Heat-Moon's (in the last selection) focus on different ideas about America.

1   In the early morning there is a city of the mind that stretches from coast to coast, from border to border. Its cross streets are the interstate highways, and food, comfort, companionship are served up in its buildings, the truck stops near the exits. Its citizens are all-night drivers, the truckers and the waitresses at the stops.

2   In daylight the city fades and blurs when the transients appear, tourists who merely want a meal and a tank of gas. They file into the carpeted dining rooms away from the professional drivers' side, sit at the Formica tables set off by imitation cloth flowers in bud vases. They eat and are gone, do not return. They are not a part of the city and obscure it.

3   It is 5 A.M. in a truck stop in West Virginia. Drivers in twos, threes and fours are eating breakfast and talking routes and schedules.

4   "Truckers!" growls a manager. "They say they are in a hurry. They complain if the service isn't fast. We fix it so they can have their fuel pumped while they are eating and put in telephones on every table so they can check with their dispatchers. They could be out of here in half an hour. But what do they do? They sit and talk for two hours."

5   The truckers are lining up for seconds at the breakfast buffet (all you can eat for $3.99—biscuits with chipped-beef gravy, fruit cup, French toast with syrup, bacon, pancakes, sausage, scrambled eggs, doughnuts, Danish, cereal in little boxes).

The travel store at the truck stop has a machine to measure heart- 6
beat in exchange for a quarter. There are racks of jackets, belts, truck
supplies, tape cassettes. On the wall are paintings for sale, simu-
lated wood with likenesses of John Wayne or a stag. The rack by the
cash register is stuffed with Twinkies and chocolate Suzy Qs.

It is 5 A.M. in New Mexico. Above the horseshoe-shaped counter 7
on panels where a menu is usually displayed, an overhead slide
show is in progress. The pictures change slowly, allowing the
viewer to take in all the details. A low shot of a Peterbilt, its chrome
fittings sparkling in the sunshine, is followed by one of a bosomy
young woman, the same who must pose for those calendars found
in auto-parts stores. She almost has on clothes, and she is offering
to check a trucker's oil. The next slide is a side view of a whole
tractor-trailer rig, its 18 wheels gleaming and spoked. It is followed
by one of a blond bulging out of a hint of cop clothes writing a
naughty trucker a ticket.

The waitress looks too tired and too jaded to be offended. The 8
jaws of the truckers move mechanically as they fork up their eggs-
over-easy. They stare at the slides, glassy eyed, as intent on chrome
as on flesh.

It is 4 A.M. in Oklahoma. A recycled Stuckey's with blue tile roof 9
calls itself simply Truck Stop. The sign also boasts showers, scales,
truck wash and a special on service for $88.50. At a table inside,
four truckers have ordered a short stack and three eggs apiece,
along with bacon, sausage and coffee. (Trucker's Super-breakfast—
$3.79).

They have just started drinking their coffee, and the driver with 10
the Roadway cap calls over the waitress, telling her there is salt in
the sugar he put in his coffee. She is pale, thin, young, has dark circles under her eyes. The truckers have been teasing her, and she
doesn't trust them. She dabs a bit of sugar from the canister on a
finger and tastes it. Salt. She samples sugar from the other canisters. They have salt too, and she gathers them up to replace them.
Someone is hazing her, breaking her into her new job. Her eyes
shine with tears.

She brings the food and comes back when the truckers are near- 11
ly done. She carries a water jug and coffeepot on her tray. The men
are ragging her again, and her hands tremble. The tray falls with
a crash. The jug breaks. Glass, water and coffee spread across the
floor. She sits down in the booth, tears rolling down her cheeks.

12   "I'm so tired. My old man . . . he left me," she says, the tears coming faster now. "The judge says he's going to take my kid away if I can't take care of him, so I stay up all day and just sleep when he takes a nap and the boss yells at me and . . . and . . . the truckers all talk dirty . . . I'm so tired."

13   She puts her head down on her arms and sobs luxuriantly. The truckers are gone, and I touch her arm and tell her to look at what they have left. There is a $20 bill beside each plate. She looks up, nods, wipes her eyes on her apron, pockets the tips and goes to get a broom and a mop.

14   It is 3:30 A.M. in Illinois at a glossy truck stop that offers all mechanical services, motel rooms, showers, Laundromat, game room, TV lounge, truckers' bulletin board and a stack of newspapers published by the Association of Christian Truckers. Piped-in music fills the air.

15   The waitress in the professional drivers' section is a big motherly-looking woman with red hair piled in careful curls on top of her head. She correctly sizes up the proper meal for the new customer at the counter. "Don't know what you want, honey? Try the chicken-noodle soup with a hot roll. It will stick to you like you've got something, and you don't have to worry about grease."

16   She has been waitressing 40 years, 20 of them in this truck stop. As she talks she polishes the stainless steel, fills mustard jars, adds the menu inserts for today's special (hot turkey sandwich, mashed potatoes and gravy, pot of coffee—$2.50).

17   "The big boss, well, he's a love, but some of the others aren't so hot. But it's a job. Gotta work somewhere. I need a day off though. Been working six, seven days straight lately. Got shopping to do. My lawn needs mowing."

18   Two truckers are sitting at a booth. Their faces are lined and leathery. One cap says Harley-Davidson, the other Coors.

19   Harley-Davidson calls out, "If you wasn't so mean, Flossie, you'd have a good man to take care of you and you wouldn't have to mow the damn lawn."

20   She puts down the mustard jar, walks over to Harley-Davidson and Coors, stands in front of them, hands on wide hips. "Now you listen here, Charlie, I'm good enough woman for any man but all you guys want are chippies."

21   Coors turns bright red. She glares at him. "You saw my ex in here last Saturday night with a chippie on his arm. He comes in

here all the time with two, three chippies just to prove to me what a high old time he's having. If that's a good time, I'd rather baby-sit my grandkids."

Chippies are not a topic of conversation that Charlie and Coors   22
wish to pursue. Coors breaks a doughnut in two, and Charlie uses his fork to make a spillway for the gravy on the double order of mashed potatoes that accompanies his scrambled eggs.

Flossie comes back and turns to the new customer in mirror   23
shades at this dark hour, a young trucker with cowboy boots and hat. "John-boy. Where you been? Haven't seen you in weeks. Looks like you need a nice omelet. Cook just made some of those biscuits you like too."

I leave a tip for Flossie and pay my bill. In the men's room,   24
where I am shunted because the ladies' is closed for cleaning, someone has scrawled poignant words: NO TIME TO EAT NOW.

Engaging the Text

1. Use the following words in sentences: transients (2), jaded (8), canisters (10), and hazing (10).
2. Find a drawing or photo to illustrate Formica (2—an impervious surface for countertops) and Peterbilt (7—a type of truck body).
3. Take the words luxuriantly (13) and poignant (24) and change them from adverb to adjective or adjective to adverb, and use each in a new sentence.
4. This essay appeared in *Time* magazine, the reason for the newspaper style, short paragraphs, and use of present tense. Does the constant use of present tense make the story more lively? Why or why not?
5. Do you get to know anything about the writer, Sue Hubbell? If so, what do you learn?

Engaging the Reader

1. What is the setting of the essay? Is it a particular part of the United States? Are specific states or regions mentioned?
2. Why do the tourists eat in a separate dining room?
3. What do you think is meant by the title "A City of the Mind"?
4. What problem does the young waitress at the Oklahoma truck stop have?

5. What is the truckers' response to this? Do you think this is typical of truckers?
6. Characterize the waitress at the Illinois truck stop. How does she differ from the Oklahoma waitress?

The Engaged Writer

1. Write about your own job or occupation from your own point of view.
2. Write about your job as if someone else were observing you, the way Sue Hubbell observes the two waitresses.
3. Compare and contrast the two waitresses in this story. How are they alike? How are they different? Can you come to any conclusions about waitressing based on your answer?
4. What problems of working women are alluded to in this essay? Examine one or more of these problems in a thoughtful essay.
5. Compare Hubbell's experience "on the road" with that of William Least Heat-Moon.

DONALD P. BAKER

Graduation in the Mountains

This newspaper account of the 1986 graduation of twelve seniors from a small high school in rural mountain Virginia compares life in this isolated area with life in a big city. Baker, a *Washington Post* staff writer, tells of the simple life, community spirit, and realistic expectations of the twelve graduating seniors in Virginia's second smallest school. The selection following this one, an excerpt from *The Autobiography of LeRoi Jones*, by Amiri Baraka, is also about a high school, but recounts the unpleasant experience of being an outsider at school.

1   Whitetop, Va.—Tim Ham, the senior class president at Mount Rogers High School, had planned to enlist in the Air Force after last week's graduation from Virginia's second smallest school, "but Dad bought a backhoe," so now he is going to remain here in the

mountainous southwestern toe of the state to do custom building work with his father.

"I'll go along with Dad," said Ham. "These mountains are good 2 enough for me."

It is graduation time in Appalachia, and like many other aspects 3 of life here, the discussions of ambitions and rituals of senior proms take on a different pace and style than those in urban and suburban areas.

Social life in the community revolves around the school, where 4 almost as many parents as students show up for the prom. And last weekend's graduation drew folks from all over the high valley that is tucked between the two highest peaks in Virginia overlooking North Carolina and Tennessee.

All 151 students in the Mount Rogers school district, from 5 kindergarten through grade 12, attend classes in a single building, part of which is built of rock gathered from nearby trout streams during the Great Depression. The school is the second smallest in the state—the smallest is on Tangier Island in the middle of the Chesapeake Bay.

Most of the 12 members of the 1986 graduating class attended 6 the senior prom. But unlike their city counterparts, none of the couples went out to dinner, before or after the dance. No one arrived in a rented limousine, though some were chauffeured to the dance in pickup trucks or drove their own four-wheel-drive vehicles that are a necessity in this rural region.

Afterward, instead of a soiree at a hotel or a long trip to the 7 beach, post-prom partying was limited to circling a few pickups and Jeeps in a meadow up on Helton Creek. The students popped the tabs on a few beer and soft drink cans and attempted to make conversation over the blare of music from dashboard radios.

A couple of sheriff's deputies, who in past years have put on 8 business suits and taken their wives to the dance, stationed themselves a respectable distance away to make sure the partying did not get out of hand.

None of this year's graduates is going directly to a four-year col- 9 lege, and most members of the class of 1986 want nothing more than to find a job nearby and spend the rest of their lives in their beloved mountains.

Allen Weaver, 20, hopes to get hired as a shipping clerk at one of 10 the textile or electronic plants over the mountain in North Carolina.

11   Karen Poe, 19, will commute to the hospital in Abingdon to become a nurse's aide.

12   Four or five members of the Class of '86 will continue their education, probably all at junior colleges.

13   The teen-agers who choose to remain will inherit a life that has changed little in recent decades.

14   "We're very isolated," said Principal Wilma R. Testerman, a native who was one of four Mount Rogers graduates in 1944. "There aren't too many places to live, and not too much to do for entertainment. Living here is difficult."

15   There is nothing remotely resembling a town in the Mount Rogers' school district. Whitetop is merely a post office designation.

16   There are no casual trips to town for groceries or services. A visit to a doctor, dentist or lawyer means a 45-minute trip to Ashe County, N.C., or to the nearest Virginia town of Independence (its weekly newspaper is called *The Declaration*), where Campbell's funeral home offers a 24-hour hot line with the latest news of deaths.

17   Most of the jobs are even further away. Residents drive up to 50 miles to textile and electrical plants, most of them in North Carolina. The few nearby jobs are at Grayson Highlands State Park, Mount Rogers National Forest and at the school.

18   Most jobs offer minimum wage—teachers and mail carriers pull up the average income. And by national standards it is a very poor area. More than 95 percent of the students at Mount Rogers get free lunches.

19   But it is a region where, as one resident said, "You can get by on $300 a month until the heater goes out."

20   Matt Dalia thought his family had "moved to the sticks" when they left Raleigh for West Jefferson, N.C., seven years ago. Now, however, that town of 2,500 is where the action is, so he and his friends make the 20-mile drive to cruise Main Street on weekends.

21   "This really is the sticks," Dalia said without ridicule of his new home area.

22   Dalia and many of his friends are undaunted by the remoteness of the region.

23   Anita Blevins, who compiled a 3.4 grade-point average but was disappointed with her scores on the Scholastic Aptitude Test, wants to get a degree in elementary education "and come back here to teach." She plans to attend Wytheville Community College

in the fall, and then transfer to Emory and Henry College, a four-year, private, liberal arts college. Each college is about an hour's drive from her home.

She is satisfied with the education she received, although the 24
parent of another college-bound senior said Mount Rogers graduates opt for community colleges because they are not prepared for the academic rigors of four-year institutions.

While Mount Rogers is fully accredited, getting and retaining 25
teachers is a problem. Turnover among the 12 teachers is reduced by nepotism (there are two couples among the dozen instructors) and natives, such as principal Testerman, who return to teach.

Testerman has managed to raise the goals of the students while 26
winning parental support by continuing a tradition of "three generations of paddling," said Rev. Bob Stampel, a Presbyterian minister who came to the area 18 years ago to raise money for a dental clinic. Stampel said that when he arrived he found "no home support for college," the school having produced no more than 30 college graduates in half a century.

"We offer all the courses required for accreditation," said Tester- 27
man, who has been principal for six years. The 70 high school students can choose from among 43 academic subjects offered by seven teachers, with only two subjects, business and art, taught by teachers without training in the fields.

Parents are anxious to volunteer for school activities, said Doyle 28
Hensley, president of the Parent Teacher Organization and postmaster at Whitetop, "but we don't have the skills" needed to augment the professional staff. Because "no one knows about computers," he said, eight terminals and keyboards are stored in a small room used only when teachers and students have a few spare minutes to experiment.

Teachers and students say there are advantages to their small, 29
"quaint" school, however.

Second-year English teacher Joe Barden, who was the prom 30
sponsor, said that "a big advantage is that you get to know the kids personally, and their parents."

"What is so remarkable is the resourcefulness of the students," 31
he said. "They take a little and do so much."

For example, many of the 50 members of the school's Albert 32
Hash Memorial Band (named for a nationally known local fiddlemaker) play instruments they made themselves.

33   The young musicians pluck dulcimers, fiddles and other string instruments, carrying on a tradition of mountain music that fills the hills and hollows.

34   Consolidation with another school is not an option because of the location. The nearest school is at Independence, a long zigzaggy drive under the best of conditions. In the spring and fall, it is a scenic drive paralleling or crossing rocky streams, the Appalachian Trail and forests of rhododendron. But during the long winter, when sudden snowstorms strike, it often is impassable.

35   Some students spend an hour a day riding in each direction on one of the school's three yellow buses.

36   The Mount Rogers Rockets sports teams compete in the Mountain Empire District, with rivals Auburn and Rocky Gap 90 to 100 miles away, and Shawsville, 120 miles.

37   "The other schools don't understand when we call and say we can't come because of snow," said Teena Morefield, who coaches girls' basketball and volleyball, teaches physical education and driving, coordinates the gifted-and-talented program and is part-time librarian. "They say, 'It's fine, here.' Well, they're not on the mountain."

38   Mount Rogers students miss an average of three weeks of classes each year because of snow.

39   The most popular school holiday is the opening day of deer hunting season in November.

40   "If you live here, you gotta love hunting, hiking, fishing, the outdoors," said Allen Weaver, adding that "everyone has a four-wheeler, and nearly everyone has a horse."

41   When Matt Dalia's parents, Vicky and Joday Dalia, moved here almost five years ago, the school was one of the big attractions. "We liked it from the moment they opened the PTO meeting with a prayer," said Vicky Dalia, whose family is Mormon.

42   The Dalias now say they are not completely satisfied with the school or the community.

43   Vicky Dalia complains about the absence of a playground, an inadequate library, a vocational shop in which the equipment often is broken, and "a couple teachers who don't know their subjects."

44   But the mountains exert a powerful, almost mystical, pull on the residents, and the Dalias, who operate a mail-order decorating business from their home, feel deep roots here, "even if we aren't related to anyone."

Postmaster Hensley said his son, John Jr., who is a sophomore   45
accounting major at Lincoln Memorial University in Harrigate,
Tenn., feels that same tug for the mountain land. Despite his college studies, "He'd rather be here than anyplace in the world," his
father said.

Engaging the Text

1. Most of the words in this newspaper feature article are easy
    to understand, though a few might be unfamiliar to city
    dwellers. Look up backhoe (1), dulcimers (33), and rhodo-
    dendron (34) as well as counterparts (6), soiree (7), and rigors
    (24). Use each in a sentence. Do you find the vocabulary here
    easy or difficult?
2. Are the sentences generally short or long, simple or complex?
    Give some examples.
3. As a newspaper article, the essay uses short paragraphs, lots
    of quotations from people, many names, and the present tense
    for narration. Compare this essay's style with Sue Hubbell's in
    "On the Road."

Engaging the Reader

1. Describe the life of the twelve graduates of Virginia's second
    smallest school. Does it differ from your own high school
    experience? How?
2. How involved are parents and teachers in the school?
3. What seems most important to these students, parents, and
    teachers? Are these common concerns to everyone, or peculiar
    to this region of the country?

The Engaged Writer

1. Write on one of the following subjects and relate it to your high
    school: prom and postprom activities, sports and after-school
    activities, available job opportunities, faculty involvement,
    and parental involvement.
2. Does the parents' and teachers' involvement in Mount Rogers
    High School differ from that in the high school you attended?
    Compare the two.

3. Compare the high school experience narrated by the various students quoted here to what you experienced in your high school.

AMIRI BARAKA

Young

LeRoi Jones, now known as Amiri Baraka, the distinguished American playwright and author, has many volumes of poetry and fiction to his credit. He has written and produced more than twenty-four plays and has compiled several anthologies. This selection from *The Autobiography of LeRoi Jones* (1984) tells of some of his high school experiences as one of the few black students in a very mixed city high school in Newark, New Jersey, around 1950.

1   And I would get out in the playground and wear some unsuspecting turkeys out, though if I ran into some quality players, which I did, I would get cooled out. But the sense in myself was of some wall—some dull and wholly uninteresting wall—between myself and the life and persons of the place. And I wondered often what I was doing there. Except there had come into my head and out of my mouth some vague "decision" to go to Barringer.

2   At the beginning of the tenth grade I did go on to Barringer. They had some junior high school system consisting of the ninth grade for some of the high schools and that's what my sojourn at McKinley had been. (These days, the 80's, McKinley, now named 7th Avenue, is like a New York City school jammed up with blacks and Latinos in the advanced stages of ghettofication.)

3   Barringer was larger and if possible an even more foreign place. It was larger and on the other side of Branch Brook Park. There was less of the narrow ghetto First Ward feeling to it because it was larger and up toward the more middle-class Italian areas. But that was another world. McKinley was ugly and baroque and teeming and narrow and ghetto Italian. Barringer was larger and more open but it seemed even more completely separated from my Dey Street life.

And we had moved again, around this time of my life. We had   4
moved all the way back across town into the Central Ward. The old
Third Ward. And right on top of The Hill. So this meant that I had
to take a bus every day all the way cross town to school. Coming
out of the geographical lookout post of the growing black ghetto,
on Belmont Avenue and Spruce Street. What they called the Four
Corners. And during them days everybody and everything black
passed across or under or over or around those streets either day
or night. It was like X marked the spot of another kind of black life.
Back over not far from where I was born and spent my earliest
days, down the hill in Douglass-Harrison, but underneath my Belmont Avenue windows I began to be aware of the Fast Life.

It was like a sociologist's joke. Up in the morning, come down   5
from our third-floor apartment. (My grandmother and uncle were
with us again, but in much smaller space.) Down into the street,
to the corner of Belmont (beautiful mountain?) to wait for the
9 Clifton bus. Hey, and there were quite a few other refugees and
cutouts from the mostly black (and a trifle Jewish) high school at
the edge of the Central Ward, South Side. It was in my head, as
well, to flee South Side. (How did that get in my head? The talk
among friends? Overhearing adults? I donno. But it came out of
my mouth, "I don't wanna go to South Side. I wanna go to Barringer.") And there were kids on that wild 9 Clifton. Some coming from even further south going to West Side and Central, even
Vo-Tech, and the last stop, way cross town in another world, Barringer. There were a few of us made that long trip every day, back
and forth, from the Central Ward and even the South Ward, all the
way to Rome. (And yes, just below the school, sat the Vatican. The
still unfinished Sacred Heart Cathedral, that towers now, and tow-
ered then with a useless romanticism wasted on most of us black
kids who went to Barringer who saw it simply as a hated landmark.)

The joke? From the Four Corners to Rome and back. And now   6
I was completely disoriented (though calmer now, at home,
because of less hostile surroundings). Because I didn't know anybody at Barringer and I didn't know anybody on Belmont Avenue.
My friends, at that time, still lived around Central Avenue School,
Baxter Terrace, on Norfolk and Sussex and Lock and Jay and Hudson and Warren. And for a time it was a drag at both ends.

7   At Barringer it was the amazingly dull process of being an outsider that I was involved with. Though there were a few black students there I got tight with. At least to joke with in school and release some of the tension built up by our being black in Italian Antarctica. (Of the two closest joke-time buddies in my homeroom in Barringer—that is, we would jive and put each other down and bump each other and grin in the hallways and maybe the lunchroom—one, Ken, is a detective lieutenant, the other a career Navy man. And even these dudes, black though they was, called me "Jones.")

8   Two of my other friends for other kinds of talk, they were in some of my other classes, the college-prep-oriented ones, were white. And they were outsiders too. We must a made a weird trio, jim. One guy, J., was tall and skinny and talked incessantly of sports. But he wasn't Italian, could not play any sports worth a damn, plus when he was in grammar school (he went to Central Avenue too!) he had a kind of strange odor about him—oh, look, it was urine—that set him off from most of us then. Though I talked to him in Central but with another relationship. In Barringer we got tight and the pee smell had mostly gone, but he had pimples all over his face and his lack of coordination made him the brunt of much bullshit (as it had in Central—but that was a mostly black school). I didn't really like the way people acted toward J. in high school though I guess I had heaped plenty of bullshit on him myself in grammar school. But now, there was, I guess, some kind of half kinship. Since now, I was on the outside, on the fringe of this social focus, and so was J., as usual. And hell, we both liked sports. And every morning he'd come to high school with the local newspaper and we'd discuss whatever was going down in the pros or high school or college, it made no difference to us. We rapped on it.

9   V., my other walking buddy, was also completely uncoordinated and a silent (though super-opinionated, egotistic, and talky with us) shy loner-type figure. He had a potbelly and looked middle-aged at sixteen and thought about smoking a pipe. V. fancied himself an intellectual and he was. But that was his defense against the mainstream life of Barringer. That he was other because his head was somewhere else.

10   He was Italian but totally disconnected from the Italian life of that place. Plus he wanted to be a writer and it was with V. that I

first exchanged young vague ideas about writing. V. had read some books. He liked *The Red Badge of Courage* (I think because he lived in a place named after Stephen Crane) and he wrote short stories and poems like Crane's.

J., I think because of V.'s influence, later began to say that he wanted to be a sportswriter. All three of us went to a writing class in Barringer our senior year given by a hard-faced unsmiling teacher named Miss Stewart (but she turned out to be a caring human being). 11

So in my homeroom I swung with two bloods and in my other classes with two white intellectuals. Maybe all three of us were and came on like intellectuals. I know I didn't feel like no goddam intellectual. I just felt drugged being isolated and alienated and surrounded by such bullshit in white Barringer. 12

Swinging down off that 9 Clifton, on the other side, at the Four Corners, I faced an entirely different reality. On the corner a liquor store (still there), the Foxes, and next to that, coming toward my house, a black frozen custard and hot dog place; next was a black cleaner's, a Polish tinsmith, a house, then our house, 154 Belmont Avenue. At the top floor, the Joneses and Russes, and on the second floor, Dr. Bell, a young black dentist who had just got out of school. (He lived there a hot minute but this was his office mostly. He was also the building's landlord.) On the first floor, a Polish oil stove place run by this Polish man and woman who must have been 100. 13

When we got to Belmont there were still a few Poles there, mostly stores. And you could get some good kielbasy—Polish sausage. And down the street in the other direction there was still a good sprinkling of Jews, probably Polish too. But the Poles lived mostly in that one block between Spruce and 17th Avenue. The remains of a larger community, just as was the sprinkling of Jews, but centered by a huge church, which is still there, for the Polish Catholics. I went to Boy Scout camp with some of the Polish kids because even though most of them had moved out of Newark their troop was located at St. Stanislaus on Belmont Avenue and so they belonged to the Robert Treat Council, which covered Newark. One of the funniest dudes from that Polish troop who regularly used to crack us up at camp was Sigmund Pilch, who was like a nonstop wisecracking slapstick artist, who I never saw once we came back into Newark after camp. 14

15   Across the street, on the corner, was the Four Kegs, where you could stand outside and peep into and see the highlife going on thick and fast on the weekends but happening at top speed any night. And down Spruce Street the straight-out ghetto, which I still had to investigate with my teenage legs and eyes and ears. And that came in on time. But early in my Barringer days and the horrible incarceration at McKinley I was stretched out like some despairing quiet animal not even sure what was wrong. But I knew.

16   I grew up on one side of town and part of my head was shaped by that ice and alienation, that hostility and silence in the face of adversity. And I grew up on the other side of town too and that is something else.

17   I was run home a few times from Barringer by the warring white boys. Tricked and insulted any number of times. Looked at funny by teachers. I looked at the white girls and their boyfriends and tried to see through the wall of our separation at what that would be like. But I never went with a white girl in high school. (Shit, that couldn't happen in Barringer.) But I didn't go with any black girl either who went to the school. I just looked and fantasized about all of 'em.

18   The awards and the honors, the straight-out teenage joys, the simple concern, was never mine and I thought that I existed in that place in a separate piece of space where I thought my thoughts and had my resentments. And I openly did not like it. That separation and white-out. I did not like it. And it did not like me. I think it did something to me too. Like how could some nonstop sardonic-mouthed joker and quick-start artist like me be banned to an island of noninterest and overlook and uncomprehending babble. Perhaps I lusted after the life of the real inhabitants of that place. In my weakest moments I must have. But most of the time I was just passing through, even as words were coming out of my mouth or doing whatever I was doing. I was not wholly there, I felt, but the part of me that was, suffered.

Engaging the Text

1. Match each word in column A with its definition in column B. If you are not sure, locate the word in the numbered paragraph of the essay and use its context clues to give you an idea of its meaning. Use your dictionary to check.

A	B
sojourn (2)	isolation
baroque (3)	swarming
teeming (3)	scornful
romanticism (5)	temporary stay
hostile (6)	extravagant style
hostility (16)	imprisonment
incarceration (15)	incoherent sounds
alienation (16)	extravagant
sardonic (18)	antagonism
babble (18)	unfriendly

2. Baraka uses some street talk and four-letter words in his writing. Do you find these appropriate? Why?
3. He also mixes with this language a very formal vocabulary. Do the two mix well? For example, look at the word "ghettofication" in paragraph 2. Do you find it in the dictionary? How is it constructed (from what roots and suffixes)? Can you figure out its meaning from that construction?
4. Baraka uses a lot of parenthetical expressions as well as whole parenthetical sentences. What kind of an impression does this give you? Why would Baraka choose this style?
5. Why does Baraka use initials for the names of his friends at school?
6. Baraka also uses some devices your teachers may have warned you against: comma spliced sentences and sentence fragments. Pick out some of these from the text.

Engaging the Reader

1. Describe Barringer High; do you think it was a typical high school of its time?
2. Why does Baraka characterize the way his family lives as "a sociologist's joke"?
3. Why did Baraka choose to go to Barringer rather than a closer high school?
4. Why is Baraka considered an outsider at his school?

The Engaged Writer

1. Compare V. and J., Baraka's two friends.
2. Compare his two sets of friends at school.

3. Compare the neighborhood where Baraka lived with the neighborhood surrounding the school.
4. Compare Mount Rogers High School, from the previous article, with Barringer High, the school Amiri Baraka attended in New Jersey.
5. If you have been in a situation in which you were considered an "outsider," describe that situation and tell what you did about it.
6. If you have two sets of friends, two types of environments in which you work, live, or go to school, write an essay comparing them as Baraka does.

ALDO LEOPOLD

Red Lanterns

Aldo Leopold (1887–1948) worked for the U.S. Forest Service and was a professor of game management at the University of Wisconsin. He became an advisor on conservation to the United Nations before he died while fighting a fire on a neighbor's farm. His book *A Sand County Almanac* (1949) has been considered a classic of its kind, a combination of descriptions of nature and challenging philosophy. Years later, in 1965, Leopold was named to the National Wildlife Federation's Conservation Hall of Fame, showing how his memory and influence have persevered.

1   One way to hunt partridge is to make a plan, based on logic and probabilities, of the terrain to be hunted. This will take you over the ground where the birds ought to be.

2   Another way is to wander, quite aimlessly, from one red lantern to another. This will likely take you where the birds actually are. The lanterns are blackberry leaves, red in October sun.

3   Red lanterns have lighted my way on many a pleasant hunt in many a region, but I think that blackberries must first have learned how to glow in the sand counties of central Wisconsin. Along the little boggy streams of these friendly wastes, called poor by those whose own lights barely flicker, the blackberries burn richly red on every sunny day from first frost to the last day of the season. Every

woodcock and every partridge has his private solarium under these briars. Most hunters, not knowing this, wear themselves out in the briarless scrub, and, returning home birdless, leave the rest of us in peace.

By 'us' I mean the birds, the stream, the dog, and myself. The 4 stream is a lazy one; he winds through the alders as if he would rather stay here than reach the river. So would I. Every one of his hairpin hesitations means that much more streambank where hillside briars adjoin dank beds of frozen ferns and jewelweeds on the boggy bottom. No partridge can long absent himself from such a place, nor can I. Partridge hunting, then, is a creekside stroll, upwind, from one briar patch to another.

The dog, when he approaches the briars, looks around to make 5 sure I am within gunshot. Reassured, he advances with stealthy caution, his wet nose screening a hundred scents for that one scent, the potential presence of which gives life and meaning to the whole landscape. He is the prospector of the air, perpetually searching its strata for olfactory gold. Partridge scent is the gold standard that relates his world to mine.

My dog, by the way, thinks I have much to learn about par- 6 tridges, and, being a professional naturalist, I agree. He persists in tutoring me, with the calm patience of a professor of logic, in the art of drawing deductions from an educated nose. I delight in seeing him deduce a conclusion, in the form of a point, from data that are obvious to him, but speculative to my unaided eye. Perhaps he hopes his dull pupil will one day learn to smell.

Like other dull pupils, I know when the professor is right, even 7 though I do not know why. I check my gun and walk in. Like any good professor, the dog never laughs when I miss, which is often. He gives me just one look, and proceeds up the stream in quest of another grouse.

Following one of these banks, one walks astride two landscapes, 8 the hillside one hunts from, and the bottom the dog hunts in. There is a special charm in treading soft dry carpets of Lycopodium to flush birds out of the bog, and the first test of a partridge dog is his willingness to do the wet work while you parallel him on the dry bank.

A special problem arises where the belt of alders widens, and 9 the dog disappears from view. Hurry at once to a knoll or point, where you stand stock-still, straining eye and ear to follow the dog.

A sudden scattering of whitethroats may reveal his whereabouts. Again you may hear him breaking a twig, or splashing in a wet spot, or plopping into the creek. But when all sound ceases, be ready for instant action, for he is likely on point. Listen now for the premonitory clucks a frightened partridge gives just before flushing. Then follows the hurtling bird, or perhaps two of them, or I have known as many as six, clucking and flushing one by one, each sailing high for his own destination in the uplands. Whether one passes within gunshot is of course a matter of chance, and you can compute the chance if you have time: 360 degrees divided by 30, or whatever segment of the circle your gun covers. Divide again by 3 or 4, which is your chance of missing, and you have the probability of actual feathers in the hunting coat.

10   The second test of a good partridge dog is whether he reports for orders after such an episode. Sit down and talk it over with him while he pants. Then look for the next red lantern, and proceed with the hunt.

11   The October breeze brings my dog many scents other than grouse, each of which may lead to its own peculiar episode. When he points with a certain humorous expression of the ears, I know he has found a bedded rabbit. Once a dead-serious point yielded no bird, but still the dog stood frozen; in a tuft of sedge under his very nose was a fat sleeping coon, getting his share of October sun. At least once on each hunt the dog bays a skunk, usually in some denser-than-ordinary thicket of blackberries. Once the dog pointed in midstream: a whir of wings upriver, followed by three musical cries, told me he had interrupted a wood duck's dinner. Not infrequently he finds jacksnipe in heavily pastured alders, and lastly he may put out a deer, bedded for the day on a high streambank flanked by alder bog. Has the deer a poetical weakness for singing waters, or a practical liking for a bed that cannot be approached without making a noise? Judging by the indignant flick of his great white flag it might be either, or both.

12   Almost anything may happen between one red lantern and another.

Engaging the Text

1. In paragraph 6, Leopold uses two forms, noun and verb, of the same root word: deductions and deduce. Find some other

verbs in this essay and make nouns out of them, for example, in paragraph 2: wander—wandering, wanderlust.
2. Other words Leopold uses come from his scientific or naturalist's vocabulary: terrain (1), solarium (3), potential (5), strata (5), olefactory (5), Lycopodium (8), and premonitory (9). Find a science textbook (zoology, geology, or botany) and look these up in the text's glossary or index.
3. Though this essay starts out with the writer's voice, it later almost speaks from the point of view of the dog. How does the writer know so much about his dog?
4. Notice the alternation of short and long sentences. Find some examples of this. Is this technique effective in describing the hunting episode? Why?
5. Leopold uses combinations of words such as "briarless" and "birdless" and participles such as "reassured" to vary his sentences. He also uses alliteration, as in "boggy bottom." Find some examples of these techniques.

Engaging the Reader

1. What are the "red lanterns" mentioned in the first paragraph?
2. Would you expect a "conservationist" to write about hunting? Why or why not?
3. What does the writer learn from his dog?

The Engaged Writer

1. If you have a dog, describe what your dog does when you go for a walk, hunt, run, or whatever you do with your dog.
2. Turn question 1 around: write from the point of view of your dog, telling what you do when your owner goes for a walk, hunt, or run with you.
3. Write about what you see at a favorite outdoor spot. Try to include the kinds of detail and action that Leopold does.
4. Write a detailed essay about a favorite sport or hobby that requires the same kind of skill that hunting does, for example,

— Surfing: how to pick those big waves
— Skiing: how to navigate sharp turns using poles
— Golf: how to get those golf balls in the cup

— Tennis: how to hit an effective serve
— Or one of these:
  • Football
  • Baseball
  • Hockey
  • Soccer

C. L. RAWLINS

Deep in Truth's Country

C. L. Rawlins, in an article in *Sierra*, describes a hike into a canyon and takes that opportunity to reflect on the meaning of *wilderness*. As he does this, he reads some poems by Emily Dickinson, which make him compare the water-washed canyon with the inner workings of the mind as expressed in language. Since Rawlins works in the Central Rockies, he looks on that environment as a lot more than just the words he uses to describe it: *pure, pristine, perfect.* This leads Rawlins to discuss words and their relation to the things they represent. The words of hymns and the mark left on a stone by a primitive camper become a part of the exploration of the word *wilderness* and an effort to draw the word closer to the objects it represents. Rawlins is the author of *Sky's Witness* (1992).

1   In April, Linda and I walked in the water's tracks down a dry canyon cut in deep meanders through Navajo sandstone. There was only one flower: locoweed, tiny staircases of gray-green leaves climbing to the folded pea blooms, white and light violet. It had snowed the week before, but the moisture had disappeared fast. New water lay pooled in a few spots where the slope of the creekbed had reached an impermeable layer of rock, and older water rested in the scooped bowls under the pour-offs from side canyons, murky and rich as good jade.

2   The law of water says go downstream. Floods had cut deeply, tumbling lava and limestone down from the mountains at the head of the drainage. The side canyons were left hanging as the main stream, with its wilder flows and sharper rocks, carved more

quickly. Water and gravity had slowly opened the earth with unequivocal beauty.

We followed each descending arc, turning east to south to west 3 until the sun seemed to circle like a hawk above our heads. The walls were steep and definite as the channel veered in slow obedience to gravity. Downstream. Deeper into the rock. In the narrowest parts the only other direction—since we couldn't fly—was upstream.

What drives a person out here? What is there in the air of small 4 towns that entices some to leave the city—a waft of clover? the repose of cottonwoods and weathered fences? And what still greater promise draws one through the small towns, along gravel roads, then rutted dirt tracks, then trails, then onto the unmarked earth itself? Wilderness has become a word to conjure with, like love. It means as many things to as many people.

Some people out here hate the word, spitting it through mouthfuls of beer and snuff—"*will*-der-nuss"—like a Baptist grandma saying "fornication." Wilderness for them is not simply the mountains, the familiar high profile, the source of wood and water. Wilderness is a word for Keep Out. Wilderness is rich kids running around naked and having fun instead of working. Wilderness is the late June flood that blows the headgate and swamps a mile of road, the hairy thing that kills five ewes in one night, the howl of wind around the haystack in February.

Yet at the same time, in the same nation, in after-dinner speeches, 6 one can hear the word "wilderness" intoned with the same pitch and reverence as the name of God. It has been chanted to the point where it fails to mean anything specific in place or time, but instead has more to do with desire: Pure. Pristine. Perfect.

Outside the wilderness much of what we see is calculated to 7 engage attention, to be bright and colorful, to flicker with brief emotion and throb with music. What we see distracts and persuades, dazzles and urges. Our senses absorb so much contrivance that anything not instantly gratifying seems perverse.

As we lose touch with our world, we become ever more 8 demanding and impatient, of wilderness and of each other. Though buffeted with stimuli, we suffer from deprivation of simple, natural truth.

That no one tells the whole truth is a postmodern axiom. We 9 are so conscious of language as a tool that we judge it by its effect: Does it increase sales? Does it draw votes? Does it bring us what we crave? A few generations of this lying-for-effect, and we have grown conscious of our loss. We need a benchmark for *what* is.

10   In the evenings, camped in the dust of an undercut rock wall, I read. In my pack is a book of poems, a small, cheap student edition that sold for thirty-five cents in the 1960s. Emily Dickinson. Born, reared, and died in Amherst, Massachusetts.

11   Why do I choose her? Why not Thoreau? Why not Muir, Stegner, Krutch, or Leopold? Or Ann Zwinger, Bruce Chatwin, or Patricia Limerick? Why not Ed Abbey, the newly risen saint of the good, red country? Emily Dickinson was the bane of my high-school English class.

12   But not every book about wilderness reads well in the wild. Too many seem like footnotes, set against what meets the eye. Not Emily:

> Had I not seen the Sun
> I could have borne the shade
> But Light a newer Wilderness
> My Wilderness has made—

When I read this I get a chill, as I do coming around a bend of this canyon, seeing what I've never seen before. There's something about following the water down, something about going into the depths of a canyon, accepting enclosure, working out the intimate details of the interior. Suddenly everything corresponds, the arc of the canyon and the braid of a soul: a perfect fit. What's strange and fine is that these elements are so diverse—careless, water-cut stone and the careful poems of a white recluse, one hundred and five years dead.

13   I spend my working life in a wilderness in the central Rockies. It used to be summer work, but has become year-round. I follow the same trails in every month of the year, from sandals to boots, to skis and back again.

14   The place itself has slowly come to mean more than grand abstractions like *pure, pristine,* or *perfect.* In fact, it has come to mean an escape from abstractions, freedom from them. There is no persuasion in a granite boulder, no parable in a lone paintbrush among the columbines.

This canyon is like my home range, mysterious with real things. 15
Everything I see or touch rings with itself: sandstone, locoweed,
scrub oak, chert. Watching and naming is my life's work, keeping
the edges sharp like the black boundary of shade from an over-
hang. An odd, smooth stone catches my eye, dove-gray among the
reds and golds. Like an egg, it rests heavy and cool in the palm,
pocked at the end where somebody, sometime, used it as a hammer. It's good to sit without saying anything and hold it in my
hand: a rock, then a tool, then a rock again. There is sanctuary in
the specific, in the heft and presence of the world.

Wilderness has also become a legal tag, which generally means 16
that one is not to use motors at ground level. In a legal wilderness, we are not allowed to whack down trees or subdivide or
bulldoze parking lots or produce explosions, broadcast music,
install security lights, speed, flash credit cards, or engage in most
of the other activities that distinguish modern American life.
Wilderness—like church—is where we are supposed to be what
we manifestly are not: quiet, calm, aware, peaceful, reverent, and
contemplative.

One of the reasons that the notion of wilderness gives us such 17
trouble is that we confuse our notions with real things, that we live
in our thoughts more than in the world that surrounds us. We are
so soaked in our messages that we have trouble distinguishing a
word from the thing itself. Our perspective is skewed, so that we
see the natural world as a mere element in our mental worlds,
wilderness as our peace of mind.

Yet I love this canyon because it is not a library or a zoo. Because 18
it isn't a book or a movie. Because everything here proceeds from
incorruptible sources. Because it tells me to do nothing that I don't
need to do. Find water. Eat. Sleep. Because I have the freedom to
act foolishly and because there are always consequences. I love this
canyon because it doesn't need me to exist.

A Color stands abroad
On Solitary Fields
That Science cannot overtake
But Human Nature feels.

"My country is Truth," says Emily. Truth is something like grav- 19
ity: It always pulls toward a common center. Language is a wooly

wilderness inside us, blooming and howling. We strive to make it do as we wish, yet something in it resists. Language, like the earth, has a center of gravity. Words draw power from what they represent. The farther a word is placed from that center, the thinner and lighter it becomes. The tortured language of politics and press releases, for instance, cracks at a touch. It encloses truth's country like brittle parentheses. "Collateral damage" does not mean the same as human deaths: The phrase tries to contain them.

20   Or think of language as heritage. Linguists draw the same kind of charts as geneticists, and speak of stocks and hybrids. Geneticists talk of DNA as a code. Language adapts, crossbreeds, and mutates. Like genes, it can also be damaged, words deformed or sterilized. Not all can be remade: The backbrain and the backcountry are rootstocks. The wild syllables nudge at the cage of lips and we slip out of the numb cadences of usefulness. I used to be afraid of the wilderness, scared to fall asleep, camped alone in the dark. Now it's my refuge, the cupped rock that holds my dream like water.

21   At the mouth of a side canyon that plunges between two gold monoliths, the slickrock has a necklace of pools. We sit by the deepest one to eat. Overhead, a hawk slips into air and gyres, with a strange, ascending cry, unlike the familiar redtail *skreeeeee*. Peregrine, Linda says. Nothing to do but watch and listen.

22   Later I look for a place to camp. Linda is tired, so she leans against a boulder in the center of the streambed, a rock that moves once every century, when the flood of floods roars down and sweeps the canyon clean, rolling the boulder another hundred steps, carving another measure of sand from its tawny flank.

23   I scout the rimrock benches and dip into a side canyon, looking for an undercut that opens south for shelter, east for morning light. I know I will not be the first to find such a place here. Even though we think of wilderness as untouched, the good camps have all been used before, like words in the language. The sandy shadow will have been lit by fires and the silence will have echoed to "Come, Come Ye Saints" in nineteenth-century English, to coyote stories in Paiute, and to forgotten songs in even older languages. We'll rest tonight among the echoes under a late-rising moon, three nights past full.

24   Having a debt to the place, owing for beauty and shelter and sleep, I'll discharge a part, what I can't keep, with this telling. The

place, like truth, will remain nameless. I am not an explorer, nor
a guide.

As Emily Dickinson said, "My business is to sing."　　25

Engaging the Text

1. Throughout the essay Rawlins uses many lists or parallel constructions of language. For example, in paragraph 6, "Pure. Pristine. Perfect"; in paragraph 5, "Wilderness is the late June flood that blows the headgate and swamps a mile of road, the hairy thing that kills five ewes in one night, the howl of wind around the haystack in February." Find some more of these lists in the essay.

2. Some of the words Rawlins uses relate the wilderness to other areas of knowledge. For example, the words stimuli (8) and geneticists (20) come from science, while unequivocal (2), entices (4), pristine (6), and perverse (7) would not be out of place in a gothic romance. Write sentences of your own using these words.

Engaging the Reader

1. What seems to be Rawlins's definition of *wilderness?* Into what parts is it divided? Outline the various parts of this definition.

2. Do you think that language tells the whole truth? Do you think it often is, as Rawlins states, "lying-for-effect"? Find some examples in advertising or political speeches of this "lying-for-effect" (one example from Rawlins is "'Collateral damage' does not mean the same as human deaths . . .").

3. Some stories need footnotes, including this one. In paragraphs 11 and 12, a number of writers need to be identified. Look in a biographical dictionary, an encyclopedia, or another reference work in your library such as *The Cambridge Guide* or *The Reader's Encyclopedia* for some information on these writers. In your journal or in your discussion group, use this information to decide why Rawlins used Emily Dickinson as a model.

The Engaged Writer

1. Describe a place you know well, using lists of three parallel phrases to describe various aspects of the place as Rawlins does in paragraphs 5 and 6.

2. Can you recall a time in your life when you were with your friends during an important national event such as the Challenger disaster, an earthquake, or another event. You knew then that everything would change after that. Write an essay about that time. Or write a journal entry for yourself about it.

COURTLAND MILLOY

Those Cocky Roaches

Courtland Milloy, a Washington, DC, newspaperman, sees a lot of inner-city life in the course of writing news and feature articles. In this article he focuses with humor on the most humble of these, the ever-present cockroach, while relating this common pest to more serious problems. In his other writing, Milloy has been an advocate for city dwellers, blacks, and others against faceless bureaucracy.

1 Inside a local eatery on a recent night, I noticed a fat brown dot walking along the counter top. As it ducked in and around the napkin holder, hid in a crack near the menu rack then made a dash for a glass of ice water, it became clear that this was no ordinary critter. This was a cockroach, the most enduring of all mankind's associates.

2 Although my appetite was gone, the waitress wasn't even embarrassed. But she did become frustrated when she tried to kill it. With a roll of newspaper in hand, she took a mighty swat, then tossed the paper into a trash can. A few seconds later, here comes the roach, walking out of the newspaper roll, a little stunned but apparently as thirsty as ever as it made its way back to the bar.

3 Talk about cocky roaches.

4 More than 300 million years before Washington had restaurants, there was the beginning of something called the Carboniferous Period—aka, "The Age of the Cockroach." On Wednesday, a group of scientists will gather for a "roach symposium" at the Mayflower Hotel here to proclaim that the jig is up for the most prolific of six-legged critters.

5 The American Cyanamid Co. has developed what it bills as a revolutionary new product called COMBAT, which looks like a renovated roach motel. Says Maria Miller, the company's product

manager, "We have devised a proven bait tray delivery system with an insecticide-laced bait that roaches can't resist."

But my experiences say those little cucarachas are here to stay. 6

As a child, I used to put them in jars with bumblebees. I can now 7 report that bees don't mess with cockroaches. I'd turn my bicycle upside down, tape the roach to the rear wheel and spin them around. The result: roaches like merry-go-rounds.

A simpler solution would have been to step on them, but I can't 8 think of a grosser noise—or a messier mess—than that of a crunched roach.

I tried aerosol sprays—and that only made them grow bigger 9 and run faster; chlordane dust and DDT made them sprout wings. You could flush them down the toilet and come back the next day only to find them doing the American crawl.

Now there are no fewer than 2,000 species of cockroaches that 10 can outrun halfbacks and fly from a kitchen to dining room in a single bound. In this city, we are under seige by the seasonal onslaught of the German cockroach (Blatella germaica), a pair of which can produce 100,000 offspring in a year.

The problem here became epidemic during the 1800s, according 11 to researchers at the Smithsonian Institution, when a horde of recently imported German roaches ran from a restaurant hide-out and invaded the U.S. Capitol, and this city has literally been bugged ever since.

It doesn't matter if you keep a clean house. Roaches like clean 12 homes—the better to embarrass you in front of your guests. In fact, according to researchers, their digestive system is so efficient that a dozen roaches can survive for a week on the nutrients contained in the glue of a postage stamp. They also like fruit, dog food, and beer, and are known to go for swims in opened bottles of Coca-Cola. They are also partial to marijuana.

Despite similarities in the taste buds of roaches and humans, the 13 roach is still the nastiest, most disgusting creature around. In some parts of Texas, the Spanish cucaracha has been known to attack when startled, fly right into your food or hair.

It's amazing, really, given all the things we know how to kill, 14 that we can't get rid of roaches. So while I still have my doubts about this new product called Combat, I'm for anything that deals with our real enemies—and I hope, one day, brings the Carboniferous Age to an end.

Engaging the Text

1. Notice how Milloy mixes straight facts with humor—for example, "the Carboniferous Period—aka, 'The Age of the Cockroach.'" What do "the Carboniferous Period" and "aka" mean? Find some other examples of this device.
2. He also uses some technical words, familiar to anyone who reads advertisements: insecticide-laced bait (5), aerosol (9), chlordane (9), and nutrients (12).
3. Notice also how he uses inflated, bureaucratic language to write about a "small" subject. Find some examples of this (e.g., "proven bait tray delivery system with an insecticide-laced bait"—"Our real enemies"—"cucarachas," the Spanish word for the insect).
4. Milloy has classified the knowledge he has gathered about the cockroach into various subtopics. What are they?

Engaging the Reader

1. Milloy starts his article in one of the ways I suggested in "Getting Started," with an anecdote to interest the reader and introduce the subject. Is this anecdote effective? What would the article lose if the anecdote were omitted?
2. What does he tell us about the history of the cockroach?
3. Does Milloy think we can ever get rid of cockroaches? Why not?

The Engaged Writer

1. Using this article as a model, write a paragraph defining or describing the fly, the mosquito, the flea, or the louse.
2. Expand the paragraph you wrote in answer to question 1 into an essay. Add quotations, history, humor, and/or details as Milloy did and come to some conclusion about the future of this beast.
3. An assignment on classification: Milloy has organized his information into actual categories: history, background, methods of eradication, and so on. In this assignment, you are to invent categories to write about that organize a mixed list of items. Tell a story in which you mention all of the following items in a logical way. The narrative should only be a tool to

enable you to mention the items, however, but it should all make sense.

— a can of shaving soap
— an ashtray
— bubble bath
— a package of Black Jack gum
— a checked flannel shirt
— a wig
— a spiral notebook
— one ficus tree
— three bottles of sangria
— a tube of toothpaste
— a set of wrenches
— a twelve-volume unabridged dictionary
— three pieces of wallboard, 6′ x 8′
— a box of continuous computer paper, 3,000 sheets
— a flute
— vitamin C tablets
— plant food
— a manual typewriter

PART
3

Diversity: Varieties of Self

With your class or peer group seated in a circle, have each member answer this question: In your life so far, what have these meant to you—race, class, and gender? You will find that each of your classmates has something different, often startling, to say. As you look around the college class of today, wherever it is located, you notice that the racial, class, and gender makeup differs widely from accounts of college classes twenty, even ten, years ago. Those groups were predominantly male, white, middle class, and young. Now diversity in the classroom calls upon teachers and students to change the way material is presented, ideas developed, and relationships understood. We have to change the paradigms—the models by which we teach, learn, and think.

The Engaging Reader as a whole might be called a text on the thorny subjects of race, class, and gender today, for many selections throughout the book deal with them. Selections from Richard Rodriguez, Booker T. Washington, W.E.B. Du Bois, Endesha Ida Mae Holland, Richard Cohen, Amiri Baraka, and Louise Erdrich, among others are a part of the book's exploration of these all-pervasive themes.

In this section, the following selections reflect that diversity, try to make some sense of it, and suggest ways to deal positively with it. Elizabeth Bishop's poem, "The Fish," though it deals with a creature, teaches a lesson in tolerance, dignity, and pride. People live in unusual and diverse places: the dump (Joan Ackermann-Blount, "In New Mexico . . ."). In old "melting pot" New York, an immigrant learns something of honor and justice (George and Helen Waite Papashvily, "Yes, Your Honesty").

Questions of race and class appear also in the Florida stories of anthropologist and storyteller Zora Neale Hurston ("Work"), while Lee Smith discusses some of the same questions for forgotten parts of the country in "The Face of Rural Poverty." Claudia Tate's interview with poet Audre Lorde brings out the diversity this one woman represents—she is black, lesbian, and a feminist—and what it means to her as a writer.

Gender differences still hamper women in today's society as Claire Safran ("Hidden Lessons . . .") points out. Carolyn Heilbrun brings up the problem of ageing and ageism in "Naming a New Rite of Passage." In the end, spirituality may bring us all together, as Leslie Marmon Silko calls up the spirits of her Native American ancestors.

ELIZABETH BISHOP

The Fish

Elizabeth Bishop was an American poet who lived in Brazil for many years after winning a fellowship that took her there to study. She won the Pulitzer Prize in 1955 for her collected poems. She has always been considered an especially sharp observer, and this poem, written in 1946, shows that skill.

1   *I caught a tremendous fish*
    and held him beside the boat
    half out of water, with my hook
    fast in a corner of his mouth.
5   *He didn't fight.*
    He hadn't fought at all.
    He hung a grunting weight,
    battered and venerable
    and homely. Here and there
10   *his brown skin hung in strips*
    like ancient wallpaper,
    and its pattern of darker brown
    was like wallpaper:
    shapes like full-blown roses

stained and lost through age. 15
He was speckled with barnacles,
fine rosettes of lime,
and infested
with tiny white sea-lice,
and underneath two or three 20
rags of green weed hung down.
While his gills were breathing in
the terrible oxygen
—the frightening gills,
fresh and crisp with blood, 25
that can cut so badly—
I thought of the coarse white flesh
packed in like feathers,
the big bones and the little bones,
the dramatic reds and blacks 30
of his shiny entrails,
and the pink swim-bladder
like a big peony.
I looked into his eyes
which were far larger than mine 35
but shallower, and yellowed,
the irises backed and packed
with tarnished tinfoil
seen through the lenses
of old scratched isinglass. 40
They shifted a little, but not
to return my stare.
—It was more like the tipping
of an object toward the light.
I admired his sullen face, 45
the mechanism of his jaw,
and then I saw
that from his lower lip
—if you could call it a lip—
grim, wet, and weaponlike, 50
hung five old pieces of fish-line,
or four and a wire leader
with the swivel still attached,
with all their five big hooks

55   *grown firmly in his mouth.*
        A green line, frayed at the end
        where he broke it, two heavier lines,
        and a fine black thread
        still crimped from the strain and snap
60   *when it broke and he got away.*
        Like medals with their ribbons
        frayed and wavering,
        a five-haired beard of wisdom
        trailing from his aching jaw.
65   *I stared and stared*
        and victory filled up
        the little rented boat,
        from the pool of bilge
        where oil had spread a rainbow
70   *around the rusted engine*
        to the bailer rusted orange,
        the sun-cracked thwarts,
        the oarlocks on their strings,
        the gunnels—until everything
75   *was rainbow, rainbow, rainbow!*
        And I let the fish go.

Engaging the Text

1. This selection is placed on the page in the form of a poem.
   What makes it a poem? Is it rhyme? Or is it rhythm? What is
   it that lets us call this piece a poem?
2. No detail is too small or too earthy for Bishop to observe. Pick
   out some of the details that make you feel you are there in the
   boat with her. Particularly note the words she uses to make the
   reader see the fish intimately: venerable (8), barnacles (16),
   rosettes (17), gills (22), entrails (30), isinglass (40), sullen (45),
   bilge (68). If any of these are unfamiliar to you, look them up
   in your dictionary. Check back with the poem and describe the
   sense in which Bishop used them.

Engaging the Reader

1. What happens in the poem? Compare the event with Aldo
   Leopold's description of hunting ("Red Lanterns").
2. Why does Bishop let the fish go?

The Engaged Writer

1. Explain the next to the last lines "until everything/was rainbow, rainbow, rainbow!"
2. Write an essay giving several reasons why you think Bishop let the fish go.
3. Using the kinds of details you picked out in question 2 in "Engaging the Text," write a description of flying a kite, hitting a fly ball, skating on a frozen pond, swimming in a lake or ocean, or another sport or activity. List your details first, then organize them into an essay—or a poem.

JOAN ACKERMANN-BLOUNT

In New Mexico: A Family Lives in Its Own World

Time magazine occasionally runs an article on the "American Scene," and this account of a self-sufficient family who lives close to the soil and avoids the expense of earning money was an unusual one. Not the usual "success story," Joan Ackermann-Blount's article describes Ron, Nora, and Laura Oest, who have no life insurance or savings but who built their own house and reclaim articles from the dump, enjoying life in a New Mexico valley.

"Chicken power," says Ron Oest, exulting in his chicken house in northern New Mexico. "That's what keeps our winter water supply from freezing. See, they roost right under the tank." Up on the roost, two dozen hens ride out the winter, unwittingly warming a thousand gallons of mountain stream water stored in the black tank that bellies down from the ceiling. It is an efficient use of passive poultry energy, harnessed by a resourceful man who supports his family handsomely on $5,000 a year. 1

"We don't have any money in the bank," explains his wife Nora, who is part Spanish, part Chiricahua Apache. She can butcher a bear and cook up a steak in the Franklin stove so tender it softens a person's attitude toward grizzlies. "We don't have any credit. No life insurance," she says with a smile, the earthy 2 enduring smile that heroines in South American novels bequeath to their daughters.

3   "People don't realize how much earning money costs," says Oest, 55. "Having a job is expensive. The clothes, the car, the house with the mortgage payments. If you spend all your time working for someone else, you don't have time to learn to do things yourself."

4   Unemployed for nearly 20 years since he was a high school speech coach and creative-writing teacher, he has had time to learn, among other things, how to build his own house, overhaul VW engines in his living room, keep bees for honey and make his own bullets out of wheel weights. He grew up in Rutherford, N.J., disliking cities and laying a 75-trap line for muskrats down through what is now the Meadowlands. A wounded Korean War vet, he collects $333 a month veteran's compensation, and that, along with $1,200 he and Nora make each year selling their crafts, is enough to buy the various items—gas, Postum, margarine—that they can't grow in their garden, hunt, sew, fish for, trade for or find in the Taos County dump.

5   Married for 18 years, the Oests met when he was teaching in a high school in Albuquerque and she was a sophomore. "She walked by and I handed her a book, and I felt myself falling in love," says Ron. After she graduated, he wrote her a poem, they dated, went to Mexico, got married and lived for three years in a 1948 yellow school bus parked in a coconut grove.

6   For the past 15 years, the Oests have lived in the Valdez Valley on three acres of land that Nora inherited from her father, land he acquired by trading a La Salle automobile to his Uncle Pedro, who needed it to get to Wyoming.

7   "The way we live now isn't that different from how I lived here as a child," says Nora, 36, whose great-great-great-grandfather on her father's side settled in the valley in the early 1800s to work the local gold mine, and whose great-great-grandfather on her mother's side was shot in the back delivering mail for the Pony Express.

8   Nora's childhood house was made of adobe, but she and Ron built their two-story, five-room house for $6,000 out of logs and cement. It is a handsome, organically grown house with unpredictable flourishes: the door handle made out of a part from a lawn mower, the recesses in the stone walls for candles, the richly ornate wood carvings throughout. Although the Oests don't have plumb-

ing, a telephone or a well, they do have electricity and a refrigerator they bought for $10 from a neighbor who later shot himself because his condominiums failed.

In their front yard, snow melts off six other refrigerators, piles 9 of tires, three Maytag washing machines, a dozen bicycles, several bed frames and various orderly piles of useful treasures, all harvested from the dump. Their toaster, broiler, blender, coffeepot, clock, heaters and just about every other electrical item in the house are also from the dump, repaired by Ron, along with down jackets, chairs, front ends for cars, wood, French windows and jars for canning.

"We've given away lots of bicycles and wagons to people less 10 fortunate than us," says Nora. She has joined Ron on the porch and sips a cup of Yerba Buena herb tea. Today even the witches, famous in this valley, must be yielding to the sun, loosening their joints in this welcome reprieve from the chill.

"Once I found a typewriter in the dump that had five rusty keys 11 and didn't work," says Ron. "I fixed it and traded it with a guy for a pig. Well, the pig had eight piglets, and I traded five of them for three VW bugs, none of which ran. I overhauled one of them to get it going; cost me $40. The next litter I traded five more piglets for another VW. We named the pig Tubby Typewriter after the typewriter."

"She was a very mellow pig," says Nora, who makes wild- 12 chokecherry wine and bakes all her breads and biscuits with homegrown wheat and rye. "When she had her first litter, we took a bottle of wine and some glasses into the pig house to help her through."

Indoors in the kitchen, the Oests' pretty daughter Laura, 8, 13 entertains a school chum. "This is my survival knife," she says, deftly slipping a 14-in. knife from its canvas sheath.

"You aren't afraid to touch it?" asks her playmate, aghast and 14 giggling, her hands stuffed into her open mouth.

"No," says Laura, who also has a pellet gun, two .22s, a .45-cal. 15 muzzle-loading rifle and muzzle-loading pistol, a bow and arrows, a wild pony named Wild Rose, and her own row of flowers and vegetables in the garden. "I use it to skin squirrels." She puts the knife back into its sheath as if she were tucking one of her Barbie dolls into bed. "Squirrels are good," she adds, reaching for one of her mother's hot homemade donuts, "but there's not much meat on them."

16   "Laura got her hunting license when she was seven," says Ron. "She was the youngest female in New Mexico ever to earn a hunting license."

17   The family often goes camping together, hunting and fishing, and Ron takes Laura to the Taos County dump to shoot bottles.

18   "When I was a kid in New Jersey," says Ron, "I used to go to the dump to hunt rats. There was this guy named Mike who lived there in a big refrigerator crate. I remember one day he was cooking up some potatoes he'd found, and he suddenly looked around and said to me, arms outstretched, 'This place is rich. *Rich.*' It really made an impression on me.

19   "I grew up in two devastating times: I was old enough as a kid to see people in the Depression, and then later I saw items rationed during the Second World War. There are times when there's nothing, and you can't get it anywhere. Why not have your own little world where you have everything you need so no one can ever say no to you?"

20   Although some aspects of their world seem idyllic, there are difficulties—constant battles to protect the environment, to keep the water in the nearby Rio Hondo clean, jaunts down to Mexico for cheaper dental work, the three-hour drive to the veteran's hospital in Albuquerque, the hopes that Laura's teeth don't grow in crooked and that her A grades will earn her a scholarship later on.

21   "Some people think it's scary to live the way we do," says Ron. "No life insurance. No savings. But if I die, the house is all paid for. We have four years' worth of food—canned, frozen and dried. We have three years' worth of firewood. No bills. We have stockpiles of clothes. Living like this you just don't ever suddenly need a lot of money."

Engaging the Text

1. The essay begins and ends with a quotation from Ron Oest. This is a useful way to get into and out of a topic. (See "Getting Started" for other tips on beginning to write.) What is the effect of these quotations?

2. Notice that the writer packs apparently irrelevant details into the same sentence. For example, in paragraph two, "'We don't have any money in the bank,' . . . who is part Spanish, part Chiricahua Apache." Find some other examples of this trick of style. Does this add to the interest of the piece?

Engaging the Reader

1. This selection, with all its rich detail, is actually an essay on values. What are some of the values the Oests have that differ from the usual American Dream?
2. Give some of the details of the Oests' lives that show what makes them "rich."

The Engaged Writer

1. Look through the essay for references to unfamiliar historical events, geographical places, or objects from the Oests' life. Look them up in an encyclopedia or dictionary, and summarize the information you obtain in a paragraph for each one. You could prepare a glossary for your classmates, reproducing it for distribution. Examples include grizzlies (2), VW Bugs (11), trap line (4), the Meadowlands (4), Korean War (4), Postum (4), Taos County (4, 17), Albuquerque (20), La Salle automobile (6), Pony Express (7), Barbie dolls (15), French windows (9), and Yerba Buena tea (10).
2. Do you and your family have an unusual life-style? A novel way of earning money—or a different set of values? Describe your family's life-style in an essay.
3. Rewrite the essay from the point of view of a more conventional neighbor. Check "point of view" in the Glossary in the back of this book.
4. Some of the letters to the editor in subsequent issues of *Time* pointed out that the Oests do not contribute to society, as does someone who pays taxes and has money in the bank and life insurance; they only take from it (pensions, material from the dump, scholarships for their daughter). Do you agree with this criticism? Express your views in a letter to the editor. See "Writing a Letter to the Editor."

CLAUDIA TATE

Audre Lorde

Claudia Tate, a writer and essayist, interviewed fourteen African American women writers for her 1983 book *Black Women Writers at Work*. One of these remarkable conversations featured Audre Lorde, whose life and work personify the idea of America's multicultural roots. She called herself a "black lesbian feminist warrior poet," and in her poetry and her lectures she envisioned a better world and struggled to achieve it for all people in our diverse society. Her words give us some guidelines on dealing with the difficult issue of "differences" of race and gender. Lorde was born in New York City of West Indian parents, became head librarian of the City University of New York, then left that position to write, to lecture on creative writing, and to be poet-in-residence at Tougaloo College. Later she became professor of English at Hunter College. She has published many books of poetry. She died in 1993.

1   CLAUDIA TATE: How does your openness about being a black lesbian feminist direct your work and, more importantly, your life?

2   AUDRE LORDE: When you narrow your definition to what is convenient, or what is fashionable, or what is expected, what happens is dishonesty by silence. It is putting all of your eggs into one basket. That's not where all of your energy comes from.

3   Black writers, of whatever quality, who step outside the pale of what black writers are supposed to write about, or who black writers are supposed to be, are condemned to silences in black literary circles that are as total and as destructive as any imposed by racism. This is particularly true for black women writers who have refused to be delineated by male-establishment models of femininity, and who have dealt with their sexuality as an accepted part of their identity. For instance, where are the women writers of the Harlem Renaissance being taught? Why did it take so long for Zora Neale Hurston to be reprinted?

4   Now, when you have a literary community oppressed by silence from the outside, as black writers are in America, and you have

this kind of tacit insistence upon some unilateral definition of what "blackness" is, then you are painfully and effectively silencing some of our most dynamic and creative talents, for all change and progress from within require the recognition of differences among ourselves.

When you are a member of an out-group, and you challenge   5 others with whom you share this outsider position to examine some aspect of their lives that distorts differences between you, then there can be a great deal of pain. In other words, when people of a group share an oppression, there are certain strengths that they build together. But there are also certain vulnerabilities. For instance, talking about racism to the women's movement results in "Huh, don't bother us with that. Look, we're all sisters, please don't rock the boat." Talking to the black community about sexism results in pretty much the same thing. You get a "Wait, wait . . . wait a minute: we're all black together. Don't rock the boat." In our work and in our living, we must recognize that difference is a reason for celebration and growth, rather than a reason for destruction.

We should see difference as a dialogue, the same way we deal   6 with symbol and image, in literary study. "Imaging" is the process of developing a dialectic, a tension between opposites that illuminates the differences and similarities between things in apparent opposition. It is the same way with people. We need to use these differences in constructive ways, creative ways, rather than in ways to justify our destroying each other.

With respect to myself specifically, I feel that not to be open   7 about any of the different "people" within my identity, particularly the "mes" who are challenged by a status quo, is to invite myself and other women, by my example, to live a lie. In other words, I would be giving in to a myth of sameness which I think can destroy us.

I'm not into living lies, no matter how comfortable they may be.   8 I really feel that I'm too old for both abstractions and games, and I will not shut off any of my essential sources of power, control, and knowledge. I learned to speak the truth by accepting many parts of myself and making them serve one another. This power fuels my life and my work.

9   C.T.: Has the social climate of the eighties suppressed the openness of the seventies?

10   LORDE: To begin with, all of these things are relative, and when we speak of the openness of the seventies, we are speaking more of an appearance than a reality. But as far as sexuality is concerned, it is true that in the seventies, black lesbians and gay men saw a slowly increasing acknowledgment of their presence within the black community. In large part this came about because of the number of us willing to speak out about our sexual identities. In the 1960s, many black people who spoke from a complex black identity suffered because of it, and were silenced in many ways. In the mistaken belief that unity must mean sameness, differences within the black community of color, sex, sexuality, and vision were sometimes mislabeled, oversimplified, and repressed. We must not romanticize the sixties while we recognize its importance. Lesbians and gay men have always existed in black communities, and in the sixties we played active and important roles on many fronts in that decade's struggle for black liberation. And that has been so throughout the history of black people in America, and continues to be so.

11   In the 1970s some of those differences which have always existed within the black community began to be articulated and examined, as we came to learn that we, as a people, cannot afford to waste our resources, cannot afford to waste each other. The eighties present yet another challenge. On one hand, there is a certain move towards conservatism and greater repression within American society, and renewed attacks upon lesbians and gay men represent only the cutting edge of that greater repression which is so dangerous to us all as black people. But because of this shift to the right, some voices once willing to examine the role of difference in our communities are falling silent, some once vocal people are heading for cover.

12   It's very distressing to hear someone say, "I can't really afford to say that or I can't afford to be seen with you." It's scary because we've been through that before. It was called the fifties. Yet more and more these days, "all of our asses are in the sling together," if you'll excuse the expression, and real alliances are beginning to be made. When we talk about "Dykes Against Racism Everywhere,"

and "Black and White Men Together," which are gay groups who have been doing active antiracist work in a number of communities, when we see the coalition of black community organizations in the Boston area that got together to protest the wholesale murder of black women in 1978 and '79, we are talking about real coalitions. We must recognize that we need each other. Both these trends are operating now. Of course, I'm dedicated to believing that it's through coalitions that we'll win out. There are no more single issues.

c.t.: Have your critics attempted to stereotype your work? 13

LORDE: Critics have always wanted to cast me in a particular role 14 from the time my first poem was published when I was fifteen years old. My English teachers at Hunter High School said that a particular poem was much too romantic. It was a love poem about my first love affair with a boy, and they didn't want to print it in the school paper, which is why I sent it to *Seventeen* magazine.

It's easier to deal with a poet, certainly with a black woman 15 poet, when you categorize her, narrow her down so that she can fulfill your expectations, so she's socially acceptable and not too disturbing, not too discordant. I cannot be categorized. That has been both my weakness and my strength. It has been my weakness because my independence has cost me a lot of support. But you see, it has also been my strength because it has given me a vantage point and the power to go on. I don't know how I would have lived through the difficulties I have survived and continued to produce, if I had not felt that all of who I am is what fulfills me and fulfills the vision I have of the world, and of the future.

c.t.: For whom do you write? What is your responsibility to your 16 audience?

LORDE: I write for myself and my children and for as many people 17 as possible who can read me, who need to hear what I have to say—who need to use what I know. When I say myself, I mean not only the Audre who inhabits my body but all those feisty, incorrigible black women who insist on standing up and saying "I *am* and you cannot wipe me out, no matter how irritating I am, how much you fear what I might represent." I write for these women for whom a voice has not yet existed, or whose voices have been silenced. I don't have the only voice or all of their voices, but they are a part of my voice, and I am a part of theirs.

18 My responsibility is to speak the truth as I feel it, and to attempt to speak it with as much precision and beauty as possible. I think of my responsibility in terms of women because there are many voices for men. There are very few voices for women and particularly very few voices for black women, speaking from the center of consciousness, from the *I am* out to the *we are* and then out to the *we can*.

19 My mother used to say: "Island women make good wives; whatever happens they've seen worse." Well, I feel that as black women we have been through all kinds of catastrophe. We've survived, and with style.

20 I feel I have a duty to speak the truth as I see it and to share not just my triumphs, not just the things that felt good, but the pain, the intense, often unmitigating pain. It is important to share how I know survival is survival and not just a walk through the rain. For example, I have a duty to share what it feels like at three o'clock in the morning when you know "they" could cut you down emotionally in the street and grin in your face. And "they" are your own people. To share what it means to look into another sister's eyes and have her look away and choose someone you know she hates because it's expedient. To know that I, at times, have been a coward, or less than myself, or oppressive to other women, and to know that I can change. All of that anxiety, pain, defeat must be shared. We tend to talk about what feels good. We talk about what we think is settled. We never seem to talk about the ongoing problems. We need to share our mistakes in the same way we share our victories because that's the only way learning occurs. In other words, we have survived the pain, the problems, the failures, so what we need to do is use this suffering and learn from it. We must remember and comfort ourselves with that fact that survival is, in itself, a victory.

21 I never thought I would live to be forty, and I feel, "Hey, I really did it!" I am stronger for confronting the hard issue of breast cancer, of mortality, dying. It is hard, extremely hard, but very strengthening to remember I could be silent my whole life long and then be dead, flat out, and never have said or done what I wanted to do, what I needed to do because of pain or fear. . . . If I

wait to be assured I'm right before I speak, I would be sending little cryptic messages on the Ouiji board, complaints from the other side.

I really feel if what I have to say is wrong, then there will be 22 some woman who will stand up and say Audre Lorde was in error. But my words will be there, something for her to bounce off of, something to incite thought, activity.

I write not only for my peers but for those who will come after 23 me, to say I was there, and I passed on, and you will pass on, too. But you're here now, so do it. I believe very strongly in survival and teaching. I feel that is my work.

This is so important that it bears repeating. I write for those 24 women who do not speak, for those who do not have a voice because they/we were so terrified, because we are taught to respect fear more than ourselves. We've been taught that silence would save us, but it won't. We *must* learn to respect ourselves and our needs more than the fear of our differences, and we must learn to share ourselves with each other.

C.T.: Is writing a way of growing, understanding? 25

LORDE: Yes. I think writing and teaching, child-rearing, digging 26 rocks (which is one of my favorite pastimes), all of the things I do are very much a part of my work. They flow in and out of each other, help to nourish each other. That's what the whole question of survival and teaching means. That we keep our experience afloat long enough, that we share what we know, so that other people can build upon our experience. There are many ways of doing that in all aspects of our lives. So teaching for me is in many respects identical to writing. Both become ways of exploring what I need for survival. They are survival techniques. Because as I write, as I teach, I am answering those questions that are primary for my own survival, and I am exploring the response to these questions with other people; this is what teaching is. I think that this is the only way that real learning occurs. Learning does not happen in some detached way of dealing with a text alone, but from becoming so involved in the process that you can see how it might illuminate your life, and then how you can share that illumination.

27 C.T.: When did you start to write?

28 LORDE: I looked around when I was a young woman and there was no one saying what I wanted and needed to hear. I felt totally alienated, disoriented, crazy. I thought that there's got to be somebody else who feels as I do.

29   I was very inarticulate as a youngster. I couldn't speak. I didn't speak until I was five, in fact, not really until I started reading and writing poetry. I used to speak in poetry. I would read poems, and I would memorize them. People would say, "Well, what do you think, Audre? What happened to you yesterday?" And I would recite a poem and somewhere in that poem there would be a line or a feeling I was sharing. In other words, I literally communicated through poetry. And when I couldn't find the poems to express the things I was feeling, that's when I started writing poetry. That was when I was twelve or thirteen.

30 C.T.: Universities seem to be one major source of income for many writers, that is in terms of writer-in-residence positions. Have you had such appointments? What has been their effect?

31 LORDE: I've only had one writer-in-residence position, and that was at Tougaloo College in Mississippi fourteen years ago. It was pivotal for me. Pivotal. In 1968 my first book had just been published; it was my first trip into the Deep South; it was the first time I had been away from the children; the first time I worked with young black students in a workshop situation. I came to realize that this was my work. That teaching and writing were inextricably combined, and it was there that I knew what I wanted to do for the rest of my life.

32   I had been "the librarian who wrote." After my experience at Tougaloo, I realized that writing was central to my life and that the library, although I loved books, was not enough. Combined with the circumstances that followed my stay at Tougaloo: King's death, Kennedy's death, Martha's accident,* all of these things really made me see that life is very short, and what we have to do must be done now.

33   I have never had another writer-in-residence position. The poem "Touring" from *The Black Unicorn* represents another aspect

*Lorde's close personal friend.

of being a travelling cultural worker. I go and read my poetry. I drop my little seeds and then I leave. I hope they spring into something. Sometimes I find out they do; sometimes I never find out. I just have to have faith, and fun along the way.

C.T.: Would you describe your writing process?   34

LORDE: I keep a journal and write in it fairly regularly. I get a lot of   35
my poems out of it. It's like the raw material for my poems. Sometimes I'm blessed with a poem that comes in the form of a poem, but other times I've worked for two years on a poem.

For me, there are two very basic and different processes for revis-   36
ing my poetry. One is recognizing that a poem has not yet become itself. In other words, I mean that the feeling, the truth that the poem is anchored in is somehow not clearly clarified inside of me, and as a result it lacks something. Then it has to be re-felt. Then there's the other process which is easier. The poem is itself, but it has rough edges that need to be refined. That kind of revision involves picking the image that is more potent or tailoring it so that it carries the feeling. That's an easier kind of rewriting and re-feeling.

My journal entries focus on things I feel: feelings that sometimes   37
have no place, no beginning, no end; phrases I hear in passing; something that looks good to me; sometimes just observations of the world.

I went through a period once when I felt like I was dying.   38
I wasn't writing any poetry, and I felt that if I couldn't write I would split. I was recording in my journal, but no poems came. I know now that this period was a transition in my life.

The next year, I went back to my journal, and here were these   39
incredible poems that I could almost lift out of it.

C.T.: What can you share with the younger generation of black   40
women writers and writers in general?

LORDE: Not to be afraid of difference. To be real, tough, loving. And   41
to recognize each other. I can tell them not to be afraid to feel and not to be afraid to write about it. Even if you are afraid, do it anyway because we learn to work when we are tired, so we can learn to work when we are afraid. Silence never brought us anything. Survive and teach; that's what we've got to do and to do it with joy.

Engaging the Text

1. Lorde discusses a number of abstract concepts here, giving vivid examples of many of them: sexism (5), racism (5), femininity (3), vulnerabilities (5). Find some more of these; if you are unsure of their meanings, check them in your dictionary.

2. Lorde cleverly slips in definitions when using a somewhat unfamiliar word. For example, in paragraph 6, she uses a word immediately followed by its definition: "dialectic, a tension between opposites that illuminates the differences and similarities between things in apparent opposition." Check through the interview and list other instances of this smooth way of explaining without appearing to.

Engaging the Reader

1. The interview format with its questions and answers differs from an essay format with a thesis and logical development of points. Also, the interviewer cannot comment or put words in the subject's mouth. Nevertheless, there are topics and subtopics in this interview. Go through the interview and write down, in as few words as possible, the main topics Lorde discusses. Do you see any unity in them? What seems to be the main theme of the interview?

2. Who is Lorde writing for? Compare her views on writing with those of Ray Bradbury, "The Impulse to Write" and Patricia Cornwell, "In Cold Blood."

The Engaged Writer

1. Lorde speaks about her writing—how she uses a journal for ideas. Start keeping such a journal, and see if some poetry comes out of it when you reread it as she does.

2. If you have had a hard time dealing with issues such as racism, sexism, or homophobia (fear of homosexuals), write about those difficulties and how you solved them, or tried to solve them.

3. Lorde speaks about other black writers and their works, as well as about her own poetry. In your library, find some poetry

by Lorde, read it, and consider whether it tells of some of the themes she touches on in her interview. Write about this in your own journal or in a paper to share with the class. You might see how the same theme can be expressed in different ways in poetry and in prose.

GEORGE AND HELEN WAITE PAPASHVILY

Yes, Your Honesty

George and Helen Waite Papashvily have collaborated on books and articles on cooking, dog training, and life on a Pennsylvania farm. But their best-known work is *Anything Can Happen* (1945) from which the following selection is excerpted. It chronicles George Papashvily's emigration from Georgia in Russia and his early years in the United States, learning English and the strange ways of the Americans. The story begins with Georgi Ivanovich (George Papashvily) as a young immigrant in New York in the 1920s. His work in a dry-cleaner's is dull, the fumes hazardous, but on Sundays he and his friends picnic in Van Cortlandt Park, grilling lamb *shashliks*. As George said, "For one day anyway we could enjoy to live like human beings."

Six months in America and already I was a jailbird. Happened this 1
way.

The weeks seemed extra long that first half year I was in New 2
York. No holidays, no feast days, no celebrations to break up the time and then when Saturday came around I had only twelve dollars, at most fourteen dollars in my pay envelope. . . .

But no matter how the week went the Sundays were good 3
because then we made all day the holiday and took ourselves in Van Cortlandt Park where there was country and trees and flowers. We could make fires and roast cubed lamb *shashliks* and walk on the grass and forget the factory. For one day anyway we could enjoy to live like human beings.

4   From six o'clock on, every Sunday morning, subway was packed full. Russians, Syrians, Greeks, Armenians, all kinds of peoples, carrying their grampas and babies and gallon jugs and folding chairs and charcoal sacks and hammocks and samovars and lunch baskets and rugs. Everyone hurrying to their regular place in the park so they could start tea and lay out the lunch, to make the day last a long, long time.

5   Well, this particular Sunday when all my trouble began was in the late spring. Bright blue day with a high sky and white lamb clouds. The kind of day that's for adventures.

6   I had my first American-bought suit on and a purple striped tie with a handkerchief to match and a real Yankee Doodle hat from straw. I felt happy and full of prance.

7   Five or six other fellows and me were visiting around the park. We went from family to family we knew and drank a glass of wine here, tried a piece of cake there, met an uncle just came from Buffalo, saw a new baby first time out and so on.

8   While we were making shortcut down a quiet path to get on other side of the park we came to a beautiful tree foaming over with white blossoms, how they call in English, dogswood.

9   "Flowers. Flowers," one Russian fellow, name of Cyrille, said. "I gonna pick. Take bouquet to my lady friend." I don't know who he was, this fellow, he joined us some place we stopped.

10   "Pick! Pick!" Everybody got the idea. "Pick flowers, take a bouquet to all the lady friends."

11   "Why spoil a tree?" I said. "Use your brains better. If you want to make friends with a nice young lady, ask her to take a walk. Tell her you gonna show her a bouquet bigger than a house, a bouquet growing right out of the ground. Something interesting. That way you get a chance to be acquainted while you're walking. Maybe you know so good on the way back you can invite for ice cream."

12   No, no won't listen. They have to break the tree down. Tear his arms and legs off like wolves. Jumping. Jumping. Who's gonna get the biggest branch? Makes me sick.

13   "Personally," I said, "I would be ashamed to give a lady flowers that I got for nothing. That I stole. I prefer better to buy. Shows more respect. Or else don't give."

14   All of a sudden that fellow, Cyrille, who had now the biggest bunch climbed down from the top branches and said to me, "I

have to tie my shoelace. Hold my bouquet for a minute, I'll be back." So I held. In that minute a policeman was there.

"Awright. Awright," he said. "Defacing public property. 15 Awright." He asked us our names and started writing them down on a piece of paper.

"What he does?" I asked Sergei. 16

"Gives us a summons." 17

"Summons?" 18

"We have to go in court." 19

"We're arrested?" 20

"Something like that. If we pay the fine, everything be O.K. But 21 if we ignore, throw away the summons, they chase us; lock us up."

"What's your name, buddy?" policeman asked me. 22

I explained the best I can I'm not picking, I'm only holding for 23 the other fellow.

But he doesn't believe me. "Don't argue," he said. "Don't argue 24 or I'll run you in right now."

I explained again. "Boys will tell you," I said. "I wasn't picking." 25

No, he doesn't believe them neither. "Don't alibi him," he said. 26

I'd be sorry to be a man like that policeman, suspicious that 27 everybody is a liar. What's the use for a person to live if he can't trust nobody?

So he wrote a ticket for me, too, and went away. And still tying 28 his shoe, that fellow Cyrille wasn't back yet.

"This is an awful, awful thing," I said. 29

"It's nothing." Sergei could laugh. 30

"Nothing! I lived my whole life at home and I was never in trou- 31 ble. Now I'm six months in America and I'm a crook. Nothing, you think? How my father likes to hear such kind of news? Arrested. What will our village say? The first man from Kobiankari ever comes in the U. S. A.—for what? To go in prison!"

"Look," Sergei said. "You don't even have to go in court. Send 32 the money. Plead guilty."

"But I'm not." . . . 33

Sergei suggested how about we go to see old Mr. Cohen, he was 34 years and years in the U. S. A. Maybe he can think of something.

"Listen," Mr. Cohen said, when we told him everything. "Fixer 35 Mixer leave alone all. Take my advices. I been a citizen for forty-seven years with full papers. President Hayes signed me in personal. Go in court. When they ask you the first question say, 'Not guilty, Your Honor'"

36   "Not guilty, Your Honor. What means 'Your Honor'?"

37   "Means the judge. All judges in U. S. A. named Your Honor."

38   "Not guilty, Your Honor. Then?"

39   "Just tell your story nice way."

40   "With my broken words?"

41   "Say the best way you can. Probably judge gonna listen and try to understand you. Of course it can happen you get a mean judge, one that's too tired to pay attention, that don't like foreigners to bother him. But very few those kind. If you get such a one, pay your fine, don't argue. But don't be disgusted with the U.S.A. Just come and tell me."

42   "What you gonna do?"

43   "Why next time, I vote against him, naturally. We don't keep him in office no more, if he don't act nice."

44   So next morning I went in court. Called the other names, Igor, Arkady, Sergei, Philip. Guilty. Guilty. Guilty. All sent money to pay their fines.

45   Now my name. I couldn't understand a word they asked me. I was nervous. My English was running out of my head like sand through a sieve. How they told me to call a judge? Your Honorable? No. Your Highness? No, that's Russian. Your?—They were asking me something. I had to answer. I took my courage in my two hands and spoke out. "Not guilty, Your Honesty."

46   Courtroom went wild. Laughing and laughing. Laughing like hyenas. The judge pounded with the hammer. Bang. Bang. Bang! His face was red like a turkey's. What I done? I was sure I was going in Sing Sing and be thrown in the deepest-down dungeon.

47   But the judge was bombasting the audience first. "Word honesty—applied by this—cause such mirth—contempt of court."

48   "Young man," now he was through with them, it be my turn, "address the Court as Sir."

49   "Yes, sir."

50   "Did I understand you to plead not guilty?"

51   "Yes, sir. Not guilty."

52   "This officer says you and your friends were violating an ordinance, destroying a tree. Breaking the limbs."

53   "Yes, sir. Some was picking. I wasn't."

54   "Have you any proof of this?"

"No sir. Friends were with me, but they can't come today. They 55
all pleaded guilty, sent you a fine. Cheaper than to lose a day's pay."

"Why didn't you do that?" 56

"Because if I'm guilty I admit it, but if I'm not guilty, no man 57
gonna make me say I am. Just as much a lie to say you guilty when
you not as to say you innocent if you did wrong."

"Yes, that's correct. How long are you in the United States?" 58

"Six months." 59

"In court here before?" 60

"No, sir." 61

"Ever in trouble at home? Assault or kill a man?" 62

"Yes, sir." 63

"How many?" 64

"Hundreds. After the first year, I never counted them any more." 65

"Where was this?" 66

"In the War. I'm a sniper. It's my job to shoot all the Germans I 67
see. Sometimes Bulgarians, too, but mostly they didn't have much
interest to show themselves, poor fellows."

"I see. I mean in civil life. When you were not a soldier, not in 68
the army. Ever hurt or strike anybody?"

"Yes, sir. Once." 69

"What?" 70

"Knocked a man's teeths out. Few." 71

"Why?" 72

"Catched him giving poisoned meat to my dog to eat." 73

"Understandable. Only time?" 74

"Yes, sir." 75

"Sure?" 76

"Yes, sir." 77

"Did you actually see this man," His Honesty asked the police- 78
man, "breaking the tree?"

"No, sir. Not exactly, but all the others admitted guilt and he 79
was with them, holding a bunch of flowers."

"I believe he's a truthful man, Officer, and this time you were 80
probably mistaken. Case dismissed."

And then His Honesty, big American judge, leaned over. And 81
what do you think he said to me, ignorant, no speaking language,
six months off a boat, greenhorn foreigner? "Young man, I like to
shake hands with you."

And in front of that whole courtroom, he did. 82

Engaging the Text

1. The writers, a Russian immigrant and his American-raised
    wife, have composed this story to suggest the speech of a
    recent immigrant, unfamiliar with standard American English.
    List as many words and phrases as you can find that are "dif-
    ferent" from standard speech. After you have done this,
    arrange them in categories according to the differences
    noticed, for example,

    — word order (words not in ordinary sequence)
    — unusual word (not the one you would use in its place,
      perhaps)
    — omitted words (articles, for example).

2. For information about Russian and other immigrants, look up
    the words Yankee Doodle (6), shashliks (3), samovars (4), and
    greenhorn (81).

Engaging the Reader

1. How did George happen to be holding the bouquet of dog-
    wood flowers when the policeman started writing tickets?
2. Explain why George called the judge "Your Honesty"?
3. Explain the judge's reaction to the incident.

The Engaged Writer

1. If you are familiar with a dialect of American English (street
    talk, regional dialect, Black English), try to tell an incident like
    Papashvily's experience with the law in that dialect.
2. Talk with a recent immigrant to the United States, asking him
    or her to tell you about a humorous or embarrassing incident
    during his or her first months here. Retell it in a short narra-
    tive like Papashvily's. Or if you are a recent arrival in the
    United States (a "greenhorn"), tell about an embarrassing inci-
    dent that happened to you because of misunderstandings like
    Papashvily's.

ZORA NEALE HURSTON

Work

Zora Neale Hurston, called in her day the most-informed person about African American folklore, was born in the all-black town of Eatonville, Florida. She eventually finished high school in Baltimore and went to Howard University. She won a scholarship to Barnard College in New York, from which she graduated in 1928. She became a student of the distinguished anthropologist Franz Boas and a member of that important literary and cultural movement, the Harlem Renaissance. Financial help from a patron enabled her to travel through the South gathering folklore, and she visited Haiti and the West Indies as well on a Guggenheim fellowship. Books such as *Mules & Men,* which came out in 1935 when racism was rampant, slowly brought the realization that African American folklore was an honored tradition, intellectually and aesthetically. The following "lies" or stories come from that book.

Kah, Kah, Kah! Everybody laughing with their mouths wide open.   1
If the foreman had come along right then he would have been good and mad because he could tell their minds were not on work.

Joe Willard says: "Wait a minute, fellows, wese walkin' too fast.   2
At dis rate we'll be there befo' we have time to talk some mo' about Ole Massa and John. Tell another one, Cliffert."

"Aw, naw," Eugene Oliver hollered out.   3

Let *me* talk some chat. Dis is de real truth 'bout Ole Massa 'cause   4
my grandma told it to my mama and she told it to me.

During slavery time, you know, Ole Massa had a nigger named   5
John and he was a faithful nigger and Ole Massa lakted John a lot too.

One day Ole Massa sent for John and tole him, says: "John,   6
somebody is stealin' my corn out de field. Every mornin' when I go out I see where they done carried off some mo' of my roastin' ears. I want you to set in de corn patch tonight and ketch whoever it is."

So John said all right and he went and hid in de field.   7

Pretty soon he heard somethin' breakin' corn. So John sneaked   8
up behind him wid a short stick in his hand and hollered: "Now,

break another ear of Ole Massa's corn and see what *Ah'll* do to you."

9   John thought it was a man all dis time, but it was a bear wid his arms full of roastin' ears. He throwed down de corn and grabbed John. And him and dat bear!

10   John, after while got loose and got de bear by the tail wid de bear tryin' to git to him all de time. So they run around in a circle all night long. John was so tired. But he couldn't let go of de bear's tail, do de bear would grab him in de back.

11   After a stretch they quit runnin' and walked. John swingin' on to de bear's tail and de bear's nose 'bout to touch him in de back.

12   Daybreak, Ole Massa come out to see 'bout John and he seen John and de bear walkin' 'round in de ring. So he run up and says: "Lemme take holt of 'im, John, whilst you run git help!"

13   John says: "All right, Massa. Now you run in quick and grab 'im just so."

14   Ole Massa run and grabbed holt of de bear's tail and said: "Now, John you make haste to git somebody to help us."

15   John staggered off and set down on de grass and went to fanning hisself wid his hat.

16   Ole Massa was havin' plenty trouble wid dat bear and he looked over and seen John settin' on de grass and he hollered:

17   "John, you better g'wan git help or else I'm gwinter turn dis bear aloose!"

18   John says: "Turn 'im loose, then. Dat's whut Ah tried to do all night long but Ah couldn't."

19   Jim Allen laughed just as loud as anybody else and then he said: "We better hurry on to work befo' de buckra[1] get in behind us."

20   "Don't never worry about work," says Jim Presley. "There's more work in de world than there is anything else. God made de world and de white folks made work."

21   "Yeah, dey made work but they didn't make us do it," Joe Willard put in. "We brought dat on ourselves."

22   "Oh, yes, de white folks did put us to work too," said Jim Allen.

23   Know how it happened? After God got thru makin' de world and de varmints and de folks, he made up a great big bundle and let it down in de middle of de road. It laid dere for thousands of

---

[1] West African word meaning white people.

years, then Ole Missus said to Ole Massa: "Go pick up dat box, Ah want to see whut's in it." Ole Massa look at de box and it look so heavy dat he says to de nigger, "Go fetch me dat big ole box out dere in de road." De nigger been stumblin' over de box a long time so he tell his wife:

"'Oman, go git dat box." So de nigger 'oman she runned to git de box. She says:

"Ah always lak to open up a big box 'cause there's nearly always something good in great big boxes." So she run and grabbed a-hold of de box and opened it up and it was full of hard work.

Dat's de reason de sister in black works harder than anybody else in de world. De white man tells de nigger to work and he takes and tells his wife.

"Aw, now, dat ain't de reason niggers is working so hard," Jim Presley objected.

Dis is de way *dat* was.

God let down two bundles 'bout five miles down de road. So de white man and de nigger raced to see who would git there first. Well, de nigger out-run de white man and grabbed de biggest bundle. He was so skeered de white man would git it away from him he fell on top of de bundle and hollered back: "Oh, Ah got here first and dis biggest bundle is mine." De white man says: "All right, Ah'll take yo' leavings," and picked up de li'l tee-ninchy bundle layin' in de road. When de nigger opened up his bundle he found a pick and shovel and a hoe and a plow and chop-axe and then de white man opened up his bundle and found a writin'-pen and ink. So ever since then de nigger been out in de hot sun, usin' his tools and de white man been sittin' up figgerin', ought's a ought, figger's a figger; all for de white man, none for de nigger.

"Oh lemme spread my mess. Dis is Will Richardson doin' dis lyin'."

You know Ole Massa took a nigger deer huntin' and posted him in his place and told him, says: "Now you wait right here and keep yo' gun reformed and ready. Ah'm goin' 'round de hill and skeer up de deer and head him dis way. When he come past, you shoot." De nigger says: "Yessuh, Ah sho' will, Massa."

He set there and waited wid de gun all cocked and after a while de deer come tearin' past him. He didn't make a move to shoot de deer so he went on 'bout his business. After while de white man come on 'round de hill and ast de nigger: "Did you kill de deer?"

34   De nigger says: "Ah ain't seen no deer pass here yet."

35   Massa says: "Yes, you did. You couldn't help but see him. He come right dis way."

36   Nigger says: "Well Ah sho' ain't seen none. All Ah seen was a white man come along here wid a pack of chairs on his head and Ah tipped my hat to him and waited for de deer."

37   "Some colored folks ain't got no sense, and when Ah see 'em like dat," Ah say, "My race but not my taste."

Engaging the Text

1. Read the stories aloud, or have someone read them aloud to you, to get the full flavor of the oral delivery.

Engaging the Reader

1. When the book came out, most people considered the storytellers on Joe Clarke's porch to be ignorant and lazy. However, if the tales are read carefully, they become an indictment of bigotry and prejudice. In which stories do you find these themes: the alleged stupidity of the black man, the injustice to the black woman, the incompetence of the "boss"?

2. One commentator on Hurston's work says: "The tales here are not the quaint, childish entertainment of a primitive tribe. They are the complex cultural communications permitted an oppressed people." Do you agree? Why or why not?

The Engaged Writer

1. If you know someone who speaks a dialect of English, tape-record stories that person tells and then transcribe them exactly as spoken.

2. For a longer paper, write about the involvement of Zora Neale Hurston in the Harlem Renaissance. Her life itself is "stranger than fiction."

LEE SMITH

The Face of Rural Poverty

Lee Smith writes comic novels, short stories, and articles about the "new South" and its multitude of characters. She does for the last part of the twentieth century what Faulkner and Hurston did for the first part—she delves into the inner souls of families and how they work, and the inner loneliness of some of their members. She has written seven novels and two short story collections, the latest being *Me and My Baby View the Eclipse* (1991, stories) and *The Devil's Dream* (1992, novel about country music). She teaches at North Carolina State University and Duke University. The following article appeared in *Fortune* in December 1990.

Let us now praise famous men. More than 50 years ago, *Fortune* 1 commissioned writer James Agee and photographer Walker Evans to memorialize the hardscrabble existences of Alabama tenant farmers; though their research never appeared in the magazine, it resulted in the classic book of that title. Since then, the lot of America's rural poor—men, women, and children—has improved greatly. Today few starve. Almost all have shelter of some sort, and life spans are considerably longer than in grandpa and grandma's day.

But . . . hidden in the hollows of Appalachia, in makeshift vil- 2 lages along the Rio Grande, in shriveled industrial towns in Pennsylvania, on the back roads of Maine, and at the edge of cotton fields in Mississippi, the world that Agee and Evans uncovered endures. What's changed is that, for most Americans, the rural poor are even more remote and invisible than they were in the 1930s.

Now it is the urban poor who are the insistent, troubling pres- 3 ence, never long out of mind. Day begins with fresh reports of the overnight death toll in ghetto drug wars. The homeless in the streets block our path and demand our help.

Yet their country cousins are no better off. The poverty rate in 4 rural counties, those without a town of 50,000, has climbed to 16%, almost as dismal as the inner cities' 18%. And their future is equally bleak. Despite scattered bright patches—rustic counties where tourism is flourishing, the handful of communities that have flowered around transplanted Japanese auto factories—much of the U.S. countryside is quietly and painfully dying.

5   That wasn't the case in the 1970s, when the long-term migration of jobs from the backwoods to the cities briefly reversed itself as corporations moved electronic assembly, apparel, and other low-tech plants to the sticks to take advantage of cheaper land and labor. For a decade rural manufacturing jobs grew at twice the rate of those in the city. But in the 1980s industry discovered even greater savings in Hong Kong, Mexico, and other foreign lands, and the backwoods boom went bust.

6   With the world economy becoming ever more global, America's nearly nine million rural poor are stuck on the part turned away from the sun. Any policy to ease their plight must start with a basic principle: People, not places, matter. Compassion does not require that U.S. taxpayers save small towns for their own sakes, despite the sentimental view that such places are reservoirs of virtue. Sometimes they are. They can also be backwaters of misery.

7   Who are the rural poor? Put aside a misconception. The victims are not those farmers besieged by drought and debt who received so much attention from politicians, rock stars, and the media a few years back. "The world's biggest myth is that there are millions of poor farmers," says Agriculture Department economist Kenneth Deavers. Farm families, who make up only about 10% of the rural population of 23 million, are by and large doing well. Their average income reached an all-time high of $43,323 in 1989, aided by $11 billion in taxpayer subsidies.

8   The poor are farmhands, who never had any land to mortgage. They are also coal miners, sawmill cutters, foundry men, and Jacks of whatever trades are hiring. Or Janes. Women make up 45% of the rural work force. A "go-getter" in many places refers not to a striver but to a fellow who picks up his wife after her shift.

9   Walk with us through a few representative towns for a look at work and life at the bottom.

10   **Belfast, Maine.** President Bush's home in Kennebunkport is the Maine that outsiders know—the one where New England patricians summer in rambling, weathered shingle houses. But Maine has the lowest per capita income in the Northeast ($15,092 in 1988, $1,398 below the national average). About 130 miles up the coast from the Bush spread is Belfast, where a typical dwelling is a second-hand mobile home on a bare patch of ground.

Storms from way off shore have battered Belfast, a port town of 11
6,200, for two decades. During the 1970s rising fuel prices made it
too expensive to heat chicken coops through the frigid winters and
to import Midwestern feed grain. By the mid-1980s, the town's two
big poultry processing plants, which once employed 1,100 people,
had both shut down.

One of Belfast's few remaining enterprises is the Stinson 12
Seafood Co., which cans herring pulled from local waters. For a
visitor accustomed to entering a suburban plant through a colon-
nade of comely shrubs and trees that lead to a smart, polished
reception lounge, Stinson comes as a shock. Alongside the
entrance, an enormous dumpster full of ripening fish heads and
tails waits to be carted off for fertilizer. A flock of seagulls almost
hides the door.

Inside, several dozen women with kitchen shears, their hands 13
rarely pausing, snip heads and tails off the fish and slap the bodies into cans. Base pay at Stinson is $4 an hour—a tad above min-
imum wage. An experienced packer raises her wages to $5 or $6
by filling 350 tins or more an hour. If she's lucky enough to clock
40 hours a week for 50 weeks a year, she can gross $12,000—still
$600 below the waterline that defines poverty for a family of four.

But at two snips to a fish and four fish to a tin, earning $5 an 14
hour requires some 20,000 scissor squeezes a day, a routine that
over time can be crippling. Ruthie Robbins, 58, has been cutting
fish for 20 years, makes $6 an hour tops, and suffers from chronic
tendonitis. "The doctor could immobilize my arm," she says, "but
then I couldn't work." Her arthritic husband earns a few extra dollars repairing lawn mowers.

Stinson's workers don't complain much. A steady job is not easy 15
to find in Belfast. Across from Robbins sits her daughter Lisa, 19,
who smiles but won't take time out to chat. Carrying on family tradition, she trims fish at a furious pace.

Tunica, Mississippi. About 30 miles south of Memphis where 16
the cotton and soybean fields begin their long flat run down the
Delta lies Tunica, which has long held the miserable distinction of
being the poorest American county in the poorest American state.

More than half of Tunica's 8,100 people live below the pover- 17
ty line. Two-thirds occupy what is euphemistically called substandard housing. That usually means an unpainted pine shack
patched with asphalt tile and protected uncertainly by a rusted

tin roof. Front porches rise and fall like waterbeds. Inside, the standard three small rooms may hold a cot, a stick or two of furniture, a hot plate, and a television set. Some dwellings have no running water, so occupants share an outdoor tap and privy with neighbors.

18   Tunica has one manufacturing plant, Pillowtex, where 300 workers earn $7 an hour on average making pillows and mattress coverings, primarily for Wal-Mart stores. But agriculture is still its mainstay.

19   Picking cotton is no longer cruel hand labor. It is hard but dignified. Black men pilot 16-foot-tall John Deere pickers that straddle two rows of cotton plants at once. Pay is $4.50 an hour with no fringe benefits, tolerable work if there were only more of it. One man on a machine can clear 400 acres in a week, a job that required 25 people or more a generation ago. At the peak, during the harvest from October through Christmas, Tunica's cotton and soybean industries employ only 1,000.

20   After that the county lapses into a coma. The pulse beats once a month, during the first week, when the welfare, Social Security, and other transfer payments that sustain half the population arrive.

21   Tunica's children look as lively as those anywhere. Better nutrition has been one of the true advances in recent decades, so physicians no longer routinely encounter the near starvation common before the 1960s War on Poverty. Give much of the credit to food stamps and to the federal WIC (Women, Infants, and Children) program, which supplies pregnant women and preschool children with fruit juice, cereal, infant formula, and other protein.

22   But when these youths reach adolescence, their spirits start to die. "Their dreams are so small," says Tunica Chamber of Commerce president Lawrence Johnson. "A 16-year-old told me the other day that no one anywhere lives as well as the Cosbys on TV, not even white folks." Only one in three graduates from high school. Some leave town. Many more turn into the men who pop cans of Budweiser in the late morning and stare blankly from dusty stoops.

23   **Las Milpas, Texas.** All the wrecked cars and splintered lumber in North America eventually roll and tumble down to the strip of Texas that lies just above the Rio Grande from Brownsville to El Paso—or so it looks from the highway. Fields of mesquite and

acres of vegetables alternate with vast junkyards that advertise: "We repair used tires, starters, windshield-wiper motors."

This frugal land is where migrant workers from Mexico spend   24 their winters in hundreds of *colonias,* or unincorporated communities, whose collective population is roughly 140,000. Some are U.S. citizens; others are resident aliens with green cards. The rest have slipped across the border illegally. Whatever their status, they pick the California lettuce, Washington State strawberries, and Illinois broccoli that end up in the nation's refrigerators.

Life in the U.S. doesn't get any more meager than in Las Mil-   25 pas. With a population of 8,800, it is larger than most other *colonias* but otherwise typical. The better homes of Las Milpas are made of sturdy cinder block, the worst are discarded school buses or huts a notch or two below even Tunica's wretched norm. When migrants return from their trek north, they push their broken '73 Mercuries and '75 Chevrolets into the welding shops for mending. Or junkman Antonio Hernandez buys the heaps for as little as $10 each and resells the serviceable parts for perhaps twice that.

Jesus Villagomez could not afford to fix his truck, so this past   26 summer he had to skip the northern harvests, where he might have earned $200 or more a week. Instead he made about $30 a week picking vegetables on local farms. The walls of his home are rigged from odd pieces of plywood; the roof is a composite of broken tin and plastic sheeting held in place by a used tire.

In a space about the size of a secretary's cubicle, Villagomez   27 lives with his wife and five children, ages 4 to 14. The parents sleep on a cot, the children on a mat ripped from the floor of a ruined car, amid a jumble of faded clothes, mud-encrusted boots, kitchen pots—and a small black-and-white TV. Even the poorest hovels of Las Milpas are electrified, as are 99.1% of all U.S. homes. But the crude "cowboy wiring," as it is known locally, that hooks the hut to a power line is a mixed blessing. Homes in the *colonias* burn with distressing frequency.

The Villagomez family shares with neighbors an outdoor water   28 tap and a toilet that empties into an overworked septic tank. Even this far south the temperature in winter frequently falls below freezing, so the family huddles even closer than the hut demands. Can this life be better than the one they left in Mexico? "Yes," says Mrs. Villagomez without hesitation. "At school the children get an education—and also lunch."

29   The notion persists that even at its worst, rural poverty is preferable to the urban kind. That's doubtful. True, poor families in the country are more likely to have both mother and father in residence (53%, vs. 38% in the cities) and at least one of those parents is more likely to have a job (65%, vs. 54%). There is also far less crime. No drug dealers terrorize Belfast, Tunica, or Las Milpas with nightly turf battles.

30   But alcohol is abundant, and cocaine use is increasing. Even little Tunica has an intersection known as Crack Corner. And guess what state leads the nation in marijuana production? Missouri, followed by Kentucky. Not all of this crop leaves for the big cities.

31   Nor is rural life necessarily healthier. Country folk have a slightly lower mortality rate than city dwellers. But they are more likely to suffer from chronic disease and disabilities. That's partly because much of their work is dangerous and also because they are less likely to be covered fully by Medicaid, which is jointly financed by federal and state governments. New York, for example, pays for physical therapy for all patients, Alabama only for some.

32   On balance, low wages probably stretch further in the country, but not much. The major edge is in housing, which is substantially cheaper, though often shoddier, than city quarters. A shabby three-room apartment in Belfast rents for less than $200 a month, compared with $450 in Boston's rundown Roxbury section. Shacks in Tunica go for less than $150 and hovels in Las Milpas for under $100. But even at those prices, three out of four poor rural families spend more than 30% of their income on shelter.

33   Food, surprisingly, is sometimes more expensive in the country. People without land don't grow their own, and groceries are pricey, driven up by the distance from distribution centers and lack of competition. On average, urban counties have 29 supermarkets each; their rural counterparts only four. A five-pound bag of Pillsbury all-purpose flour was recently selling for $1.39 at a Giant Food market in Washington, D.C., $1.59 at Junior's supermarket in Las Milpas, and $1.79 at the Piggly Wiggly in Tunica.

34   The sharp run-up in gasoline prices in recent months has been particularly burdensome for low-wage rural workers, who must commute over long distances in older cars that chug-a-lug fuel. At roughly minimum wage, four or five hours of toil a week go just to pay for the daily 50-mile round-trip routine in states like Kentucky, North Carolina, Maine, and, of course, Texas.

But the great—and growing—disadvantage for country folk, 35 even in the many places where the work ethic remains solid, is that opportunity is vanishing. Bad roads have long been a barrier to manufacturers. Now rural telecommunications systems that lag in everything from Touch-Tone dialing to fiber optics are discouraging service companies, which are also shipping overseas low-wage, low-skill jobs, such as key punching. As for rural education systems, "They are mostly abysmal," says Susan Sechler of Washington's Aspen Institute, which studies rural poverty.

Small wonder the brightest and most ambitious youngsters 36 leave. "They see the flour barrel is empty and know it's time to go," says Robert Simmons, 44, who fled Tunica for Memphis, where he sells real estate. "The ones who stay behind are afraid to take a chance." As the local talent pool dries up, outsiders become even more reluctant to locate a new plant in Smallville.

Is there any way to break this vicious cycle? Market forces offer 37 a few glimmers of hope. Las Milpas is likely to benefit from the prospering *maquiladoras* just across the Rio Grande, where U.S. and other foreign companies assemble cars, TV sets, and other goods for the American market. Those plants need warehouses and support facilities on the Texas side.

Recreation and retirement will keep some areas alive. The 38 Ozarks and the Great Smoky Mountains already draw the elderly who are looking for inexpensive and safe quarters surrounded by pleasant scenery. As the population ages, those places could boom. Jobs in construction, resort management, and nursing would multiply.

William Galston, a senior scholar at the University of Mary- 39 land's Institute for Philosophy and Public Policy, advises rural America to offer government services at lower cost than the cities. "If I were a small town," says Galston, "I'd look at the controversy about prison overcrowding in the population centers and offer my help."

Still, only a small fraction of the countryside will be required to 40 fill those needs. For the rest, the best thing the government could do would be to persuade residents to migrate—not to a troubled megalopolis like New York, but to Columbus, Ohio; Jacksonville, Florida; Austin, Texas; and dozens of other promising smaller cities.

41   That's not likely to happen. By temperament Americans are reluctant to write off regions as finished. Says Agriculture Department economist Robert Hoppe: "It's antigrowth, defeatist." Legislators are also unenthusiastic about programs that encourage constituents to clear out. A final problem: The less educated people are, the more attached they tend to be to a place.

42   But while government cannot force such folk to move on, it should at least stop giving them incentives to stay where they have no future. In Tunica, for example, Washington and the Mississippi state legislature have spent almost $7 million over the past several years constructing and subsidizing apartments. Humane though it is, this program merely houses people more comfortably in a place that is unlikely to ever generate enough jobs for them.

43   Instead, new policy initiatives should focus on helping individuals. Some already do, most notably the earned-income tax credit. This tax break is especially beneficial to the rural poor, who are more likely to be working than their city brethren. In the recent budget bill, Congress and the Bush Administration agreed to enrich the credit, so that in 1991 a wage earner who makes as much as $11,250 and has two dependent children will be eligible for a cash payment from the U.S. Treasury of up to $1,235. That's a 30% increase over 1990.

44   Why not take a similar approach to housing? Rather than build apartments in dead-end towns like Tunica, give people housing vouchers similar to food stamps they could exchange for rent. Recipients would then at least have the choice of using them in places where they might find work.

45   ˙ For all of human history, people have migrated from where opportunity has died to where it is being born. For those unable or unwilling to face such hard economic realities, government can do little more than offer more resources and more encouragement. "This isn't living, it's existing," says PamaLee Ashmore, a 32-year-old food cooperative manager, of her life in Belfast, Maine. She hopes her two children will move on—someday.

Engaging the Text

1. Notice the use of alliteration—similar consonant sounds at the beginnings of words, such as "backwoods boom went bust" in paragraph 5. Try some of these the next time you write.

2. Many words have interesting histories. Columnists, such as William Safire, have written about word histories in newspapers and magazines. Some of the words from this essay that have fascinating origins are hardscrabble (1), euphemistically (17), and megalopolis (40). An unabridged dictionary in your library will have copious information on these words.

Engaging the Reader

1. Notice the way facts, statistics, and human interest stories are woven together in this essay. Originally it was illustrated with photographs by the well-known photographer Mary Ellen Mark. Does the article need the photos? Or is the writing enough to give us the picture?
2. Does this December 1990 article show that rural poverty is being helped? Or is it getting worse? Cite information from the article to support your view.
3. Is it better to be poor in the city or in the country? Why?

The Engaged Writer

1. Compare the lives of the children growing up in Tunica, the poorest town in the poorest county in the country, with the children growing up in the projects in Chicago in Alex Kotlowitz's *There Are No Children Here*.
2. Several articles in *The Engaging Reader* discuss aspects of poverty. For a longer paper, read some of them and form a thesis about the causes, results, solutions, or government actions toward poverty or a statement of another theme connected with poverty. Read "Backing Up What You Say" and the sample "From Source to Paper" in the Writer's Guide, and write a documented paper using at least three articles on poverty from this book.
3. Find the original article in *Fortune* (December 31, 1990) and write a paper about one of the photographs by Mary Ellen Mark that illustrate the article. From the details given in the article, try to imagine that person's life.

CLAIRE SAFRAN

Hidden Lessons: Do Little Boys Get a Better Education Than Little Girls?

Myra and David Sadker, professors at American University, find that even teachers who think they are nonsexist pay more attention to boys than girls. Other studies bear out that teaching methods make a difference between expectations for women and men students in colleges as in the lower grades. Claire Safran reports on these studies in an article that also brings up other controversies on the way teachers educate children and treat male and female students.

1 Our public school teachers are targets once again of the researchers. This time, they have been charged with sex-biased instructional methods.

2   Drs. David and Myra Sadker of American University in Washington, D.C., sent observers to 100 classrooms in five states to sit in on teaching sessions. The Sadkers' researchers cited instances of boys being taught differently from girls in elementary schools, where women teachers far outnumber men, through secondary schools, where more than half the teachers are male.

3   The bias generally is unintentional and unconscious, says Myra Sadker, dean of the School of Education at American University. She notes: "We've met teachers who call themselves feminists. They show me their nonsexist textbooks and nonsexist bulletin boards. They insist there is equity in their classrooms. Then," she continues, "I videotape them as they're teaching—and they're amazed. If they hadn't seen themselves at work on film, they'd never have believed that they were treating boys and girls so differently."

4   Such videotaping of teachers is among the functions of 12 U.S. Department of Education Centers for Sex Equity in educational districts across the country.

5   From nursery school to beyond graduate school, studies show that teachers call on male students in class far more often than they

call on female students. That difference in involvement in the learning process is crucial, say educators, who add that the students who are active in class are the ones who go on to higher achievement and a more positive attitude.

Many teachers unwittingly hinder girls from being active in 6 class. Dr. Lisa Serbin of Concordia University in Montreal studied nursery schools in Suffolk County, N.Y. She tells how a teacher poured water into containers of different heights and widths, then told a little boy to try it—to learn for himself how water can change its shape without changing its amount.

"Can I do it?" a little girl asked. 7

"You'll have to wait your turn," the teacher replied, giving the 8 pitcher to a second boy. The girl asked again, but it was time to put the materials away.

"You can help me do that," the teacher offered. 9

Who gets to pour the water is important. Learning is connected 10 to instruction and direction, and boys get more of that than girls do all through school. Why? Partly because teachers tend to question the students they expect will have the answers. Since girls traditionally don't do so well as boys in such "masculine" subjects as math and science, they're called on least in those classes. But girls are called on most in verbal and reading classes, where boys are expected to have the trouble. The trouble is in our culture, not in our chromosomes. In Germany, everything academic is considered masculine, most teachers are men, and girls have the reading problems. In Japan, there's no sex bias about reading, and neither sex has special problems with it.

In most U.S. schools, there are remedial classes for reading—the 11 "boys' problem"—and boys quickly catch up to the girls. But there are very few remedial classes in math and science—the "girls' problems." Thus boys have the most skill in these subjects, which can lead to better-paying jobs later.

According to the National Assessment of Educational Progress, 12 an organization in Denver that surveys both public and private schools nationally, girls get better math grades than boys do at age 9, but their scores decline as they progress while boys' math scores rise. Researchers say such things happen because boys are taught to take a more active part in learning than girls.

This differing of the educational process for the sexes starts at 13 home. For example, in one study, preschool youngsters were shown a drawing of a house and asked, "How far can you go from your own house?" Most girls pointed to an area quite near the house and said that was how far their parents permitted them to go and how far they actually went. Most boys pointed to a much wider perimeter of permission and generally said they exceeded it. In the classroom, unconscious sex bias takes various forms:

> Girls tend to be called on if they sit close to the teacher—first row—right under his or her nose. Boys tend to be called on wherever they sit. (*Girls' Lesson:* Be dependent—stay close to the teacher, and you'll be rewarded. *Boys' Lesson:* Be independent—sit anywhere; you'll be rewarded.)
>
> The Sadkers report this interchange. Fourth-grade teacher to a girl: "That's a neat paper. The margins are just right." To a boy: "That's a good analysis of the cause of the Civil War." (*Girl's Lesson:* Form, not content, is all that's expected of you. *Boy's Lesson:* Analytical thinking is what's expected of you.)
>
> Dr. Carol Dweck, professor of education at Harvard University, cites these comments by a teacher to students who have given incorrect answers. To a girl: "That's wrong." To a boy: "You'd know the right answer if you'd done your homework." (*Girl's Lesson:* The failure may be due to your own lack of ability. *Boy's Lesson:* You can do better if you make the effort.) Told that effort brings success, both sexes try—and succeed. Otherwise, both stop trying. Educators call this concept "attribution to effort."

14 Some teachers are learning to recognize—and then change—their methods. And small changes can make large differences. The Sadkers, for example, found that if teachers wait a few seconds after asking a question before they call on a student, more students will participate and their answers will be more complete.

15   Parents disturbed by sex bias in classrooms might first test themselves for it at home. Those who want to help combat teachers' sex bias might arrange to observe classes in their children's schools, and they might discuss sex bias at PTA meetings. On this issue, awareness is the first step.

Engaging the Text

1. You will want to know and use the following words if you write or talk about gender issues. Study their definitions until you are sure you can use them easily: sex-biased (1), unintentional (3), feminists (3), equity (3), and perimeter (13).

2. This essay reports informally on several studies done by educators and psychologists. How do you know what parts are written by Safran and what parts come from the studies she reports? Underline the signal phrases she uses to introduce these studies.
3. Pick out what you consider the two or three most important statements in this article. Why are they important? What does the author do to indicate their importance?

Engaging the Reader

1. What did the Sadkers find through their research? What was the method used?
2. What do some teachers do to hinder girls from being active in class?
3. What suggestions does Safran offer to change this bias?

The Engaged Writer

1. Have you observed in your high school or college classroom any examples of conscious or unconscious bias (gender, class, or race) in the treatment of students? If so, develop a short account of one of them.
2. Take one of the statements you picked out of the article in response to question 3 in "Engaging the Text" and develop an essay from it, using some supports of your own.
3. Feminists often state that it is incorrect to assume that the masculine pronoun (he, him, his) also includes the feminine, that it is *generic*. For example, "every student will bring his calculator to math class." Do you agree? If not, how would you change this practice?

SARA PACHER

The Restoration of Jimmy Carter

This essay's subtitle, "From President to Chairman of the Boards," adds another pun to the one in the main title. Jimmy Carter was president of the United States from 1977–1981. His presidency ended in the frustration about the hostages in Iran. He and his wife

Rosalynn returned to their home in Plains, Georgia, to become involved in projects such as Habitat, a group helping communities to build homes for the homeless, with volunteers as well as the occupants doing the work of building. Most recently, Carter has represented the U.S. in peacekeeping negotiations, most notably engineering the restoration of the Haitian elected president. *Mother Earth News* reported in 1987 on Carter's new life after being president. Part of that article follows.

1   Maybe it's because I, too, was born and raised in a small south Georgia town, but I found sitting down to talk to Rosalynn and Jimmy Carter as comfortable as lazing in a porch swing on a summer afternoon, sipping minty iced tea. Just such a swing overlooks a roaring mountain stream at the Carters' log cabin retreat in the Blue Ridge Mountains. Along with the cabin's other furniture, the swing was designed and built by the former president, a master woodworker who selects and cuts the trees for such projects from his 160-acre farm. He strips off the bark (which he sometimes uses for caning) and shapes the wood into furniture and other items destined to become heirlooms.

2   "My daddy was a good man with tools," he recalls, "so learning how to use them was as natural as breathing for us. If something broke, we had to fix it ourselves. You didn't call somebody in to repair something or replace it with something new. We had these skills—all farmers did during the Depression years—and we had very well equipped shops, both for woodworking and blacksmithing."

3   Over the years, Carter has made some 50 household items, about half of which he has given away as gifts. But some pieces still sit around the family's Plains house and have been in use for over 30 years. His wife is quick to point out, however, that his skills improved as time went on. "When we came home from the Navy in 1953, he built a sofa and a lounge chair for the back porch. He used nails in them. Now he builds everything without nails. He's studied woodworking and worked at it, and he's made really beautiful furniture for our home—including a pencil-post bed and tables by the side."

4   His woodworking aptitude served Carter well during his political campaigns, particularly when meeting factory workers. "You don't have to say but a few things to people who work in a factory

before they realize that you, yourself, have been a laborer. It may be a different kind of skill from theirs, but there's a rapport, sort of like in a fraternity, among people who work with their hands."

Once he campaigned his way to the presidency, Carter occa-   5
sionally managed to slip in a few hours at the carpenter's shed at Camp David, because, in his opinion, "What we need in our lives is an inventory of factors that never change. I think that skill with one's own hands—whether it's tilling the soil, building a house, making a piece of furniture, playing a violin or painting a painting—is something that doesn't change with the vicissitudes of life. And for me, going back to the earth or going back to the woodshop have always been opportunities to reinforce my basic skills. No matter if I was involved in writing a book, conducting a political campaign, teaching at Emory University or dealing with international affairs, I could always go back—at least for a few hours at a time—to the woodshop. That's meant an awful lot to me. It's a kind of therapy, but it's also a stabilizing force in my life—a total rest for my mind.

"When I'm in the woodshop," he continues, "I don't ever think   6
about the chapter I'm writing or the paragraph I can't complete or the ideas that don't come. I'm thinking about the design of a piece of furniture, how the wood's going to fit together, what joint I'm going to use and whether or not my hand tools are sharp."

In Jimmy and Rosalynn Carter's recently published book, *Every-*   7
thing to Gain: Making the Most of the Rest of Your Life (Random House, $16.95), they explain candidly how they used back-to-basics skills to confront and resolve their "traumatic" political defeat, an abrupt departure from Washington and their fears of an empty future.

"In the book," Jimmy says, "we try to relate our lives, not to the   8
White House or to the governor's mansion, but to Plains—for a couple of reasons. One, to show the attraction of a small town, and, second, to make it clear that the book is not just about a couple who happened to have been the First Family of the nation; it's also written for the average person who loses a job, has an unexpected career change, has to move to a place not of his or her choice, has a last child leave home. Or for a married couple who suddenly find themselves at retirement age and living together for the first time all day long—not just at night. I think there's a lot in it for people to learn—not only how to add 11 more years to their lives by

changing personal habits, but what to do with those 11 years: how to make them challenging and exciting and gratifying and filled with adventure—even in a town as small as Plains."

9   The Carters plunged enthusiastically into such projects as laying a sidewalk and putting a hardwood floor in their unfinished attic. Rosalynn has picked up additional carpentry skills in working with one of their favorite organizations, Habitat for Humanity, a volunteer housing program for the poor with 171 projects in this nation, as well as others in 17 foreign countries. . . . She doesn't, however, spend much time in the Plains woodshop.

10   "She's welcome," her husband asserts, "but she's got her own things to do."

11   "I work in the yard, tend flower beds, trim shrubbery," she says.

12   "And we both spend a good bit of time on our farm," adds Carter. "We take care of the timberlands. Sometimes we go for long walks in the woods. I may see a particular hickory or white oak tree that I think would be suitable for four or five—perhaps, seven or eight—chairs or stools or for some other piece of furniture. Out of one, say, 12-inch hickory, you can make 10 chairs if the tree is straight and the grain is good. I usually select a tree close to home, though, since I have to tote the pieces back to the woodshop area.

13   "One of my favorite kinds of woodworking involves green wood, but there's a tremendous amount of hard labor involved in that. You also have to develop an intimacy with the woodlot to start with—and then between you and a particular tree. You have to envision what your project is going to be like and then try to handle the different rates at which the wood dries, so the joints get tight and become indestructible. It's the kind of technical problem that appeals to me," says the former nuclear engineer.

14   It wasn't until Carter left the White House (prematurely, he thinks) that he acquired a complete collection of woodworking tools and machines (a gift from his former staff), and he's obviously made good use of them. Still, his favorite tools are a drawknife and spokeshaves. And he uses a simple, old-fashioned method of bending his wood.

15   "Get a pot of water and a length of six-inch-round metal stovepipe with a 90° elbow—you can find it in any hardware store. You just put the elbow in the boiling water and let the steam go through the pipe. Then you put a towel or newspaper in the end

to hold the steam in and incline the pipe a little bit so that, as the steam condenses, it can run back into the pot. It's a wood-steamer that might cost $4." For long pieces, he attaches another length of pipe.

His favorite place to shop for such hardware? He was quick to answer. "Highland Hardware in Atlanta is one of the best stores I know in the country. Really tops! The store brings in the best woodworkers in the nation to teach two- and three-day seminars. I've attended some of those." 16

Nor does Carter foresee a time when such training centers and the skills they teach will become anachronistic. "Take cars. There are obviously so many new electronics components to an automobile that you have to have special equipment of a highly costly nature to do rudimentary repairs. But the basic skills of working with an engine or working with tools, I think, will always be valuable. Somebody's got to make the tools to repair the machines, make the dies and the stamps for the first model to be tested." 17

Obviously, most of today's young people don't grow up routinely learning to use their hands "as naturally as breathing," as Carter did. But he thinks they still have an advantage his parents' generation lacked. 18

"Back then, you'd start working at the age of 16 or 18 and work until you died or were physically incapable of working anymore. You began work at sunrise and worked until dark. But, nowadays, you work 40 hours a week, get a couple of weeks off for vacation and then retire at 55, 60 or 65. You have so much spare time to take on additional exciting things. Sometimes they can be quite productive things; sometimes just enjoyable; sometimes dedicated to serving others. In *Everything to Gain* we try to present a panorama of activities an average person can undertake. We try to point out that no matter what stage of life you may be in—young, middle-aged or retired—there's the possibility of a constantly expanding arena of interest, excitement, challenge, gratification and adventure. In this book we encourage people to take on new things that might look very difficult, but that become very gratifying once the person is involved." 19

"If you have a crisis of any kind," Rosalynn adds, "one of the best things to do is to learn something new." 20

Engaging the Text

1. Two of the special words in the article have to do with the woodworking that Carter is enthusiastic about: drawknife and spokeshaves (14). See if you can find a drawing of these two implements. Try a collegiate or unabridged dictionary.

2. Other words cluster around the other topic of the selection: feelings about retirement and making a valuable contribution to the world: rapport (4), vicissitudes (5), therapy (5), stabilizing (5), traumatic (7), anachronistic (17), and gratification (19). Use three of these words in sentences of your own about your feelings about your job or vocation.

3. What are the two puns in the title and subtitle of the article?

4. How does Pacher get into the subject of her article? Is this an effective introduction? (See "Getting Started.")

Engaging the Reader

1. What do you find out about the former president's skill at carpentry?

2. Do you think you would like to read the Carters' 1987 book *Everything to Gain?* Why or why not?

3. What does Carter have to say about the subject of retirement?

The Engaged Writer

1. In paragraph 15, Carter describes a simple method of bending his wood. From your knowledge of some skill—from changing a tire to making a picture frame—write a short paper giving the essential method of making some object.

2. Write an essay on the pros and cons of retirement as you see it from Carter's experience and any other observations you have made.

3. What problems have resulted in this country from the large number of retirees? How can they be solved?

4. The essay goes on, after our section here, to discuss the contribution Carter made as president as well as the work he has done for Habitat. For information on Habitat, write to Habitat for Humanity, Habitat and Church Streets, Americus, GA 31709. The subject might be a good one for a research project.

5. Another subject for research is Carter's distinguished career in international relations since leaving the presidency. Write an essay describing this career.

CAROLYN HEILBRUN

Naming a New Rite of Passage

Carolyn Heilbrun is a professor of the humanities at Columbia University and, under the name of Amanda Cross, a mystery writer. Her scholarly work has included biographies and feminist works such as *Toward a Recognition of Androgyny and Reinventing Womanhood.* Her autobiographical study, *Writing a Woman's Life,* draws on the experiences of celebrated women to show that biographers have suppressed the truth of the female experience in order to meet society's expectations. The following speech for a college reunion tells us that middle-age women pass through a "rite of passage" that shows them who they really are and opens a new life to them.

When I was invited to give this address, I was told that the 1 Reunion theme of the Ada Comstock Scholars was "Late Bloomers." And that seemed to me a fine opportunity to speak to you, in fact rather seriously, about an idea that has been compelling my attention of late—the idea of naming, creating, trying to bring into existence a new phase in women's lives.

When dreaming, I dream big. So I am hoping also for a new rite 2 of passage, perhaps even an initiation for women, into what can be, I am convinced, the best part of a female life, something worth looking forward to from the passions, the dizzy joys, the careless raptures, the unceasing demands upon us when we are young. I hope you will not shudder if I tell you I am about to attempt the impossible and to glorify middle-aged women.

Old is a dirty word in our language. If I say even I am old, out- 3 rage is heard from all corners. "You are not old," they say. "You are vigorous, powerful, doing wonderful things, affecting events." "Exactly," I want to answer. And I am, thank God, no longer young. "But you don't really look your age," they argue in a last-ditch stand. "Yes, I do," I say. "I look the way I feel at the age I am."

4   But I cannot redeem the word old. It is a down word, a depressant, a doom. So we speak of midlife, which suggests the time when we can be called neither young, nor very old. This is the span I want to recover for women, the extended moment that can become a new rite of passage, a new initiation. The only occasion I can think of to match it is the swearing in of a federal judge. She has ascended to a new position, a new rank, a new chance for effectiveness, and she can remain there until she dies or chooses to turn her mind to something else. No one asks where the male gaze would place her on a scale of one to 10. She lives outside the male gaze. Her value is not determined by whether she turns men on, whether their eyes light up on beholding how she looks. Their eyes light up when they recognize the person she is.

5   Signs of age come upon women in our society like marks of the devil in earlier times. And it seems we must fight them, either by painful and irreversible acts upon our bodies, or allow ourselves to be captured by regret, resentment, and despair. For no one, certainly not for any woman, do the marks of age come easily, or without terror. Simone de Beauvoir writes, "They are all young, these people who suddenly find they are old. One day I said to myself, I'm 40. By the time I recovered from the shock of that discovery, I had reached 50." The shock of that discovery is a choice. Either to live as a different woman, or to die as an old woman pretending to be young.

6   Her biographer, Deirdre Bair, writes of Beauvoir's wonderful new life in her fifties, sixties, and seventies. Bair writes, "It gave her enormous pleasure to see that most of the people who now sought her advice, her presence, and her efforts on their behalf, were women." They wanted her help in their battles of equality. Instead of trying to recapture the old life, designed in the hope that men would look on her with desire, she moved into the new world of age, where her voice, her ability to affect events, increased. Beauvoir, in short, moved from anger and aging to the discovery of a new life, in which she rejoiced for almost three decades. Men were still there. Younger men might be lovers, younger women heirs, companions, perhaps lovers. But she had undergone the rite. She had passed from youth to age without trying artificially to keep her youth. Momentarily, as we saw, she bemoaned it, as all passing pleasures are bemoaned, but she allowed herself to be transformed, not by plastic surgery, or the infusion of silicon, or the

removal of ribs or fat, but by looking to another country, a foreign country, where they do things differently. That is L.P. Hartley's phrase; he is speaking of the past. I speak of the future.

Neither the gaze of men, nor her former need for them to gaze, 7 will any longer define the life of a woman who has undertaken this rite of passage. John Berger has described all that has finished, and I quote, "Men act, and women appear. Men look at women. Women watch themselves being looked at. This determines not only most relations between men and women, but also the relation of woman to herself. The surveyor of woman in herself is male, the surveyed female. Thus she turns herself into an object, and most particularly an object of vision, a sight."

As she ages, a woman must escape, if and for a time, in cam- 8 ouflage, from that gaze. She may love men, cherish them as friends and comrades, sons, husbands, fathers. But they will not define how she will look. They may not guess what she will be. Men will still say, if I am not turned on by just looking at you, you are no longer woman. And she will answer, only youth has that talent, and I will not impersonate youth. I will not live in drag for your sake.

Women athletes and dancers, like their male counterparts, know 9 they must prepare for a life when the youthful confidence of their bodies has deserted them. None believes she can imitate youth. All women should live as dancers, recognizing physical facts, eschewing the tricks that promise but cannot deliver extended youth. We women need to learn to move with confidence into this new, as yet unnamed life. A life, a birth and not death, where a woman lives by what she does, not by how she looks or who looks at her. In the disguise of age, she explores and then lives in this new world. As real as men in the world she formerly occupied, she will take the reality she recognized only in them and claim it for herself.

This rite of passage is no easier than most initiations, and it 10 takes longer. It recognizes stages. The first is often hair. Because for too many, our body is all that tells us our life is ready to move on. I am asked by most of the women around 40 I know (and more of the women I know are around 40), "Should I dye my hair?" I suppose we all begin the same way, plucking out the grey hairs, combing them from sight, and then comes the question, "Should I dye it?" My answer is, dye it if you feel more comfortable that way. My own statistical example suggests that many women will stop dye-ing their hair after a few years, but a few will persist even to their death beds. It doesn't really matter. So long as we don't think we can successfully impersonate youth, we should do with hair dye and makeup what offers us the chance to take our bodies for granted. For as one enters upon this new life, this time when one becomes an explorer of a new landscape, one should not underestimate the importance of camouflage.

11   One wears camouflage in the jungle, I understand, so that one will be overlooked by snipers. The same protection is recommended for this risky journey. But camouflage is only skin deep. Its salient characteristic is that one can shed it when in safety. To make actual changes in one's body, as with cosmetic surgery, is to go unsuccessfully into the jungle in a disguise assuring defeat. No one finds it easy or even tolerable to overlook the fact that as older women we will have to be what we do. As women we will watch ourselves grow invisible to youth worshippers and to the male gaze. Despair is inevitable but must be wrestled with. The hardest initiation lies ahead—an initiation as in a fairy tale, readying one for a quest. To get to that new place, a woman must pass through the stage of invisibility. You will be mysteriously unseen. You will not be noticed immediately upon your entrance in a store, a party, a meeting. You will move invisible for a time, to learn to see, and to forget being seen. As you grow slowly visible in the new life you have chosen, you will be heard more and seen less. Your voice will ramify; your body will become the home of a new spirit.

12   Many women hovering near 50 have whispered to me, and I to them, of how the world opened up—of the mysterious change, the surge of freedom, the possibility of new adventures. We say, "I have passed through the magic circle of invisibility into the land of new accomplishment and new passion." Beauvoir said, "Aging changes the individual's relationship with time and therefore her relationship with the world and her own history."

13   One knows, as no young person ever does, that she will die and that life must be lived now. One knows also that one is truly old, in the bad old sense of old—finished—only when one no longer believes in the possibility of change. And the way to believe in the possibility of change is to stop fearing it. When we are younger, especially if we are parents or have the care of the young in our keeping, we tend to be protective, to guess what may be risked, to

consider what is worth risking, to ward off dangers. In the time I speak of here, we go forward to meet dangers, knowing that we risk only ourselves, and that danger is another name for life.

I do not yet know a great deal about the time of life I'm trying   14 to name and redeem and half-invent, but I know a few of its signs, the signals by which the period declares itself. There is a new, overwhelming pleasure in being alone. Not isolated, not an outcast, not cringing from the world, but joyfully alone, because earlier life has offered so little opportunity for this. Even in the midst of a happy and vital relationship, there must be times when one is alone and silent, if life is to be lived at all. This is the need we women find hard to meet early in our lives, and find difficult even to recognize.

Together with a need to be alone is the need for one's own   15 space. Perhaps you all know as many women as I do who rejoiced in their first room of one's own. I suspect that such rooms are a bit more common today than they were when I set out from college, but particularly for those who have lived in close relationships or with large families, such space is still miraculous. Oddly enough, it is most often found outside where one's loved ones are. A room in a house that has been a community will often just become another family room. The point is to be in a space where one can move around unattached by cords, visible or invisible. Those rare women, like Simone de Beauvoir, who have always lived alone from the moment they left their parents' home may find a kind of togetherness empowering, though I doubt it. Beauvoir herself was besottedly in love with Nelson Algren—she was as besottedly in love as one can well be. But even she had difficulty living with him when he turned up in Paris. She wanted him, but not in her space. In midlife, one wants to own one's space, one's time, one's peace.

Intensity is the hallmark of these years I'm trying to define.   16 There is no longer time for meaningless conversations, for social events where time merely passes, where obligations no longer important are merely fulfilled. One leaves one's space to take part in something that, if ever so slightly, changes the world. It may well be something unlike a judgeship, which the media never notices—but which nonetheless affects the lives of individuals. Since I have been working on a biography of Gloria Steinem, I have met many of these women because Steinem herself has met and encouraged them. They're all midlife women who have found something marvelous to do, and done it. What all this means is that one begins to live, as Oliver Wendell Holmes advised, "as one takes part in the events of one's time. For not to do so," he said, "is not to have lived at all."

17   As you can tell, I have not really worked all this out. It's still churning in my mind, and I hope you'll forgive me for having tried it out on you, but I know that whatever your age, you are looking or will be looking toward 75, the age when the period of which I speak may be called over—although exact figures are as preposterous as most definitions of the normal. They are all approximations, statistical probabilities only. And in this midlife period you will not be old or young, you will be a different woman. But if you are not young, you will nonetheless feel so to yourself, although those seeing you may not guess. There is a line in Gabriel Garcia Marquez's novel *Love in the Time of Cholera* I particularly cherish. Someone accuses a character in the book of being rich. "No," he answers, "I am not rich. I am a poor man with money, which is not the same thing." So when someone tries to compliment us who have been initiated into this special time of life by telling us we look young, we must say, "No, not young, I am an older woman with pizazz, which is not the same thing."

18   Often I ask myself, if a woman like the woman I used to be should come to me for advice, what advice would I give her? Be yourself, I would say. You look as you look, you are what you are. Go forth and dissolve anxiety about what you think they will think of the impression you make. You want properly to have your being in the world where there is hope for risk, anxiety, and troubles, and not mere safety. That is your life, the life women should want.

19   We all bring into our lives as older women the baggage of the male gaze, the fear of disappointing people, the anxiety about not being dressed right, the knowledge of not seeming desirable. We must drop that baggage. We must go into the adventures, the meetings, the interviews, to meet people, to affect people, to learn, and not to brood on how one appears, to disappoint. I would say, allow yourself happiness. Let good news please you, mildly perhaps, but not always with dread, as though the truth is likely to be found out, or pain is to follow. Troubles enough will come. It is unlikely that we can anticipate them.

In *The Handmaid's Tale,* the teller thinks back on how much that   20
was wonderful in life she took for granted. The play *Our Town*
bears the same message. The age in a woman's life I speak of is
where one can savor simple pleasures and have the time to discover what they really are.

Above all it is an age when a new life begins. First we fear to   21
lose the old life—we don camouflage. Then we agree to invisibility, the secret passage, the secret life. Then a new world opens out.
I myself am in that new world now. And I'm still trying to discover
how I got here. I did not leap in like a diver. Perhaps I waded in,
like a child who has never before seen the water. What I want to
say to you is—knowing I hardly have the words with which to say
it properly—come on in. The water's fine.

Engaging the Text

1. Though Heilbrun is a college professor, her vocabulary in this
    speech, given at a reunion, reminds us more of her mystery
    writing style. She uses such words as raptures (2), irreversible
    (5), camouflage (8), eschewing (9), and besottedly (in love—
    15). Use these five in sentences that could come from a mys-
    tery novel. How do your sentences compare with those in the
    text?

Engaging the Reader

1. Heilbrun discusses two alternatives for women going into
    middle age: keep artificially young or go through a stage of
    invisibility as a sex object into visibility as a person. Talk in
    your peer groups about these two alternatives or write about
    such a choice in your journal.

The Engaged Writer

1. If you are a woman or a man returning to college, or starting
    a new career, write a paper giving your reasons for doing so.
2. There are many cultural differences in how people look at
    youth and age. For example, in Europe, and to a greater extent
    in the Far East, old age is a time of dignity and honor. If you
    have observed some of these differences, write an essay com-
    paring the two cultures.

LESLIE MARMON SILKO

The Man to Send Rain Clouds

Leslie Marmon Silko won a MacArthur Prize Award for 1981–1986; this "genius" award allowed her to write *The Almanac of the Dead* (1991). Previously she had written other stories, poems, and sketches centering around her Native American people, the Lakota Pueblo. She was born in Albuquerque, New Mexico, and after her education she returned to the Pueblo to live and write. Her style is that of a storyteller, using a mixture of fable, legend, poem, and narrative, as in *Storyteller* (1981), a collection of poems, stories, legends, photos, and reminiscences about her family and her ancestors from which this selection comes.

1   They found him under a big cottonwood tree. His Levi jacket and pants were faded light blue so that he had been easy to find. The big cottonwood tree stood apart from a small grove of winterbare cottonwoods which grew in the wide, sandy arroyo. He had been dead for a day or more, and the sheep had wandered and scattered up and down the arroyo. Leon and his brother-in-law, Ken, gathered the sheep and left them in the pen at the sheep camp before they returned to the cottonwood tree. Leon waited under the tree while Ken drove the truck through the deep sand to the edge of the arroyo. He squinted up at the sun and unzipped his jacket—it sure was hot for this time of year. But high and northwest the blue mountains were still in snow. Ken came sliding down the low, crumbling bank about fifty yards down, and he was bringing the red blanket.

2   Before they wrapped the old man, Leon took a piece of string out of his pocket and tied a small gray feather in the old man's long white hair. Ken gave him the paint. Across the brown wrinkled forehead he drew a streak of white and along the high cheekbones he drew a strip of blue paint. He paused and watched Ken throw pinches of corn meal and pollen into the wind that fluttered the small gray feather. Then Leon painted with yellow under the old man's broad nose, and finally, when he had painted green across the chin, he smiled.

"Send us rain clouds, Grandfather." They laid the bundle in the 3
back of the pickup and covered it with a heavy tarp before they
started back to the pueblo.

They turned off the highway onto the sandy pueblo road. Not 4
long after they passed the store and post office they saw Father
Paul's car coming toward them. When he recognized their faces he
slowed his car and waved for them to stop. The young priest rolled
down the car window.

"Did you find old Teofilo?" he asked loudly. 5

Leon stopped the truck. "Good morning, Father. We were just 6
out to the sheep camp. Everything is O.K. now."

"Thank God for that. Teofilo is a very old man. You really 7
shouldn't allow him to stay at the sheep camp alone."

"No, he won't do that any more now." 8

"Well, I'm glad you understand. I hope I'll be seeing you at 9
Mass this week—we missed you last Sunday. See if you can get old
Teofilo to come with you." The priest smiled and waved at them
as they drove away.

Louise and Teresa were waiting. The table was set for lunch, and 10
the coffee was boiling on the black iron stove. Leon looked at
Louise and then at Teresa.

"We found him under a cottonwood tree in the big arroyo near 11
sheep camp. I guess he sat down to rest in the shade and never got
up again." Leon walked toward the old man's bed. The red plaid
shawl had been shaken and spread carefully over the bed, and a
new brown flannel shirt and pair of stiff new Levi's were arranged
neatly beside the pillow. Louise held the screen door open while
Leon and Ken carried in the red blanket. He looked small and
shriveled, and after they dressed him in the new shirt and pants
he seemed more shrunken.

It was noontime now because the church bells rang the 12
Angelus. They ate the beans with hot bread, and nobody said anything until after Teresa poured the coffee.

Ken stood up and put on his jacket. "I'll see about the grave- 13
diggers. Only the top layer of soil is frozen. I think it can be ready
before dark."

Leon nodded his head and finished his coffee. After Ken had 14
been gone for a while, the neighbors and clanspeople came quietly to embrace Teofilo's family and to leave food on the table

because the gravediggers would come to eat when they were finished.

15   The sky in the west was full of pale yellow light. Louise stood outside with her hands in the pockets of Leon's green army jacket that was too big for her. The funeral was over, and the old men had taken their candles and medicine bags and were gone. She waited until the body was laid into the pickup before she said anything to Leon. She touched his arm, and he noticed that her hands were still dusty from the corn meal that she had sprinkled around the old man. When she spoke, Leon could not hear her.

16   "What did you say? I didn't hear you."

17   "I said that I had been thinking about something."

18   "About what?"

19   "About the priest sprinkling holy water for Grandpa. So he won't be thirsty."

20   Leon stared at the new moccasins that Teofilo had made for the ceremonial dances in the summer. They were nearly hidden by the red blanket. It was getting colder, and the wind pushed gray dust down the narrow pueblo road. The sun was approaching the long mesa where it disappeared during the winter. Louise stood there shivering and watching his face. Then he zipped up his jacket and opened the truck door. "I'll see if he's there."

21   Ken stopped the pickup at the church, and Leon got out; and then Ken drove down the hill to the graveyard where people were waiting. Leon knocked at the old carved door with its symbols of the Lamb. While he waited he looked up at the twin bells from the king of Spain with the last sunlight pouring around them in their tower.

22   The priest opened the door and smiled when he saw who it was. "Come in! What brings you here this evening?"

23   The priest walked toward the kitchen, and Leon stood with his cap in his hand, playing with the earflaps and examining the living room—the brown sofa, the green armchair, and the brass lamp that hung down from the ceiling by links of chain. The priest dragged a chair out of the kitchen and offered it to Leon.

24   "No thank you, Father. I only came to ask you if you would bring your holy water to the graveyard."

25   The priest turned away from Leon and looked out the window at the patio full of shadows and the dining-room windows of the nuns' cloister across the patio. The curtains were heavy, and the

light from within faintly penetrated; it was impossible to see the
nuns inside eating supper. "Why didn't you tell me he was dead?
I could have brought the Last Rites anyway."

Leon smiled. "It wasn't necessary, Father." 26

The priest stared down at his scuffed brown loafers and the 27
worn hem of his cassock. "For a Christian burial it was necessary."

His voice was distant, and Leon thought that his blue eyes 28
looked tired.

"It's O.K. Father, we just want him to have plenty of water." 29

The priest sank down into the green chair and picked up a 30
glossy missionary magazine. He turned the colored pages full of
lepers and pagans without looking at them.

"You know I can't do that, Leon. There should have been the 31
Last Rites and a funeral Mass at the very least."

Leon put on his green cap and pulled the flaps down over his 32
ears. "It's getting late, Father. I've got to go."

When Leon opened the door Father Paul stood up and said, 33
"Wait." He left the room and came back wearing a long brown
overcoat. He followed Leon out the door and across the dim
churchyard to the adobe steps in front of the church. They both
stooped to fit through the low adobe entrance. And when they
started down the hill to the graveyard only half of the sun was visible above the mesa.

The priest approached the grave slowly, wondering how they 34
had managed to dig into the frozen ground; and then he remembered that this was New Mexico, and saw the pile of cold loose
sand beside the hole. The people stood close to each other with little clouds of steam puffing from their faces. The priest looked at
them and saw a pile of jackets, gloves, and scarves in the yellow,
dry tumbleweeds that grew in the graveyard. He looked at the red
blanket, not sure that Teofilo was so small, wondering if it wasn't
some perverse Indian trick—something they did in March to
ensure a good harvest—wondering if maybe old Teofilo was actually at sheep camp corraling the sheep for the night. But there he
was, facing into a cold dry wind and squinting at the last sunlight,
ready to bury a red wool blanket while the faces of his parishioners
were in shadow with the last warmth of the sun on their backs.

His fingers were stiff, and it took him a long time to twist the 35
lid off the holy water. Drops of water fell on the red blanket and
soaked into dark icy spots. He sprinkled the grave and the water

disappeared almost before it touched the dim, cold sand; it reminded him of something—he tried to remember what it was, because he thought if he could remember he might understand this. He sprinkled more water; he shook the container until it was empty, and the water fell through the light from sundown like August rain that fell while the sun was still shining, almost evaporating before it touched the wilted squash flowers.

36   The wind pulled at the priest's brown Franciscan robe and swirled away the corn meal and pollen that had been sprinkled on the blanket. They lowered the bundle into the ground, and they didn't bother to untie the stiff pieces of new rope that were tied around the ends of the blanket. The sun was gone, and over on the highway the eastbound lane was full of headlights. The priest walked away slowly. Leon watched him climb the hill, and when he had disappeared within the tall, thick walls, Leon turned to look up at the high blue mountains in the deep snow that reflected a faint red light from the west. He felt good because it was finished, and he was happy about the sprinkling of the holy water; now the old man could send them big thunderclouds for sure.

Engaging the Text

1. Silko chooses words that set the scene in a certain part of the country: cottonwoods (1), arroyo (1), pueblo (3), church bells rang the Angelus (12); the old carved door with its symbols of the Lamb (21); twin bells from the King of Spain. Check on the meanings of these words and phrases, and identify the part of the country.

2. In keeping with the story-telling tradition, Silko puts hints in her story about the two cultures she is portraying. In one of these appear a small gray feather (2), pinches of corn meal and pollen (2). In the other are Louise's wish to have the priest sprinkle holy water (19), and the priest's apparent refusal, at first, to do so, and the priest's reaction at what he thinks may be some perverse Indian trick (34). Look through the story for other cultural indicators that Silko uses to develop her theme.

Engaging the Reader

1. What do you think the following passage means? "He sprinkled the grave and the water disappeared almost before it

touched the dim, cold sand; it reminded him of something—he tried to remember what it was, because he thought if he could remember he might understand this." What do you think "it" is?

2. What parts of the story tell you of one culture represented here, the Catholic one? And what parts tell about the Native American spiritualism? With your classmates, make two lists of these evidences of different cultures.

3. Silko reports what happens here. Nowhere does she make a judgment, or seem to advocate one course of action or another. Yet is it easy to see that we have a subtle story of the interaction between two cultures. Is there any evidence that the two are trying to understand one another?

4. What is the theme or thesis of this story? Is it expressed directly in the story? If not, how is it communicated to us?

The Engaged Writer

1. With the list you made in question 2 under "Engaging the Reader," write a comparison of the two cultures represented here.

2. Compare old Teofilo's death with that of the "Most Decorated Hero" of Louise Erdrich's story. What differences do you see in the way the two stories are handled?

3. How would you advise the priest to act so that he can understand his Native American parishioners? Do you see any evidence that he is trying to do so? Use these thoughts as the basis for an essay on the theme of cross-cultural understanding.

4. Write down a story told to you by one of your parents or grandparents. The story can be a fable, a fairy tale, or an exploit of one of your ancestors. Stories like these often get better in the telling, so do your best.

5. Now that you have finished the section on diversity, write in your journal or for an essay what the concepts of race, class, and gender have meant in your own life so far.

PART

4

Heritage: Diversity
of Culture

The selections in the first three parts of *The Engaging Reader* give examples of how human beings become aware of themselves and then form relationships with others and with their surroundings. This section, the heart of the book, explores the heritage that each of us brings from background, ancestors, environment, and experience. These form our heritage, and comprise what we share and what we find unique in our diverse culture.

We have chosen three branches of that many-limbed culture of America to explore and relate to each other: varied occupations, the influence of music, and attitudes toward change. One part of our diverse culture brings baggage from the legendary past. The first selection is from an Apache legend about the origins of the potter's craft (The Jicarilla Apache, "How the Apaches Got Clay"). The next article looks at old-time ways of delivering babies (Endesha Ida Mae Holland, "Granny Midwives"), while the following one reviews a production of a play by Holland about her mother's work as a midwife in rural Alabama (Margaret Spillane, "From the Mississippi Delta").

Reviewing plays leads to appraisal of music, and the next group of selections deals with diverse musical traditions of the Americas. First is Mark Holston's "Rhythm Four Strings," with its history of the Caribbean rhythms and musical instruments. Then a scholarly study of the Blues traces its origins in African-American culture (Portia K. Maultsby, "African Cultural Traditions in the Blues"). Allan Bloom's controversial question, "Is Rock Music Rotting Our Kids' Minds?" concludes the segment on music.

The following section of Part 4 shows how people react to change in the culture they were born in, and how they adapt to new circumstances. In the first, Polingaysi Qoyawayma's "No Turning Back," a young Native American woman realizes she can never return completely to the ways of her ancestors. In the next, a young girl in Sarajevo experiences the horrors and dislocations of war and bombardment (Zlata Filipovic, "Zlata's Diary"). Then, a teacher comes to an Arizona trading post to learn much about the Navaho culture (Zane Grey, "At Kaidab Trading Post"). Finally, Carl Sandburg, in his poem "Chicago," gives insight into the growing, rude, difficult city.

THE JICARILLA APACHE

How the Apaches Got Clay

Recording the work of the past is the mission of the American Folklore Society, whose members and scholars collect information such as this traditional story, told orally for many years before it was finally written down in 1938. The Pueblo Indians of New Mexico were famous potters, an art that continues today. The Apaches picked up the art of pottery from their Pueblo Indian neighbors and soon were making clay pipes for smoking and pots for cooking. Potters always regard clay beds for pottery as very special; not just any clay will do. The Apache women smoked pipes before heading for the sacred clay deposits. They permitted men to help them haul the clay to the work site, but custom forbade men from bringing flint weapons with them. Flint was a male material, clay a female, and the Apache thought pots made from clay in contact with flint might break in the firing. The following account is from *Memoirs of the American Folklore Society,* vol. 31.

1   In the beginning of the world there was an old man and an old woman. They had nothing to do and they prayed to the one who made the earth to give them something to live on. Then one day a spirit came and stood before them.

2   First he took them to a rock and said, "That is gold. It is worth much, but I cannot give it to you, for you do not know how to work it."

Then he showed them another rock, saying, "That is silver. That, 4
too, is valuable, but you do not know of it or what to do with it,
so I cannot give it to you. Some day people will come from across
the ocean, from the east. They will feed you, give you clothes and
food. That is why I will send them. And they will like this silver
and gold."

Then the spirit took the old man and the old woman to the other 5
side of the mountain. A big hole was there. "Go over there and dig
out that clay," the spirit told the two old people. "I will show you
how to make pots and bowls with it. You will live by this means."

Then the spirit called the woman over to him and touched both
her hands with his, instructing her, "Now work the clay from your
own knowledge and with your own understanding."

So the old man and woman went together to dig the clay and 6
then the woman made a clay bowl and she did very good work.
She made bowls of all shapes. But she did not know what to call
the different bowls or the proper use for each shape.

That night the man and woman prayed and the spirit appeared 7
to the woman in a dream and told her how to use the pots and
what to call them. The spirit also told her that she must teach all
the children what she knew.

Engaging the Text

1. Notice the formula story: "In the beginning," the requisite
   three choices, the dream solution to the problem. Why is this
   story told in such a formal, unchanging way?

Engaging the Reader

1. Why does the story begin "In the beginning of the world"?
2. How many alternatives does the spirit show the old man and
   the old woman?
3. What is the third choice? Why will this benefit them?
4. Why does it seem important to the woman to know the names
   of the pots and how to use them?

The Engaged Writer

1. Can you remember a story beginning "Once upon a time"? If
   so, write it down from memory.

2. If you are from another culture and you learned some of its legends and stories by heart, try to write out one of them for your classmates. Perhaps your instructor will collect some of these stories and reproduce them for the whole class. This publication might be a very successful class project.

ENDESHA IDA MAE HOLLAND

Granny Midwives

Endesha Ida Mae Holland, an assistant professor in American studies and women's studies at SUNY Buffalo, became an award-winning playwright with *Miss Ida B. Wells, Second Doctor Lady*, and *From the Mississippi Delta*. This selection is the result of her trip to Alabama to interview two of the few remaining lay, or "granny," midwives in the state—women who learned to deliver babies by apprenticeship to another midwife and who lacked other formal education. Holland's mother had been such a midwife. The following selection from Holland's 1987 *Ms.* magazine article gives an account of one of her interviews.

1   It's a kind of poetic justice, I think to myself as we leave Birmingham, Alabama, bound for Huntsville, to talk to one of the last granny midwives in the state. Perhaps this story will serve as the fee that I never paid for the delivery of my son, who was brought into the world by a granny midwife—my mother. I thrill to this notion of repayment.

2   My late mother, Ida Mae Holland, was professionally called the "Second Doctor Lady" because of her skill. The Second Doctor Lady was a great asset to our Mississippi delta community. She would go to see about pregnant women at any hour, anytime; she saved old newspapers and baby clothes from the white families to carry with her on home deliveries, and she could turn a breech baby around in a woman's stomach.

3   Before I had my baby, I would accompany my mother to remote areas outside of town to endless "shotgun shacks" (where each room was built directly behind the other) when she went to deliver babies. I can still hear her instructions to this day: "Bear down now,

Mag, not so hard, and Johnson, you git in yonder and take your pances off so dat I kin lay dem on de bed so dat her pains won't be so hard." As a child, I often wondered what would happen if Miss Mag's husband wasn't the baby's daddy—and what might happen if his old greasy, smelly pants couldn't help ease the pain of Magnolia Johnson, the mother of 12 children already. After the delivery was over, Mama would holler to me where I was supposed to be waiting in the yard, although I was usually closer to the window, where I had a good view of what was happening: "Gal, you come in here and write dis here baby's name down on dis here piece of paper." Mother couldn't read or write, so I would hurry with my seventh-grade education along with my resolve never to have a baby, and astonish the gathered women with my ability to read and write.

Since hospitals often refused to offer obstetrical care to black   4
women, my mama's work was vital. The men of the town respected her and the women needed her. But this was not unusual. Many times midwives became almost sainted in the communities. A family could always depend on their assistance, whether it was for prenatal counseling, the laying on of hands and tallow grease, lessons in food preparation, child-care training, or especially their presence at the labor bed.

Despite their importance, in 1987 these Alabama granny mid-   5
wives find themselves barred from using a lifelong accumulation of skills and knowledge. The state health department stopped issuing new permits for lay midwives 10 years ago and gradually has phased out any who still remained in practice. Now, none are left. I went to Alabama to interview two of its last living granny midwives so that their work—the work of my mother, and of hundreds of other women like her—will not be forgotten. I felt a responsibility, and that made me feel real good inside.

My researcher, Nicole Williams, who is white, and I parked our   6
car in front of a housing project in Huntsville and made our way toward an old man sitting on the front porch in an old chair.

"'Cuse me, sir"—his eyes never left my face—"is this where   7
Mrs. Pearl Caudle live?" I asked.

"Show is. She in dere, yawl come on in," said the old man with   8
an air of expectancy. The screen door to the ground-level apartment was thrown wide and a nut-brown face with shoulder-length frizzed hair, oversize glasses, and the most elegant hands I had seen in a long time beckoned us on inside.

9   "Yawl come on in here," said Mrs. Caudle; then she excused herself for a moment.

10   Nicole tests the tape recorder. I look at the pictures on the walls. Shiny black faces peer out. A plaque from Delta Sigma Theta Sorority proclaims to anyone who sees it that Pearl Caudle is a humanitarian. I can smell corn bread getting a little brown and Mrs. Caudle is rattling her cookpots. Suddenly, the room, the sounds, and the smells transport me back to my Mississippi delta days.

11   *"Gal, you see how hard hit is to have a baby," Mama would say to me. "You see what running 'round wit de boys gits you and letting dem look underneath your closes." I would dutifully swear never to let the boys look under my clothes.*

12   "Here I is now, honey. So ask me what you want to," Mrs. Caudle announces as she comes back into the room.

13   I start right in telling her about my mother in order to establish a bond. Mrs. Caudle relaxes.

14   "I was born and raised in Alabama," she tells us. "I don't know nothing 'bout living nowhere but in Alabama." We sit looking into each other's faces with a strong sense of kinship.

15   "Tell me something, Mrs. Caudle: you say you been delivering babies since you were twenty-two years old, and now you're seventy-eight. You must have caught a lot of babies?"

16   "'Course, indeed I have! I delivered so many, brought 'em in 'fore I knowed anything 'bout de health department and certificates and all. I was 'bout forty 'fore I knowed anything 'bout it but just delivering dem babies. But now it's five hundred or more since I had the authority. But I done so much 'fore I had my authority."

17   "What made you start?"

18   "Oh, I can't hardly tell you what made me start up. All my life, I always did believe in helping people; and if I couldn't help 'em, I wasn't gonna harm 'em." I could tell right off that Mrs. Caudle had summed up her philosophy of life, so I marked the question off the page further down.

19   "Can I take some pictures?"

20   "Wait a minute, honey," she says. Mrs. Caudle goes swiftly into the bedroom and returns, pinning her lay midwife's pin to her bosom.

21   I start taking pictures of her and the pictures on the wall. She walks alongside me, giving a running commentary on her portrait gallery. She points to children of all ages. "Yeah, these my grand-

children, but it ain't all of 'em, 'cause I got twenty-one. I delivered them and I delivered they mothers. Don't know how many great grands I got." She surely knows the value of the picture she points to next: "Here is all three of us, right here. I and Ellen Thompson and Miss Maudie Drake." They were the last lay midwives issued permits in the state of Alabama.

The next picture we come to is one that reflects the fine looks 22 and youth of the old man sitting on the porch. "And that's the man I been with for more than fifty years."

"How did you and Mr. Caudle meet?" I ask, not being one to 23 overlook a cue.

"I don't know. Ask him. We first met some sort of way, I don't 24 know, and then I married him." Mr. Caudle takes his cue and enters. He sits quietly on the other end of the sofa. Mrs. Caudle continues: "I delivered all of 'em—white and black. Some of 'em coulda went to the hospital. I delivered some who didn't have a prayer. I didn't charge nothing when I first started. Sometimes I would ask for a quarter; some of the people had it, some didn't. After a while I started gitting three dollars and then five. When I went under the supervision of the law—when I got my author- ity—I had to charge them [the families] twenty-five dollars and some of them didn't have twenty-five cents. But now they can go to the hospital 'cause they got welfare and Social Security taking care of 'em."

"Before welfare and Social Security, I bet you were some kinda 25 busy, Mrs. Caudle."

"Honey, I tell you that many a time I come home from some 26 woman's house and didn't even get a chance to come into the house, 'cause I had to get in the car waiting to take me to help some other woman. Plenty of times."

"Why did the health department cancel your permit?" I gently 27 ask.

"They just decided to stop," Mrs. Caudle says with a sad face. 28 "We're all kinda old. I'm 'bout the youngest one 'mongst 'em; and if I'm seventy-eight years old, you know about them. Maudie Drake and Mrs. Thompson is over me. We been bringin' babies and raisin' babies. Just start to slow up. It couldn't be helped in any way. Social Security and welfare been taking care of 'em. And they [the public health officials] just figured we wasn't doing enough.

29   "Let me tell you, honey, I never lost a mother or a baby. 'Course some of 'em dies in the hospital after the baby was born. But I ain't never lost one. Now, I have gone to mothers and the baby be already dead. And I ain't never left one with no big navel." From my days of being with the Second Doctor Lady, I know how unprofessional it is to leave a big navel on a baby.

30   "Did you train anybody else under you?"

31   "Don't know if I did or didn't. 'Course a lot of people say they want to train under me, but they soon quit or die off—so I don't know if I did nor not. Now some of my great granddaughters say that they want to be a midwife. But I can't do nothing now, can't give 'em no book to read, or show 'em how it's done, nothing like that unless they got a permit [to practice]." Mrs. Caudle laments the passing away of the old era.

32   "I tell you, I done delivered some of 'em that was coming butt first—but I just would work till I turn the baby 'round and then it would come out right. Yes, ma'am, my sister's child, he the first I ever seen come feet first—big old fat black baby, just as pretty as he could be, and he's a big old fat black man today."

33   "Were you afraid?"

34   "Naw! I ain't scared of nothing but snakes. But when I see that hand come first, somebody gonna take her to the hospital and I'm gone go with 'em."

35   "What will you do now, Mrs. Caudle, since you can't practice midwifery?"

36   "I tell you the truth, I ain't gonna let nobody die if I can help it. I'm gonna obey the law, but if a baby's comin' into the world, and I know good and well they ain't able to go to the hospital—then it be bad for me to let that baby die—or the mother. So what I'm gone do is call somebody. Just call somebody and tell 'em I did it. Ain't that fair? I tried my best to be obedient, but I got to do my duty."

37   As we prepare to take our leave, we hug and kiss Mrs. Caudle and say many good-byes. My last view of the old man and old woman is filled with pain. Indeed, I think, it's just the way Kathleen O'Donohue, director of the Women's Community Health Center of Huntsville, has said. "When lay midwives are not allowed to practice, it's like watching them tear down an old treasured landmark."

Engaging the Text

1. The essay is in the form of an interview. In paragraph 10 you find out about the use of a tape recorder and in paragraph 6 that Holland was accompanied by an assistant, a researcher. Does this interview technique "show" in the essay? How?
2. Comment on the use of dialect in the interview. Does it enhance the story? Does it make it more (or less) understandable?
3. Holland shows a sense of humor, a touch that enlivens any piece of writing. Pick out some examples of this.
4. Compare Holland's interview technique with that of Claudia Tate ("Andre Lorde").

Engaging the Reader

1. What do you learn about the writer's mother?
2. What has happened to Alabama's "granny" midwives? Can they still practice?
3. What are the reasons given for the health department's actions?
4. What do you know about the practice of midwifery today?

The Engaged Writer

1. From the details given in the interview, write a short character sketch of Mrs. Pearl Caudle.
2. Using a tape recorder, interview a classmate or friend on one of the following topics:

   — Should we have sex education in public schools?
   — Should granny midwives continue to practice?
   — What was your most satisfying job?

3. After taping the interview, organize it into an essay as Holland does for this article.
4. What kind of health care plan would be ideal for our country? Look at those proposed and evaluate them.

MARGARET SPILLANE

From the Mississippi Delta

As part of the theater section in the July 1991 issue of *The Nation,*
Margaret Spillane, a writer and painter from New Haven, commented on a play then running at the Hartford Stage in Hartford,
Connecticut. It was an autobiographical play by Endesha Ida Mae
Holland, author of "Granny Midwives," the previous selection. The
review comments on the acting, the story, and some particularly
astounding dramatic moments in the play. The play appeared in
theaters around the country in 1991. It dramatized the story of Holland's growing up as the daughter of one of the last "Granny Midwives" in the Mississippi Delta.

1   Across town from Company One, another kind of lust and revolution is blazing brightly. At the Hartford Stage, three African-
American actresses who are the cast of *From the Mississippi Delta*
assume the characters, colors and genders of a wide variety of
Delta people. Throughout the play these three wear the same
threadbare secondhand dresses, the kind that well-heeled folks feel
generous about offering as gifts to their domestic servants rather
than cutting the clothes into dustrags. But upon such skinflint gifts
and short-change wages, many a domestic worker has applied her
stamina and her stubborn persistence to shape a world in which
her own knowledge of beauty and justice can have authority.

2   And such is the case in *Delta.* Three brilliant ensemble players—
Cheryl Lynn Bruce, Sybil Walker and Jacqueline Williams—summon up the work climate and family lives of black women in rural
Mississippi. Performing on a stage of spare design—an ironing
board, a chair, a window frame hanging in midair, some potted
petunias—the actresses commit their talents first and foremost in
service to the story, never allowing an individual performance to
shine more brightly than the tale itself. That exquisite forbearance
lets emerge the story's own raw power to heal, to give hope, to
mete out justice.

3   Most of the tales in *Delta* revolve around the lives of two brave
and resourceful women, Aint Baby and her daughter, Phelia. Performing small material transformations is what these women's

lives are all about: Early in her work life Aint Baby does ironing for white women and becomes renowned for pressing so sharp a crease in a pair of trousers that they could stand up by themselves. Later Aint Baby becomes certified as a midwife. Phelia might have struggled on a path similar to her mother's were it not for another transforming influence: the arrival of the civil rights movement in her town.

Playwright Endesha Ida Mae Holland made this autobio-   4 graphical play as she would make a quilt, taking modest pieces of fabric that would otherwise go ignored and patiently and deliberately organizing them into something both resplendent and enduringly useful. This is not to say that all the panels of this quilt are equally well crafted. In the second act, several scenes—one of a fire, another of a funeral—seem to have been stitched in with more concern for their lyrical shape than for the horror at the heart of each.

But *Delta* also contains two of the most astonishing dramatic   5 moments I have ever seen onstage. One happens during the story of how 11-year-old Phelia, hired ostensibly to baby-sit in a well-off white family's home, is lured upstairs and summarily raped. The whole incident takes only a few seconds, on a stage completely empty except for two actresses—one playing the utterly immobile white woman standing by at her husband's bidding, and the other as the child suddenly flung down on her back, her face a mask of uncomprehending pain, her ambushed limbs a wreath of fierce angles.

The other astonishing scene: Aint Baby presiding at the birth of   6 a couple's thirteenth child. I know of no other work of art that has better depicted childbirth as the risk that it always is, with the shadow of fatal possibilities always flickering at the doorway. And this midwife's wisdom extends far beyond the clinical skills for which she got her certification. With an eloquence issuing from the sinews in her neck and the muscles of her arms, with her fingertips measuring herbs and her lips shaping an invocation, Aint Baby is a fierce vessel enclosing centuries of African healing wisdom. On the night I attended not a soul in the audience dared breathe as this medicine woman wrenched mother and child from the threshold of death and planted them solidly among the living.

Lest some Heritage Foundation bootstrap-boosting honcho   7 wander into the Hartford Stage glowing with the idea that *From the*

Mississippi Delta is a paean to individual enterprise, let me disabuse that bozo right here. Aint Baby regards her midwife's certificate not as an emblem of superiority over her neighbors but as a means to guarantee that their community will carry on. Even Phelia's eventual triumph in the larger world—earning academic honors at a university up North—is no flight from home ground. When Phelia users her cap-and-gowned moment of glory to name every single person from the Delta and beyond who ever extended love and wisdom to her, she seems to rise atop a pyramid made of their names, their unseen lives unearthed by the act of naming.

Engaging the Text

1. Notice the colorful mix of words used in this short review: skinflint (1), stamina (1), forbearance (2), invocation (6).
2. What does Spillane mean in this sentence: "Lest some Heritage Foundation bootstrap-boosting honcho . . . disabuse that bozo right here" (paragraph 7)?

Engaging the Reader

1. Notice the metaphor of a quilt (paragraph 4) that Spillane uses to discuss the structure of the play and the way Holland incorporates incidents into it. Make an outline of the review's structure. Is it like a quilt? How?
2. What is the thesis—or main point—of the review?
3. Would you enjoy seeing this play? What details in the review influenced your response?
4. Check your local paper, you college paper, or a national magazine such as *Time* or *Newsweek* for play or film reviews. What general topics do they cover? How do they compare with Spillane's review?

The Engaged Writer

1. Using Spillane's review as a model for topics covered, structure, and inclusion of detail, write a review of a play, a film, or a television play that you have seen recently.
2. If you have seen *From the Mississippi Delta*, write a response agreeing or disagreeing with Spillane's review.

MARK HOLSTON

Rhythm Four Strings

Music is both a profession and a pleasurable hobby, for the listener
as well as the performer. The following article highlights a particular instrument, a Puerto Rican guitar called a *cuatro*. The history of
the instrument shows its deep connection with Caribbean folkloric
music. Mark Holston, a lifelong musician, has written about jazz
and Latin American music for a number of publications, including
Americas, in which this article appeared in 1991.

Ask any Puerto Rican to name the typical instrument most iden-   1
tified with the island, and the answer will be immediate: the small
guitar known as the *cuatro*. But press the same person to provide
any details about the instrument's origin, and the response is likely to be silence. Only in recent years have musicologists begun to
probe the history of the enigmatic string instrument, but the studies so far have proven little more than what all Puerto Ricans take
for granted. The *cuatro* and the Caribbean island's folkloric music
are so intertwined they are all but one and the same.

Some may envision a homesick sailor aboard one of Christopher   2
Columbus' ships on the 1492 voyage, strumming a small Spanish
guitarra. The romantic notion that some form of guitar was among
the first objects of European culture to be introduced to the New
World may or may not be historically accurate; but there is no
doubt that within a few years of the Spaniards' arrival, the guitar
was a part of everyday life in such growing settlements as Havana,
Santo Domingo and San Juan.

Most certainly, those first guitars were not what we associate   3
today with the classical Spanish guitar tradition. The Spanish guitar of the fifteenth century was a much smaller instrument,
endowed with just four (cuatro) strings. It matters little that the
shape has changed over the centuries or that the *cuatro* may now
have as many as ten strings. The personality of the instrument and
the role it plays in Puerto Rican life remains much the same today
as it has been for almost five centuries.

While Puerto Ricans defend the *cuatro* as exclusively their own,   4
Venezuela claims its particular version, as well as a strikingly sim-

ilar instrument called the *tiple*. Indeed, throughout Latin America, and the world, cousins of the *cuatro* have evolved, each finding its own form and distinctive high pitched voice.

5   The *cavaquinho* is as revered by Brazilians as the *ukulele* is by Hawaiians. In the interior of Panama, *campesinos* strum the *mejorana*. High in the Andes of Peru and Bolivia, native craftsmen use the shell of the armadillo as the sound chamber for their distinctive *charango*. Mexicans call their version of the armadillo-based string instrument a *mandola de concha*. In the outback of Brazil's northeast, the *vaqueiros*, or cowboys, favor a small guitar with a short neck called the *viola sertaneja*. Even Cuba's *tres* and the banjo of the rural U.S. South owe their lineage to the same family of small string instruments dubbed by some as "the poor man's guitar."

6   In this day of assembly lines, the *cuatro* and its kin remain major exceptions to the standards of mass production. The best *cuatros* are still crafted in much the same manner as they were hundreds of years ago. In small villages throughout Puerto Rico, local artisans who learned their skills from their fathers, work with materials as old as the mountains of *El Yunque* to fashion instruments as individual as the towns from which they come. From trees with names as magical as the titles of folk ballads come special ingredients, each suited to a particular part of the *cuatro*'s body. *Guaraguao, jiquey, majú, laurel, tulipán* and *yagrumo* woods all come together in rich harmony to craft the *cuatro*'s finished form.

7   "The *cuatro* is my blood," says Puerto Rico's internationally known guitarist, Yomo Toro. The rotund musician, now a resident of New York, has expanded the use of the humble folk instrument far beyond the customary role it plays in Puerto Rico's *jíbaro* (country) music. Toro, who has spent years in the service of such legends of tropical music as Celia Cruz, Willie Colón, Tito Puente and Rubén Blades, has also performed with mainstream pop artists like Paul Simon and Linda Ronstadt. When the music calls for that perfect touch of typical Puerto Rican flavor, Toro is usually the first to be called.

8   When Toro started using the *cuatro* in tropical music groups, he surprised a lot of traditionalists, but he proved that the instrument adapts easily to many styles. "You can use it to play *salsa*, or classical music, or anything you want. It sounds beautiful," he says. Toro recalls the day a *cuatro* was first placed in his hands. Like many Puerto Rican children with a knack for making music, his

small hands could make sense of the miniature fret and closely spaced strings. By the time he reached adulthood, with hands so large they enveloped the instrument, Toro's fingers had been trained to negotiate the *cuatro*'s delicate neck with all the skill and confidence associated with the world's great classical guitarists. His experience is not unique. In fact, such early exposure is almost a requirement if one is to achieve any degree of expertise on the instrument. "You must start very young," Toro states. "Even an accomplished guitarist will know he has met his match if he picks up a *cuatro* for the first time as an adult."

Making the instrument all the more difficult to play is the fact 9 that, in reality, the *cuatro* has become a *cinco*. Not that anyone calls it that, but most modern *cuatros* have five strings, or actually, 10 strings, five sets of two with each pair tuned to the same note.

Where Yomo Toro has found popularity adapting the traditional 10 *cuatro* style to the world of tropical music, others have expanded the instrument's potential into very nontraditional styles. Edwin Colón Zayas, a young Puerto Rican who has impressed even the veteran Toro, has set out to prove the *cuatro* has no limitations. He has brought the finesse of a classically trained guitarist to *cuatro* interpretations of compositions by Chopin and Rimsky-Korsakov (the demanding *Flight of the Bumble Bee*), the seldom heard Argentine *zamba* rhythm, and even the very Polish *Beer Barrel Polka*.

Taking perhaps even more liberties, a Puerto Rican group called 11 "Jibaro Jazz" has proven the *cuatro* is as adept at pure improvisation as is the most modern electric guitar. At the other end of the stylistic spectrum, a group called "Mapeyé" is a self appointed keeper of the flame. "Mapeyé is respect to tradition and history," writes Puerto Rican critic Gloria Paniagua. "Mapeyé is indigenous, the evocation of the black earth and reddishness of our mountain land—a lesson of nationhood, of resistance, of love to those who deserve to be loved." Such is the range of emotion the music in its purest form evokes.

Across the Caribbean, Venezuelan Mauricio Reyna has devoted 12 himself to broadening the base of interest in his country's version of the instrument, the *cuatro Venezolano*. Son of famous *cuatro* soloist Freddy Reyna, Mauricio has been kept busy by the Venezuelan Institute of Culture and Cooperation spreading the message of *cuatro* to islands throughout the Caribbean with a series of workshops. He has also introduced the sound of the *cuatro* to motion picture audiences through his score for the Venezuelan film *Un Domingo Feliz*, a screenplay by Colombian writer Gabriel García Márquez.

13   Reyna's passion for the instrument is not unlike that of his Puerto Rican neighbors. "It is the purest," he notes, making reference to the *cuatro*'s similarity to the original Spanish guitar.

14   But even as master artists like Toro and Colón Zayas continue to seek new ways to challenge the capabilities of the *cuatro*, the instrument will continue to find comfort in its traditional role around the plazas of small Puerto Rican towns. That is where the men who cut and craft the native woods into the finished *cuatro* live next door to those whose talents will always ensure a ready audience. In those unpretentious moments, under an open sky, when the simple folk tunes of many generations are enjoyed once more, the *cuatro* renews its true soul.

Engaging the Text

1. All of the following words can refer to feelings about music. Study their definitions, and use them in sentences about a kind of music you enjoy: enigmatic (1), indigenous (11), and evocation (11).

2. What are musicologists (1)? Use the word when you discuss this article.

3. This definition essay uses many Spanish words because it explores the music of Spanish-speaking Puerto Rico. However, the words are explained in the text; they are the names of various instruments (paragraphs 2–5) and of the woods used to craft the *cuatro*'s body (paragraph 6).

Engaging the Reader

1. If you are a musician, write about your instrument in the same way Holston defines and analyzes the *cuatro* and its music.

2. If you are a part of any specialized business that uses its own vocabulary (music, computers, construction), explain some of the words in that vocabulary to your classmates.

The Engaged Writer

1. This essay provides informative, accessible information about a specialized kind of music. The writer needed to know and understand the music and its instruments, know the players

and their histories and styles, and give information about albums. Choose a topic about which you already are somewhat informed, gather facts and figures about the subject from your library, and write a paper giving the kind of information contained in Holston's article. Examples of these subjects might be types of airplanes, different word processing programs, performances of fourwheel-drive automobiles, rap music, or the history of a type of instrument you play. When you write this paper, be sure to refer to your library sources (see "Backing Up What You Say" in the Writer's Guide).

PORTIA K. MAULTSBY

African Cultural Traditions in the Blues

Portia Maultsby is an ethnomusicologist, and as a scholar has written a documented paper on the African background of American "Blues" music. Maultsby is a Professor of Afro-American Studies and Music at Indiana University, and has written on African-American music. This article appeared in a special edition of *Maryland Humanities* entitled "Celebrate the Blues!" As an extended definition, this paper explains how African sources influence how African Americans compose, react to, and live for music today.

For nearly four centuries, African Americans often were characterized as a people without a culture. This interpretation is documented in early scholarly discourses on black language, religious practices, and music that describe the salient features of African-American culture as imitations and variations on Euro-American culture. By the 1960s some scholars began to challenge this theory, documenting Africa as the cultural source of many African-American values and traditions.[1]

This African heritage "must be viewed in terms of creative processes which allow for continuity and change."[2] As African cultures evolved in the New World, responding to migration, technological advancements, and new political, economic, and social arrangements, they maintained traditions from their African past and innovated to meet the demands of a changing environment. Tradition and innovation are both illustrated in the array of styles that constitute the African-American music.

3   African cultural traditions define the way African Americans create, interpret, and experience music. The creative process mirrors the social organization of African communities. Within this structure, the nuclear family, relatives, neighbors and friends interact as a unit. This organization of black life underscores the conception of musical performance as a celebratory community event. Audience members become active participants, blurring the traditional distinction between performer and audience. Audiences interact with performers, singing familiar verses and "hook lines," responding, "sing to me," "I hear ya," "tell the truth," and so on, and displaying physical gestures.

4   Promotional materials also highlight the spontaneous, interactive, and celebratory character of African-American musical performances. They read: "come and jam with," or "come and get down with" for secular concerts and "come and be moved by" for religious gatherings.

5   Contemporary performers, in meeting the cultural expectations of black audiences, adapt recorded versions of their songs with ad lib "rapping" (secular) or "sermonettes" (sacred) to establish rapport with the live audience. When the singing actually begins, the style of the performance complements the "we are here to party" or "we are here to be moved" attitude of the audience or congregation.

6   The audience is encouraged to participate in any way, sometimes even to join performers on stage. Soul singer Sam Moore, of the duo Sam and Dave, recalls how he "would stop the band and go hand-clapping in the audience [and] make them stand up."[3] Through music, African Americans express themselves as individuals and share the creative experience with one another.

7   In African and African-derived communities, music is an integral part of daily life. Associated with a variety of activities, it is assigned specific functions that determine the content, structure, and style of a song. Children's game songs, for example, entertain, develop motor skills, and facilitate play. The lyrics often feature call-response structures to facilitate musical exchanges between the children. Hand-clapping and stomped dance patterns accompany many game songs, providing an intricate rhythmic foundation.

Similarly, African Americans perform work songs to ease the   8
burden of hard, physical labor and to coordinate effort. The songs'
call-response structure encourages all workers to participate.
Pounding hammers or axes often supply rhythm and timing.

The degree to which music fulfills its intended function deter-   9
mines its artistic merit. Cultural values, which determine the
guidelines for song interpretation, play an important role in this
process. And the performers' style and aesthetic qualities are central to the evaluative process.

African-American performances are distinguished from those of   10
other cultures by a distinctive black music aesthetic, whose elements may be categorized as (1) style of delivery; (2) quality of
sound; and (3) mechanics of delivery.[4]

Style of Delivery

The style of delivery refers to the physical mode of presentation,   11
where body movements, facial expression, and clothing are
intrinsic to the performance. In African and African-derived communities, music-making represents a celebration of life and sym-
bolizes vitality. African-American performers demonstrate this
concept through the dramatic manner in which they deliver a
song. They become totally consumed, displaying an emotional
intensity and a physical involvement that is dramatized through
use of the entire body.

The vitality of African-American life is evident, too, in costumes   12
of bold, vivid colors. The costumes and the ways in which performers physically communicate with their audiences create a rit-
ualistic ambience.

Quality of Sound

The quality of sound is a unique blend produced by the manipu-   13
lation of timbre, texture, and shading in ways uncommon to Western practice. These sounds include lyrical, raspy, guttural, percus-
sive timbres, alternating straight and vibrato tones, and weaving
moans, shouts, grunts, hollers, and screams into the melody. The
underlying concept adheres to African cultural and aesthetic principles. As Francis Bebey suggests:

The objective of African music is not necessarily to produce sounds agreeable to the ear, but to translate everyday experiences into loving sound. In a musical environment whose constant purpose is to depict life, nature, or the supernatural, the musician wisely avoids using beauty as his criterion because no criterion could be more arbitrary.[5]

14   Musical sounds in African-derived cultures not only imitate those of nature and the supernatural but also the emotions of joy, despair, and sadness associated with daily life. Vocal sounds are reproduced on instruments when performers make them "holler," "cry," "grunt," "scream," "moan," and "whine." The vocal dimension of instrumental sounds is reflected in phrases like "make it talk," "talk to me," and "I hear ya talkin'" used by black people to say that their aesthetic expectations have been met.

Mechanics of Delivery

15   African-American performers employ a variety of improvisatory devices to interpret songs in a manner that "moves the soul" or "speaks to the spirit." This process involves manipulating time, text, and pitch. Performers expand time by extending the length of notes and by repeating words, phrases, and entire sections of the songs. They play with rhythm and increase rhythmic complexity by adding layers of handclaps, instrumental accompaniment, and vocal parts of varying ranges. They change the pitch through the use of bends, slides, melismas, passing tones, and other forms of melodic embellishment. And they build intensity by highlighting the polar extremes of a single voice.

16   When performers create and interpret songs within the aesthetic boundaries formulated by black people, audiences respond immediately and often so audibly that they momentarily drown out the performer. The audiences' verbal comments and demonstrative physical gestures are signs that performers meet their aesthetic expectations.

17   African-American music represents the continuum of an African consciousness in America. Its uniqueness is defined by an approach to the creative, interpretative, and experiential process. This approach preserves values, traditions, and ideas fundamen-

tal to African cultures. The African-American musical tradition, therefore, can only be analyzed, interpreted, and evaluated within this context and theoretical framework.

Notes

[1] John Blassingame, *The Slave Community*, rev. ed. (New York: Oxford Press, 1979); Alan Dundes, ed., *Mother Wit from the Laughing Barrel* (Englewood Cliffs, N.J.; Prentice-Hall, 1973); George Pullen Jackson, *White Spirituals in the Southern Uplands* (1933; reprint ed., New York: Dover Publications, 1965); Guy B. Johnson, *Folk Culture on St. Helena Island* (1930; reprint ed., Hatboro, Pa.: Folklore Associates, 1968); Joseph E. Holloway, ed., *Africanisms in American Culture* (Bloomington: Indiana University Press, 1990); Lawrence Levine, *Black Culture and Black Consciousness* (New York: Oxford University Press, 1977); Albert J. Raboteau, *Slave Religion* (New York: Oxford University Press, 1978); Newman White, *American Negro Folk Songs* (Cambridge: Harvard University Press, 1928); Norman E. Whitten, and John F. Szwed, eds., *Afro-American Anthropology* (New York: Free Press, 1970).

[2] J. H. Kwabena Nketia, "African Roots of Music in the Americas: An African View," in *Report of the 12th Congress* (London: American Musicological Society, 1981), pp. 82–88.

[3] Sam Moore, interview with author, 25 February 1983.

[4] Mellonee Burnim, "The Black Gospel Music Tradition: A Complex of Ideology, Aesthetic, and Behavior," in *More Than Dancing*, ed. Irene V. Jackson (Westport Conn.: Greenwood Press, 1985), pp. 154–65.

[5] Francis Bebey, *African Music: A People's Art*, trans. Josephine Bennett (New York: Lawrence Hill, 1975), p. 115.

Engaging the Text

1. Since this article appeared in a humanities journal, its language and structure are quite formal. It uses, therefore, a vocabulary of scholarship: salient features (1), celebratory (3), facilitate (7), aesthetic qualities (9), intrinsic (11), improvisatory (15), polar extremes (15), experiential process (16). Make sure you know what these mean by rewording the sentences in your own words. For example, the first sentence in paragraph 16 can be paraphrased as "When musicians sing and play African style, their hearers react right away and often so loudly that you can't hear the music for a moment."

2. The essay also demonstrates a knowledge of the audience reaction: note particularly paragraph 3, 5, and 14 for descriptions of how audiences receive and participate in the Blues.

Engaging the Reader

1. If you need to write a research paper for any course, this one can be a model. It uses superscribed numbers[1] to refer to a list at the end of the article such as this one. There is a simplified method that uses a short reference in parentheses (Burnim 154).
2. See if you can find some musical examples to illustrate this essay: some albums of "Blues" that show the audience reactions Maultsby is talking about.

The Engaged Writer

1. Audiences have become aware, in recent years, of the differences in responses from African-American audiences and others in America. Write a paper explaining why conduct that might seem loud or rude to some is really a aesthetic appreciation and involvement in a musical art.
2. If you have heard blues by artists like Wendell Holmes or Bobby Parker, write a review of what they do, basing it on the "context and theoretical framework" of Maultsby's article.
3. Taking the lists you looked at under *Engaging the Text*, develop a short essay explaining what is actually meant by such things as "hooklines," "sing to me," "I hear ya," "tell the truth," or any others you can think of from your own experience. What, for example is "rapping"? Give examples.
4. This section includes two other articles besides this one on different musical traditions in America: Caribbean, African, and Rock. One involves history, one ethnology, and the other is an anti-rock diatribe. Answer Bloom's article on the deleterious effects of rock by giving examples of cultural innovativeness from the other two articles.

Notes

[1] John Blassingame, *The Slave Community*, rev. ed. (New York: Oxford Press, 1979).

ALLAN BLOOM

Is Rock Music Rotting Our Kids' Minds?

Allan Bloom's *The Closing of the American Mind* set the educational establishment on edge in 1987 with its violent criticism of American education in this generation. In it Bloom faults the schools and colleges for lack of moral leadership, as well as for failing to teach the traditions of our civilization. He also blames parents and the entertainment industry for far-reaching effects on students' lives. Bloom was Professor of Social Thought at the University of Chicago. The following is an excerpt from the section "Music" in *The Closing of the American Mind.*

Picture a thirteen-year-old boy sitting in the living room of his family home doing his math assignment while wearing his Walkman headphones or watching MTV. He enjoys the liberties hard won over centuries by the alliance of philosophic genius and political heroism, consecrated by the blood of martyrs; he is provided with comfort and leisure by the most productive economy ever known to mankind; science has penetrated the secrets of nature in order to provide him with the marvelous, lifelike electronic sound and image reproduction he is enjoying. And in what does progress culminate? A pubescent child whose body throbs with orgasmic rhythms; whose feelings are made articulate in hymns to the joys of onanism or the killing of parents; whose ambition is to win fame and wealth in imitating the drag-queen who makes the music. In short, life is made into a nonstop, commercially prepackaged masturbational fantasy.

This description may seem exaggerated, but only because some would prefer to regard it as such. The continuing exposure to rock music is a reality, not one confined to a particular class or type of child. One need only ask first-year university students what music they listen to, how much of it and what it means to them, in order to discover that the phenomenon is universal in America, that it begins in adolescence or a bit before and continues through the college years. It is *the* youth culture and, as I have so often insisted, there is now no other countervailing nourishment for the spirit. Some of this culture's power comes from the fact that it is so loud. It makes conversation impossible, so that much of friendship must be without the shared speech that Aristotle asserts is the essence of friendship and the only true common ground. With rock, illusions of shared feelings, bodily contact and grunted formulas, which are supposed to contain so much meaning beyond speech, are the basis of association. None of this contradicts going about the business of life, attending classes and doing the assignments for them. But the meaningful inner life is with the music. . . .

3   My concern here is not with the moral effects of this music— whether it leads to sex, violence or drugs. The issue here is its effect on education, and I believe it ruins the imagination of young people and makes it very difficult for them to have a passionate relationship to the art and thought that are the substance of liberal education. The first sensuous experiences are decisive in determining the taste for the whole of life, and they are the link between the animal and spiritual in us. The period of nascent sensuality has always been used for sublimation, in the sense of making sublime, for attaching youthful inclinations and longings to music, pictures and stories that provide the transition to the fulfillment of the human duties and the enjoyment of the human pleasures. Lessing, speaking of Greek sculpture, said "beautiful men made beautiful statues, and the city had beautiful statues in part to thank for beautiful citizens." This formula encapsulates the fundamental principle of the esthetic education of man. Young men and women were attracted by the beauty of heroes whose very bodies expressed their nobility. The deeper understanding of the meaning of nobility comes later, but is prepared for by the sensuous experience and is actually contained in it. What the senses long for as well as what reason later sees as good are thereby not at tension with one another. Education is not sermonizing to children against their instincts and pleasures, but providing a natural continuity between what they feel and what they can and should be. But this is a lost art. Now we have come to exactly the opposite point. Rock music encourages passions and provides models that have no relation to any life the young people who go to universities can possibly lead, or to the kinds of admiration encouraged by liberal studies. Without the cooperation of the sentiments, anything other than technical education is a dead letter.

Rock music provides premature ecstasy and, in this respect, is 4
like the drugs with which it is allied. It artificially induces the exal-
tation naturally attached to the completion of the greatest endeav-
ors—victory in a just war, consummated love, artistic creation, religious devotion and discovery of the truth. Without effort, without
talent, without virtue, without exercise of the faculties, anyone and
everyone is accorded the equal right to the enjoyment of their
fruits. In my experience, students who have had a serious fling
with drugs—and gotten over it—find it difficult to have enthusiasms or great expectations. It is as though the color has been
drained out of their lives and they see everything in black and
white. The pleasure they experienced in the beginning was so
intense that they no longer look for it at the end, or as the end. They
may function perfectly well, but dryly, routinely. Their energy has
been sapped, and they do not expect their life's activity to produce
anything but a living, whereas liberal education is supposed to
encourage the belief that the good life is the pleasant life and that
the best life is the most pleasant life. I suspect that the rock addiction, particularly in the absence of strong counterattractions, has
an effect similar to that of drugs. The students will get over this
music, or at least the exclusive passion for it. But they will do so
in the same way Freud says that men accept the reality principle—
as something harsh, grim and essentially unattractive, a mere
necessity. These students will assiduously study economics or the
professions and the Michael Jackson costume will slip off to reveal
a Brooks Brothers suit beneath. They will want to get ahead and
live comfortably. But this life is as empty and false as the one they
left behind. The choice is not between quick fixes and dull calculation. This is what liberal education is meant to show them. But
as long as they have the Walkman on, they cannot hear what the
great tradition has to say. And, after its prolonged use, when they
take it off, they find they are deaf.

Engaging the Text

1. In paragraph 1, we find a concentration of extreme writing,
   including the words consecrated, culminate, pubescent, orgasmic, and onanism. This sample of Bloom's writing shows both
   his huge vocabulary and his harsh judgments. Do you consider this first paragraph overwritten?

2. Bloom varies his sentences—using short and long ones, complex and simple ones. Identify some of these kinds of sentences in the selection.

Engaging the Reader

1. In this selection from his book, we are first introduced to a student doing homework while listening to rock music on his headphones. What is the effect of this music?
2. What is Bloom's main concern with rock music? Do you agree with him? Why or why not?

The Engaged Writer

1. Write a paper about a rock star you may have heard, trying to imagine what Bloom might say about him or her.
2. Do you agree with Bloom that "the meaningful inner life" of students "is with the music"?
3. Bloom takes a definite stand against the contemporary music scene. In the rest of the chapter, he discusses Michael Jackson and Mick Jagger, whom he calls "the hero and the model for countless young persons at universities." If you consider Bloom's views (especially in paragraph 1) overwritten or inaccurate, write a paper disagreeing with him. If you agree with Bloom's stand, write about why you do so.
4. In the *Magazine Index* or ProQuest, look up some articles about the argument concerning the effect of rock music. See if you can get at least one article on each side. Take a stand on this issue, and write a documented paper quoting from some of the sources you have found.

POLINGAYSI QOYAWAYMA

No Turning Back

Polingaysi Qoyawayma (Elizabeth Q. White) began life in a Hopi village, where she at first accepted its traditions and values. After she began to work for a missionary family, she was inspired to continue her education, but her family resisted having her sent away to an Indian boarding school. Finally, she prevailed and became a teacher to her people. After she retired, she became a prize-winning potter. She told her story in 1964 to Vada F. Carlson, an Arizona journalist; that is why the autobiography speaks of Polingaysi in the third person. The following section of *No Turning Back* occurs after she returns to the village from boarding school when her uncle chastises her as "no longer a true Hopi." She remembers her initiation ceremony when she became a member of the tribe and now begins to wonder who, indeed, she really is.

In the traditional Hopi pattern, children are advised, instructed, 1 scolded, and sometimes punished, by their maternal uncles. Polingaysi's relations with her mother's brothers had been pleasant, but after she became a member of the Frey household, her old uncle in Moenkopi village began showing disapproval of her. Cousins repeated small remarks he had made about her and she became increasingly aware of his annoyance.

One day he sent word for her to come visit him. She went, to 2 find him in a state of indignation. He began scolding at once.

"You proud and stubborn girl! Why are you straying from 3 the Hopi way of life? Don't you know it is not good for a Hopi to be proud? Haven't I told you a Hopi must not pretend to hold himself above his people? Why do you keep trying to be a white man? You are a Hopi. Go home. Marry in the Hopi way. Have children." His eyes were angry and his mouth contemptuous. "I have said you were Hopi, but you are no longer a true Hopi. You don't know the Hopi way. In a year or so, even if you do go back to Oraibi, you won't know anything. Leave these white people who are leading you away from your own beliefs. Go. Go now."

Tears streamed down Polingaysi's cheeks as she listened to the 4 man's bitter words. All her inner confusion, all her painful indecision, swelled in her breast until she could bear it no longer. She lashed back at him.

"I won't! I won't go back to the life of a pagan. Never, never 5 again. I've worked for this education you ridicule. At Riverside, I scrubbed miles of dirty floors while I was learning a little about reading and writing and arithmetic. After I learned to sew, I made dresses for others, bending over the sewing machine while the other girls slept, to earn money for my own dresses.

6   "I've worked hard for everything I have. It has not been easy for me to learn this new way of living. Do you think I'll go back to sleeping on the floor and eating out of a single pot? Do you think I want to have a household of children who are always hungry and in rags, as I was in my childhood? No! I don't care what you think of me. I don't care what my Hopi people think. Not any more. I'm going to keep on learning, no matter how much you despise me for it."

7   Trembling violently, she turned on her heel and left his house, amazed at her temerity. How could she have dared talk in those defiant terms to an uncle? It frightened her. She could see the chasm between her two worlds widening; his words had stung like the lashes of the Whipper Kachina on the day of her initiation into the Kachina cult.

8   She had expected those initiatory lashes. Only Hopi children initiated into the Powamua fraternity escape them. She had looked forward to them as an opening of the door to wisdom.

9   As she walked swiftly toward the Frey home on the hillside, smarting under the injustice of her uncle's reproaches, she recalled the day of her initiation.

10   Feeling important and excited, she had walked between her ceremonial "parents" to the kiva, her shoulder blanket clutched close to shield her body from the February chill. The arms of the ladder had seemed to reach out to her, and she had gone into them and down the rungs into the dim warmth of the kiva.

11   Other initiates sat on the plastered stone bench between their sponsors, feet drawn up, simulating young eagles in the nest. Before she joined them she saw the feathers dangling from a peg on the wall, and the beautiful little sand mosaic beneath them. It was only after she was seated that she saw the larger sandpainting on which she would later stand for whipping.

12   She began to be afraid. The other children also were fearful. Then an old man, naked except for a G-string, came down the ladder and began addressing the initiates. He spoke rapidly and in low tones. Although she listened intently, Polingaysi could not hear all of his words, but she realized that he was telling the ancient history of the Hopis and of their migrations from the beginning.

13   There was an air of expectancy on the part of the older people as the old man left the kiva, and suddenly there was a fearful din

at the kiva opening, a sound of running feet, a beating of yucca lashes against the standard.

Hearts racing, the candidates for initiation stared at the kiva 14 opening. Two Hu Kachinas, their bodies painted black with white spots, rushed down the ladder carrying armfuls of yucca lashes. They wore nothing except red moccasins, breech clout, mask, and foxskin ruff. The masks were black and bulging-eyed, with horns at each side, white spots on the cheeks, and a white turkey track in the center of each forehead.

Crow Mother, Ang-wu-sna-som-ta-qa, which is to say "Man 15 With Crow Wings Tied To," followed, wearing a woman's dress and ceremonial robe with moccasins, and carrying additional pale green yucca lashes for the whippers. Her mask had great black crow wings at each side.

At once a little boy was led forward by his sponsors, his naked 16 body trembling. Stepping into the large sandpainting, he raised one hand above his head and covered his genitals with the other. The lashes curled about his body, leaving welts, then his godfather pulled him aside and took the remainder of the whipping for him.

When her turn came, Polingaysi was grateful that she was a girl 17 and was allowed to wear her blanket dress. The whipping she received was not painful, but the emotional strain sent her to the bench weeping and weak. It seemed cruel to her that Crow Mother should urge the whippers to strike harder. However, when the whippers whipped each other at the conclusion of the rites, she felt better. Justice had been done.

The Powamua chief then dismissed the Kachinas with gifts of 18 breath feathers and cornmeal and began his lecture. The initiates were now at the threshold of knowledge, he told them. They would learn more secrets soon, but must not tell the younger, uninitiated children what had taken place. Telling, they were warned, would bring reprisals from the angry Kachinas.

Reaching the Freys' houseyard, Polingaysi looked down into 19 the narrow streets of the old village of Moenkopi, the rock houses huddled on the lower slopes of the sand-dune-bordered wash.

"That initiation!" she thought angrily. "What was it but a pagan 20 rite? I must forget it."

Not yet calm enough to talk with the Freys about her clash with 21 the old uncle, she went to her room. Turning toward the mirror, she surveyed her solemn reflection unapprovingly.

22   "Maybe I'm not a true Hopi. But what am I? Am I a true anything? Am I sincere? Do I really want to waste my time in trying
to bring the gospel to my stubborn, superstition-bound Hopi people? They will only despise me for it."

23   She began taking the pins from her long and heavy black
hair, intending to wash it. Suddenly she realized how automatic
the gesture had been, how Hopi. Wash the hair. Purify the life
stream.

Engaging the Text

1. The list of words for this selection tells the emotional story
    of Polingaysi's indignation (2), her uncle's contemptuous
    (3) anger, and her feelings of temerity (7) at her defiant (7)
    attitude. Look up these words if you need to in order to
    understand this woman's daring in breaking away from
    tradition.

2. Some of the vocabulary, mostly explained in the text, refers to
    the Hopi initiation rites that Polingaysi went through as a
    child. These are kiva (10), sandpainting (11), Kachinas (14), and
    Moenkopi (19).

3. Pick out some of the words and phrases Polingaysi uses that
    show how she feels about these incidents. For example, in
    paragraph 7 she describes the "chasm between her two
    worlds."

Engaging the Reader

1. In this essay, two incidents, several years apart, are discussed
    as if they were happening together. Is this confusing, or is it
    effective? Do you think the experiences are deliberately told
    that way?

2. Why is the conversation with Polingaysi's uncle so important
    to her?

3. What is her reply to him? Describe any other important con-
    versations in this autobiography.

4. How does the incident with her uncle make her think of her
    initiation into the Kachina cult?

5. Review the story's references to old traditions. Does Polin-
    gaysi's final action show that she is a "true Hopi"?

The Engaged Writer

1. Using some of the words and phrases you picked out in question 3 in "Engaging the Text," write a paper showing how Polingaysi feels about what is happening to her. Put quotation marks around the words you use from Polingaysi's account and introduce them with signal phrases.
2. Have you ever been given advice, meant for the best, by someone in authority—a parent, teacher, or other person you respect? However, you knew this advice was wrong for you and you decided to reject it. Write an account of that incident, giving your feelings about the problem as Polingaysi does.

ZLATA FILIPOVIĆ

Zlata's Diary: A Child's Life in Sarajevo

Zlata Filipović, thirteen in 1991, lived in Sarajevo during the worst of the shelling and destruction of that city, and kept a diary from September 1991 to October 1993. A cherished only child from a cultured middle-class family whose life had centered around school, music, friends, and skiing, Zlata lived without water or electricity during the war, saw her friends killed, her parents demoralized, and her home destroyed. Newspaper reporters who met her found that she had kept the diary she addressed as "Mimmy." Impressed with its clarity and Zlata's courage, they arranged publication of the diary in Croat by UNESCO. Now it has appeared throughout the world.

Wednesday, April 29, 1992

Dear Mimmy,

I'd write to you much more about the war if only I could. But I   1
simply don't want to remember all these horrible things. They make me sick. Please, don't be mad at me. I'll write something.

I love you,

Zlata

Saturday, May 2, 1992

Dear Mimmy,

2 Today was truly, absolutely the worst day ever in Sarajevo. The shooting started around noon. Mommy and I moved into the hall. Daddy was in his office, under our apartment, at the time. We told him on the intercom to run quickly to the downstairs lobby where we'd meet him. We brought Cicko [Zlata's canary] with us. The gunfire was getting worse, and we couldn't get over the wall to the Bobars', so we ran down to our own cellar.

3   The cellar is ugly, dark, smelly. Mommy, who's terrified of mice, had two fears to cope with. The three of us were in the same corner as the other day. We listened to the pounding shells, the shooting, the thundering noise overhead. We even heard planes. At one moment I realized that this awful cellar was the only place that could save our lives. Suddenly, it started to look almost warm and nice. It was the only way we could defend ourselves against all this terrible shooting. We heard glass shattering in our street. Horrible. I put my fingers in my ears to block out the terrible sounds. I was worried about Cicko. We had left him behind in the lobby. Would he catch cold there? Would something hit him? I was terribly hungry and thirsty. We had left our half-cooked lunch in the kitchen.

4   When the shooting died down a bit, Daddy ran over to our apartment and brought us back some sandwiches. He said he could smell something burning and that the phones weren't working. He brought our TV set down to the cellar. That's when we learned that the main post office (near us) was on fire and that they had kidnapped our President. At around 8:00 we went back up to our apartment. Almost every window in our street was broken. Ours were all right, thank God. I saw the post office in flames. A terrible sight. The fire-fighters battled with the raging fire. Daddy took a few photos of the post office being devoured by the flames. He said they wouldn't come out because I had been fiddling with something on the camera. I was sorry. The whole apartment smelled of the burning fire. God, and I used to pass by there every day. It had just been done up. It was huge and beautiful, and now it was being swallowed up by the flames. It was disappearing. That's what this neighborhood of mine looks

like, my Mimmy. I wonder what it's like in other parts of town? I heard on the radio that it was awful around the Eternal Flame. The place is knee-deep in glass. We're worried about Grandma and Granddad. They live there. Tomorrow, if we can go out, we'll see how they are. A terrible day. This has been the worst, most awful day in my eleven-year-old life. I hope it will be the only one. Mommy and Daddy are very edgy. I have to go to bed.

Ciao!

Zlata

Sunday, May 3, 1992

Dear Mimmy,

Daddy managed to run across the bridge over the Miljacka and get to Grandma and Granddad. He came running back, all upset, sweating with fear and sadness. They're all right, thank God. Tito Street looks awful. The heavy shelling has destroyed shop windows, cars, apartments, the fronts and roofs of buildings. Luckily, not too many people were hurt because they managed to take shelter. Neda (Mommy's girlfriend) rushed over to see how we were and to tell us that they were OK and hadn't had any damage. But it was terrible.   5

We talked through the window with Auntie Boda and Bojana just now. They were in the street yesterday when that heavy shooting broke out. They managed to get to Stela's cellar.   6

Zlata

Tuesday, May 5, 1992

Dear Mimmy,

The shooting seems to be dying down. I guess they've caused enough misery, although I don't know why. It has something to do with politics. I just hope the "kids" come to some agreement. Oh, if only they would, so we could live and breathe as human beings again. The things that have happened here these past few days are terrible. I want it to stop forever. PEACE! PEACE!   7

I didn't tell you, Mimmy, that we've rearranged things in the apartment. My room and Mommy and Daddy's are too   8 dangerous to be in. They face the hills, which is where they're shooting from. If only you knew how scared I am to go near the windows and into those rooms. So, we turned a safe corner of the sitting room into a "bedroom." We sleep on mattresses on the floor. It's strange and awful. But, it's safer that way. We've turned everything around for safety. We put Cicko in the kitchen. He's safe there, although once the shooting starts there's nowhere safe except the cellar. I suppose all this will stop and we'll all go back to our usual places.

Ciao!

Zlata

Thursday, May 7, 1992

Dear Mimmy,

9 I was almost positive the war would stop, but today . . . Today a shell fell on the park in front of my house, the park where I used to play and sit with my girlfriends. A lot of people were hurt. From what I hear Jaca, Jaca's mother, Selma, Nina, our neighbor Dado and who knows how many other people who happened to be there were wounded. Dado, Jaca and her mother have come home from the hospital, Selma lost a kidney but I don't know how she is, because she's still in the hospital. AND NINA IS DEAD. A piece of shrapnel lodged in her brain and she died. She was such a sweet, nice little girl. We went to kindergarten together, and we used to play together in the park. Is it possible I'll never see Nina again? Nina, an innocent eleven-year-old little girl—the victim of a stupid war. I feel sad. I cry and wonder why? She didn't do anything. A disgusting war has destroyed a young child's life. Nina, I'll always remember you as a wonderful little girl.

Love, Mimmy,

Zlata

Engaging the Text

1. The last entry in Zlata's published diary is "We haven't done anything. We're innocent. But helpless!" What do you think she means by this?

2. In the section chosen from her diary, Zlata uses simple, short words and sentences. But her account gives a picture of what war looks like from the inside. Pick out some words and phrases that make up that picture.

Engaging the Reader

1. Zlata originally started writing her diary after reading *The Diary of Anne Frank*. Essentially, she, like Anne Frank in similar stressful circumstances, needed a friend and a confidante. If you don't know Anne Frank's diary, look it up, and talk with your classmates or your writing group about its similarities with Zlata's diary.

2. On television and in the press, we have seen more vividly than ever before how current events impact on the ordinary person. In groups, recall and list some of these events and some of the ordinary citizen's reaction to them.

The Engaged Reader

1. Read Gail Godwin's "A Diarist on Diarists" and write the commentary you think Gail Godwin would have written on Zlata's Diary, had it been published when Godwin wrote her essay. Try to imitate Godwin's style, vocabulary, and sentence length.

2. In your library, find newspaper articles from the dates of Zlata's diary (you can find these using an electronic database or a newspaper index, such as that of the *New York Times* or *Washington Post*). From the information you find, reconstruct the events that made Zlata write as she did. You are, in effect, annotating her diary and its reporting of events on a personal level with the events as they were reported to the world by the press.

3. This child's-eye view of war can be contrasted with that of the "Most Decorated Hero" of Louise Erdrich's story in Part Two and the nostalgic view of war in Ed Malles' "Hallowed Ground" in Part Five. Write a paper on the theme of war, using these three views as starting points. Quote from them to support your own points, signalling what you are going to do ("according to . . .") and weaving these quotes into your own arguments. You may also use library sources, if your paper is to be a major one.

ZANE GREY
———

At Kaidab Trading Post

Zane Grey won worldwide recognition as America's most famous writer of Westerns. His descriptions of the Western scene are extraordinarily faithful—his stark landscapes and trading posts exist today. His son Loren feels that *The Vanishing American* was one of his father's finest novels. This story caused a lot of controversy on its publication in a magazine in 1922 because of Grey's stern portrayal of dishonest and profit-seeking missionaries who defrauded the Indians they were supposed to help. The Wetherills, friends of Grey, ran a famous trading post on the Navajo reservation where they spent their lives helping the Indians. The following selection, part of Chapter 4 of *The Vanishing American* (1922), tells of the arrival of a young schoolteacher at the trading post, welcomed by the Withers, who were modeled on Grey's friends John and Luisa Wetherill.

1 Close at hand Kaidab trading post showed striking aspects of life and activity. Marian looked and looked, with mounting delight and wonder.

2   First there were a number of the shaggy Indian ponies, unhaltered, standing with uplifted heads, and black rolling eyes askance on the mail-carrier's car. Several were without saddles, having a blanket tied on their backs; one was a cream color almost pink, with strange light eyes and wonderful long mane and tail; most of them were a reddish bay in color, and there was a fiery little black that took Marian's eye.

3   Huge bags of burlap containing wool were being packed into a wagon by Indian freighters. And Indians were lounging around, leaning against the stone wall of the trading post. The look of them somehow satisfied Marian. Raven black hair, impassive faces of bronze, eyes of night, lean and erect figures clad in velvet and corduroy, with glints of silver and bead ornament—these circumstances of appearance came somewhere near fitting Marian's rather sentimental anticipations.

4   Before the open front of one building, evidently a storehouse, other Indians were packing wool in the long sacks, a laborsome

task, to judge from their efforts to hold the sack erect and stomp down the wool. The whole interior of this open house appeared busy and littered with harness, rope, piles of white sacks, piles of wool and skins. The odor of sheep struck Marian rather disagreeably. The sun was hot and fell glaringly upon the red blankets. Flies buzzed everywhere. And at least a dozen lean, wild-looking, and inquisitive-eyed dogs sniffed around Marian. Not one of them wagged its tail. White men in shirt sleeves, with sweaty faces and hands begrimed, were working over a motorcar as dilapidated as the mail carrier's. Two Indian women, laden with bundles, came out of the open door of the trading post. The older woman was fat and pleasant-faced. She wore loose, flowing garments, gaudy in color, and silver necklaces, and upon her back she carried a large bundle or box. When she passed Marian caught a glimpse of a dark little baby face, peering out of a hole in that box. The younger female was probably a daughter, and she was not uncomely in appearance. Something poignant and bright haunted her smooth, dark face. She was slender. She had little feet encased in brown moccasins. She wore what Marian thought was velveteen, and her silver ornaments were studded with crude blue stones. She glanced shyly at Marian. Then an Indian came riding up to dismount near Marian. He was old. His lean face was a mass of wrinkles, and there was iron gray in his hair. He wore a thin cotton shirt and overalls—white apparel much the worse for wear. Behind his saddle hung a long bundle, a goatskin rolled with fur inside. This he untied and carried into the trading post. More Indians came riding in; one of the ponies began to rear and snort and kick; the dogs barked; whisks of warm and odorous wind stirred the dust; the smell of sheep wool grew stronger; low, guttural voices of Indians mingled with the sharper, higher notes of white men.

A sturdily built, keen-eyed man stalked out of the post, with a 5 hand on the Indian mail-carrier's shoulder. He wore a vest over a flannel shirt, but no coat or hat. His boots were rough and dusty.

"Take her bags in," he said to the Indian. 6

Then, at his near approach, Marian felt herself scanned by a 7 gaze at once piercing and kindly.

"Glad to welcome you, Miss Warner," he said. "Been expecting 8 you for two hours. I'm John Withers."

Marian offered her hand. "Expecting me?" she queried 9 curiously.

10   "News travels fast in this country," he replied, with a smile. "An Indian rode in two hours ago with the news you were coming."

11   "But my name?" asked Marian, still curious.

12   "Mrs. Withers told me that and what you looked like. She'll shore be glad to see you. Come. We'll go in."

13   Marian followed him into the yard beside the trading post, where somewhat in the background stood a low, squat, picturesque stone house with roof of red earth. Her curiosity had developed into wonder. She tingled a little at an implication that followed one of her conjectures. How could Mrs. Withers know what she looked like? Withers ushered her into a wonderful room that seemed to flash Indian color and design at her. Blankets on floor and couch, baskets on mantel and wall, and a strange-painted frieze of Indian figures, crude, elemental, striking—these lent the room its atmosphere. A bright fire blazed in the open stove fireplace. Books and comforts were not lacking. This room opened into a long dining room, with the same ornamental Indian effects. And from it ran a hallway remarkable for its length and the variety and color of its decorations.

14   Marian's quick eyes had only time for one look when a woman of slight stature and remarkable face entered.

15   "Welcome to Kaidab, Miss Warner," she said warmly, with extended hands. "We're happy to meet you. We hope you will stay long."

16   "Thank you, Mrs. Withers—you're very kind. I—I am very glad to get here," replied Marian, just a little confused and nervous.

17   "You've had a long, cold ride. And you're red with dust. Oh, I know that ride. I took it first twenty-five years ago on horseback."

18   "Yes, it was hard. And cold—I nearly froze. But, oh, it was wonderful!"

19   Withers laughed his pleasure at her words. "Why, that's no ride. You're just on the edge of real wild country. We're going to show you."

20   "John, put Miss Warner's bags in the second room. And send some hot water. After she's comfortable and rested we can talk."

21   Marian found the room quaint and strange as the others. It had a clean, earthy smell. The walls appeared to be of red cement, adobe, Marian supposed, and they were cold. While washing and changing her dusty clothes Marian pondered over her singular impressions of Mrs. Withers. She was no ordinary woman. For

some reason not apparent to Marian, her hostess had a strong personal regard for her. Marian had intuitively felt this. Besides, she must have been a woman used to welcoming strangers to this wild frontier. Marian sensed something of the power she had felt in women of high position, as they met their guests; only in the case of Mrs. Withers it was a simplicity of power, a strange, unconscious dignity, spiritual rather than material. But Marian lost no time in making herself comfortable or conjecturing about Mrs. Withers. She felt drawn to this woman. She divined news, strange portents, unknown possibilities, of which hurried her back to the living room. Mrs. Withers was there waiting for her.

"How sweet and fair you are!" exclaimed Mrs. Withers, with an   22
admiring glance at Marian's face. "We don't see your kind out here. The desert is hard on blondes."

"So I imagine," replied Marian. "I'll not long remain 'Benow—   23
di cleash.' . . . Is that pronounced correctly?"

Mrs. Withers laughed. "Well, I understood you. But you must   24
say it this way . . . 'Benow di cleash!'"

Her voice had some strange, low, liquid quality utterly new to   25
Marian.

"Mrs. Withers, you know where I got that name," asserted   26
Marian.

"Yes, I'm happy to tell you I do," she rejoined earnestly.   27

Marian slowly answered to the instinct of the moment. Her   28
hands went out to meet those offered by Mrs. Withers, and she gazed down into the strange, strong face, with its shadows of sorrow and thought, its eyes of penetrating and mystic power.

"Let us sit down," continued Mrs. Withers, leading the way to   29
the couch. "We'll have to talk our secrets at odd moments. Somebody is always bobbing in. . . . First, I meant to tell you two things—that I know will make us friends."

"I hope so—believe so," returned Marian, trying to hold her calm.   30

"Listen. All my life I've been among the Indians," said Mrs.   31
Withers in her low voice. "I loved Indians when I was a child. I've been here in this wild country for many years. It takes years of kindness and study to understand the Indian. . . . These Indians have come to care for me. They have given me a name. They believe me—trust me. They call on me to settle disputes, to divide property left by some dead Indian, to tell their troubles. I have learned their dreams, longings, their religion, their prayers and

legends and poetry, their medicine, the meaning of their dances. And the more I learn of them the more I love and respect them. Indians are not what they appear to most white people. They are children of nature. They have noble hearts and beautiful minds. They have criminals among them, but much less proportion than have the white race. The song of Hiawatha is true—true for all Indians. They live in a mystic world of enchantment peopled by spirits, voices, music, whisperings of God, eternal and everlasting immortality. They are as simple as little children. They personify everything. With them all is symbolic."

32   Mrs. Withers paused a moment, her eloquent eyes riveted upon Marian.

33   "For a good many years this remote part of the Indian country was far out of the way of white men. Thus the demoralization and degradation of the Indian were retarded, so far as this particular tribe is concerned. This Nopah tribe is the proudest, most intelligent, most numerous, and the wealthiest tribe left in the United States. So-called civilization has not yet reached Kaidab. But it is coming. I feel the next few years will go hard with the Indian—perhaps decide his fate."

34   "Oh—there seems no hope!" murmured Marian.

35   "There indeed seems none, if you look at it intelligently and mercilessly. But I look at this question as the Indian looks at everything. He begins his prayer, 'Let all be well with me'—and he ends it, 'Now all is well with me.' He feels—he trusts. There really is a God. If there were not I would be an infidel. Life on the desert magnifies all. . . . I want you to let me help you to understand the Indian. . . . For the sake of your happiness!"

Engaging the Reader

1. Grey begins the selection by naming two categories, life and activity, followed by their development in three descriptive paragraphs. List the details he uses for development of each main point.

2. In paragraph 4, many descriptive adjectives set the scene Marian encounters at the trading post and develop the point Grey is making. These are dilapidated, uncomely, poignant, velveteen, and guttural. Look them up if you are not clear about their meanings.

3. Other words in the selection support the next point Grey develops—Marian's feelings: conjectures (13), intuitively (21), and portents (21). Use these in sentences of your own.
4. Grey uses series of short, "kernel" sentences (notice the group beginning with "She" in the long fourth paragraph). What effect do these sentences give?
5. Grey uses many colorful descriptions to set his scenes. He also uses many abstract words that may sound romantic and idealistic. List some of these.

Engaging the Reader

1. The novel tells the story of the difficult romance—the dilemma of different cultures—between Marian and Nophaie, a Navajo. What hints do you receive of that story in the excerpt here?
2. Judging by the hints given, what do you think happens in the rest of the book? Use your imagination!

The Engaged Writer

1. In your library, look for Longfellow's poem "Hiawatha," mentioned in paragraph 31. Write a short description of what it is and what Mrs. Withers means when she refers to it.
2. Where would you find information about the career of Zane Grey and about past and present Western trading posts? Write a short paper on what you find out about these subjects.
3. Describe in a few paragraphs, using the way Grey describes the trading post, the Withers, and the Indians as a model, a group of people you have observed: an ethnic group, a family of immigrants, residents on an Indian reservation, the inhabitants of a small village in another country, or a military outfit.
4. If you have moved from one country to another, or if you are a recent immigrant in the United States, write your version of Marian's "culture shock."
5. How would you explain the work customs in your office or in your part of the country to someone who came from another area?

CARL SANDBURG

Chicago

Carl Sandburg, the very popular poet, used common, ordinary speech in his poems, calling them "simple poems for simple people." His career was varied: fireman, roving reporter, party organizer, newspaper editor, and traveling poet. He became famous with a many-volumed life of Abraham Lincoln. His poems talk about workers, outcasts, and like Walt Whitman, the American people in both urban and rural culture. The evocative titles of the works that made him famous were *Chicago Poems* (1914), *Cornhuskers* (1918), *Smoke and Steel* (1920), and *Slabs of the Sunburnt West* (1922). From these you can see his love for ordinary, exciting, raw American life. The poem "Chicago" first appeared in the magazine *Poetry* in 1914.

    Hog Butcher for the World,
    Tool Maker, Stacker of Wheat,
    Player with Railroads and the Nation's Freight Handler;
    Stormy, husky, brawling,
5   City of the Big Shoulders:

They tell me you are wicked and I believe them, for I have seen
    your painted women under the gas lamps luring the farm
    boys.
And they tell me you are crooked and I answer: Yes, it is true I
    have seen the gunman kill and go free to kill again.
And they tell me you are brutal and my reply is: On the faces of
    women and children I have seen the marks of wanton
    hunger.
And having answered so I turn once more to those who sneer at
    this my city, and I give them back the sneer and say to them:
10 Come and show me another city with lifted head singing so
    proud to be alive and coarse and strong and cunning.
Flinging magnetic curses amid the toil of piling job on job, here
    is a tall bold slugger set vivid against the little soft cities;
Fierce as a dog with tongue lapping for action, cunning as a
    savage pitted against the wilderness,

Bareheaded,
Shoveling,
Wrecking, 15
Planning,
Building, breaking, rebuilding,
Under the smoke, dust all over his mouth, laughing with white
teeth,
Under the terrible burden of destiny laughing as a young man laughs,
Laughing even as an ignorant fighter laughs who has never lost 20
a battle,
Bragging and laughing that under his wrist is the pulse, and
under his ribs the heart of the people,
  Laughing!
Laughing the stormy, husky, brawling laughter of Youth, half-
naked, sweating, proud to be Hog Butcher, Tool Maker,
Stacker of Wheat, Player with Railroads and Freight Handler
to the Nation.

Engaging the Text

1. Sandburg rejected traditional rhyming, rhythmic verse and
   wrote in utterly free patterns. He can often be said to have
   composed prose paragraphs. Indicate in the poem where these
   "paragraphs" begin and end.
2. Why do you think Sandburg capitalizes certain words in his
   lines?
3. Sandburg uses poetic devices:

   — personification—giving human characteristics to a nonhuman city, Chicago
   — simile—comparing two dissimilar things using "like" or
   "as" ("fierce as a dog," line 12)
   — repetition—especially of participles (such as "brawling,"
   line 4)

   Find some other examples of these in the poem.

Engaging the Reader

1. List some of the words Sandburg uses to describe his city.
2. What are some of the criticisms other people make about
   Chicago? Does he agree? How does he respond to these critics?

The Engaged Writer

1. List some characteristics of your city, using some of the comparisons and personification Sandburg uses.
2. Describe your city or home town, in prose or verse, using the list you made to answer question 1 in this section.

PART
5

Controversies

More than any other kind of writing, argumentative writing demonstrates the cooperation, even the complicity, between reader and writer. It raises a real question about an issue on which there is much disagreement or which might be unpopular or painful to hear.

In "Controversies" four controversial topics are explored in three or four diverse ways. These topics are: poverty, its results and possible solutions; the preservation of the environment; the civil rights movement; and the mercy killing dilemma. These articles show various sides of these topics.

In writing on a controversial topic, the writer investigates the facts, states them carefully, and tries to write them in such a way that the reader can agree with or at the very least accept them as reasonable. This kind of writing may start with a thesis statement. You can also build up to that thesis, however, leading the reader along paragraph by paragraph with logic and reason until most readers would hate to disagree.

You can start such a persuasive paper by setting up a point of view different from your own, or from the attitude to be expressed in your essay, and work from there, having defused the early argument. For example, Roger Rosenblatt ("The Quality of Mercy Killing") starts with the facts of Rosswell Gilbert's killing of his wife and the sentence he received for that crime. He then goes on to discuss the circumstances and ends with compassion for Gilbert and examination of a serious issue: mercy killing.

Another method is to start with a very broad question, then progressively zero in to one of interest to the reader. Grace Cangialosi describes her work with the homeless, while Sara Rimer interviews mothers in a welfare hotel. Michael Satchell describes a way to help the poor and homeless with surplus food. When you read their articles, you have a pretty good idea which side of a controversy they are on.

The question of the preservation of our environment calls forth warnings from science (Carl Sagan, "The Warming of the World") and about the dangers of exploitation (Paul Quinnett, "Enough of Roads"). Close to home is Melody Ermachild Chavis's story about "Street Trees" and the efforts to reclaim our cities. Then our national heritage of parks and battlefields is the subject of Ed Malles' "Hallowed Ground."

In a landmark speech in 1895, Booker T. Washington ("Cast Down Your Bucket Where You Are") discusses the place of African Americans in American political, social, and economic life. In "Response to Mr. Washington" W. E. B. Du Bois violently disagrees with him. Following these historic arguments, Martin Luther King's "I Have a Dream" speech has become a part of the culture of all Americans. Today, the scholar Henry Louis Gates, Jr. remembers his heritage in "The Last Mill Picnic."

In the end, the reader gets a chance to respond to published views: letters from the readers of the Rosenblatt article "The Quality of Mercy Killing" air their opinions. Students who reacted to the article in the first edition of this book also show how the public, the reader, gets involved in these controversies.

GRACE CANGIALOSI

Wild Willie

Grace Cangialosi is an Episcopal priest in a rural Virginia congregation. While studying for the ministry, she worked in Washington D.C. for the ecumenical Church of The Saviour as a volunteer. After hearing about the plight of the homeless and the effort of the church to help them, Cangialosi volunteered to drive for one night a week as part of a team of two to scout the city streets and distribute blankets and hot coffee to homeless people in parks and on streets. She says, "Just so casually do we make momentous decisions. Just so easily do we take one step that will forever alter our perceptions of the world." By taking this step, she moves from clock time into another kind of time, spiritual time, that will influence her life. Wild Willie, along with other homeless people and her fellow volunteer, Paul, will forcefully affect her life. Her experiences on the DC streets appear in *A Kairos Winter* (1994), from which this sketch comes.

The First Night

The evening has arrived for my first trip out with Paul. I have   1
worn jeans and a heavy jacket and a wool cap against the cold, but inside I am shivering. After the Jubilee Church service at the Potter's House Paul and I go over to Christ House to make coffee and gather some blankets. It isn't terribly cold tonight, but there will be some, Paul says, who will need blankets. So we fill the back of the car with blankets and load in the cups and a jug of very strong, very sweet, coffee. Paul explains that the sugar will give a little extra energy.

Wild Willie

There are many men out here whose faces I will always remem-   2
ber, men with whom I held conversations, men for whom I look as we approach our various stops. But there is one man who, above all others, came to epitomize life on the streets for me, although he never spoke a word to me. Perhaps it is because I know the end of his story. Perhaps it is because he evoked in me a fear that, given enough years of inhuman treatment, a person can finally begin to seem, to act, inhuman.

"Wild Willie," Paul called him—others referred to him as "The   3
Wolfman." He occupied a roaring heat grate in a small triangular park at Virginia and E, N.W. The roar of the steam generators beneath him had long since robbed him of his hearing, so it was only by gesture and props that we could communicate our mission—"Do you want coffee? A blanket?" He took the coffee and placed it with several other partially filled cups around the grate's cement edging. He didn't want a blanket. Paul knew he wouldn't want a blanket, said he never used one. I was disbelieving; he wore a green plaid polyester sport jacket. But then, considering the clouds of steam billowing up around him, creating a bizarre, hellish atmosphere, I realized that he was probably warm enough.

Paul said he had been out here longer than anyone. I was stunned by his vacant stare as I handed him the coffee. What happened to destroy the life in those pale eyes, that face framed with its unkempt beard and wild mane of grey hair?

4   We saw Willie most nights as we made our rounds, always on the same grate. One night there was another man with him, but most of the time he was alone, staring into the darkness. A couple of times he was not there, and I worried. Paul would promise to ask about him. When I awakened at night to the glow of falling snow, Willie was the first person I thought about. Questions would flood my mind: Does he have something to put over him to keep the snow off? Does he even waken? Does it matter that he is wet? When the *Washington Post* carried a story about yet another homeless person found frozen to death on the street, I read carefully to see if it was Willie—or any of the other men I now knew at sight.

5   In October, 1988, Willie got his story in the *Post*. He was found dead of a heart attack on the grate where he had spent ten years. The headline read,

"A Life and Death in Anonymity"

and then underneath,

"For 10 Years, Man Occupied Grate with 'Dignity to Himself.'"

6   And there, at the top of the article, was a picture of Willie, reclining on one elbow, wearing a jacket and pants, hair wild around his head. I wept then, and I weep now, as I take the picture from my desk and look at it again. It is part of the small gallery of pictures in my office—pictures of those who have irrevocably informed and shaped my life. Willie never knew me; he never spoke to me; but he has become a part of me.

Engaging the Text

1. Check a dictionary for the meanings of the words *kairos* and *chronos* as applied to time. Then see if those definitions explain why the title of the book is *A Kairos Winter*.
2. Notice that the narration is told by the author in the first person ("I"), and that the verbs are in present tense: "I am shivering" (1). What effect does this have on the reader?

Engaging the Reader

1. In your groups, talk about some experience you had that changed your life. As Cangialosi does, concentrate on the experience, not on yourself. Notice that we know little about her from this selection.

The Engaged Reader

1. Look through the following two articles on how other groups attempt to stem the effects of poverty and privation: the food banks and the self-help groups. Can you find other examples of volunteer effort that has made a difference, in combatting poverty, the spoiling of the environment, disease, ignorance, or any of the other ills that plague humanity? Choose one of them to write a paper about.

2. Write a sketch of a vivid, striking, unusual person that you have seen only a few times and in some special circumstances. This person is not someone you know well, but a person who has made such an impression on you (like Wild Willie) that you will never forget.

MICHAEL SATCHELL

How People Survive on Leftovers

Feeding and sheltering the homeless has been a recent area of controversy, especially in big cities. The following article from *Parade* magazine (1985) discusses some of the ways activist groups try to help solve the problem (also disclosed in Sara Rimer's article, "At a Welfare Hotel, Mothers Find Support in Weekly Talks"). Billions of dollars worth of food are wasted or spoiled. Now some of it is recovered by volunteer workers to feed people.

At 3 A.M. on a wet, bone-chilling night, Carol Fennelly is grubbing around in a garbage dumpster at the Maryland Wholesale Produce Market, south of Baltimore. Bundled against the cold, she quickly fills four large cardboard boxes with green peppers, then moves to the loading dock. A few words with a merchant yield three cases of blemished tomatoes and some bananas too ripe to make it to a supermarket shelf.

2   By 4 A.M., Fennelly and two coworkers have enough to fill their van—15 cases each of broccoli and pears, 12 of tomatoes, four each of peppers and bananas and a couple of boxes of grapes.

3   By 10 that morning, the produce has been cleaned and sorted by Fennelly and fellow members of a religious activist group called the Community for Creative Non-Violence. Some 150 needy people are lined up outside its free food pantry in Washington, D.C., soon to receive the recovered produce, along with donated day-old bread, packets of chicken giblets and U.S. government cornmeal. Later, street people may drop in for a cup of coffee and doughnuts to tide them over. Still more produce—salvaged from small truck farms, market loading docks and supermarket dumpsters—will supply an evening meal. Nearly 1000 men and women are fed here each day.

4   In the war against hunger, members of small groups such as this one are shock troops on the front lines of a growing national movement to reclaim food for the poor that otherwise would be thrown away.

5   About a fifth of the food produced in the U.S. is wasted, a federal study revealed. Much is lost or spoiled during storage, transportation and processing, still more during meal preparation and as plate waste. Little is recoverable.

6   More than $6 billion worth of food at the wholesale and retail level is wasted—or used to be. Recently, the food banks have begun recovering some of this: surplus items, mislabeled goods, food whose shelf life has expired, and marred but edible items. Situated in population centers and equipped with warehouses, freezers and coolers, the food banks ask large food companies for donations, which they then distribute to soup kitchens, emergency feeding programs and food pantries, as well as to various social welfare agencies.

7   By asking the agencies to contribute from 5 cents to 12 cents a pound for such goods, the food banks are largely self-supporting. The agencies, which often purchase food at wholesale or retail prices, in turn have a cheap, reliable supply of consumables. And the companies making the food donations are eligible for a tax write-off on the items.

"It's a tremendous idea, and everyone benefits," says Bill 8
Ewing, director of marketing for Second Harvest, a network of 74
food banks. Begun as a small operation in Phoenix in 1967, Second
Harvest has expanded nationwide since 1977. Last year, the organization distributed 85 million pounds of food across the U.S.

While food banks are geared to function efficiently by gather- 9
ing, storing and distributing in large quantities, small neighbor-
hood-based programs also are a vital link in the food chain. It takes
little more than desire and hard work to have a significant impact.

In November 1982, Celeste McKinley of Las Vegas went to a 10
garbage dumpster behind a supermarket, seeking waste produce
to feed her pet cockatoo. "I couldn't believe what they were throwing away," she recalls. "Most of the food was still attractive and
edible but no longer shelf-perfect. It was a terrible waste."

McKinley began soliciting surplus from supermarkets in the 11
city. Today, she operates Gleaners, Inc., a free food pantry fur-
nishing groceries to more than 15,000 needy families a month.

In New York, an organization called City Harvest operates a dif- 12
ferent type of salvage program, providing the physical link
between food supplies and the agencies that need them. Six people, one office, a telephone and two vans net 2 million pounds of
surplus food a year from a network of restaurants, bakeries, food
suppliers and other sources.

"We have no warehouse—don't need one," says Helen Palit, the 13
founder of City Harvest. "The whole thing is done by telephone.
Food suppliers have always wanted to give away their surplus,
but they never knew where to send it or who would pick it up."

Manhattan is an especially rich resource. On any day, Palit may 14
get donations of 100 pounds of pâté and 20 wheels of Brie cheese
from a gourmet supplier, or thousands of pounds of lamb from a
wholesaler who overbought, or surplus meals from expensive
restaurants where the tab for one might run $100 or more. Food
banks in other cities have similar luck.

Unfortunately, the salvage operations still claim only a fraction of 15
the food being thrown away. Many possible donors remain
untapped, while others are reluctant to contribute their surplus. Fast-
food chains, for example, routinely toss out any items that sit much
longer than 10 minutes under a heat lamp. The chains have resisted
suggestions to freeze these foods and donate them to the hungry.

16   Though it is seen as a holding action to help just a few of the 35.3 million Americans living below the poverty level, the foodbank movement is growing. As Celeste McKinley says, "We help feed people, and it doesn't cost the taxpayers one cent."

Engaging the Text

1. Study the definitions of the following words and use them in sentences of your own: bone-chilling (1), blemished (1), activist (3), salvaged (3), salvage (12), and reluctant (15).
2. The article starts with a dramatic incident—a woman grubbing through a garbage dumpster. Find some other examples in *The Engaging Reader* of startling or dramatic beginnings.
3. The article quotes workers and directors of various operations in big cities. Notice how the quotations are handled: as part of Satchell's sentences, smoothly integrated with a signal phrase:

   — "We have no warehouse—don't need one," *says Helen Palit, the founder of City Harvest.*
   — *As Celeste McKinley says,* "We help feed people, and it doesn't cost the taxpayers one cent."

Engaging the Reader

1. What motivates Carol Fennelly and other volunteers to grub through dumpsters?
2. What are the two methods used to recover surplus food?
3. What are some of the sources for salvageable food?
4. What other sources remain untapped?

The Engaged Writer

1. Look through your local telephone directory to see if your community has a group that salvages food from chains and markets for the needy. Call them to get addresses and other information on their work. Write a report for your classmates.
2. Write a letter to the president of a large fast-food chain, such as the one mentioned in paragraph 15 of the article. Urge the company to donate leftover food to an activist group. Use arguments and facts drawn from this article. See "Writing a Letter to the Editor" for some suggestions on writing your letter.

3. What are some of the other issues brought up by, but not discussed in, the article that relate to the homeless and their needs? Should, for example, the homeless be lodged in hotels (Rimer, "At a Welfare Hotel") while housing stands vacant?
4. From your reading of the pieces by Rimer ("At a Welfare Hotel") and Satchell, write an essay comparing the methods of dealing with the depressed underclass.
5. Can you find other methods, here or elsewhere, of coping with this problem, aside from Rimer's and Satchell's suggestions?

SARA RIMER

At a Welfare Hotel, Mothers Find Support in Weekly Talks

Discussion of "welfare mothers" is inevitably controversial. This 1986 article reveals the concerns of women residents in the Martinique Hotel in New York City. The Martinique, a welfare hotel, shelters 400 homeless families, but within it shine glimmers of real community, especially the Coffee Hour.

"I'm getting ready to walk away and leave them all here—the 1 baby, too," the mother of four said in an agitated voice. "I can't take it. I tell you, I'm getting ready to crack some heads."

"You know what you do when you feel that way?" another 2 mother said. "You talk to God."

"You get a babysitter," said another mother. "Then you go and 3 find someone to talk to."

This was not just any group of women discussing the pressures 4 of motherhood. These women knew the mother of four was deadly serious because all of them had felt just as desperate at some point.

This was another weekly meeting of a group of mothers who 5 are struggling to raise their children at the Martinique Hotel, a welfare hotel at Broadway and 32d Street that is crowded with 400 homeless families.

6   The meeting of the group, formed two years ago by the Hudson Guild, a 90-year-old Manhattan settlement house, is known as Coffee Hour. It has become an oasis of talk and understanding in a place where the first lesson a mother learns is to trust no one and where each week brings crises and continued stress—everything from sudden loss of food stamps to the inability to find an apartment within the welfare rent allotment. The women have become the closest thing to a community inside the Martinique.

7   "I met all my friends at Coffee Hour," said Azalee Green, the mother of five. "Coffee Hour is like a family."

8   Like many of the other women, Gloria Magriz said she had spent most of her first two months at the Martinique in her room with her three children, going out only to do errands.

9   "I was scared," Miss Magriz, 22 years old, said. "You have no friends when you come here. You can't trust people."

10 .   Coffee Hour, open to all women at the Martinique, helped bring her out of her room. "I listened to the other women," she said. "Their problems sounded bigger than mine. They had kids taken away from them. Or their husbands beat them, or they didn't have enough food so their kids went hungry."

11   Sometimes as many as 20 women come to Coffee Hour, sometimes only six or seven. Some bring their babies. Lately, they have been meeting huddled in their winter coats in the hotel's cold ballroom, warming themselves with coffee and cookies provided by the Hudson Guild. They keep talking despite constant interruptions—children running through the room, announcements that the ballroom is needed for the free lunch program.

"Such Survivors"

12 The group discussions are led by Evelyn Vega, a Hudson Guild social worker who offers counseling and referral services to families at the hotel. Each week, the women discuss a different topic from a list they have submitted. Suggestions include:

"How to help each other."
"How to understand my son's problems at school and home."
"How to get an apartment for my kids."
"How to love our family."

"These women are such survivors," Miss Vega said. "They love 13 their children so much."

The women talk in sad, angry voices of the other mothers whom 14 they watch giving up, escaping in drugs or simply leaving their children to fend for themselves. Last summer one mother died of a drug overdose. The women raised money to buy suits for her sons, 12 and 14 years old, to wear to her funeral.

Last month, an 18-year-old mother of three left her children, 15 whose ages range from 3 months to 3 years. Another member of the group, Pat Stanley, is taking care of them in hopes their mother will return. Miss Stanley has three rooms for her own 11 children.

"I sympathize with her," Miss Stanley said. "I know what it is 16 to be depressed. One time I got so depressed I didn't leave my apartment for 10 days."

Stigma of Hotel Life

At one meeting, a 19-year-old pregnant mother of two broke 17 down. She said she felt too overwhelmed to accomplish the smallest task, like cleaning the rugs in her room. After the meeting, the other women cleaned her rugs.

One subject that comes up repeatedly is the stigma that comes 18 with living in a welfare hotel. It is particularly hard on children, who are taunted for being "hotel kids." At a recent meeting, Miss Stanley said her 11-year-old son, who prides himself on being tough, had come home from school close to tears.

"His teacher made a remark about him being at the Mar- 19 tinique," she said. "She said, 'I heard about the robbing and mugging that goes on there.'"

Some of the Coffee Hour mothers have become role models for 20 the others. One of them is Miss Green—"the mother of the Martinique," as some call her—whose efforts to transform her hotel room into a home are discussed in admiring tones.

A Makeshift Kitchen

The rooms at the Martinique don't come with cooking facilities, 21 only small refrigerators. Dishes are washed in bathroom sinks. But Miss Green managed to convert her closet into a makeshift kitchen, with a hotplate and two nightstands pushed together for a counter.

22   "She's got her room so nice," said another Coffee Hour mother, Shirley Dingle. "She says, 'Why not fix it up? Who knows how long we're going to be here?'"

23   Inspired by her friend, Miss Dingle, 35, decorated the walls of her room with framed color photographs of her four children. With a string and a yellow curtain, she improvised a room divider for privacy.

24   Like the other families at the hotel, the mothers in the group have come to the Martinique through a variety of circumstances—burned out of their apartments, evicted, or forced to leave buildings that have been abandoned. Still others had to leave the overcrowded apartments of relatives with whom they were living.

"Give Each Other Strength"

25   When new families arrive, the women from Coffee Hour offer comfort and advice. "This is a neighborhood," Miss Green tells them. "There are good streets and bad streets, weak families and good families."

26   At a recent meeting, there was one newcomer, a woman with eight children, who said she had been evicted the week before from her apartment in Brooklyn. The other women explained Coffee Hour to her.

27   "It's a place where us ladies can get together and talk about our problems," Miss Dingle said.

28   "We give each other strength," Miss Stanley said.

29   "I'll be riding in the elevator and people say, 'You gotta be careful in here,'" the new woman told them. "I don't trust anyone. I won't loan anything to anyone—not even a cigarette."

30   The other women said they had felt that way, too. "But you got to remember the times when there are five days before your check comes," one said, "and you're digging through your ashtrays, looking for a cigarette. You can't make it alone in here."

Engaging the Text

1.   What is the origin and first meaning of the word *stigma* (18)? Can you see how it arrived at its present meaning from its earlier one?

2.   What do these technical terms mean: *settlement house* (6) and *referral services* (12)?

3. Substitute another word for the underlined one in this sentence from paragraph 23: "With a string and a yellow curtain, she improvised a room divider for privacy."
4. The selection is written mostly in dialogue. Does it tell the story more effectively than description? Explain your answer.
5. The selection begins with a startling statement by one of the women, an excellent way to involve the reader in a story. Find a few more examples of exciting or startling first sentences like this from other selections in *The Engaging Reader* or from articles in your daily newspaper and bring them to class to share with your classmates.

Engaging the Reader

1. Why are the women living at the Martinique? What are some of their feelings about living there?
2. What is the Coffee Hour and how did it get started?
3. What benefits does it bring to the women? How do their lives change through joining this group?
4. What hope is there for these women?

The Engaged Writer

1. Why were the women afraid to leave their rooms, often staying there for days or even weeks? Explain.
2. If you belong to a group like the "Coffee Hour"—a mutual-help group of any kind—write down a group conversation and then arrange it into an essay modeled on Rimer's. You might want to use a tape recorder—with the permission of your group—to record the conversation. Then edit the conversation later.

CARL SAGAN

The Warming of the World

Carl Sagan must have been the most popular scientist of the 1980s. His book and television series, *Cosmos* (1980), enjoyed a huge audience. In recent years, he was outspokenly critical of the arms race and the threat of nuclear destruction. In this 1985 newspaper essay, Sagan sees the need for attention to the problem of the earth's warming. We burn wood, coal, and oil, so the climate is changing and the oceans rising. How will this affect us?

1   When humans first evolved—in the savannahs of East Africa a few million years ago—our numbers were few and our powers feeble. We knew almost nothing about controlling our environment—even clothing had yet to be invented. We were creatures of the climate, utterly dependent upon it.

2   A few degrees hotter or colder on average, and our ancestors were in trouble. The toll taken much later by the ice ages, in which average land temperatures dropped some 8°C (centigrade, or Celsius), must have been horrific. And yet, it is exactly such climatic change that pushed our ancestors to develop tools and technology, science and civilization. Certainly, skills in hunting, skinning, tanning, building shelters and refurbishing caves must owe much to the terrors of the deep ice age.

3   Today, we live in a balmy epoch, 10,000 years after the last major glaciation. In this climatic spring, our species has flourished; we now cover the entire planet and are altering the very appearance of our world. Lately—within the last century or so—humans have acquired, in more ways than one, the ability to make major changes in that climate upon which we are so dependent. The Nuclear Winter findings are one dramatic indication that we can change the climate—in this case, in the spasm of nuclear war. But I wish here to describe a different kind of climatic danger, this one slower, more subtle and arising from intentions that are wholly benign.

4   **A delicate balance of invisible gases.** It is warm down here on Earth because the Sun shines. If the Sun were somehow turned off, the Earth would rapidly cool. The oceans would freeze, eventually the atmosphere itself would condense out and our planet would be covered everywhere by snowbanks of solid oxygen and nitrogen 10 meters (about 30 feet) high. Only the tiny trickle of heat from the Earth's interior and the faint starlight would save our world from a temperature of absolute zero.

5   We know how bright the Sun is; we know how far from it we are; and we know what fraction of the sunlight reaching the Earth

is reflected back to space (about 30 percent). So we can calculate—with a simple mathematical equation—what the average temperature of the Earth should be. But when we do the calculation, we find that the Earth's temperature should be about 20°C below the freezing point of water, in stark contradiction to our everyday experience. What have we done wrong?

As in many such cases in science, what we've done wrong is to 6 forget something—in this case, the atmosphere. Every object in the universe radiates some kind of light to space; the colder the object, the longer the wavelength of radiation it emits. The Earth—much colder than the Sun—radiates to space mainly in the infrared part of the spectrum, not the visible. Were the Sun turned off, the Earth would soon be indetectable in ordinary visible light, though it would be brilliantly illuminated in infrared light.

When sunlight strikes the Earth, part is reflected back into the 7 sky; much of the rest is absorbed by the ground and heats it—the darker the ground, the greater the heating. The ground radiates back upward in the infrared. Thus, for an airless Earth, the temperature would be set solely by a balance between the incoming sunlight absorbed by the surface and the infrared radiation that the surface emits back to space.

When you put air on a planet, the situation changes. The Earth's 8 atmosphere is, generally, still transparent to visible light. That's why we can see each other when we talk, glimpse distant mountains and view the stars.

But in the infrared, all that is different. While the oxygen and 9 nitrogen in the air are transparent in both the infrared and the visible, minor constituents such as water vapor (H_2O) and carbon dioxide (CO_2) tend to be much more opaque in the infrared. It would be useless for us to have eyes that could see at a wavelength, say, of 15 microns in the infrared, because the air is murky black there.

Accordingly, if you add air to a world, you heat it: The surface 10 now has difficulty when it tries to radiate back to space in the infrared. The atmosphere tends to absorb the infrared radiation, keeping heat near the surface and providing an infrared blanket for the world. There is very little CO_2 in the Earth's atmosphere—only 0.03 percent. But that small amount is enough to make the Earth's atmosphere opaque in important regions of the infrared spectrum. CO_2 and H_2O are the reason the global temperature is not well below freezing. We owe our comfort—indeed, our very existence—to the fact that these gases are present and are much more transparent in the visible than in the infrared. Our lives depend on a delicate balance of invisible gases. Too much blanket, or too little, and we're in trouble.

11　**The greenhouse effect—what it is and isn't.** This property of many gases to absorb strongly in the infrared but not in the visible, and thereby to heat their surroundings, is called the "greenhouse effect." A florist's greenhouse keeps its planty inhabitants warm. The phrase "greenhouse effect" is widely used and has an instructive ring to it, reminding us that we live in a planetary-scale greenhouse and recalling the admonition about living in glass houses and throwing stones. But, in fact, florists' greenhouses do not keep warm by the greenhouse effect: they work mainly by inhibiting the movement of air inside, another matter altogether.

12　　We need look only as far as the nearest planet to see an example of an atmospheric greenhouse effect gone wild. Venus has in its atmosphere an enormous quantity of carbon dioxide (roughly as much as is buried as carbonates in all the rocks of the Earth's crust). There is an atmosphere of CO_2 on Venus 90 times thicker than the atmosphere of the Earth and containing some 200,000 times more CO_2 than in our air. With water vapor and other minor atmospheric constituents, this is enough to make a greenhouse effect that keeps the surface of Venus around 470°C (900°F)—enough to melt tin or lead.

13　　When humans burn wood or "fossil fuels" (coal, oil, natural gas, etc.), they put carbon dioxide into the air. One carbon atom (C) combines with a molecule of oxygen (O_2) to produce CO_2. The development of agriculture, the conversion of dense forest to comparatively sparsely vegetated farms, has moved carbon atoms from plants on the ground to carbon dioxide in the air. About half of this new CO_2 is removed by plants or by the layering down of carbonates in the oceans. On human time-scales, these changes are irreversible: Once the CO_2 is in the atmosphere, human technology is helpless to remove it. So the overall amount of CO_2 in the air has been growing—at least since the industrial revolution. If no other factors operate, and if enough CO_2 is put into the atmosphere, eventually the average surface temperature will increase perceptibly.

What are the dangers? There are other greenhouse gases that are 14 increasingly abundant in the Earth's atmosphere—halocarbons, such as the freon used in refrigerator cooling systems; or nitrous oxide (N_2O), produced by automobile exhausts and nitrogenous fertilizers; or methane (CH_4), produced partly in the intestines of cows and other ruminants.

But let's for the moment concentrate on carbon dioxide: How 15 long, at the present rates of burning wood and fossil fuels, before the global climate becomes significantly warmer? And what would the consequences be?

It is relatively simple to calculate the immediate warming from 16 a given increase in the CO_2 abundance, and all competent calculations seem to be in good agreement. More difficult to estimate are (1) the rate at which carbon dioxide will continue to be put into the atmosphere (it depends on population growth rates, economic styles, alternative energy sources and the like) and (2) feedbacks— ways in which a slight warming might produce other, more drastic, effects.

The recent increase in atmospheric CO_2 is well documented. . . . 17 Over the last century, this CO_2 buildup should have resulted in a few tenths of a degree of global warming, and there is some evidence that such a warming has occurred.

The National Academy of Sciences estimates that the present 18 atmospheric abundance of CO_2 is likely to double by the year 2065, although experts at the academy predict a one-in-20 chance that it will double before 2035—when an infant born today becomes 50 years old. Such a doubling would warm the air near the surface of the Earth by 2°C or 3°C—maybe by as much as 4°C. These are average temperature values; there would naturally be considerable local variation. High latitudes would be warmed much more, although a baked Alaska will be some time coming.

There would be precipitation changes. The annual discharge of 19 rivers would be altered. Some scientists believe that central North America—including much of the area that is now the breadbasket of the world—would be parched in summer if the global temperature increases by a few degrees. There would be some mitigating effects; for example, where plant growth is not otherwise limited, more CO_2 should aid photosynthesis and make more luxuriant growth (of weeds as well as crops). If the present CO_2 injection into the atmosphere continued over a few centuries, the warming would be greater than from all other causes over the last 100,000 years.

20   As the climate warms, glacial ice melts. Over the last 100 years, the level of the world's oceans has risen by 15 centimeters (6 inches). A global warming of 3°C or 4°C over the next century is likely to bring a further rise in the average sea level of about 70 centimeters (28 inches). An increase of this magnitude could produce major damage to ports all over the world and induce fundamental changes in the patterns of land development. A serious speculation is that greenhouse temperature increases of 3°C or 4°C could, in addition, trigger the disintegration of the West Antarctic Ice Sheet, with huge quantities of polar ice falling into the ocean. This would raise sea level by some 6 meters (20 feet) over a period of centuries, with the eventual inundation of all coastal cities on the planet.

21   There are many other possibilities that are poorly understood, including the release of other greenhouse gases (for example, methane from peat bogs) accelerated by the warming climate. The circulation of the oceans might be an important aspect of the problem. The scientific community is attempting to make an environmental-impact statement for the entire planet on the consequences of continued burning of fossil fuels. Despite the uncertainties, a kind of consensus is in: Over the next century or more, with projected rates of burning of coal, oil and gas, there is trouble ahead.

22   **The importance of thinking globally.** The problem is difficult for at least three different reasons:

23   (1) We do not yet fully understand how severe the greenhouse consequences will be.

24   (2) Although the effects are not yet strikingly noticeable in everyday life, to deal with the problem, the present generation might have to make sacrifices for the next.

25   (3) The problem cannot be solved except on an international scale: The atmosphere is ignorant of national boundaries. South African carbon dioxide warms Taiwan, and Soviet coal-burning practices affect agricultural productivity in America. The largest coal resources in the world are found in the Soviet Union, the

United States and China, in that order. What incentives are there for a nation such as China, with vast coal reserves and a commitment to rapid economic development, to hold back on the burning of fossil fuels because the result might, decades later, be a parched American sunbelt or still more ghastly starvation in sub-Saharan Africa? Would countries that might benefit from a warmer climate be as vigorous in restraining the burning of fossil fuels as nations likely to suffer greatly?

Fortunately, we have a little time. A great deal can be done in 26 decades. Some argue that government subsidies lower the price of fossil fuels, inviting waste; more efficient usage, besides its economic advantage, could greatly ameliorate the CO_2 greenhouse problem. Parts of the solution might involve alternative energy sources, where appropriate: solar power, for example, or safer nuclear fission reactors, which, whatever their other dangers, produce no greenhouse gases of importance. Conceivably, the long-awaited advent of commercial nuclear fusion power might happen before the middle of the next century.

However, any technological solution to the looming greenhouse 27 problem must be worldwide. It would not be sufficient for the United States or the Soviet Union, say, to develop safe and commercially feasible fusion power plants: That technology would have to be diffused worldwide, on terms of cost and reliability that would be more attractive to developing nations than a reliance on fossil fuel reserves or imports. A serious, very high-level look at patterns of U.S. and world energy development in light of the greenhouse problem seems overdue.

During the last few million years, human technology, spurred 28 in part by climatic change, has made our species a force to be reckoned with on a planetary scale. We now find, to our astonishment, that we pose a danger to ourselves. The present world order is, unfortunately, not designed to deal with global-scale dangers. Nations tend to be concerned about themselves, not about the planet; they tend to have short-term rather than long-term objectives. In problems such as the increasing greenhouse effect, one nation or region might benefit while another suffers. In other global environmental issues, such as nuclear war, all nations lose. The problems are connected: Constructive international efforts to understand and resolve one will benefit the others.

29   Further study and better public understanding are needed, of course. But what is essential is a global consciousness—a view that transcends our exclusive identification with the generational and political groupings into which, by accident, we have been born. The solution to these problems requires a perspective that embraces the planet and the future. We are all in this greenhouse together.

Engaging the Text

1. Though this selection is on a highly scientific subject, its vocabulary is not especially obscure. Sagan almost always explains—gracefully and without condescension—the meanings of the terms he uses. Notice these and keep this method in mind for a future documented paper. Most of the difficult words in this selection, those that Sagan has not defined in context, are technical words, such as technological (27), that refer to the subject of global warming. Some of these are infrared (6—referred to often, hence important to understand), savannahs (1), climatic (3), transparent (8), opaque (9), admonition (11), inhibiting (11), irreversible (13), and photosynthesis (19). As you read or summarize Sagan's argument, be sure to look up these words if they are unfamiliar to you.

2. Sagan has become a popular writer, partly because of interest in his topics (stars and big bangs), but most especially because of his style. His own voice (familiar to TV viewers of his series "Cosmos") comes through in his essays. Look especially at the last paragraph, where Sagan pleads eloquently for a "global consciousness" to solve the serious problem he outlines. What does this paragraph tell you about Sagan himself?

3. Sagan lightens his scientific writing with familiar sayings (such as the one in paragraph 11) and even jokes (paragraph 18). Find these and list some other examples of his personal style in this essay.

Engaging the Reader

1. What is the "greenhouse effect" Sagan describes?
2. What are the two kinds of changes humans are able to make in their climate?
3. Why is Earth's climate not 20°C below freezing, as calculations might indicate?

4. What might be some of the effects of an increase of CO_2 in the atmosphere? What can be done about these long-term effects—or should we not be concerned with them?

The Engaged Writer

1. Write a summary paragraph of this essay (see "Writing a Summary of What You Read"). After you do this, check your work with the model summary that appears in the "Writer's Guide."
2. Can you think of some other reasons why we should begin to think globally about problems resulting from adding more CO_2 to the atmosphere? Discuss them.
3. How serious is the problem Sagan discusses? What can we do about it? From what you have read here and from your previous responses, try to answer these questions.
4. Look up recent discussions on this subject in a magazine or newspaper index or a CD-ROM computerized magazine and newspaper search program in your college library (your instructor or librarian can help you find these). A "Topic Searcher" on the greenhouse effect appears in the "Writer's Guide." Do you find any new material on this subject (dated since 1985)? Write a paper incorporating your findings.

PAUL QUINNETT

Enough of Roads

Audubon Magazine advocates a conservationist approach and celebrates wildlife. It was a surprise, then, to read an article there on road building. Published in 1985, the article tells tales of the old-time piercing of roads through the wilderness. The author concludes by wondering "once you have built a road, how you would go about unbuilding it."

When a friend of mine's grandfather graduated from the University of Califor- 1
nia with a degree in civil engineering, his old professor remarked to him, "Son,
I'm afraid you have wasted your time. They've built all the highways they're
ever going to build."
The year was 1911.

2   As a young man I took a small but steady offense at where roads were put. I took this offense even though, as a surveyor, I drew a good check every other Friday afternoon for putting roads where the boys back at the main office told us to put them. If we were told to put an access road through a stand of virgin timber, we put it through the timber. If we were told to put a road up a trout stream, we put it up the trout stream. And though, as a fisherman, I didn't like putting roads hip-and-thigh with rushing trout streams, I did it—for the money.

3   Now, as I understand things, the U.S. Forest Service is planning to build or rebuild some 30,000 miles of roads where, you'd have to assume, there are none. This proposition troubles me deeply.

4   There is not as much to putting a road up the side of a trout stream as people might think. You just locate the flood-plain, get above it as best you can, and start driving stakes—centerline, off-sets, grades, curves—and set the whole of it off with bright orange flags atop lengths of lath. A good survey crew can lay in a mile of road in a day or week, depending on elevations and what nature has put in its way.

5   Simpler still is the survey of a timber access road. My old party chief could, with a handheld level and a pocketful of short stakes, walk an access road right up the side of a mountain in a matter of hours. The new kid on the crew, I once asked him if his methods weren't a little sloppy. "Close enough for government work," he said.

6   After the stakes are in, the guys with the heavy equipment show up—D9 Cats, earthmovers, small cranes to lay in the culverts—followed by men with shovels and picks. There is a great deal of noise and a little shooting by the dynamite crew to get the big stone small enough to move. In no more than a tick on the clock of history, the canyon, the stream, the shape of things, is changed—as far as I know, forever.

7   When the crews are finished and the equipment gone, stream and canyon and floodplain look like the victims of some awful violence: lunch sacks tossed in the underbrush, oil spills from the grease monkeys, broken cables strewn about, beer cans and whisky bottles where the crews got a head start on an evening's drinking. But the road is there, graded smooth and tilting up the canyon like so many pool tables laid end to end. You can pull the whole of it in a Volkswagen in second gear.

For a time the stream runs milky tan, fresh dirt leaching from 8 its wounds. Standing there in the quiet of the last evening of the work, you can look up and down the valley and see the white scars left by Caterpillar blades against the trees, awkward piles of roots and slash, and the bright broken rock where the heavy stuff cracked it open and ground it up. "Helluva job," someone says. And you say, "Yep. Helluva job." But you won't go fishing in that stream—not today, maybe not ever.

To an engineer, a finished road is a thing of beauty—a plan he 9 drew on quarter-inch grid paper around and over the hard facts supplied him by the survey crew—an idea come to reality. He can go see it, walk on it, look up and down its surfaces, and say to himself, "This is one I built." Maybe, as it must be for architects, there is some palpable sense of accomplishment at seeing a canyon tamed so that wheels can roll where, only days before, they could not. I've imagined that this feeling, this sense of Divine Providence to subdue the Earth, was part of what drove the railroaders who carved and blasted and laid the steel from coast to coast in the last century.

As I remember them, the men who pushed the dirt with the big 10 D9 Cats felt the same way about their work. Looking at them, up in their seats chewing on cigars and pushing and pulling the levers that raise and lower the blades, they seemed to love the power of their great machines and the way those tightly harnessed horses could shove a tree over, roll a giant stone. And there was always talk about the Cat men: who was good with a blade and who was not so good. A good man with a blade could move more dirt in less time than a man who was only average. The paymasters on some of the jobs I worked brought whisky for the crews on the last payday of the job and passed it out to everyone. Two bottles for the Cat man who moved the most dirt.

And then, when a job was finished, all hands would head down 11 to a local tavern and buy round after round of ice-cold beer, paying off bets, saluting the end of something, looking like those fellows you see in the beer commercials who, coming in off an oil rig, clearly deserve the best of brews. At nineteen, I was proud to be among them.

For the road builders I knew, the Why of a new road was of less 12 interest than the How. "How are we going to get around that granite?" "Should we bridge it here or farther up?" "How many yards

do you think it will take to get a good fill on that feeder stream?"
This is what they talked about, as I imagine road builders always
have. Politics, economic implications, environmental effects—none
of these subjects ever came up.

13   Hiking one summer morning to an old Roman watchtower on
the Costa del Sol in southern Spain, my brother observed to me
that the cobblestones on which we were walking were laid by
Roman slaves. The towers were built to keep an eye on the
Carthaginians and to serve as an early warning system should the
empire fall under attack by sea. The cobblestone roads, narrow but
in fine repair for miles at a stretch, connected the towers so that
men and supplies could move quickly from the villages to the towers and battlements. And from each tower you could see another,
on your right and on your left, and on and on for mile upon mile
of coastline. The Carthaginians are gone, along with the Romans.
But the roads remain. A proper road will, it seems, outlast the
motive that inspired it and the government that built it.

14   Out in the west is where the new roads are planned. They are
planned, if I understand the situation correctly, to enable logging
outfits to get to the trees. Mother Nature has always put the best
trees just out of reach of the men who want them, and when you
stop to think about it, she has taken the same precautions with her
other treasures: gold, silver, oil, water, old bull elk, the finest
trout—the visions of which fan the fires of man's lust and inspire
him to savage the land.

15   I am a westerner, have always been one. I own two cowboy hats
and know how to get to Libby, Montana, and why I would want
to go there in the first place. I'm a hunter and a fisherman, and I
love a good road as much as the next sportsman. But, I think, there
is this business of too much of a good thing. Maybe we have roads
enough.

16   Thinking over the places I hunt and fish (Washington, Montana,
Idaho, and Utah), there are already so many roads through the
woods that, from the window of a light plane, they have become
the land's most distinguishing feature. Great sutures in the Earth,
they appear to hold the planet together like some kind of Frankensteinian handiwork. They circle, run straight, hug the sides of
canyons, climb over ridges, coast down the other sides, and eventually connect up to yet other roads which, in turn, join still others until the woods are divided into great portions of green sur-

rounded by surface seams of gravel and crushed rock. Even when you try not to look, your eye follows them. And you wonder, peering down, how things might have looked before the road builders came.

There are, too, all sorts of roads: the good, the bad, and the [17] ugly. There are roads that take you up where you couldn't (or wouldn't) walk. Hunting mule deer one September in the Henry Mountains in southern Utah, I was inspecting the dates and names of hunters from another time inscribed on the aspen trees of a place called Nasty Flats when an old-timer came by and said, "Back in the twenties we came up here by horse. They didn't have no roads then. A good hunt took thirty days." And, looking down over the desert country back toward the Green River, you could see that a fall mountain hunt was as much a journey as a shoot. The new road in from the highway, as slick as red clay might get after a rainstorm, is still a great advantage to a hunter on a three-day pass from his city.

And of the good roads, you would have to say something about [18] the one you find just at dark after wandering lost in the bush with that little tingle of fear working down your spine. "A road," you say aloud, putting your feet on something level and man-made. "I can get home on a road."

Or that perfect, unkempt logging road grown up with short [19] grass and edged with thimbleberry bushes where the grouse wander out of the creek beds to sun or scratch and where you can walk them up easy and lay them flat in the grasses with the double gun.

Or the good road that runs the length of Rock Creek in Montana [20] and that takes you by the great pools and glides and turnouts on the points so that, watching the surface on an August afternoon, you can see where a rainbow is sipping spent mayflies caught in the slicks.

Or the good summer roads. The summer roads where I live now [21] are soft-bottomed and unfit for travel after the first snow. They are clearly marked, "Summer Road Only." But these, if you have a four-wheel-drive, are where you want to go. You know the warning sign keeps the two-wheelers out of the backcountry where the quail and pheasants have not been hunted and will hold well for the pointers.

But all the roads are not good. And all are not beautiful. West- [22] ern Montana, where I hunt elk each fall, has miles and miles of such roads. These are business roads. You can make money on roads of this quality. A logging outfit makes money moving logs. To move a log at a profit you need a road that would pass inspection in Los Angeles: a road that is well surfaced, straight, properly banked, and wide enough to allow two logging trucks to pass each other at high speed—the higher the speed the better. The more logs that can be moved from the mountain to the mill between dawn and dark, the greater the profit margin. I imagine these are the roads intended by the Forest Service, the best roads my tax money can buy.

23   "We have to close 'em every fall after the loggers are out," a game warden told me several years ago when I came upon him locking up a heavy gate to road number 2262. "Otherwise road hunters just pound the hell out of them. What's your reaction?"

24   "Fine with me," I said.

25   "That's refreshing," he said. "Because once you put a road in, everybody thinks they have a right to drive on it. And you know how elk hate a busy road."

26   The Thompson River, just up Clark Fork from the town of Thompson Falls, has two roads, one on each side. The loggers use the right bank, everyone else the left. You use a logging road at your own risk. The signs say so. And the risk is substantial. Smart people keep their CBs turned on when they're on a loggers' road and listen for the truckers to sing out the mile markers so they can clear out if someone is coming. If they don't, they can end up looking like a grasshopper on the grill of an eighteen-wheeler.

27   I was fly-fishing on the Thompson one afternoon in September; the heavy dust kicked up from both roads hung in the air and settled back on everything until, after an hour or so, I had to bang my hat against my leg to shake the stuff off. I don't go to Montana to stand between two streams of noisy traffic and get buried in road dust. So I don't fish the Thompson anymore.

28   But where they really want the new roads to go is where they don't have any now. They want, I imagine, to turn roadless to roaded. This will, of course, make that backcountry we might one day wish to leave alone under the 1964 Wilderness Act quite touchable and ineligible for protection. And, should the citizens rise up someday and say, "Whoa," it will be too late to undo what has been done—even though this administration, like the Romans, will have become but a footnote to history.

I have wondered, once you have built a road, how you would 29
go about unbuilding it. I don't know that it has ever been tried. But
I have watched the men in the D9 Cats push the dirt ahead of
them, angling the blade so that the soil peels left or right and down
a slope, where it fans out like so much loose sand and slides in
amongst the trees and brush, covering the ferns and mosses. And
standing there, seeing the work I helped organize, I have wondered how even the best Cat man could put it back again. I don't
see how anyone could, not even God.

Engaging the Text

1. Many of the new words in this article come from the road
   builder's vocabulary: hip-and-thigh (2), lath (4), culverts (6).
   Some, though, deal with sensations or thoughts: palpable (9),
   implications (12), and tingle (18). One unusual word choice comes
   from one of the first horror stories, a novel by Mary Shelley called
   Frankenstein (the film adaptations are familiar to late-night movie-
   watchers). Find Frankensteinian (16) in the article where Quinnett
   uses it as an adjective and see if it fits his meaning.
2. This essay's style seems free and loose, starting with reminiscences of road building and going on to talk of present-day
   hunting and fishing. One reason it seems so artless is that various words act like good lubricants to keep the action moving
   from paragraph to paragraph. Quinnett demonstrates clever
   use of transitional words and phrases to link paragraphs
   together. Some of these "links" include:

   — repeating a word, phrase, or idea from one paragraph in
      the beginning of the next paragraph
   — use of a transitional word: however, nevertheless, then,
      now, next, but
   — repeating the same words at the beginning of several
      paragraphs: "Or the . . . roads . . ."

   Underline these linking or transitional words in the essay.
   How would the essay be changed if they were left out?

Engaging the Reader

1. From the article, tell who Quinnett is and what he does.
2. How are roads built through the wilderness?

3. What kinds of roads does Quinnett compare American roads to? Why?
4. What kinds of roads does he describe?

The Engaged Writer

1. Write about the results of your deductions on who Paul Quinnett is and what he does.
2. Describe a new road or street or highway being built in your neighborhood and the changes you think it will make. There has to be a new road near you, or at least a planned road or one you think should be built, or not built.
3. Part of this essay is a process essay, telling how roads are built through the timber of the West. Write an essay, using this one as a model, describing a process you know well: building a house, painting a room, scraping the hull of a boat, putting together a woodworking project, sewing a dress, laundering clothes, or any other process you are familiar with from your work, daily life, or hobbies.
4. Where would you look to find out what the 1964 Wilderness Act mentioned in paragraph 28 is? Write a short essay on your search and its results.
5. Compare Quinnett's view of conserving the wilderness with Carl Sagan's concerns for the atmosphere.

MELODY ERMACHILD CHAVIS

Street Trees

Melody Ermachild Chavis is a private investigator in Berkeley, California. Her work is with death-row inmates. She also coordinates a garden project with young and old in her community. This article appeared in *Sierra* magazine in 1994, and was one of the winners in *Sierra*'s 1994 Nature-Writing Contest.

1   I was drawn to my upstairs bedroom window by shouting in the street. The shouter was a middle-aged black man in shabby pants, and he strode, fast, right down the middle of the street. Storming

across the intersection, the man beat the air with his fists and shouted into the sky. "Somalia!" he cried. "Somalia!"

Ours is a neighborhood where poverty and addiction have ² made misery for years, and this was when airlifts of food to the Horn of Africa were all over the nightly news. "I know what you mean," I thought. "Why there? Why feed them but not you?"

Then he walked up to the newly planted tree under my win- ³ dow, grabbed its skinny trunk with both hands, yanked it over sideways, and cracked it in half on his knee. He threw the tree's leafy top onto the sidewalk and stomped off, cursing. I pressed my palms to the glass as he disappeared up the sidewalk.

The tree was just a baby, one of the donated saplings our neigh- ⁴ borhood association planted with help from the children on our block. Men from the public-works department had come and cut squares in the sidewalk for us, reaming out holes with a machine that looked like a big screw. The kids planted the trees, proudly wielding shovels, loving their hands in the dirt.

I had made name tags for each tree, with a poem printed on ⁵ each one, and we asked the kids to give each tree a name. "Hi, my name's *Greenie*, I'm new and neat, just like the children on our street." If we made the trees seem more like people, I thought, the kids would let them live.

Both trees and people around here are at risk of dying young. ⁶ After our neighborhood was flooded with crack cocaine and cheap, strong alcohol, things got very rough. In the last five years, 16 people have been murdered in our small police beat. Most of them were young black men, and most of them died on the sidewalks, where the trees witness everything: the children, the squealing tires and gunshots, the blood and sirens.

My neighbors and I did all we could think of to turn things ⁷ around, including planting the trees.

But the dealers still hovered on the corners and the young trees ⁸ had a hard time. Idle kids swung on them like playground poles, and peeled off strips of bark with their nervous little fingers.

One of the saplings planted in front of my house had fallen vic- ⁹ tim to a car, and now the other one had been murdered by a man mad about Somalia.

Discouraged, I let the holes in the cement choke with crab- ¹⁰ grass. In the center of each square, a pathetic stick of dead trunk stuck up.

11   When things are bad, I stand in my kitchen window and look into my own garden, a paradise completely hidden from the street outside. For 15 years I've labored and rested in my garden, where roses clamber on bamboo trellises. There are red raspberries and rhubarb. Lemon, apricot, apple, and fig trees are sheltered by young redwoods and firs that hide the apartment house next door. I planted the apricot tree 13 years ago when it was a bare stick as tall as myself. Now I mark the seasons with its changes. In early spring the apricot blooms white, tinged with pink, and feeds the bees. When our chimney fell in the earthquake, I used the bricks to build a low circular wall I call my medicine wheel. Inside it I grow sage, lavender, rosemary, and oregano. A stone Buddha sits under fringed Tibetan prayer flags, contemplating a red rock.

12   Not far from my house is a place I'm convinced is a sacred site. Within one block are a large African-American Christian church, a Black Muslim community center, and a Hindu ashram. Someone put a Buddha in a vacant lot near there, too, and people built a shrine around it. All this is close to the place where the Ohlone people once had a village.

13   I dream of those who lived here before me—an Ohlone woman, members of the Peralta family whose hacienda this was, and a Japanese-American farmer who had a truck garden here until he lost it when he was interned during World War II.

14   I often feel I'm gardening with my dear old next-door neighbor Mrs. Wright. An African-American woman from Arkansas, Mrs. Wright came to work in the shipyards during the war. When she bought the house next door this was the only neighborhood in town where black people were allowed to live. She was foster mother to many children, and she was sadly disapproving of the young people who used drugs when that started. Mrs. Wright farmed every inch of her lot, and had it all in food, mainly greens, like collards and kale. She gave most of the food away.

15   Her life exemplified the adage, "We come from the earth, we return to the earth, and in between we garden." I miss her still, although she died six years ago, in her 70s, after living here nearly 50 years. I was almost glad she didn't live to see the night a young man was shot to death right in front of our houses.

16   A map of the neighborhood 15 years ago, when my family came, would show community places that are gone now: bank, pharmacy, hardware and small, black-owned corner stores. There

are a lot of vacancies now, jobs are gone, and people travel to malls to shop. Many families run out of food the last days of the month.

On my map I can plot some of what killed this community's   17 safety: the too-many liquor outlets—nine within four blocks of my house; the drug dealers who came with crack about 1985. Clustered near the drugs and alcohol are the 16 murder sites: the 15 men, the one woman.

"I want to get away from all this," I think often. But *really* get-   18 ting away would mean selling our home and leaving, and so far, my husband and I have been unwilling to give up, either on our neighbors or on our hopes for helping make things better.

But we do get away, to the mountains. We've been walking the   19 John Muir Trail in sections the last few summers. I've never liked the way it feels good to go to the mountains and bad to come home. That's like only enjoying the weekends of your whole life.

According to my mail, "Nature" is the wilderness, which I'm   20 supposed to save. And I want to. But right here and now, if I go outside to pick up trash, I might have to fish a used syringe out of my hedge. That's saving nature too. The hard task is loving the earth, all of it.

The notes I stick on my refrigerator door remind me of the unity   21 and sacredness of life. There's a quote from Martin Luther King, Jr. on "the inescapable network of mutuality." I know I can't take a vacation from any part of this world.

Still, the habit of my mind is dual. This I hate: (the littered side-   22 walk); this I love: (the alpine meadow). I could get into my car and drive to that meadow. But when I drive back, the sidewalk will still be dirty. Or, I could stay here, pick up a broom, and walk out my front door.

The sidewalk yields clues that people have passed this way, like   23 trail markers in the mountains: candy wrappers the kids have dropped on their way back from the store; malt liquor cans and fortified-wine bottles inside brown bags. Sometimes there are clothes, or shoes, or car parts. I tackle it all in thick orange rubber gloves, wielding my broom and dustpan, dragging my garbage can along with me. I recycle what I can. "This is *all* sacred," I tell myself. "All of it."

There are bigger waste problems. But when I think about the   24 ozone hole, I find that it helps me to clean up. Thinking globally without acting locally can spin me down into despair.

25   Or into anger. I know that other people somewhere else made decisions that turned our neighborhood, once a good place, into a bad one. Like the alcohol-industry executives who decided to aim expensive ad campaigns at African-American teens. I know decisions happen that way to the old-growth forests, too.

26   I went to a lecture at the Zen Center not far from my house, to hear the head gardener there. She talked about what is to be learned from gingko trees. I've always liked their fan-shaped leaves, bright gold in the fall, but I hadn't known they were ancient, evolved thousands of years ago. They exist nowhere in the wild, she said, but were fostered by monks in gardens in China and Japan. Somehow, gingkos have adapted so that they thrive in cities, in polluted air. They remind me of the kids around here, full of life in spite of everything. I've seen teenage boys from my block, the kind called "at risk," "inner city," sometimes even "thugs," on a field trip to an organic farm, patting seedlings into the earth like tender young fathers putting babies to bed.

27   The day after the lecture, I went to the nursery, ready to try planting trees again in the holes in the sidewalk. Now in front of my house are two tiny gingkos, each inside a fortified cage of four strong metal posts and thick wire mesh. To weed them, I kneel on the sidewalk and reach in, trying not to scratch my wrist on the wire.

28   Kneeling there, I accept on faith that this little tree will do its best to grow according to its own plan. I also believe that every person wants a better life.

29   One evening last summer I lay flat out in a hot spring in the broad valley on the east side of the Sierra. I imagined one of the little street gingkos growing upright from my left palm. Out of my right palm, an ancient bristlecone pine of the White Mountains. This is how the trees live on the earth, as out of one body. They are not separate. The roots of the city tree and the summit tree pass through my heart and tangle.

Engaging the Text

1.   Chavis uses some vivid sentences, including some astonishing lists: "Most of them were young black men, and most of them died on the sidewalks, where the trees witness everything: the children, the squealing tires and gunshots, the blood and sirens." Look carefuly at this sentence and note the combinations of opposites: men and children, sounds, sights.

2. The writer uses images from around the world to illustrate her view of her garden: Tibet, Africa, India, Native American, Japanese. List some of these.

Engaging the Reader

1. Describe a scene, such as your garden, your room, your class-room, in the same terms Chavis does: an exact description with all the images and cross-references the sights call to your mind. Be loose. Be imaginative.
2. Exchange these "scenes" with one of your classmates and find something to add, building on your classmate's experience.
3. What does Chavis mean by saying, "The hard task is loving the earth, all of it" (20)?

The Engaged Writer

1. Chavis writes about nature from the point of view of a city dweller. C. L. Rawlins defines "wilderness" as an outdoor worker in the vast open spaces. Compare their two perspec-tives, both as to differences and similarities, and give exam-ples, quoting from each one to back up your main points.
2. Chavis ties her own reminisences to larger issues, such as city violence, the ozone hole, deteriorating city neighborhoods. Choose one of these issues to write about in a documented paper, starting out with a reference (quoting accurately) from "Street Trees."
3. What kind of a "tree" would you like to plant (see paragraphs 28–29) to make the world safer for city youth? And for your-self and your descendants?

ED MALLES

Hallowed Ground

As America rediscovers its heritage, we find an increasing number of groups of many ethnic backgrounds putting on demonstrations of cultures of the past. No group is more active or more meticulous in staging reenactments than Civil War "buffs." Every year they re-enact major battles of the Civil War, and during the rest of the year they painstakingly research and provide reproductions of uniforms, equipment, and weapons used in the original battles. Even more important, the actual battle sites have become scenes for a completely different kind of battle: the interests of preservationists like the people in Malles' article and those of commercial interests who want the land for housing, industry, or theme parks. Groups like the Association for the Preservation of Civil War Sites work to preserve these sites for future generations—and this article tells about these efforts.

1   On battlefields across the South, our forefathers forged a nation with their blood and their tears.

2   Today, a new army has returned to these fields to fight for those who came before them, to fight to preserve the memory of their sacrifice.

3   Like the armies of so long ago, they are people from all walks of life united by a common goal. Then, and now, they fight for the same thing—to preserve their heritage.

4   When you meet **Thomas Cartwright** and **Chuck Isaacs,** both men have an academic air—tall, bearded, with glasses—and indeed they both hold degrees in American History. But their voices are pure Tennessee, rich and strong and made for storytelling, and their manner welcoming. If you ask these foot soldiers of the new army why it's important to preserve the site of the Battle of Franklin, Tennessee, the answer is easy. It's their home.

5   "I grew up on the battlefield," Chuck says. "When I was a kid, we didn't play cowboys and Indians; we played Civil War. My dad built a big diorama of the battlefield (which I nearly broke crawling around on) that's on display at the Carter House museum now." Similarly, Thomas grew up in nearby Nashville and remembers his grandmother taking him to visit the battlefield to hunt for relics; and Thomas, over the years, amassed "thousands of minié balls." Both men grew up drinking deeply of the history of this place.

6   For Chuck and Thomas, this early love deepened; playing Civil War became studying it in college. Later, Thomas became curator of the Carter House, the focal point of the battle. The house stands today, scarred and pocked with the long-quiet violence of the battle, looking down over the city of Franklin. A busy two-lane road

runs past it now, and homes and businesses surround it, but the house still testifies to the memories of that other time.

"We're not still 'fighting the war' when we struggle to preserve 7 these sites. They're just part of our lives," Thomas says. And Chuck agrees. "We're not trying to make it grand and wonderful. It's not. What took place here was hell on earth. But it is important. It shouldn't be forgotten."

To help keep it alive, Thomas and Chuck, an executive at a local 8 bank, stay active in reenactments and benefits, raising money for markers and for preservation of the nearby sites from the Nashville Campaign of 1864. "So much of what's around the Carter House is already used—for businesses and homes, schools and roads," says Thomas. "But if we can at least preserve what we have and place markers to let people know what happened here, well, that's something."

One of the main ways they share with visitors is through a busi- 9 ness, Battlefield Tours, Inc., that they run together. This is their pas-sion, for both men are storytellers. The statistics, the dry numbers of casualties, aren't the point. Instead, the people who fought, who survived or died, are the reason they insist that we shouldn't forget.

"For all the thousands of men who fought here, there are just as 10 many stories. We try to bring them to life," Thomas says. Like a reflection of their childhood games, oftentimes Chuck or Thomas will don a uniform to portray a particular soldier when they con-duct tours of the cemetery.

"We stop by a grave and say, 'This is so and so. This is a partic- 11 ular person,'" Chuck explains. "Not a statistic or just someone nameless. Whoever's playing his part will do something to show who this was—tell his story, read his last letter to the family. It real-ly brings it home."

"We want to take them back in time," Thomas continues. "Bring 12 it to life, where they can hear the guns, smell the smoke. Let peo-ple know how they lived, what they wore."

The land first pulled Chuck and Thomas into this, their life's 13 work. And the land is crucial if this part of their heritage is to sur-vive. "To walk the same battlefield, see the terrain," Chuck says, "I want that for my children. Once it's gone, it's gone."

Both men attend to the day-to-day business of their jobs, of the 14 tours, of the next fundraising event. But both are aware, every day, of the time after they're gone. Thomas says, "I tell children's groups it's their turn before long, their turn to keep the memories alive. And that's what it's all about—remembering it was people on both sides who all earned the right to be remembered."

15   **Holly Robinson** is a leader. This former history professor exudes energy and confidence and seems eager for challenges. "If I can face 100 18-year-olds at 8 A.M. and interest them in Western Civilization, I can do anything," she declares with a laugh.

16   If Chuck and Thomas are foot soldiers fighting for their home in this new army, Holly is definitely a general, looking over the lay of the land and devising strategy. Holly's voice is a powerful weapon. Trained by years of lecturing, it will reach you and force your attention, backed by her steely conviction. A small woman with intense gray eyes and a ready smile, when speaking passionately she seems a giant.

17   No comprehensive survey of Civil War sites had been done since the Army War College survey of 1926–1930. Each of the thousands of sites found across the South has its own characteristics.

18   When Manassas battlefield site in Virginia was threatened with development in the late 1980s, Congress was spurred to appoint a knowledgeable, bipartisan commission, The Civil War Sites Advisory Commission, to take a long, objective look at the state of Civil War sites across the country. Holly Robinson was elected chairperson.

19   "We had a wonderful, talented group of members," Holly says. "We received no pay, just government per diem for our expenses, and we issued our report on time and within budget." And Holly, not one to slow down for long, was elected chairperson of the newly formed Georgia Civil War Commission before the ink was even dry on the national study.

20   A report might not seem so important, but this one was. By evaluating all the remaining battlefields, a blueprint now exists to help guide legislation, to help focus the energy of everyone involved in battlefield preservation.

21   While holding open meetings in 11 states and visiting 50 separate battlesites, Holly was greatly encouraged by the response she saw everywhere. "All the people I met, in small towns and large, were so excited about their history and their heritage. They loved showing it off. And always, in battlefield preservation, it's the local people who really matter. They make it work."

Holly used her energy, along with her experience as a teacher, 22
to educate everyone she met about the benefits of preservation. "It
can do so much good for a community. If the heritage of a place is
preserved, it can attract visitors, stimulate economic development,
and raise the quality of life. With preservation, you always have
to make sure it helps the community."

Born in Virginia and raised an Air Force brat, Holly knows what 23
it means to struggle to hold onto one's sense of heritage. Not having a constant of place makes it that much more difficult. And she
feels our heritage as a nation is strongly connected to the Civil War.

The recent fascination with the Civil War she sees as a "new 24
interest in who we are and where we came from. Preserving this
helps teach everyone—present and future generations—about our
culture, to understand why we are the way we are."

A site can teach us such things: "It's inspirational," Holly says, 25
"to actually stand on the same ground where those people fought
and died. Their sacrifice was so incredible." But it runs even deeper than this. "We don't want to celebrate battlefields," she says.
"We preserve them so that we can understand the gritty courage,
the profound dedication, of the people who fought there. We want
to consecrate, not glorify."

Like a gentleman farmer called out to fight, **Will Greene** also 26
has his place in this new army as a fierce cavalry leader. A tall, affa-
ble man, Will's experience as a national park ranger shows in his
mellow voice and easy conversation. When it comes to business,
though, the toughness necessary to lead shines through. This is
dedication, serious dedication.

As one of the founding members of the Association for the 27
Preservation of Civil War Sites (APCWS), and as its current president, Will has watched it grow from 800 members in 1987 to more
than 6,500 members today. Before this, Will, a long-time transplanted Virginian, had worked for 17 years in the park service.
And when the time came to step up, to make his passion into a full-
time job, Will answered the call.

What's the key to getting more and more people involved in 28
battlefield preservation? Will agrees with Holly—education.
"Only a small number of people are for pure preservation," Will
says. "More people are for having the battlefields for educational
reasons and an even greater number for having a site tie in to com-

munity development. You show all these people the advantages, and they'll get involved."

29   His work carries a certain pressure of time. For many of the battlefields, time is running out as sites are being developed—and lost. "Of course there's a renewed interest in the Civil War and in preservation," he says. "When something becomes scarce, people are willing to fight for it. And you have to do first things first—you have to save the sites."

30   Too often, Will feels, it's difficult to impress upon people how valuable the actual battlefield is. He explains, using an analogy: historic homes. "People visiting a historic home, a Monticello, always ask 'What's original? Is this the real item?' It's the same with the battlefields. They are original; they are the real item.

31   "Make no mistake—if you lose a site, you don't lose its history. That's always there. But you do lose its ability to touch people. History loses its third dimension and becomes a two-dimensional memory."

32   That's the real importance of these sites. All the books and diagrams and numbers and facts in the world can't convey the emotional impact of the site itself. That special place grips you and pulls you into the past. "You stand on the battlefield," Will says, "and you start to wonder: What made these people do what they did? What were their values? What do they have to teach us? What do we have today that would motivate us to do what they did?"

33   As the leader of one of the nation's most powerful preservation groups, Will has his wish list, an idea of what he'd like to accomplish. Pragmatically, he knows every site can't be saved, but he envisions "as many of these special places as possible woven into the educational fabric of our country, ranging from national parks to plaques outside historic homes."

34   Like everyone involved, Will can't help but think in terms of the future. All of these soldiers are fighting today, but their hearts are in tomorrow. They stand guard over our heritage and aim to leave it for the next generation.

35   "Day to day," Will says, "it's hard to tell you've accomplished anything. You win; you lose. And it's a slow process, the business of doing this. But then you take a little time and go stand on that battlefield that you helped protect—a piece of our heritage—and you know."

Engaging the Text

1. Notice the stirring beginning, reminiscent of the Gettysburg Address and Churchill's wartime speeches: "On battlefields across the South, our forefathers forged a nation with their blood and their tears." What's the point of starting this way? How does it affect the reader—you?

2. Notice the three-part structure of the essay, in which three different groups take unique ways of preservation. Notice also the conclusion, in three parts, where at the end of each section (paragraphs 14, 25, and 35) each of the people interviewed summarizes the principles behind individual involvement in his or her own words.

Engaging the Reader

1. Are there any preservation efforts in your town or region? Where would you find this information? Look in newspapers to see if old buildings, parks, factories, or even battlefields are being restored—or destroyed. What kinds of efforts does the article suggest to preserve or use them wisely?

2. What are the dangers or the long-term results of the different kinds of pollution detailed in Sagan, "The Warming of the World," Quinnett, "Enough of Roads," and Chavis, "Street Trees," and in this article? List them and then in a second column, speculate on some solutions for these problems. Are there any similarities in the list of solutions?

3. What kinds of preservation do the people interviewed for this article advocate? List the various ways they are preserving the heritage of the past without necessarily compromising the present needs.

The Engaged Writer

1. If you find such preservation efforts, or the need for them, in your discussion of question 1 under *Engaging the Reader,* write a letter to the editor of a local newspaper giving arguments in favor of preservation. See "Writing a Letter to the Editor" in the Writer's Guide for suggestions on this kind of letter.

2. Write a paper on the solutions you found for pollution problems you listed in #2, *Engaging the Reader.*

Youth

3. Compare the efforts of Thomas Cartwright, Chuck Isaccs, Holly Robinson, and Will Greene to save the battlefield sites with that of Marjory Stoneman Douglas to save the Everglades and its natural environment.

4. Which is more important—people living today who need homes and recreation, or the heritage of the past which needs extraordinary efforts at preservation? List the arguments pro and con on this issue to see where you stand on it, and then write an argumentative paper upholding your side of the controversy.

BOOKER T. WASHINGTON

Cast Down Your Bucket Where You Are: The Atlanta Exposition Address

Booker T. Washington was born a slave about 1856 in Virginia. Deprived in youth, he struggled for an education, finally succeeding in studying at Hampton Institute. He became the first principal at Tuskegee Institute and, through diplomacy in fundraising, made it a thriving college. He emerged as a national personality when he was asked to give a speech at the Atlanta Exposition of 1895. His speech seemed to trade civil, social, and political rights for economic opportunity for blacks, yet it's important to understand the temper of the times and the oppression and violence, all of which kept blacks from exercising their rights. His speech appeared in his memoir *Up From Slavery* in 1901.

MR. PRESIDENT AND GENTLEMEN OF THE BOARD OF DIRECTORS AND CITIZENS.

1 One-third of the population of the South is of the Negro race. No enterprise seeking the material, civil, or moral welfare of this section can disregard this element of our population and reach the highest success. I but convey to you, Mr. President and Directors, the sentiment of the masses of my race when I say that in no way have the value and manhood of the American Negro been more fittingly and generously recognized than by the managers of this

magnificent Exposition at every stage of its progress. It is a recognition that will do more to cement the friendship of the two races than any occurrence since the dawn of our freedom.

Not only this, but the opportunity here afforded will awaken 2 among us a new era of industrial progress. Ignorant and inexperienced, it is not strange that in the first years of our new life we began at the top instead of at the bottom; that a seat in Congress or the state legislature was more sought than real estate or industrial skill; that the political convention of stump speaking had more attractions than starting a dairy farm or truck garden.

A ship lost at sea for many days suddenly sighted a friendly 3 vessel. From the mast of the unfortunate vessel was seen a signal, "Water, water: we die of thirst!" The answer from the friendly vessel at once came back, "Cast down your bucket where you are." A second time the signal, "Water, water; send us water!" ran up from the distressed vessel, and was answered, "Cast down your bucket where you are." And a third and fourth signal for water was answered, "Cast down your bucket where you are." The captain of the distressed vessel, at last heeding the injunction, cast down his bucket, and it came up full of fresh, sparkling water from the mouth of the Amazon River. To those of my race who depend on bettering their condition in a foreign land or who underestimate the importance of cultivating friendly relations with the Southern white man, who is their next-door neighbour, I would say: "Cast down your bucket where you are"—cast it down in making friends in every manly way of the people of all races by whom we are surrounded.

Cast it down in agriculture, mechanics, in commerce, in 4 domestic service, and in the professions. And in this connection it is well to bear in mind that whatever other sins the South may be called to bear, when it comes to business, pure and simple, it is in the South that the Negro is given a man's chance in the commercial world, and in nothing is this Exposition more eloquent than in emphasizing this chance. Our greatest danger is that in the great leap from slavery to freedom we may overlook the fact that the masses of us are to live by the productions of our hands, and fail to keep in mind that we shall prosper in proportion as we learn to dignify and glorify common labour and put brains and skill into the common occupations of life; shall prosper in proportion as we learn to draw the line between the superficial and the substantial,

4.

the ornamental gewgaws of life and the useful. No race can prosper till it learns that there is as much dignity in tilling a field as in writing a poem. It is at the bottom of life we must begin, and not at the top. Nor should we permit our grievances to overshadow our opportunities.

5   To those of the white race who look to the incoming of those of foreign birth and strange tongue and habits for the prosperity of the South, were I permitted I would repeat what I say to my own race, "Cast down your bucket where you are." Cast it down among the eight millions of Negroes whose habits you know, whose fidelity and love you have tested in days when to have proved treacherous meant the ruin of your firesides. Cast down your bucket among these people who have, without strikes and labour wars, tilled your fields, cleared your forests, builded your railroads and cities, and brought forth treasures from the bowels of the earth, and helped make possible this magnificent representation of the progress of the South. Casting down your bucket among my people, helping and encouraging them as you are doing on these grounds, and to education of head, hand, and heart, you will find that they will buy your surplus land, make blossom the waste places in your fields, and run your factories. While doing this, you can be sure in the future, as in the past, that you and your families will be surrounded by the most patient, faithful, law-abiding, and unresentful people that the world has seen. As we have proved our loyalty to you in the past, in nursing your children, watching by the sick-bed of your mothers and fathers, and often following them with tear-dimmed eyes to their graves, so in the future, in our humble way, we shall stand by you with a devotion that no foreigner can approach, ready to lay down our lives, if need be, in defence of yours, interlacing our industrial, commercial, civil, and religious life with yours in a way that shall make the interests of both races one. In all things that are purely social we can be as separate as the fingers, yet one as the hand in all things essential to mutual progress.

Engaging the Text

1. In a passionate yet eloquent speech, Washington uses down-to-earth metaphors, parables, and even slang, such as "gewgaws" (4). What does the metaphor of the fingers and the hand mean

(5)? Is this an effective figure of speech? Does Washington use many of these figures of speech? If so, list some of them.

2. The story about the water buckets is a parable—an anecdote in which the words in the story have a literal meaning but also refer to a message the writer wishes to get across about some moral value or lesson. What does Washington mean by the parable of the water buckets?
3. How does Washington's choice of language reflect his "philosophy of conciliation"? See particularly enterprise (1), heeding the injunction (3), and underestimate (3).

Engaging the Reader

1. What does Washington say were the aims of black people right after the Civil War?
2. What is the point of the story about the ship at the mouth of the Amazon?
3. What careers does Washington say blacks should train themselves for?
4. What message does he have for whites?
5. What attitude does he seem to have toward foreign workers? Why?

See the next selection by Du Bois for writing assignments.

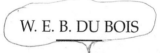

W. E. B. DU BOIS

Response to Mr. Washington

Born in 1868 in Massachusetts, W. E. B. Du Bois had an excellent education at Fisk, Harvard, and the University of Berlin. He became a scholar and professor and dedicated himself to studies of "the Negro problem." At first an admirer of Booker T. Washington, he later rejected Washington's conciliatory philosophy, and in *The Souls of Black Folk* (1903) he called on blacks to take their rightful place in civil and social America as well as to demand economic equality. He joined the Communist Party in 1961 as his political philosophy developed and moved to Ghana to live and teach just before his death in 1963. The following selection is from *The Souls of Black Folk* (1903).

1 Mr. Washington represents in Negro thought the old attitude of adjustment and submission; but adjustment at such a peculiar time as to make his programme unique. This is an age of unusual economic development, and Mr. Washington's programme naturally takes an economic cast, becoming a gospel of Work and Money to such an extent as apparently almost completely to overshadow the higher aims of life. Moreover, this is an age when the more advanced races are coming in closer contact with the less developed races, and the racefeeling is therefore intensified; and Mr. Washington's programme practically accepts the alleged inferiority of the Negro races. Again, in our own land, the reaction from the sentiment of war time has given impetus to race-prejudice against Negroes, and Mr. Washington withdraws many of the high demands of Negroes as men and American citizens. In other periods of intensified prejudice all the Negro's tendency to self-assertion has been called forth; at this period a policy of submission is advocated. In the history of nearly all other races and peoples the doctrine preached at such crises has been that manly self-respect is worth more than lands and houses, and that a people who voluntarily surrender such respect, or cease striving for it, are not worth civilizing.

2   In answer to this, it has been claimed that the Negro can survive only through submission. Mr. Washington distinctly asks that black people give up, at least for the present, three things,—

First, political power,
Second, insistence on civil rights,
Third, higher education of Negro youth—

and concentrate all their energies on industrial education, the accumulation of wealth, and the conciliation of the South. This policy has been courageously and insistently advocated for over fifteen years, and has been triumphant for perhaps ten years. As a result of this tender of the palmbranch, what has been the return? In these years there have occurred:

1. The disfranchisement of the Negro.
2. The legal creation of a distinct status of civil inferiority for the Negro.

3. The steady withdrawal of aid from institutions for the higher training of the Negro.

These movements are not, to be sure, direct results of Mr. Wash- 3 ington's teachings; but his propaganda has, without a shadow of doubt, helped their speedier accomplishment. The question then comes: Is it possible, and probable, that nine millions of men can make effective progress in economic lines if they are deprived of political rights, made a servile caste, and allowed only the most meagre chance for developing their exceptional men? If history and reason give any distinct answer to these questions, it is an emphatic *No.* And Mr. Washington thus faces the triple paradox of his career:

1. He is striving nobly to make Negro artisans business 4 men and property-owners; but it is utterly impossible, under modern competitive methods, for workingmen and property-owners to defend their rights and exist without the right of suffrage.

2. He insists on thrift and self-respect, but at the same time 5 counsels a silent submission to civic inferiority such as is bound to sap the manhood of any race in the long run.

3. He advocates common-school and industrial training, and 6 depreciates institutions of higher learning; but neither the Negro common-schools, nor Tuskegee itself, could remain open a day were it not for teachers trained in Negro colleges, or trained by their graduates.

Engaging the Text

1. Du Bois writes with the elegance of the scholar and professor of the new science of sociology. Some of the words from Du Bois's vocabulary as a sociologist are programme (1), impetus (1), intensified (1), self-assertion (1), conciliation (2), disfranchisement (2), servile (3), meagre (3), paradox (3), artisans (4), suffrage (4), and depreciates (6). Check the meanings of these words in a dictionary.

2. Find where these words occur in the text and substitute a plain synonym for some of them. Does the text read as well?

Engaging the Reader

1. Name the points on which Du Bois disagrees with Washington. Which ones do you agree with? Why?
2. Do you agree with Washington that, for a good end, one should give up some of one's principles or demands, or with Du Bois, that one should not compromise for fear of giving up much more? In other words, do the means ever justify the end?

The Engaged Writer

1. Explain the following:

   — In the history of nearly all other races and peoples the doctrine preached at such crises has been that manly self-respect is worth more than lands and houses, and that a people who voluntarily surrender such respect, or cease striving for it, are not worth civilizing.

   —W. E. B. DU BOIS

   — It is at the bottom of life we must begin, and not at the top.

   —BOOKER T. WASHINGTON

2. What does Washington say blacks should trade for economic progress? What does Du Bois insist has been the outcome of this philosophy? Do you agree with Du Bois?
3. What light do you think this controversy between Washington and Du Bois sheds on the later civil rights movement of the 1960s?
4. Show how Washington's and Du Bois's views shaped the world in which Henry Louis Gates grew up. Which philosophy, that of Washington or that of Du Bois, has been more influential in charting the course of integration since 1964?

MARTIN LUTHER KING, JR.

I Have a Dream

Probably one of the most influential orations of modern times, this
speech was delivered after the Freedom March of August 1963 at the
Lincoln Memorial in Washington D.C. King, a clergyman, was a
major leader in the civil rights movement and his speech has been
quoted again and again, along with replays on television of its delivery. He believed, like Mahatma Ghandi, that equality was to be
achieved through non-violent means. He received the Nobel Peace
Prize in 1964 and was assassinated in Memphis, Tennessee in April
1968.

I am not unmindful that some of you have come here out of exces- 1
sive trials and tribulation. Some of you have come fresh from narrow jail cells. Some of you have come from areas where your quest
for freedom left you battered by the storms of persecution and
staggered by the winds of police brutality. You have been the vet-
erans of creative suffering. Continue to work with the faith that
unearned suffering is redemptive.

Go back to Mississippi; go back to Alabama; go back to South 2
Carolina; go back to Georgia; go back to Louisiana; go back to the
slums and ghettos of the northern cities, knowing that somehow
this situation can, and will be changed. Let us not wallow in the
valley of despair.

So I say to you, my friends, that even though we must face the 3
difficulties of today and tomorrow, I still have a dream. It is a
dream deeply rooted in the American dream that one day this
nation will rise up and live out the true meaning of its creed—we
hold these truths to be self-evident, that all men are created equal.

I have a dream that one day on the red hills of Georgia, sons of 4
former slaves and sons of former slave-owners will be able to sit
down together at the table of brotherhood.

I have a dream that one day, even the state of Mississippi, a 5
state sweltering with the heat of injustice, sweltering with the heat
of oppression, will be transformed into an oasis of freedom and
justice.

no violation

6   I have a dream my four little children will one day live in a nation where they will not be judged by the color of their skin but by content of their character. I have a dream today!

7   I have a dream that one day, down in Alabama, with its vicious racists, with its governor having his lips dripping with the words of interposition and nullification, that one day, right there in Alabama, little black boys and black girls will be able to join hands with little white boys and white girls as sisters and brothers. I have a dream today!

8   I have a dream that one day every valley shall be exalted, every hill and mountain shall be made low, the rough places shall be made plain, and the crooked places shall be made straight and the glory of the Lord will be revealed and all flesh shall see it together.

9   This is our hope. This is the faith that I go back to the South with.

10   With this faith we will be able to hew out of the mountain of despair a stone of hope. With this faith we will be able to transform the jangling discords of our nation into a beautiful symphony of brotherhood.

11   With this faith we will be able to work together, to pray together, to struggle together, to go to jail together, to stand up for freedom together, knowing that we will be free one day. This will be the day when all of God's children will be able to sing with new meaning—"my country 'tis of thee; sweet land of liberty; of thee I sing; land where my fathers died, land of the pilgrim's pride; from every mountain side, let freedom ring"—and if America is to be a great nation, this must become true.

12   So let freedom ring from the prodigious hilltops of New Hampshire.

Let freedom ring from the mighty mountains of New York.

Let freedom ring from the heightening Alleghenies of Pennsylvania.

Let freedom ring from the snow-capped Rockies of Colorado.

Let freedom ring from the curvaceous slopes of California.

But not only that.

Let freedom ring from Stone Mountain of Georgia.

Let freedom ring from Lookout Mountain of Tennessee.

Let freedom ring from every hill and molehill of Mississippi, from every mountainside, let freedom ring.

And when we allow freedom to ring, when we let it ring from 13
every village and hamlet, from every state and city, we will be able
to speed up that day when all of God's children—black men and
white men, Jews and Gentiles, Catholics and Protestants—will be
able to join hands and to sing in the words of the old Negro spiritual, "Free at last, free at last; thank God Almighty, we are free at last."

Engaging the Text

1. Some vocabulary words you may need to check in order to
   comment on this speech are: creed (3), interposition and nullification (7), prodigious (12), curvaceous (12).
2. King's knowledge of documents like the Declaration of Independence shows in this speech (paragraph 3); his Bible training likewise (8).
3. List as many of the parallel structures—opposites like "jangling discords . . . beautiful symphony" (10) you can find in
   this speech. Diagramming it on paper or the board might help
   you appreciate its intricate and interlocking structure.

Engaging the Reader

1. The fact that King was a clergyman, Harvard-educated but
   steeped in the gospel tradition of the South, influenced the
   form of this oration. Notice the parallel structures and the repetition throughout it: "I have a dream" (6 times); "Let freedom
   ring" (9 times).
2. Look at the views expressed by Booker T. Washington (accom-
   modation) and W.E.B. Du Bois (complete equality), and compare them with King's vision of a future for America.
3. Do you think that future dream has been realized? Why or
   why not? Incorporate the thinking of Henry Louis Gates, Jr.
   from the article following this one into your thinking.

The Engaged Writer

1. After comparing the views of Washington, Du Bois, and King,
   write a paper on what has happened in the civil rights movement since 1963.
2. Write about you own dream for the future of America, using
   some parallel structures and repetitions as King does.

3. Which philosophy, King's, Du Bois' or Washington's, has been more influential in charting the course of integration since 1964?

HENRY LOUIS GATES, JR.

The Last Mill Picnic

Henry Louis Gates, Jr., was born in a small mill town in West Virginia where the African-American (or "colored") population formed a tightly-knit community. He received his doctorate at Cambridge University in England and is now Professor of English and Chairman of Afro-American Studies at Harvard University. A well-known scholar and speaker, he is the author of many books and articles, among others, *Loose Canons* and *The Signifying Monkey*. In this selection from *Colored People: A Memoir* (1994) he looks back with nostalgia on what happened when "the last wave of the civil rights movement" hit his town.

1 Some colored people claimed that they welcomed the change, that it was progress, that it was what we had been working for for so very long, our own version of the civil rights movement and Dr. King. But nobody really believed that, I don't think. For who in their right mind wanted to attend the mill picnic with the white people, when it meant shutting the colored one down?

2 Just like they did Howard High School, Nemo's son, Little Jim, had said. I was only surprised that he said it out loud.

3 Everybody worked *so* hard to integrate the thing in the mid-sixties, Aunt Marguerite mused, because that was what we were supposed to do then, what with Dr. King and everything. But by the time those crackers made us join them, she added, we didn't want to go.

4 I wish I could say that the community rebelled, that everybody refused to budge, that we joined hands in a circle and sang "We Shall Not, We Shall Not Be Moved," followed by "We Shall Overcome." But we didn't. In fact, people preferred not to acknowledge the approaching end, as if a miracle could happen and this whole nightmare would go away.

It was the last colored mill picnic. Like the roll called up yon- 5
der, everybody was there, even Caldonia and Old Man Mose. But
Freddie Taylor had brought his 45s and was playing the best of
rhythm and blues like nobody could believe. "What Becomes of
the Brokenhearted?" was the favorite oldie of the day, because
Piedmont was a Jimmy Ruffin town. Mellow, and sad. A coffee-
colored feeling, with lots of cream. Jerry Butler's "Hey, Western
Union Man" and Marvin Gaye's "I Heard It Through the
Grapevine" were the most requested recent songs.

We had all come back for it, the diaspora reversing itself. There 6
was a gentle hum or rumble that kept the same pitch all through
the day, a lazy sort of pace as we walked back and forth along the
arc of parked cars and just-mowed grass at Carskadon's Farm.
Timothy grass and raspberry, black-eyed Susans big as saucers,
thistle and dandelion, and everywhere sumac. The greensward
was an allergist's nightmare, cow pies were a perpetual threat.
Still, we walked.

They had tried to shut down Walden Methodist first, but Big 7
Mom, the matriarch, had simply refused to stop attending her
church of eight decades. And "the boys"—her sons, the Cole-
mans—had of course supported her. Other than her doctor, Big
Mom almost never saw white people. Nor did she care to be with
or worship with them. People huddled together and lobbied her,
then huddled together and lobbied her some more, to no avail. Big
Mom wasn't going to stop attending Walden Methodist. And that
was that. Since she had a weak heart and high blood pressure, had
lost most of her sight because of a degenerating retina, couldn't
hear unless you spoke in her ear—and had, above all else, a steely
sense of resolve—*nobody* messed with Big Mom.

The white minister at the newly integrated United Methodist 8
Church, over in the Orchard, would preach his normal sermon and
then traipse over to Back Street and minister to Big Mom, Mr.
Ozzie, Mr. Doug Twyman, Mr. Lynn Allen, and a Coleman son or
two. Miss Toot and her daughters, Frieda and Eudie, would still
sing gospel, including "The Prodigal Son." White people can't
preach too good, was all that Big Mom would volunteer about her
experience with integration. I know she thought that God was
white: there were all those pictures hanging on her walls. But that
was another matter.

9   They might have kept Walden Methodist, but there was no hope for the mill pic-a-nic. And what was worse was that nobody had known what to do to reverse it. The mill administration itself made the decision, it said, because the law forbade separate but equal everything, including picnics. So the last wave of the civil rights era finally came to the Potomac Valley, crashing down upon the colored world of Piedmont. When it did, its most beloved, and cementing, ritual was doomed to give way. Nobody wanted segregation, you understand; but nobody thought of this as segregation.

10   So much was the way I remembered these occasions from my earliest childhood, and yet a new age had plainly dawned, an age that made the institution of a segregated picnic seem an anachronism. All of the people under thirty-five or so sported newly coiffed Afros, neatly rounded and shiny with Afro-Sheen. There were red and black and green dashikis everywhere, blousing over bell-bottomed trousers. Gold peace symbols dangled over leather vests, bare nigger toes poked out of fine leather sandals. Soul handshakes filled the air, as did the curious vocatives "brother" and "sister." I found myself looking for silk socks and stocking-cap waves, sleeveless see-through T-shirts peeking over the open neck of an unbuttoned silk shirt, Eye-talian style. Like Uncle Joe liked to wear when he dressed up. For bottles of whiskey and cheap wine in brown paper bags, furtively shared behind the open trunks of newly waxed cars, cleaned for the occasion, like Mr. Bootsie and Jingles and Mr. Roebuck Johnson used to do. Even the gamblers didn't have much to say, as they laid their cards down one by one, rather than slapping them down in the bid whist way, talking shit, talking trash, the way it used to be, the way it always was. The way it was supposed to be.

11   Miss Sarah Russell was there, carrying that black Bible with the reddish-orange pages—the one that printed the Sacred Name of Jesus and His words in bold red letters—still warning everybody about the end of the world and reminding us that Jesus wasn't going to be sending us a postcard or a telegram when He returned to judge us for our sins. He'd be coming like a thief in the night. The signs of the times are near, she shouted, the signs of the times. Don't nobody know the season but for the blooming of the trees. There's war and then there's the rumors of wars. My God is a harsh master, and the Holy Ghost has unloosed the fire of the spirit, and we know that fire by the talking in tongues.

Whenever Miss Sarah came around, Mr. Bootsie, Mr. Johnson,   12
and Mr. Jingles would never drink out of whatever it was they kept
in those brown paper bags. She appreciated that.

Mr. Bootsie and Mr. Marshall were running their card game at   13
its usual place in the arc of parked automobiles, hoping that Miss
Sarah would just keep walking by, as she made the rounds, ful-
filling her obligation to remind her friends about Jesus' imminent
return, and sharing a cool glass of lemonade and maybe a crisp
fried chicken leg as she paused to catch her breath. Miss Ezelle had
on a bright-red dress—she always *did* look good in red—and she
was telling Mr. Buddy Green to lower his voice and not talk about
how much money he was losing at poker until Miss Sarah got out
of the way.

Greg and I, spying Miss Sarah over by the gamblers' card table,   14
made a beeline down to the river, figuring that Jeannie and Tanya
Hollingsworth had probably decided to go swimming by now.
And Miss Sarah Russell, despite all the symbolism of water in the
Bible, would never have been caught dead down by the river,
where all that bare brown flesh, glistening in the sunshine, could
prove too distracting even to the saved.

No one was at the river yet, so we headed back up the bank,   15
passed Nemo's cast-iron vat, where he boiled the corn, and headed
over to watch the last softball game, the game that pitted the alumni of Howard High School against the alumni of Everyplace Else.
Roebuck Johnson was there, standing next to Mr. Comby Curl, the
latter's wavy hair shining even more brightly than usual and sliced
neatly by the part that he had shaved himself with that same
straight-edged razor that made the back of my neck break out in
shaving bumps. Involuntarily, I rubbed the back of my neck with
my left hand, to see if they had disappeared yet. They were still
there from yesterday's haircut. Roebuck was watching the game
because he loved sports and also to escape the prying eye of all of
his competing interests and loyalties. But it was exhilarating to
watch the Howard team, headed by Earkie and Raymond, beat the
hell out of the team from Elsewhere, just like they did every year.
Only this time, the beating seemed more relentless. Poochie Taylor—who many people thought was the best natural athlete in a
kingdom of natural athletes—tore the leather off the softball.
"Couldn't stand to be away from the Valley," was what they said
when he came home from spring training in the big leagues.

Everybody had wanted him to make it to the World Series, just to beat the racist Yankees. Instead, he went to work up at the mill and then got his own church as a pastor. Everybody said he was sincere, unlike some of the other born-agains.

16   I was surprised that no one made any speeches, that no one commemorated the passing of the era in a formal way. But it did seem that people were walking back and forth through Carskadon's field a lot more times than they normally did, storing up memories to last until the day when somebody, somehow, would figure out a way to trick the paper mill into sponsoring this thing again. Maybe that's why Miss Ezelle seemed to take extra care to make her lips as red as Sammy Amoroso's strawberries in late August, and why Uncle Joe had used an extra dab of Brylcreem that morning, to give his silver DA that extra bit of shine. And why Miss Toot's high-pitched laughter could be heard all over that field all the day long, as she and Mr. Marshall beat all comers in a "rise and fly" marathon match of bid whist. So everyone could remember. We would miss the crackle of the brown paper bag in which Mr. Terry Conway hid his bottle of whiskey, and the way he'd wet his lips just before he'd tilt his whole body backwards and swig it down. The way he'd make the nastiest face after he drank it, as if he had tasted poison itself. When the bottle ran out, Mr. Terry would sleep himself back to health in the cool dawn splendor of a West Virginia morning.

17   Nor were there any fights at the colored Legion that night, not even after Inez Jones, with George Mason's white handkerchief dangling between her legs, did the dirty dog to end all dirty dogs.

18   The colored mill picnic would finish its run peaceably, then, if with an air of wistful resignation. All I know is that Nemo's corn never tasted saltier, his coffee never smelled fresher, than when these hundreds of Negroes gathered to say goodbye to themselves, their heritage, and their sole link to each other, wiped out of existence by the newly enforced anti-Jim Crow laws. The mill didn't want a lawsuit like the one brought against the Swordfish.

19   Yeah, even the Yankees had colored players now, Mr. Ozzie mumbled to Daddy, as they packed up Nemo's black cast-iron vat, hoping against hope to boil that corn another day.

Engaging the Text

1. Paragraph 5 mentions some of the popular songs and singers of the time when Gates was growing up. Look some of them up, play them, and see why he chose them to illustrate his chapter.
2. Notice the meticulous way Gates refers to all the older people as "Miss" or "Mr."
3. The essay is full of references to African-American culture besides Dr. King (1): "We Shall Overcome" (4), the roll called up yonder (5), sing gospel (8), Afros, Afro-Sheen (10), dashikis, soul handshakes, gold peace symbols, compared with "silk socks and stocking-cap waves" (10). Find some others, and explain them to others in your writing group.

Engaging the Reader

1. Read the first paragraph of this essay and see if you agree with Gates, who regrets the integration of the annual mill picnic. Originally two events, one for white and one for colored, the Civil Rights laws did away with the former principle of "separate but equal."
2. Why does Gates regret the old mill pic-a-nic? Why do you think the black mill workers and their families worked hard for integration, then "preferred not to acknowledge the approaching end, as if a miracle could happen and this whole nightmare would go away" (4)?
3. Why does Gates call his chapter "The Last Mill Picnic"?
4. Paragraph 10 gives some specific examples of what Gates means by saying that "a new age had plainly dawned, an age that made the institution of a segregated picnic seem an anachronism."

The Engaged Writer

1. Taking as model Gates's detailed description of the picnic, describe some event you attended: Fourth of July Fireworks at the Washington Monument, a rock or blues concert, a wedding or a funeral, and describe the scene and the participants the way Gates does. Leave yourself out, if possible, to make the experience more objective.

2. Compare Gates' experience with the mill picnic and high school (2) with Amiri Baraka's experiences in an integrated city high school.
3. Gates's whole theme seems to be the "passing of an era." In the rest of the book, he regrets the sense of community of the past and also the divisiveness of races today. After having read the section here about civil rights: Washington, Du Bois, King and now Gates, write a paper on what your dream for a future American society would be as regards race and race relations.

ROGER ROSENBLATT

The Quality of Mercy Killing

Many newsmagazines comment on issues in editoriallike essays, as does *Time* magazine. Roger Rosenblatt, writer and TV commentator, published this essay in August 1985, using a specific case as an example. He discusses the dilemma of society and the law when a person has "killed for love"—a mercy killing, or euthanasia. The title refers to some famous lines from Shakespeare's *The Merchant of Venice:*

> *The quality of mercy is not strained,*
> *It droppeth as the gentle rain from heaven*
> *Upon the place beneath: it is twice blessed:*
> *It blesseth him that gives and him that takes.*
> (act 4, scene 1)

1 If it were only a matter of law, the public would not feel stranded. He killed her, after all. Roswell Gilbert, a 76-year-old retired electronics engineer living in a seaside condominium in Fort Lauderdale, Fla., considered murdering his wife Emily for at least a month before shooting her through the head with a Luger as she sat on their couch. The Gilberts had been husband and wife for 51 years. They were married in 1934, the year after Calvin Coolidge died, the year after Prohibition was lifted, the year that Hank Aaron was born. At 73, Emily had Alzheimer's disease and osteoporosis; her spinal column was gradually collapsing. Roswell

would not allow her to continue life as "a suffering animal," so he committed what is called a mercy killing. The jury saw only the killing; they felt Gilbert had mercy on himself. He was sentenced to 25 years with no chance of parole, which would make him 101 by the time he got out. The Governor has been asked to grant clemency. Most Floridians polled hope that Gilbert will go free.

Not that there ever was much of a legal or practical question 2 involved. Imagine the precedent set by freeing a killer simply because he killed for love. Othello killed for love, though his passion was loaded with a different motive. Does any feeling count, or is kindness alone an excuse for murder? Or age: maybe someone has to be 76 and married 51 years to establish his sincerity. There are an awful lot of old people and long marriages in Florida. A lot of Alzheimer's disease and osteoporosis as well. Let Gilbert loose, the fear is, and watch the run on Lugers.

Besides, the matter of mercy killing is getting rough and out of 3 hand. Nobody seems to use poison anymore. In Fort Lauderdale two years ago, a 79-year-old man shot his 62-year-old wife in the stairwell of a hospital; like Emily Gilbert, she was suffering from Alzheimer's disease. In San Antonio four years ago, a 69-year-old man shot his 72-year-old brother to death in a nursing home. Last June a man in Miami put two bullets in the heart of his three-year-old daughter who lay comatose after a freak accident. An organization that studies mercy killings says that nine have occurred this year alone. You cannot have a murder every time someone feels sorry for a loved one in pain. Any fool knows that.

Yet you also feel foolish watching a case like Gilbert's (if any 4 case can be said to be like another) because, while both feet are planted firmly on the side of law and common sense, both are firmly planted on Gilbert's side as well. The place the public really stands is nowhere: How can an act be equally destructive of society and wholly human? The reason anyone would consider going easy on Gilbert is that we can put ourselves in his shoes, can sit at his wife's bedside day after day, watching the Florida sun gild the furniture and listening to the Atlantic lick the beach like a cat. Emily dozes. He looks at her in a rare peaceful pose and is grateful for the quiet.

Or he dreams back to when such a scene would have been 5 unimaginable: she, sharp as a tack, getting the better of him in an argument; he, strong as a bull, showing off by swinging her into the air—on a beach, perhaps, like the one in front of the condominium where old couples like themselves walk in careful slow motion at the water's edge. Since the case became a cause, photographs of the Gilberts have appeared on television, she in a formal gown, he in tails; they, older, in a restaurant posing deadpan for a picture for no reason, the way people do in restaurants. In a way the issue here *is* age: mind and body falling away like slabs of sand off a beach cliff. If biology declares war, have people no right to a pre-emptive strike? In the apartment he continues to stare at her who, from time to time, still believes they are traveling together in Spain.

6   Now he wonders about love. He loves his wife; he tells her so; he has told her so for 51 years. And he thinks of what he meant by that: her understanding of him, her understanding of others, her sense of fun. Illness has replaced those qualities in her with screams and a face of panic. Does he love her still? Of course, he says; he hates the disease, but he loves his wife. Or—and this seems hard—does he only love what he remembers of Emily? Is the frail doll in the bed an impostor? But no; this is Emily too, the same old Emily hidden somewhere under the decaying cells and in the folds of the pain-killers. It is Emily and she is suffering and he swore he would always look after her.

7   He considers an irony: you always hurt the one you love. By what act or nonact would he be hurting his wife more? He remembers news stories he has read of distraught people in similar positions, pulling the plugs on sons and husbands or assisting in the suicides of desperate friends. He sympathizes, but with a purpose; he too is interested in precedents. Surely, he concludes, morality swings both ways here. What is moral for the group cannot always be moral for the individual, or there would be no individuality, no exceptions, even if the exceptions only prove the rule. Let the people have their rules. What harm would it do history to relieve Emily's pain? A little harm, perhaps, no more than that.

8   This is what we see in the Gilbert case, the fusion of our lives with theirs in one grand and pathetic cliché in which all lives look pretty much alike. We go round and round with Gilbert: Gilbert suddenly wondering if Emily might get better, if one of those white-coated geniuses will come up with a cure. Gilbert realizing that once Emily is gone, he will go too, since her way of life, however wretched, was their way of life. He is afraid for them both. In *The Merchant of Venice* Portia says that mercy is "twice blessed;/It

blesses him that gives and him that takes." The murder committed, Gilbert does not feel blessed. At best, he feels he did right, which the outer world agrees with and denies.

Laws are unlikely to be changed by such cases: for every modification one can think of, there are too many loopholes and snares. What Gilbert did in fact erodes the whole basis of law, which is to keep people humane and civilized. Yet Gilbert was humane, civilized and wrong: a riddle. In the end we want the law intact and Gilbert free, so that society wins on both counts. What the case proves, however, is that society is helpless to do anything for Gilbert, for Emily or for itself. All we can do is recognize a real tragedy when we see one, and wonder, perhaps, if one bright morning in 1934 Gilbert read of a mercy killing in the papers, leaned earnestly across the breakfast table and told his new bride: "I couldn't do that. I could never do that."

Engaging the Text

1. Some of the vocabulary in this essay refers to the medical or technical aspects of the murder case: Luger (1), Alzheimer's disease (1), osteoporosis (1), clemency (1), pre-emptive strike (5), and precedents (7). Others refer to feelings involved, such as thinking "Is the frail doll on the bed an *impostor?*" (6) or "*distraught* people" (7). Be sure you understand these key words, looking them up in a dictionary if necessary.

2. This essay is an editorial—that is, it states a judgment or view of a controversial issue. What seems to be Rosenblatt's position on this case? How does he let you know this?

3. Rosenblatt uses many examples and case histories to illustrate his points. List some of these.

4. Rosenblatt also uses literary allusions to Shakespearean plays. Discuss these allusions. Do they make the essay more relevant? If so, how?

5. Dreams, flashbacks, and imaginary conversations also help to make the point (paragraphs 5 and 9). Is the writer justified in attributing these to Gilbert? Why or why not?

Engaging the Reader

1. Why did Roswell Gilbert kill his wife Emily?

2. What is the feeling of various parts of the public about this case?

3. What was Gilbert's dilemma? The impossible choice he had to make?

4. Since this article was written, other commentators have noted that Gilbert's sentence of 25 years in prison is the same penalty as some notorious serial killers have received. Do you agree with this penalty? If not, what penalty should have been imposed?

The Engaged Writer

1. Write a paper on how the situation described relates to Shakespeare's lines from which Rosenblatt got his title.

2. Explain the "riddle" in the last paragraph.

3. Before reading the letters that follow, write a paper arguing against Rosenblatt's apparent stand on the issue, or agreeing with it.

Letters Responding to "The Quality of Mercy Killing"

Two weeks after Roger Rosenblatt's essay appeared in *Time* magazine (September 1985), some letters to the editor were published that responded to "The Quality of Mercy Killing." The letters represent some of the many possible arguments for and against Gilbert's action and the public and official support he received. One letter, not reproduced here, told of the writer's care of her crippled father who suffered from Alzheimer's disease. She made the point that though the law may judge Gilbert, his real judges are those who have been in the same position he was. The letter seemed sympathetic to Gilbert. Another writer with a similar experience expressed reserved sympathy but also the view that Gilbert had given up his responsibility for caring for Emily and should bear the consequences of his act. Two of the four letters published appear here.

1 To think that Florida Governor Bob Graham was in favor of granting clemency to Gilbert horrifies me. If he is eventually pardoned, not one sick older woman in Florida will be safe. Murder is murder regardless of motive, and should be punished.

RENEE KERNS
MOHAVE VALLEY, ARIZ.

The case of Roswell and Emily Gilbert highlights a problem of 2
a rapidly increasing segment of our population, which is not only
very old but often beleaguered by incurable illnesses. These people are kept alive by modern technology, contrary to nature, which
should be the ultimate ruler over life and death. Consequently we
are faced with the awesome cost of caring for thousands of hope-
lessly sick people, while our standard of ethics remains mired in
Victorian thinking. The only way out of the dilemma is suicide by
the incurably ill before total incapacity prevents such action, or in
the case of a truly loving couple, suicide by joint resolve. Because
this alternative exceeds human ability, such bravery remains rare.
Therefore governments will have to be the final arbiter, whether
we like it or not. Incidentally, I am 73 years old.

HENRY T. BARTELS
WHITING, N.J.

Engaging the Text

1. The letter writers represented here use different writing styles.
   What differences can you notice in them? Notice arbiter, beleaguered, and mired in the Bartels letter.
2. Which writer sounds more angry? Which more reasonable?
   Why do you think they display these attitudes?

Engaging the Reader

1. What attitudes are expressed by the letter writers?
2. Summarize these attitudes in a sentence for each letter.

The Engaged Writer

1. Following the guidelines in "Writing a Letter to the Editor,"
   write a letter to the editor of *Time* magazine, agreeing or disagreeing with the Rosenblatt article, with the penalty imposed
   on Gilbert, or with any one of the responding letters here.

Some Student Responses to This Assignment

To the Editor:

Roswell Gilbert, who killed his wife by mercy killing, did the
right thing. In this day and age, people can be kept alive indef-
initely by machines. Technological advance is such that after a

person is pronounced clinically dead, he or she can be kept alive. But these people will never walk or be aware of their surroundings. This is creating an unbearable burden on the family in terms of the medical expense and the care these people need. It is also straining the health care facility.

Mercy killing is really one of the many possible answers. After 51 years of marriage, and watching his wife suffer, Mr. Gilbert must have been devastated. His life, too, was being destroyed. I am sure Mrs. Gilbert would approve the action of her husband. It is easy for society to pass judgment against Mr. Gilbert; however, no one was offering any help.

It is really a travesty of justice that he was sent to jail.

Frehiowet Sertse

Dear Editor:

The article by Roger Rosenblatt, "The Quality of Mercy Killing," is an extremely interesting one. It looks at the dilemma that our society faces when someone breaks the law by killing a loved one for mercy. When I first read the article I was shocked beyond belief that such a thing could take place. In Ethiopia, where I come from, such things do not exist. While it is true that we do have many kinds of illnesses that affect our old people, we can never interfere with the will of God. In our culture, when someone is terminally sick and is suffering very much, we simply put the person in the hands of God after we have done all we can as human beings. This ill person is taken to various sacred places, churches, and sanctuaries, and the entire family and friends show their concern through prayer and offerings to the saints and to God. No one ever considers killing the sick person as an act of mercy.

In the United States, however, the culture is quite different. Families are not as close as they are in our culture. Many individuals and married couples are too detached from their family base because of the system and the social life. Because of this, the government should establish some kind of an institution to help people with such problems of hopelessness. The article seems almost supportive of the idea of mercy killing. I think this is because it focuses on the despair of Mr. Roswell Gilbert as an individual. This is not the problem of the individual; it is a social and cultural problem. Mr. Gilbert should have been able to look to his society and culture for a solution to the problem instead of finding the answer in himself.

By presenting the problem as a social dilemma, the article makes us think that "mercy killing" may be considered a solution if it does not break the law. Mercy killing is not in the hands of human beings but in the hands of God so it should not be made a choice at all.

I agree that breaking the law in a mercy killing is a serious problem for the future of our society. I also understand the suffering of Mr. Gilbert. I believe that both Mr. Gilbert and his wife are victims of a society and culture that has lost the capacity to help such people.

Fanaye Gebrekidan

PART
6

Risks: Taking Chances

The first time you took a step (at about one year of age), you took a big risk. People who break through tradition, sexism, prescribed roles, and the tyranny of kings take risks in their lives. From a Hopi woman to the urban pioneer who slugged the mugger; from the framers of the Constitution to the 1848 Seneca Falls women—all who speak out strongly put their careers and even their lives on the line. Even recreational skiers and mountain climbers take risks. They may come, as N. Scott Momaday ("The End of My Childhood") expresses it, "within an eyelash of eternity."

In this section of *The Engaging Reader* a recurring theme is individuals having to make judgments and act on them, even though they may have suffered by doing so. By acting, taking a stand, taking a risk, these people often made their lives more meaningful and rich. Elinore Pruitt Stewart, the pioneer "Woman Homesteader," did this. On the other hand, many had to retrench and retreat from risk, often through no fault of their own, as did the Divers in J. Anthony Lukas's "When a Citizen Fights Back."

Some people take risks for fun, to test their skills, as the extreme skiers (Jeff Lowe, "On the Edge") do on untracked mountain peaks. Others, like Stephen Hawking, work on the leading edge of theoretical science at enormous personal risk ("Public Attitudes Toward Science"). Some find a cause and devote long lives to it, as Marjory Stoneman Douglas did for the Everglades (Dava Sobel, "Marjory Stoneman Douglas").

Others must compromise to live meaningfully. Sometimes this means leaving home, as Annie John does to get an education (Jamaica Kincaid, "A Walk to the Jetty"). The writers of the Declaration of Independence and the Constitution of the United States had to turn their backs on the secure government of the English King and take their chances with the raw new American Republic. The section continues, appropriately, with the Preamble and Bill of Rights, the first ten amendments to the United States Constitution, and with the Resolutions of the Seneca Falls Women's Rights Convention of 1848. It ends with Edith Wharton's "A First Word," a good conclusion to the section. All of the readings in this section recount examples of strong-minded people who forced themselves out of their ruts, took risks, took their lives in hand, and made connections with the larger world they helped to form.

N. SCOTT MOMADAY

The End of My Childhood

Native American writers were honored when N. Scott Momaday won the Pulitzer Prize in 1969 for his novel *House Made of Dawn*. Momaday is the leader of a new group of Native American writers who combine their college education with their native tribal lore. Momaday is a professor and scholar who has won many other honors besides the renowned Pulitzer. His autobiographical *The Names* (1976), like Leslie Silko's *Storyteller*, celebrates his ancestors and their traditions. The following excerpt is from *The Names*.

1   At Jemez I came to the end of my childhood. There were no schools within easy reach. I had to go nearly thirty miles to school at Bernalillo, and one year I lived away in Albuquerque. My mother and father wanted me to have the benefit of a sound preparation for college, and so we read through many high school catalogues. After long deliberation we decided that I should spend my last year of high school at a military academy in Virginia.

2   The day before I was to leave I went walking across the river to the red mesa, where many times before I had gone to be alone with my thoughts. And I had climbed several times to the top of the mesa and looked among the old ruins there for pottery. This time I chose to climb the north end, perhaps because I had not gone that way before and wanted to see what it was. It was a difficult climb, and when I got to the top I was spent. I lingered among the ruins

for more than an hour, I judge, waiting for my strength to return. From there I could see the whole valley below, the fields, the river, and the village. It was all very beautiful, and the sight of it filled me with longing.

I looked for an easier way to come down, and at length I found 3 a broad, smooth runway of rock, a shallow groove winding out like a stream. It appeared to be safe enough, and I started to follow it. There were steps along the way, a stairway, in effect. But the steps became deeper and deeper, and at last I had to drop down the length of my body and more. Still it seemed convenient to follow in the groove of rock. I was more than halfway down when I came upon a deep, funnel-shaped formation in my path. And there I had to make a decision. The slope on either side was extremely steep and forbidding, and yet I thought that I could work my way down on either side. The formation at my feet was something else. It was perhaps ten or twelve feet deep, wide at the top and narrow at the bottom, where there appeared to be a level ledge. If I could get down through the funnel to the ledge, I should be all right; surely the rest of the way down was negotiable. But I realized that there could be no turning back. Once I was down in that rocky chute I could not get up again, for the round wall which nearly encircled the space there was too high and sheer. I elected to go down into it, to try for the ledge directly below. I eased myself down the smooth, nearly vertical wall on my back, pressing my arms and legs outward against the sides. After what seemed a long time I was trapped in the rock. The ledge was no longer there below me; it had been an optical illusion. Now, in this angle of vision, there was nothing but the ground, far, far below, and jagged boulders set there like teeth. I remember that my arms were scraped and bleeding, stretched out against the walls with all the pressure that I could exert. When once I looked down I saw that my legs, also spread out and pressed hard against the walls, were shaking violently. I was in an impossible situation: I could not move in any direction, save downward in a fall, and I could not stay beyond another minute where I was. I believed then that I would die there, and I saw with a terrible clarity the things of the valley below. They were not the less beautiful to me. It seemed to me that I grew suddenly very calm in view of that beloved world. And I remember nothing else of that moment. I passed out of my mind, and the next thing I knew I was sitting down on the ground, very cold in the shadows, and looking up at the rock where I had been within an eyelash of eternity. That was a strange thing in my life, and I think of it as the end of an age. I should never again see the world as I saw it on the other side of that moment, in the bright reflection of time lost. There are such reflections, and for some of them I have the names.

Engaging the Text

1. Momaday describes the river, the mesa (1), the ruins, all the items of his walk very exactly. Then at the moment in which he is suspended in the cleft in the rock he deliberately avoids describing what happened. We literally do not know how he ended up "sitting down on the ground, very cold in the shadows, and looking up at the rock where I had been within an eyelash of eternity." Why does he do this?
2. See if you can find a drawing or photo of a mesa (1). This word is Spanish and means *table*. Why do you think the early Spanish settlers in the Southwest called these unusual formations *mesas*? Other technical words concerning mountain formations and climbing are chute, negotiable, and vertical (3).
3. Momaday's language is simple but solemn: he uses phrases like "the sight of it filled me with longing" and "I realized that there could be no turning back." Why do you think he chose these phrases? What does his use of these phrases tell us about him?

Engaging the Reader

1. Why does Momaday's family decide that he should go away to school for his last year of high school?
2. Why do you think he went on a walk the day before he was to leave for school?
3. Where did he walk? What happened to him there?
4. What did he learn from this experience?
5. What do you think he means by "the names"?

The Engaged Writer

1. What events in your life have forced you to change established habits, as Momaday had to change when he went away to school? Write about one of these.

2. If you have gone from one culture to another, write about one of the biggest changes you noticed in the new environment.
3. Was there a moment in your life when you knew your "childhood ended"? Write about it.
4. Have you made a great decision in your life and realized that "there was no turning back"? Describe this event in an essay, developed, like Momaday's, as a story or illustration of that theme.
5. If you have been in a position of great immediate danger, as Momaday was on the cliff, write about what you decided to do and the consequences of that decision.

JAMAICA KINCAID

A Walk to the Jetty

Jamaica Kincaid was born in St. John's, Antigua, in the West Indies. She later became a staff writer for the *New Yorker*. Her stories have appeared in several magazines, and she has won prizes for her novels. Her novel *Annie John* (1985) tells a growing-up story about a girl on an island much like Antigua. Kincaid's *A Small Place* (1988) tells about her return home from the United States years later. This excerpt from *Annie John* begins when Annie goes away to study, taking a big risk in her young life.

My heart now beat fast, and no matter how hard I tried, I couldn't 1 keep my mouth from falling open and my nostrils from spreading to the ends of my face. My old fear of slipping between the boards of the jetty and falling into the dark-green water where the dark-green eels lived came over me. When my father's stomach started to go bad, the doctor had recommended a walk every evening right after he ate his dinner. Sometimes he would take me with him. When he took me with him, we usually went to the jetty, and there he would sit and talk to the night watchman about cricket or some other thing that didn't interest me, because it was not personal; they didn't talk about their wives, or their children, or their parents, or about any of their likes and dislikes. They talked about things in such a strange way, and I didn't see what they found

funny, but sometimes they made each other laugh so much that
their guffaws would bound out to sea and send back an echo. I was
always sorry when we got to the jetty and saw that the night
watchman on duty was the one he enjoyed speaking to; it was like
being locked up in a book filled with numbers and diagrams and
what-ifs. For the thing about not being able to understand and
enjoy what they were saying was I had nothing to take my mind
off my fear of slipping in between the boards of the jetty.

2   Now, too, I had nothing to take my mind off what was happening to me. My mother and my father—I was leaving them forever.
My home on an island—I was leaving it forever. What to make of
everything? I felt a familiar hollow space inside. I felt I was being
held down against my will. I felt I was burning up from head to toe.
I felt that someone was tearing me up into little pieces and soon I
would be able to see all the little pieces as they floated out into nothing in the deep blue sea. I didn't know whether to laugh or cry. I
could see that it would be better not to think too clearly about any
one thing. The launch was being made ready to take me, along with
some other passengers, out to the ship that was anchored in the sea.
My father paid our fares, and we joined a line of people waiting to
board. My mother checked my bag to make sure that I had my pass-
port, the money she had given me, and a sheet of paper placed
between some pages in my Bible on which were written the names
of the relatives—people I had not known existed—with whom I
would live in England. Across from the jetty was a wharf, and some
stevedores were loading and unloading barges. I don't know why
seeing that struck me so, but suddenly a wave of strong feeling
came over me, and my heart swelled with a great gladness as the
words "I shall never see this again" spilled out inside me. But then,
just as quickly, my heart shriveled up and the words "I shall never
see this again" stabbed at me. I don't know what stopped me from
falling in a heap at my parents' feet.

3   When we were all on board, the launch headed out to sea. Away
from the jetty, the water became the customary blue, and the
launch left a wide path in it that looked like a road. I passed by
sounds and smells that were so familiar that I had long ago
stopped paying any attention to them. But now here they were,
and the ever-present "I shall never see this again" bobbed up and
down inside me. There was the sound of the seagull diving down
into the water and coming up with something silverish in its

mouth. There was the smell of the sea and the sight of small pieces of rubbish floating around in it. There were boats filled with fishermen coming in early. There was the sound of their voices as they shouted greetings to each other. There was the hot sun, there was the blue sea, there was the blue sky. Not very far away, there was the white sand of the shore, with the rundown houses all crowded in next to each other, for in some places only poor people lived near the shore. I was seated in the launch between my parents, and when I realized that I was gripping their hands tightly I glanced quickly to see if they were looking at me with scorn, for I felt sure that they must have known of my never-see-this-again feelings. But instead my father kissed me on the forehead and my mother kissed me on the mouth, and they both gave over their hands to me, so that I could grip them as much as I wanted. I was on the verge of feeling that it had all been a mistake, but I remembered that I wasn't a child anymore, and that now when I made up my mind about something I had to see it through. At that moment, we came to the ship, and that was that.

The goodbyes had to be quick, the captain said. My mother 4 introduced herself to him and then introduced me. She told him to keep an eye on me, for I had never gone this far away from home on my own. She gave him a letter to pass on to the captain of the next ship that I would board in Barbados. They walked me to my cabin, a small space that I would share with someone else— a woman I did not know. I had never before slept in a room with someone I did not know. My father kissed me goodbye and told me to be good and to write home often. After he said this, he looked at me, then looked at the floor and swung his left foot, then looked at me again. I could see that he wanted to say something else, something that he had never said to me before, but then he just turned and walked away. My mother said, "Well," and then she threw her arms around me. Big tears streamed down her face, and it must have been that—for I could not bear to see my mother cry—which started me crying, too. She then tightened her arms around me and held me to her close, so that I felt that I couldn't breathe. With that, my tears dried up and I was suddenly on my guard. "What does she want now?" I said to myself. Still holding me close to her, she said, in a voice that raked across my skin, "It doesn't matter what you do or where you go, I'll always be your mother and this will always be your home."

5   I dragged myself away from her and backed off a little, and then I shook myself, as if to wake myself out of a stupor. We looked at each other for a long time with smiles on our faces, but I know the opposite of that was in my heart. As if responding to some invisible cue, we both said, at the very same moment, "Well." Then my mother turned around and walked out the cabin door. I stood there for I don't know how long, and then I remembered that it was customary to stand on deck and wave to your relatives who were returning to shore. From the deck, I could not see my father, but I could see my mother facing the ship, her eyes searching to pick me out. I removed from my bag a red cotton handkerchief that she had earlier given me for this purpose, and I waved it wildly in the air. Recognizing me immediately, she waved back just as wildly, and we continued to do this until she became just a dot in the matchbox-size launch swallowed up in the big blue sea.

6   I went back to my cabin and lay down on my berth. Everything trembled as if it had a spring at its very center. I could hear the small waves lap-lapping around the ship. They made an unexpected sound, as if a vessel filled with liquid had been placed on its side and now was slowly emptying out.

Engaging the Text

1. In this story, as in many distinctive pieces of writing, we say we can hear the writer's "voice." What is unusual or distinctive about Annie's "voice"? Look at sentence length, vocabulary (words such as *guffaws*, paragraph 1), descriptions, and metaphors. List these as you find them, and then use a few from your list in sentences of your own.

Engaging the Reader

1. Why is Annie afraid of slipping between the boards of the jetty?
2. Is Annie happy or sad about leaving home? What is the feeling she has?
3. How is she traveling?

The Engaged Writer

1. Annie describes scenes very simply, yet underneath we can feel the emotion she must have had. Choose a scene from your

own life in which you made a change, such as leaving home or making a big decision about a career or personal relationship. Tell it in the same kind of simple language that Annie uses.

2. What kinds of changes do young people make today? Take one of them as a theme and write an essay on how to cope with it. Some of these changes include

    — leaving home
    — getting married
    — taking a new job
    — changing style of living
    — doing a dangerous sport—rock climbing, hang gliding, and so on
    — joining the service
    — risking one's life in a tight situation

3. Compare Annie John's experience in leaving home with N. Scott Momaday's.

ELINORE PRUITT STEWART

The Arrival at Burnt Fork and Filing a Claim

Elinore Rupert was a widow with a small daughter when she left her work in Denver, Colorado, in 1909 to prove up a claim—to file for free land under the Homestead Act. She had worked as a "washlady" for a woman named Juliet Coney in Denver; while waiting to prove her claim, she worked as housekeeper for a Wyoming rancher named Clyde Stewart. As soon as she arrived in Wyoming, she started a correspondence with her former employer, Mrs. Coney; the letters here are the beginning of that correspondence. In a very short time she married Mr. Stewart and had several more children. She did claim her land and had many adventures while living on the frontier. Her cheerful disposition and clever wit carried her through many ups and downs of frontier life and show abundantly in these excerpts from her letters which first appeared in 1913–1914 in *The Atlantic Monthly*. In 1991, a film, *Heartland*, was based on her story.

I

The Arrival at Burnt Fork

BURNT FORK, WYOMING,
April 18, 1909.

Dear Mrs. Coney,—

1   Are you thinking I am lost, like the Babes in the Wood? Well,
I am not and I'm sure the robins would have the time of their
lives getting leaves to cover me out here. I am 'way up close to
the Forest Reserve of Utah, within half a mile of the line, sixty
miles from the railroad. I was twenty-four hours on the train
and two days on the stage, and oh, those two days! The snow
was just beginning to melt and the mud was about the worst I
ever heard of.

2   The first stage we tackled was just about as rickety as it could
very well be and I had to sit with the driver, who was a Mormon and so handsome that I was not a bit offended when he
insisted on making love all the way, especially after he told me
that he was a widower Mormon. But, of course, as I had no chap-
erone I looked very fierce (not that that was very difficult with
the wind and mud as allies) and told him my actual opinion of
Mormons in general and particular.

3   Meantime my new employer, Mr. Stewart, sat upon a stack
of baggage and was dreadfully concerned about something he
calls his "Tookie," but I am unable to tell you what that is. The
road, being so muddy, was full of ruts and the stage acted as if
it had the hiccoughs and made us all talk as though we were
affected in the same way. Once Mr. Stewart asked me if I did not
think it a "gey duir trip." I told him he could call it gay if he
wanted to, but it didn't seem very hilarious to me. Every time
the stage struck a rock or a rut Mr. Stewart would "hoot," until
I began to wish we would come to a hollow tree or a hole in the
ground so he could go in with the rest of the owls.

4   At last we "arriv," and everything is just lovely for me. I have
a very, very comfortable situation and Mr. Stewart is absolutely
no trouble, for as soon as he has his meals he retires to his room
and plays on his bagpipe, only he calls it his "bugpeep." It is "The
Campbells are Coming," without variations, at intervals all day

long and from seven till eleven at night. Sometimes I wish they would make haste and get here.

There is a saddle horse especially for me and a little shotgun 5 with which I am to kill sage chickens. We are between two trout streams, so you can think of me as being happy when the snow is through melting and the water gets clear. We have the finest flock of Plymouth Rocks and get so many nice eggs. It sure seems fine to have all the cream I want after my town experiences. Jerrine is making good use of all the good things we are having. She rides the pony to water every day.

I have not filed on my land yet because the snow is fifteen 6 feet deep on it, and I think I would rather see what I am getting, so will wait until summer. They have just three seasons here, winter and July and August. We are to plant our garden the last of May. When it is so I can get around I will see about land and find out all I can and tell you.

I think this letter is about to reach thirty-secondly, so I will 7 send you my sincerest love and quit tiring you. Please write me when you have time.

Sincerely Yours,

Elinore Rupert.

II

Filing a Claim

May 24, 1909

Dear, Dear Mrs. Coney,—

Well, I have filed on my land and am now a bloated land- 8 owner. I waited a long time to even *see* land in the reserve, and the snow is yet too deep, so I thought that as they have but three months of summer and spring together and as I wanted the land for a ranch anyway, perhaps I had better stay in the valley. So I have filed adjoining Mr. Stewart and I am well pleased. I have a grove of twelve swamp pines on my place, and I am going to build my house there. I thought it would be very romantic to live on the peaks amid the whispering pines, but I reckon it would be powerfully uncomfortable also, and I guess my twelve can whisper enough for me; and a dandy thing is, I have all the nice snow-water I want; a small stream runs right through the center of my land and I am quite near wood.

9   A neighbor and his daughter were going to Green River, the county-seat, and said I might go along, so I did, as I could file there as well as at the land office; and oh, that trip! I had more fun to the square inch than Mark Twain or Samantha Allen <u>ever</u> provoked. It took us a whole week to go and come. We camped out, of course, for in the whole sixty miles there was but one house, and going in that direction there is not a tree to be seen, nothing but sage, sand, and sheep. About noon the first day out we came near a sheep-wagon, and stalking along ahead of us was a lanky fellow, a herder, going home for dinner. Suddenly it seemed to me I should starve if I had to wait until we got where we had planned to stop for dinner, so I called out to the man, "Little Bo-Peep, have you anything to eat? If you have, we'd like to find it." And he answered, "As soon as I am able it shall be on the table, if you'll but trouble to get behind it." Shades of Shakespeare! Songs of David, the Shepherd Poet! What do you think of us? Well, we got behind it, and a more delicious "it" I never tasted. Such coffee! And out of *such* a pot! I promised Bo-Peep that I would send him a crook with pink ribbons on it, but I suspect he thinks I am a crook without the ribbons.

10   The sagebrush is so short in some places that it is not large enough to make a fire, so we had to drive until quite late before we camped that night. After driving all day over what seemed a level desert of sand, we came about sundown to a beautiful cañon, down which we had to drive for a couple of miles before we could cross. In the cañon the shadows had already fallen, but when we looked up we could see the last shafts of sunlight on the tops of the great bare buttes. Suddenly a great wolf started from somewhere and galloped along the edge of the cañon, outlined black and clear by the setting sun. His curiosity overcame him at last, so he sat down and waited to see what manner of beast we were. I reckon he was disappointed for he howled most dismally. I thought of Jack London's "The Wolf."

After we quitted the cañon I saw the most beautiful sight. It   11
seemed as if we were driving through a golden haze. The violet
shadows were creeping up between the hills, while away back
of us the snow-capped peaks were catching the sun's last rays.
On every side of us stretched the poor, hopeless desert, the sage,
grim and determined to live in spite of starvation, and the great,
bare, desolate buttes. The beautiful colors turned to amber and
rose, and then to the general tone, dull gray. Then we stopped
to camp, and such a scurrying around to gather brush for the
fire and to get supper! Everything tasted so good! Jerrine ate
like a man. Then we raised the wagon tongue and spread the
wagon sheet over it and made a bedroom for us women. We
made our beds on the warm, soft sand and went to bed. . . .

After two more such days I "arrived." When I went up to the   12
office where I was to file, the door was open and the most taci-
turn old man sat before a desk. I hesitated at the door, but he
never let on. I coughed, yet no sign but a deeper scowl. I stepped
in and modestly kicked over a chair. He whirled around like I
had shot him. "Well?" he interrogated. I said, "I am powerful
glad of it. I was afraid you were sick, you looked in such pain."
He looked at me a minute, then grinned and said he thought I
was a book-agent. Fancy me, a fat, comfortable widow, trying to
sell books!

Well, I filed and came home. If you will believe me, the Scot   13
was glad to see me and didn't herald the Campbells for two
hours after I got home. I'll tell you, it is mighty seldom any one's
so much appreciated. . . .

Well, I must quit writing before you vote me a nuisance. With   14
lots of love to you,

Your Sincere Friend,

Elinore Rupert.

Engaging the Text

1. Stewart refers several times to popular books and authors of
   the time (showing, perhaps, that she read a lot in the prairie
   evenings). Some of these are the *Babes in the Wood* (1), Mark
   Twain and Samantha Allen (9), Shakespeare and "Songs of

David" (9), and Jack London's "The Wolf" (10). How do these authors and books relate to Stewart's life?

2. Some of her slang shows how words have changed from her day to today, for example, *making love* (2) at that time meant simply "coming on" and *gay* (3) meant humorous, fun-filled. Give some other examples of words that have changed meaning.

3. Could Garrison Keillor ("How to Write a Personal Letter") have used the letters of the "woman homesteader" as examples?

4. In spite of the chatty tone, Stewart uses colorful descriptions of the West of that time (1909). Note the words in some of these descriptions: cañon and buttes (10). Find some other descriptive passages in *The Engaging Reader* (for example, in Zane Grey's "At Kaidab Trading Post"), and notice their effectiveness.

Engaging the Reader

1. Compare these letters with Sigal D'Avanzo's "Dear Mom," a modern equivalent of moving to a new land. Take the tone of the letters into consideration.

2. How does Stewart fit into this section called "Risks"?

3. What resources would a widow with a small child have today? How would they compare with the opportunities Stewart found when she became a widow?

The Engaged Writer

1. Why do you think Stewart so often refers to nursery rhymes or stories in her letter? Find the stories she refers to and write a short paper about one of them, relating it to Stewart's life.

2. Changes in definition, such as those for *making love* and *gay* referred to in "Engaging the Text" could furnish good material for a short essay. Write one about some other words that have changed their meanings today.

3. Find an account in a newspaper or magazine of a person who lives a rather unusual life. Write a short letter from that person to an imaginary friend in another part of the country.

4. Write a letter to a friend about an important step you took in your life. Date your letter shortly after the occurrence and write it as if it had just happened, as Stewart did. Refer to Garrison Keillor's "How to Write a Personal Letter" for advice on the composition of this letter.

JEFF LOWE

On the Edge

Jeff Lowe writes for *Backpacker* magazine, where this article appeared in 1988. In addition, he is involved in many other outdoor and wilderness projects. He subtitled the article "The perfect way to find yourself is by skiing in the red zone"—referring to the dangerous areas forbidden to skiers. What follows is a poetic tribute to pushing the human body beyond its limits.

The memory actually grows more vivid with time. Once again, the 1 rock walls lining the couloir flash by my peripheral vision like spectators lining a race course. The gully is steep, an honest 45 degrees—twice as steep as the most reckless black-diamond ski run at a resort—the snow, hard. Rebound off a firm edge-set, suck up the knees, start another jump turn. For a wonderful, weightless moment I'm in the fall line. Then I reach my skis down again to reestablish contact with the snow and finish carving the turn. Icy ridges the size of speed bumps jolt them as I traverse the gully, then dive into the next turn.

The tight rock walls contain and amplify the sound of edges 2 scraping on impenetrable snow. The elemental grinding reaches me more by way of ski, foot, and spine, than by ear. Soon quadriceps start to incandesce. The pain begins as a flicker, then bursts into flame, warning, "Be careful now, don't overdo it. You can't afford to make a mistake!" But I'm seduced by the rhythm into executing just one more turn, then another, then another. . . .

That's the feeling of extreme skiing: so intense, so alive, your 3 heart keeping time in your chest, your legs pumping and releasing, over and over, the essence of commitment palpable in the smell of your sweat. There's nothing to equal the deep, animal satisfaction that results when mind and body operate in total integration.

Extreme skiing has a much shorter history than its spiritual ally, 4 mountaineering. Ski-mountaineering on the easier peaks began in Europe in the 1800s, but Mont Blanc, at 15,782 feet the Alps' highest peak, was not skied all the way from the summit until Lionel Terray and Bil Dunaway did it in 1953. Truly extreme skiing, where you get only one fall ever, began in the 1960s when Sylvain Saudan knocked off difficult routes such as the Eiger's precipitous west flank. Saudan's exploits triggered a surge of interest, which slowed somewhat after Heini Holzer's fatal fall on Pitz Roseg in 1970.

5   Extreme skiing in the United States didn't begin until the late 1960s and early 1970s, when Bill Briggs skied the Grand Teton, and Fritz Stammberger did North Maroon Bell. Today, a small but growing band of skiers quietly seek out steep chutes in the Rockies and Sierra each spring.

6   After Holzer's fall, a decade passed before the sport really heated up again anywhere. The unquestioned star today is Jean-Marc Boivin, a gifted mountaineer who, in the winter of 1986, climbed four major Alpine north faces in one day, descending by parapente or hang-glider in between. Last winter, Boivin introduced this French concept of *enchaînement* to extreme skiing as well, with the descents of four major routes in a single day. As Boivin shows, extreme skiing is a child of mountaineering, not of resort skiing.

7   July Fourth came and went last year, but for some reason my itch for one last ski trip before the hot, dry days of August simply had to be scratched. For many years I'd been eyeing a striking run in Colorado's San Juan Mountains: the northwest couloir of 14,150-foot Mt. Sneffels. I recruited Lou Dawson as a ski partner and Glenn Randall as a photographer, and on the 6th of July, headed south to the San Juans.

8   Ironically, heavy snowfall makes winter skiing in Colorado couloirs a game of Russian roulette with five bullets in the chamber. One January, for example, an avalanche swept two strong but overzealous Telluride skiers clean out of the gully. Astonishingly, the hammer landed on an empty chamber, and neither was hurt. But the best time for extreme skiing remains late spring or early summer, when the snow is too firm to avalanche, but has not yet melted out or turned to ice.

9   On our July morning, we still had to catch the snow before the sun softened it too much. With the grunts appropriate to 4 A.M., we crawled out of our bags by headlamp. Breakfast was a truncated and tasteless affair—a banana in three bites, plus half-a-quart of grapefruit juice. The enormous wonder of the star-flecked, cobalt sky was almost lost on us as we swung excessively heavy packs onto our backs, skis thrust between the compression straps, and headed up the steep, dirt road leading deeper into the basin.

Mt. Sneffels's bulk hid our destination. Here on the south side, 10 a few scruffy patches of snow lingered, faintly visible in the starlight, but none would have offered decent skiing. We could only hope that the northwest couloir was still skiable.

In the soft, pre-dawn light, I marvelled again at Lou's new hair- 11 cut: a crewcut with a stripe shaved down the middle of his reddish hair. The reverse Mohawk, combined with his long, thin legs, and arms ending in big hands like bundles of kielbasas, made him look like a cross between a dirt farmer and a punk-rocker. Lou has written a ski touring guide called *Colorado High Routes,* and is working on a guide to skiing Colorado's 14,000-foot peaks.

Glenn, on the other hand, resembled a slightly aging choir boy. 12 Now 30, he might still look like every mother's high school dream son if it weren't for a string of expeditions that have etched his features as vividly as the rocks and mountains on which he plays and works. Although he was in taut shape, having only recently returned from two Alaskan ski-mountaineering expeditions, he decided to descend on crampons to have a more secure platform for photography.

We turned up a snow-filled gully and climbed toward a saddle 13 in the east ridge that overlooks the great basin below Sneffels's north face. The sun rose as we climbed, though we felt its warmth only when we emerged from the gully onto the saddle.

Acres of snow plunging down to 12,000 feet were like a paint- 14 ing to our eyes. And the snow was solid—proof, we assumed, that our intended route of descent in the northwest gully would still offer excellent skiing. The snowfields, already tinged red with the dust of many hot summer days, contrasted sharply with the meandering greens of the valley far below. We turned up the steep, rocky, east ridge, and continued climbing in the sunshine, past dazzling microgardens of alpine phlox, gentian, and cinquefoil.

The air on the summit was crisp, though wispy mare's tails 15 hinted at deteriorating afternoon weather. The gully snowpack was good—at least as far as we could see. And the pitch didn't look too extreme. After all, we'd seen the runout, and assumed that if someone fell, he'd just slide onto flat snow eventually. The hidden middle portion? We didn't even think about it.

Many of the most active Colorado skiers are so reticent that no 16 one claims the first descent of Sneffel's northwest couloir, but it seems to have occurred within the last couple of seasons. I asked

Lou how many times the couloir had been skied. "Oh, a lot," he replied offhandedly, "maybe a hundred." This may be an exaggeration, but it confirms my suspicion that for all its lunatic appearance, extreme skiing is a growing sport. Everywhere I went in Colorado's Front Range last spring, there were already tracks of skiers, often on extremely technical runs.

17   After a hasty bite to eat, we rappelled from the summit into the northwest gully. Lou and I lurched like drunken spiders in our rigid ski boots. I had walked up in lightweight hikers, then switched to my trusty San Marco alpine boots. Lou had chosen slightly softer Dynafit alpine-touring boots, more comfortable for hiking, a little less supportive for skiing.

18   When we reached snow, Lou and I chipped out a platform on which to don our skis. Looking down into the couloir was like staring down the muzzle of a 12-gauge. For 50 feet below us, the early July sun touched the surface, softening it agreeably. Then the snow steepened and plunged into the kind of shade that is banished only briefly at midday in high summer. The snow there looked unyielding and repellent.

19   Glenn cramponed down 100 feet and reported good conditions in the sun, but much harder snow than expected in the shade. "You want steel on your feet for this stuff," he said. Lou had self-arrest grips on his ski poles. I had no illusions about what would happen in a fall—one way or another, a fast trip to the bottom—and carried ordinary alpine ski poles.

20   Risk is in the game. Controlling that risk is part of the exhilaration, and part of the responsibility, of the extreme skier. It comes down to an educated feathering of the personal edge; it's when you're operating within the final few percentage points of your abilities that magical rewards can happen.

21   Enough talk. I eased out onto the slope and set my edges hard to check the quality of the snow. It felt good here in the sun. Denying a strong reluctance to begin, I made the first jump turn as decisively as I could. The next came more easily, but once in the shade, my skis were clacking like castanets on the solidly frozen snow. The edges just barely bit deep enough to hold me as I made my turns, then pulled off to the side to watch Lou. He dispatched the first turns as if he were skiing on a big egg, barely leaving the snow as he initiated each one, landing gently. We joined together, then continued. Glenn led the way to check conditions.

Eight hundred feet below the summit, we rounded a turn and 22
stopped in shock. A massive rockfall had cut loose from the
gully's west wall some days—or weeks—before. Tons of cascad-
ing stone had stripped the gully of snow, leaving behind only
ancient ice, pocked with boulders the size of truck tires. "I don't
think you guys will be skiing this," yelled Glenn somewhat
gratuitously.

We could see that below the rockfall zone, even the ice had 23
melted out completely. Our ski adventure was over almost before
it had begun.

Or was it? Last August I had climbed the northwest ridge. I 24
remembered looking down into a gully that, if memory served me
well, should lie just to the west of this one. It had snow, even at
summer's end. If only we could reach it, it might still be skiable.

I looked around. A notch cut the west wall of the gully just 200 25
feet below us. Lou and I switched to crampons, and we descended
through the wasteland below, then traversed to the notch.

Relief! Below us, snow filled the gully from rim to rim. True, it 26
was heavily suncupped, but its moderate angle made it eminent-
ly skiable—even if every turn would have to be a jump. The day
would be a good one yet.

A few hundred feet lower, we dropped over a lip and saw that 27
this gully too had melted out. Skiable snow began again after only
a hundred feet of talus, but no runout and a steepening angle gave
each turn that unmistakable edge of seriousness.

We climbed down through rock and clamped on the skis one 28
last time. Sharp towers graced the east wall of the gully, framing
vistas of the farmlands near Montrose in the notches between
them. The angle eased for a little way, then plunged again in the
steepest section of all. As we eased over the lip, we saw that at last
we had a runout onto sunny, soft snow not far below.

Lou went first. Without hesitation, he plunged through a series 29
of turns. Then, in the very steepest part, he stopped. Pulling an
inclinometer from his pocket, he measured the slope: 48 degrees.
Then he pocketed his instrument and flawlessly descended to the
safety of the open slope.

I followed, leaning out over my skis and ramming my pole tip 30
into the snow as I sprung into each turn. Each movement had to
be aggressive, decisive, just to stay upright and among the living.
Each landing had to be exactly centered to drive in the ski edges

at precisely the right angle. Sitting back or leaning in would cause a dangerous loss of control.

31   The first turn felt perfect. So did the next. And the next. And the elusive feeling of freedom started expanding my chest. This was why I had come.

32   Too soon it was over. The gully began to open out, then ended suddenly and completely. Full sunshine washed over us as we entered a broad snowfield, and it felt like blinders had been removed from our eyes.

33   We popped off the boards and looked back at what we'd done. To our knowledge, no one had ever skied the variation we'd found—a fitting cap to a day full of surprises.

34   All skiers must define extreme skiing for themselves. One might consider Sneffels in July casual; a second might consider it court-ing death. The point is neither the angle nor the difficulty in any absolute sense, but the inner experience. Few people actually know where their limits are. Finding yours, then expanding them in a remote mountain environment that imposes self-sufficiency, is what extreme skiing is all about. Too few realize they can share the experience, that the mountains of western North America offer ter-rain that is suitable for anyone from beginner to expert.

35   As I wearily strapped my skis to my pack, I realized abruptly that we had to go back over the saddle in the east ridge to return to the truck. Great. Traipse up 1500 feet more of loose scree and soft snow? No problem.

36   With a rueful chuckle, I swung my leaden pack onto my back and started up. After all, as Lou said, it really had been "just another lousy day in paradise."

Engaging the Text

1.   Lowe writes about a very technical sport such as skiing with both the terms specific to the sport and a vital language full of metaphors and similes that we usually associate with poetry. Some of his technical terms are black-diamond ski run (1), couloir (7), quadriceps (2), precipitous (4), chutes (5—see also Momaday), cramponed (19), *enchaînement* (6), Telluride (8—a place), rappelled (17), and inclinometer (29). In addition, Lowe uses other colorful words from other experiences to enliven his writing: lurched (17), repellent (18—note similarity in pro-

nunciation to rappelled), meandering (14), incandesce (2—as a verb), palpable (3), truncated (9), and cobalt (9).
2. The author makes us feel as if we are physically there, even if we are not expert skiers. How does he do this? Point out some passages where his writing is especially vivid.
3. In addition, Lowe describes his companions, Lou and Glenn, very clearly. List some of these details, such as the "reverse Mohawk" (11).
4. Explain the meaning of some of the metaphors Lowe uses: "Russian roulette with five bullets in the chamber" (8) and "an educated feathering of the personal edge" (20). He also uses similes: "like bundles of kielbasas" (11) and "like drunken spiders" (17). You don't have to be a skier to appreciate these.

Engaging the Reader

1. What does the title "On the Edge" mean? On the edge of what?
2. In your peer group, see if anyone has had an adventure to which the first sentence of "On the Edge" applies. Ask him or her to describe that experience.
3. Discuss some of the technicalities Lowe mentions; for example, why does he say it is better to do this extreme skiing in late spring or early summer?

The Engaged Writer

1. Describe one particular action you took recently that could have been dangerous. Use details the way Lowe does.
2. Describe a person you know with as few details as Lowe uses to make us see his two companions very vividly.
3. Would you be willing to take up this sport of extreme skiing Lowe advocates to find "where your limits are"? If so, write why you would do it; if you are unwilling, explain why.
4. Write about some incident that you have read about in the newspapers or seen on TV that illustrates the "inner experience" of being "on the edge" that Lowe champions.
5. Compare the dangers Lowe runs with those of some of the other writers in this section: N. Scott Momaday ("The End of My Childhood"), J. Anthony Lukas ("When a Citizen Fights Back"), or the writers of the Seneca Falls Resolutions, for example.

DAVA SOBEL

Marjory Stoneman Douglas: Still Fighting the Good Fight for the Everglades

Marjory Stoneman Douglas exemplifies many of the themes of this book: self-realization, ecological concerns, and changing gender roles. She began as a competent newspaper writer and realized fame as a novelist and nature writer. Her campaign to save the Everglades, the "river of grass" in South Florida, has pitted her against powerful and moneyed authorities and made her a symbol of the fight for natural preservation for the whole country. Dava Sobel wrote this commemorative article for *Audubon* magazine to celebrate Douglas's one-hundred-first birthday and to note that she is the only surviving member of the original 1927 Everglades Park Committee. Dava Sobel has been a science reporter and magazine writer; she has been working on a book about extraterrestrial intelligence.

1 Just before her one-hundred-first birthday, Marjory Stoneman Douglas felt compelled to take a day off work to meet with federal officials at Everglades National Park in Homestead, Florida, just about an hour's drive from her home in Coconut Grove.

2   The meeting came up at a busy time for Mrs. Douglas—not that she's ever idle. Though legally blind, she'd been working with the help of a friend and two secretaries, trying among other things to complete her biography of W.H. Hudson, the naturalist and author of *Green Mansions.* But Mrs. Douglas apparently lives by the rule that when the Everglades call for her, she goes to them. This has been true most of her adult life, especially for the last twenty years. As she tells it, she became passionately committed to the Glades in the beginning of her eightieth year—"about the time I started the W.H. Hudson project, about the time I lost so much of my eyesight I could hardly have seen the Everglades outdoors."

3   Mrs. Douglas arrived for the March 1st meeting at park headquarters wearing her white spring coat, her ladylike Panama hat, and a single strand of white beads. A picture taken of her that day,

sitting next to William K. Reilly, administrator of the Environmental Protection Agency, and Robert S. Chandler, superintendent of the park, appeared with a page-one story about the proposed $700 million restoration of the Everglades in *The New York Times.* In the photo, Mrs. Douglas has her face set in an attentive yet imperturbable expression behind her thick glasses. The two gentlemen appear well-pleased to be in her company, though perhaps they would be hard pressed to tell her anything she didn't already know.

The only surviving member of the original 1927 committee to 4 put the Everglades under Park Service protection, Mrs. Douglas had a hand in creating Everglades National Park, which was finally chartered twenty years later. Since then, she's engaged both hands—and sometimes both feet, too, it seems—in saving the complex ecosystem of the Everglades from certain destruction by agricultural and real-estate interests. She'd be the first to tell you she hasn't spent a whole lot of time tromping around the mangroves and the sawgrass. ("It's too buggy, too wet, too generally inhospitable—the sawgrass would cut you to pieces—for camping or hiking or the other outdoor activities which naturalists in other places can routinely enjoy.") Still, on her infrequent visits over the years, she has witnessed the nuptial flight of the white ibis, fed marshmallows to the alligators, and walked close enough to a rare Florida panther to see the shadows of its whiskers.

"I know it's out there and I know its importance," she has said 5 of the park and its environs. "I suppose you could say the Everglades and I have the kind of friendship that doesn't depend on constant physical contact."

Even Mrs. Douglas, an accomplished reporter, short-story 6 writer, and author of several books, never could decide whether to call the Everglades an "it" or a "they." That grammatical confusion is symbolic of the mystique of the Everglades—singular in its uniqueness, plural in their vastness and diversity.

Instead of communing with the Glades, Mrs. Douglas spoke for 7 them in tireless efforts at public education, from her position as founder and first president of the group she named "Friends of the Everglades." Thanks to her devoted friendship, the Everglades seem headed for brighter days because the state, the federal government, the Army Corps of Engineers, and the South Florida Water Management District are all taking steps toward restoring the landscape now thought to be on the brink of biological collapse.

8   This is the last battle to be won. In years past, Mrs. Douglas has rescued the Glades from plume hunters who ransacked the rookeries for the millinery trade, from developers who wanted to erect bridges, suburbs, and even a jetport on the marshes. This time she's convinced most everyone of the value of what she's been saying all along—that the Everglades must have their free flow of water restored. That has been her mantra, because the water *is* the Everglades.

9   The Army Corps of Engineers did more than anyone else to disturb the course of the waters, Mrs. Douglas maintains. One of the Corps' first offenses was to straighten the meanders of the Kissimmee River into a canal in the early 1900s. This benefited the big sugarcane growers, who then polluted Lake Okeechobee by backpumping their irrigation water into it, "along with all the pesticides, fertilizer, dead cats, and old boots that the water had absorbed."

10   While some environmentalists defend this or that endangered species of waterbird, Mrs. Douglas clings to a radical view:

11   "It's the whole thing that's got to be preserved," she says. "We've got to restore the Kissimmee River, we've got to clean up Lake Okeechobee and maintain the sheet flow of the Everglades."

12   It follows from her simple formula that the return of a vast sheet of water—inching southwestward from the Kissimmee River and Lake Okeechobee, down and across one hundred miles of what she calls "the great pointed paw of the state of Florida," out to the Gulf of Mexico—will bring back the birds, the rainfall, and the many natural treasures that have been gradually disappearing from the Glades over the past century. But Mrs. Douglas will have to live at least another ten years to reap the fruits of her own hard work.

13   One of the first things I asked when I met her was how she had managed to hold fast to her goal when it seemed she might never prevail. She answered with a question of her own: "Why should I give up?"

14   It was she who divined the true character of these wetlands as a river, not a swamp, and gave the place its enduring epithet in the title of her 1947 book, *The Everglades: River of Grass.*

15   "There are no other Everglades in the world," she wrote then.

They are, they have always been, one of the unique regions of the 16
Earth, remote, never wholly known. Nothing anywhere else is
like them: their vast glittering openness, wider than the enormous visible round of the horizon, the racing free saltness and
sweetness of their massive winds, under the dazzling blue
heights of space. . . . The miracle of the light pours over the green
and brown expanse of sawgrass and of water, shining and slow-
moving below, the grass and water that is the meaning and the
central fact of the Everglades of Florida. It is a river of grass.

All her poetic loquacity goes into her writing. In our interview, 17
she speaks in the clipped tones and sparse phrases of the "damn
Yankee" she professes to be, even after seventy-five years in Florida. (Though born in Minnesota, Mrs. Douglas was raised in New
England and schooled at Wellesley College.) Hers is not an impo-
lite or impatient terseness. Rather, it has the feel of personal conservation, as though she is speaking sparingly to save her own
energy for the work still at hand. She consents to every public
appearance, every requested photo session or television taping,
out of a sense that her small, frail body remains a powerful instrument for swaying public opinion to her cause.

But if her answers were often shorter than I would have liked, 18
they did not lack for color or clarity. I asked her, for example, why
she had kept her married name, when her marriage to enigmatic
Kenneth Douglas (a writer thirty years her senior) lasted only a
brief period between 1913 and 1915, with Mr. Douglas absent
much of that time.

"I think it's easier, when you travel alone and all that, to be a 19
Mrs. rather than a Miss," she replied, hailing from an era before
"Ms." was invented.

"Yes," I agreed, "there are times when it's hard to be a woman." 20
"I don't think it's hard to be a woman," she corrected me. "It's 21
a challenge."

"So keeping your married name was one way to meet that chal- 22
lenge—to give yourself protection in the world?"
"Mmhm." 23
Looking back, she doesn't regret the marriage, but she doesn't 24
regret leaving it, either. And while her autobiography candidly
describes the pleasure that she found in marital relations, Mrs.
Douglas has since drawn a clear distinction between being *alone,*

which she often chooses to be, and being *lonely,* a condition with which she seems utterly unfamiliar.

25   "I say sex is more bother than it's worth," she told me. "Ever since Freud, everybody thinks they have to have sex or they'll explode with a loud noise. Well I don't think that's true. Sex is not so important as all that."

26   "You feel that the lack of it leaves one more energy to put into other things?"

27   "Yes it does," she answered. "Yes it does."

28   Despite her two last names, her advanced age, and the great respect she commands, people tend to call her by her first name, and she does not object. New acquaintances, even strangers recognizing her in a restaurant, are immediately on a first-name basis with her. Florida Governor Lawton Chiles, who recently decreed her birthday on April 7th to be the start of a two-week state celebration of environmental awareness, was simply doing the accepted thing when he named the tribute "Plant a Tree for Marjory."

29   Marjory herself, mindful of the hoopla surrounding her one-hundredth birthday in April 1990, had asked this year that people buy her no presents, throw her no parties. She wanted each well-wisher to plant a tree for her, she said. When I told her that the governor had parlayed her desire into a two-week campaign, complete with a phone number that Floridians could call to be counted among the commemorative planters, she smiled and said, "How lovely."

30   We were sitting in the large room of her small house, with its cool, stucco walls the color of old parchment, and dark, partially exposed beams overhead. Several tabletops and bookcases supported an assortment of statues and trophies—many in the form of wood storks, herons, and egrets—awarded for her Everglades work. They were not *displayed* so much as set down where space allowed. One of them had been pressed into service as a hat rack.

31   The scores of books that once lay stacked and scattered everywhere, attesting to Marjory's lifelong obsession with reading, have all been tucked neatly in the bookcases now that she is blind. In their place, almost as many "Talking Books"—some on cassettes, some on records—covered a settee and spilled into an unruly mound on the floor. I noticed a few Dorothy Sayers titles among them, along with Graham Greene, P.G. Wodehouse, and *The Norton Book of Travel.*

"This is where you work?" I asked, reveling in the feel of the 32
place.

"Yes, of course," she said. "Where else would I?" 33

The house resembles Marjory in many ways—spare, sensible, 34
serviceable. She moves about inside it like a sighted person, by
virtue of having lived here for sixty-five years. The kitchen has the
original appliances by the look of them, which is no great hardship
for Marjory, since she's always preferred dining out to cooking.
The bedroom is not much larger than the perimeter of the unmade
single bed, and a window holds the cat flap through which her
tomcat, Willie Terwilliger, comes and goes as he pleases. She has
a dressing room next to the bedroom, and a small extra bedroom
where her Uncle Charlie spent the last years of his life, and where
she put up her friend Marion Manley, who lost her money in the
big land bust, for several years during the Depression.

It is a welcoming and comfortable home. Its high ceilings and 35
four-way draft provide an adequate alternative to air conditioning,
even in the 90-degree heat of our afternoons together. From the
arched wooden front door to the small terrace out back, where Marjory says she never spends much time because of all the work she
has to do, there is nothing extravagant about this house—except
perhaps for the color of the bathroom. It is positively flamingo.

I commended Marjory for her decision to build a small house 36
without air conditioning. I asked if she'd been thinking about the
environment even then, in 1926.

"Well, of course," she shot back. But even though she was envi- 37
ronmentally aware far ahead of her time, she was at that moment
referring to the suitability of the house to its southern surroundings: "I had to be thinking about the environment. Of course I did.
You couldn't build a house down here without taking the Florida
conditions into account."

I suggested that a lot of people had done so, nevertheless. 38

"More fools they. A lot of damn Yankees. I'm a damn Yankee 39
myself, but not to that extent."

"So you've been living as the Floridians do?" 40

"No, I've been living the way I want to live in Florida." 41

When she sets her jaw, her lips make a hard line that tilts up to 42
the left, dividing her face asymmetrically. Her word for her look
is "crooked," and she's remarked how it has grown "crookeder"
with age. But when she laughs, she looks rounded and playful.

43   The magazine's photographer, daunted by the darkness of Marjory's rooms, moved a large rattan chair outdoors for his purposes. Marjory took my arm for direction once we were beyond her doorstep, but elbowed my ribs, as one might spur a horse, to get me to walk faster. Then she sat still, in front of the mahogany tree dripping with ball moss, and posed as directed while two, perhaps three rolls of film clicked by.

44   "I dare say that's enough," she called out, feeling the heat. But the photographer wanted to drive her out to Watson Island, where he could take more pictures against the backdrop of the Miami skyline. Marjory predates the skyline, having arrived here when Miami was a town of some fifteen thousand inhabitants. She consented good-naturedly to the trip.

45   "How does the Miami of today compare with the town you knew?" I asked *en route*.

46   "Oh, it's better as a big city. We have very many more privileges and accommodations."

47   Half an hour later I found myself walking her to a photo chair again, which this time had been set up at the very edge of a pier, not six inches from the water. A couple of brown pelicans flew down to perch on the nearby pilings as I explained to Marjory the precariousness of her situation.

48   "Remember, one false move and you're in the drink," I said.

49   "Oh that's all right," she said. "I can swim."

50   Afterward, over her daily cocktail, she recounted how she'd often thought of compiling a book, to be called *Just One More,* that would show pictures of intrepid photographers in the most death-defying feats of photojournalism.

51   "My first time up in an airplane," she recalled, laughing, "I flew with a photographer who went out across the wing—it was a biplane—to take photographs of the regatta down below, while the pilot maintained precisely the right angle to keep him from falling off. He just had one foot around the strut and all the courage in the world."

52   She's written so many things, in so many genres—newspaper articles, columns and editorials, poetry, short stories, novels, histories, natural histories—that a humor book about photographers would probably surprise no one. But her current project, titled *W.H. Hudson, Environmentalist,* is a scholarly work to be published by the University of Florida Press. In the course of her research,

Marjory traveled to England seven times. The trips allowed her to rummage through a deskful of Hudson's letters and other materials at his old publishing house, J.M. Dent, and to wander in his footsteps through Hampshire and Cornwall. She also made three trips to the Argentine, where Hudson's great-niece, Violeta, became her hostess, friend, and helper, turning over more letters and family records. By the last trip, to the site of Hudson's *Idle Days in Patagonia,* Marjory's eyesight had deteriorated so badly that she needed to have a wheelchair meet her plane at the large airports. At the smaller airports between Buenos Aires and Patagonia, she would alight from the tiny aircraft and say aloud in Spanish to no one in particular, "I don't see very well. Please help me."

She has proved herself to be a thorough researcher who devotes 53 at least as much time to studying as to writing about her subjects. Anyone could swear by her hard-won historical and scientific information. But Marjory gives equal credence to her own common sense and strongly held opinions—no matter what the experts say. It was on such grounds that she vehemently protested the state game commission's program to put radio collars on the Florida panther. Fewer than fifty of these animals survive today in the Big Cypress National Preserve, adjacent to the Everglades. They are a subspecies of cougar, and unquestionably among the most critically endangered mammals in the world. The commission wanted to track their movements so as to mount better efforts to protect them. But Marjory was outraged at the plan, even before one of the rare animals died while being treed by dogs and shot with a tranquilizer dart in preparation for collaring.

It was a snap decision for her, and irreversible, too, forged from 54 observation of her own housecats. They didn't care much for collars, as though they knew they might easily snag such an encumbrance on some brush, and choke and die.

"I don't like collars on cats," Marjory declared. "Panthers are 55 cats, too." Her opinion of the program could be summed up as follows: "I don't care what the federal and state governments say, I think it's stupid."

What she did for the panther was to tell her Indian friends to 56 stop killing them for their whiskers, or bristles, which they carried in their medicine bags. It was an awful waste to kill the whole beast just for the hairs on its face, she argued, proposing a different strategy. Any panthers accidentally killed by speeding cars should be given to the Indians to use and dispose of as they wished.

57   "I'd heard they do that with the eagles in the West," she explained matter-of-factly. "I thought the same idea would work here."

58   People think of Marjory Stoneman Douglas as a great environmentalist, and she is, though she came to that calling late in life and almost by accident. Certainly she showed an early sympathy for nature, as she relates in her autobiography, *Marjory Stoneman Douglas: Voice of the River:*

59   Upstairs in the sitting room, father read to me, mostly from "Hiawatha." When he came to Hiawatha building the canoe and saying to the birch tree, 'Give me of your bark, oh, birch tree,' and the birch tree sighing and bending over to give up its bark, he was astonished by the fact that I burst into loud sobs. I couldn't make him understand I was sorry for the birch tree, because why should the birch tree have to give up his bark just because Hiawatha wanted to build a canoe? I couldn't stand it. I cried and I guess father skipped the canoe part after that.

60   But it wasn't the love of the wilderness that brought her to South Florida in 1915. She came down here to get a divorce and to be reunited with her father, Judge Frank B. Stoneman, editor of the *Miami Herald,* whom she hadn't seen for twenty years since she was a child of five.

61   Judge Stoneman was already stumping for the preservation of the Everglades before his daughter arrived. At the time, most Floridians saw the Everglades as a snake-infested swamp that would benefit from nothing so much as a thorough draining. He spoke out against draining in his editorials. He didn't have much scientific evidence to support his position, but he clung to it nevertheless, showing great foresight in his belief that the Everglades water should be left to seek its own level. One imagines, from Marjory's description of him, that Frank Stoneman valued the Everglades for their mere existence and their sheer beauty. For their right to be. And in this she wholeheartedly agreed with him.

62   As it happened, a job soon opened up for Marjory on the society pages of the *Herald.* Here she found her calling. She had always wanted to be a writer, had written in high school and majored in

English composition in college, but it took the society editor's sudden leaving to land Marjory in her dream career.

Marjory's native ability and the small size of the newspaper's 63 staff (which included actor Joseph Cotton on the classified-ad desk) combined to push her into other beats. In 1916, during World War I, she was sent to do a story on the first woman enlistee from Florida in the Naval Reserve.

"Look," she telephoned her father to say, "I got the story on the 64 first woman to enlist. It turned out to be me."

"I admire your patriotism," he replied, "but it leaves us a little 65 short-handed."

"I was overqualified for yeoman work in the Navy," she told me 66 during the interview. So she put in for an early honorable discharge and then served overseas in France on assignment for the American Red Cross.

Back in Florida in 1920, she became an assistant editor at the 67 *Herald* with her own column, "The Galley." An editorial she wrote in verse, expressing her outrage about a young man who was arrested for vagrancy and then beaten to death in a labor camp, convinced the state legislature to abolish beatings in the camps. Another cause she wrote about in her column was the establishment of Everglades National Park, and as a result she was invited to join the park committee.

Her life on the newspaper thrust her into the tumult of the 68 growing metropolis of Miami, but the work and the pressure proved overwhelming. She left the newspaper and made a living writing short stories for *The Saturday Evening Post* and other magazines. She set some of the stories in and around the Everglades, and never lost interest in them over the fifteen years she spent working as a full-time freelance writer. She contributed to *Black Mask*, the same magazine that had published Dashiell Hammett's stories before he became famous. Another of her contemporaries was Ernest Hemingway, about whom she had this to say: "I didn't subscribe to the Hemingway thinking. I was more or less tied into the mainstream from which Hemingway was estranged. I couldn't write in that bare, stark way in which a story begins like a slap in the face."

She wrote her own stories with style and power, as in this 69 excerpt from "Pineland," published in the *Post* on August 15, 1925:

70   All around them the white brilliance of the Florida noon poured down upon the uneven road from the burial place, caught on the bright spear points of palmettos and struck into nakedness the shabby houses among stumps of pine trees of this outskirt of Miami. The light and the hot wind seemed whiter and hotter for the figure of Sarah McDevitt in her mourning.

71   Eventually she grew tired of writing stories, and was six months into a novel when the opportunity to write the Everglades book literally fell into her lap. In 1941 her friend Hervey Allen, an editor at Rinehart, offered her the chance to contribute to a series of books about the rivers of America. He suggested she take on the Miami River, but she protested on the ground that it was "only about an inch long." The Everglades, on the other hand, about which she still knew very little, were somehow connected to the Miami River, and would no doubt make a richer story.

72   "All right," she remembers Allen saying, "write about the Everglades." The only problem was, the series was supposed to be about rivers.

73   "Do you think I could get away with calling it a river of grass?" Marjory asked the state hydrologist, the first expert she consulted in her research. He said she could, and she threw herself into the project for the next five years.

74   The book was an enormous success and has sold ten thousand copies a year since 1947. Reading it makes its continuing popularity easy to understand:

75   The water moves. The sawgrass, pale green to deep-brown ripeness, stands rigid. It is moved only in sluggish rollings by the vast push of the winds across it. Over its endless acres here and there the shadows of the dazzling clouds quicken and slide, purple-brown, plum-brown, mauve-brown, rust-brown, bronze. The bristling, blossoming tops do not bend easily like standing grain. They do not even in their own growth curve all one way but stand in edged clumps, curving against each other, all the massed curving blades making millions of fine arching lines that at a little distance merge to a huge expanse of brown wires, or bristles or, farther beyond, to deep-piled plush. At the horizon they become velvet. The line they make is an edge of velvet against the infinite blue, the blue-and-white, the clear fine primrose yellow, the burning brass and crimson, the molten silver, the deepening hyacinth sky.

The book is not just a celebration of nature but a detailed chron-　76
icle, from the bloody skirmishes between Native Americans and
European settlers in the Glades to the later struggles of the wetlands wildlife against the onslaught of dams, drainage, and
drought.

"The book reads beautifully," I complimented her. "The descrip-　77
tions are so lyrical that I would guess you must have written them
out in longhand."

"I did, yes. And then I hired a typist. I did so much writing on　78
a typewriter for the newspaper that it affected my style. So I wrote
the book in longhand."

I was fascinated with this revelation about Marjory's writing　79
process.

"With a fountain pen?" I pursued.　80

"Oh, my heavens, woman, of course! What a question!"　81

The book brought her great acclaim and united her name with　82
the Everglades forever. But it wasn't until 1970, after the environmental movement of the sixties had taken hold, that the Everglades became "a central force" in Marjory's existence. The pre-
cipitating issue was the threatened building of a jetport inside the
Everglades. An acquaintance of Marjory's, Joe Browder of National
Audubon Society, was working hard to oppose the plan, but
with little popular support. Marjory bumped into one of Browder's assistants in a grocery store and said she applauded their
efforts.

The young woman asked Marjory what *she* was doing to help　83
in the situation. Marjory made reference to her book, and meeting
a blank stare, she offhandedly said she'd try to help if possible.
Browder himself came to collect on her promise the next day.
Together they hatched the idea of an organization that would take
a stand for the Everglades.

Marjory was still mulling over this prospect when she met an　84
old sailing buddy at a picnic. She asked his opinion of an Everglades support group that anyone could join for a nominal fee—
say one dollar. "It's a great idea," he said, and stuck a dollar in her
hand right then and there. That was the charter membership
induction into the Friends of the Everglades. By the end of the year
there were five hundred members, and the ranks eventually
swelled into the thousands. The jetport was never built.

I learned something more of Marjory by venturing into the　85
Everglades on bicycle and on foot, where I found an abundance of

alligators lounging all along the length of the roadways, only a few yards away from me. I stood as close as a midwife to an egg-laying turtle, and spied through binoculars on an anhinga mother in an eye-level nest with two naked snake-necked chicks.

86   From the high vantage point of a chartered Cessna in late April, at the tail end of the dry season in the Everglades, I saw the miles of sawgrass looking brown and flat. The scant water was concentrated in networks of squiggly rivulets outlined in mangroves, and hammocks of hardwood trees reached up from scattered slight elevations in the land. Only a few teardrop-shaped islands in Rogers River Bay were white with egret nests. Parallel lines cut by airboats crisscrossed the sloughs, and alligator trails, also visible from above, wandered wavily across the landscape.

87   Between the midmorning heat and the engines' droning, I fancied I saw metaphors for Marjory in the panorama below. She is a river herself, I thought, meandering through so many lives and times, flooding them with her good writing and good will.

88   I had one more question to ask her: "Tell me, of all the eras you've lived through, are you enjoying *now* most of all?"

89   "Well, naturally," she replied.

Engaging the Text

1. Read with care the italicized portions of the text from Marjory Stoneman Douglas's books. How do they differ from the informal reportorial style of the author of the article, Dava Sobel? Can you point to any specific word choices, grammatical constructions, or sentences that make up Douglas's style?
2. How do words such as loquacity and terseness (paragraph 17) explain something of Douglas's character today?
3. The article is partly conducted in dialogue, as an interview. Compare the technique Sobel uses to that used by Endesha Ida Mae Holland ("Granny Midwives").

Engaging the Reader

1. What were the succeeding issues that engaged Douglas in the fight for the Everglades over the years? What is the "last fight to be won" (paragraph 8)?
2. If there is an issue that your college is excited about (there usually is), interview one of your classmates on that issue,

reporting both your questions and your classmate's statements in the interview style Sobel uses with Marjory Stoneman Douglas. Tape your interview, or take notes on what is said by both of you.

3. Compare Marjory Stoneman Douglas's remarks on the course of her life (paragraphs 88 and 89) with Edith Wharton's ("A First Word").

The Engaged Writer

1. Using the notes you made on the interview with your classmate (question 2 in "Engaging the Reader"), write an essay in which you use this interview and its contents to prove a point about the issue you've been considering. This essay should have a thesis, as the article on Douglas does.

2. Plan and carry out an interview with one of the following:

> — an older member of your family
> — a member of your church or club
> — a person who has been involved in some important event in the past: the civil rights movement, a political campaign, a war or military campaign
> — a well-known person you have an opportunity to meet and interview

Treat the material as Sobel does—stick to a thesis; do not wander from the point; and use many illustrations, including the transcribed interview, long quotations, and descriptive details.

J. ANTHONY LUKAS

When a Citizen Fights Back

This story of one otherwise peaceable, responsible citizen was part of a Pulitzer-prizewinning book, *Common Ground: A Turbulent Decade in the Lives of Three American Families* (1985). Colin Diver and his family attempted to be "urban pioneers"—to move into a deteriorating neighborhood with hope of new life. A crime spree finally led Diver to strike back on his own behalf.

1   Impelled by the same sense of responsibility which had led them to confront truck traffic, commuter congestion, substandard housing, and rampant prostitution, Colin and Joan gradually assumed command of the war on crime. They kept a careful list of every crime committed in their corner of the South End. Friends and neighbors called at all hours to report incidents, which Joan inscribed in a loose-leaf notebook. In neat schoolgirl's script she recorded the informant's name, the location, date, and time of the crime, the number and description of the assailants, their weapons (if any), the victim's name, the goods or money taken, and whether or not the crime had been reported to the police.

2   The level of criminal activity remained fairly constant through the Christmas season, but as 1975 ended, the situation on the Divers' block deteriorated radically.

3   It started on Tuesday, December 30, when a man up the street was mugged in the alley behind his house.

4   At 5:00 P.M. the next day—New Year's Eve—a gang of boys with sticks stopped an elderly man on the sidewalk and took his wallet.

5   Half an hour later the same gang grabbed an old woman's purse.

6   At 5:45 on January 6 the Divers' next-door neighbor, Linda Trum, was returning home with her three-year-old daughter when two young men came up behind her. One of them put his arm around her neck and, as she struggled, her assailant said, "Don't scream. Just give us your money." She said she wasn't carrying any. The men rifled her pockets, then ran off down the block.

7   At 9:45 that same night, Colin and Joan were watching television when they heard a scream from the alley behind the house. Colin grabbed the Slugger, the bat with which he had once helped win the Lexington Little League championship, and ran into the alley. There he found a woman named Terry Baksun, whose purse had been snatched. Colin looked up the alley, but the mugger had fled.

8   After dinner the next night the Divers had an appointment to look at a new Kirby vacuum cleaner. The salesman—a college student named Bobby Jacobs—was aggressive but charming, and Colin and Joan smiled to themselves as he ran the machine up and down their dining room, demonstrating a bewildering array of tubes and brushes.

At 8:20 P.M., their eldest son, Brad, hollered down the stairs, "I 9
think I heard a scream outside."

Colin gestured to Jacobs to turn off the vacuum cleaner. 10

"Are you sure, Brad?" 11

"I think so." 12

Colin ran to the door, grabbed the Slugger from its niche, and 13
dashed out onto the sidewalk, where he found a twenty-five-year-
old black woman named LeSola Morgan.

"What's the matter?" Colin asked. 14

"He took my pocketbook." 15

"Who did?" 16

"Some guy. He hit me in the face and grabbed my purse." 17

"Which way'd he go?" 18

"Down there," she said, pointing toward Tremont Street. 19

As Colin started off in that direction, he saw a man run out of 20
the alley by the library carrying a large black handbag.

"That's my pocketbook," yelled LeSola Morgan. 21

"Stop!" Colin hollered. "Stop! Thief!" 22

The man ran harder, thundering past the library. 23

Taking up the chase, as he had so often in the past, Colin noticed 24
something unusual about his quarry. Most of the others he'd pursued through these streets were kids who ran like NFL ends, gone
before he got anywhere near them. But this one was different: a
man in his late twenties or thirties, lumbering down the sidewalk
like a rogue elephant. And Colin was actually gaining on him!

At Tremont Street, the man dodged a screeching taxi, darted 25
past a honking panel truck, and charged across the busy thor-
oughfare. Colin hesitated for a moment. Tremont was a significant
boundary to his world, the southern border of the gentrified South
End. Beyond it stretched a row of tenements, occupied principal-
ly by Puerto Ricans, Dominicans, and Cubans. The O'Day Playground halfway down the block was the center of the South End's
heroin trade, a dangerous place at any time of the day or night. On
other chases in months past Colin had always stopped at Tremont,
unwilling to carry his pursuit into alien territory. But he was fed
up. After six crimes of violence on his block in barely a week, he
had to catch one of these bastards! Without further reflection, he
hurtled across Tremont and sprinted after the fleeing figure.

It was a dismal night, cloudy and cold. Streetlights glowed in 26
the fog. A fine drizzle lay an icy slick along the pavement, but

Colin kept his footing, quickly making up the ground he'd lost. The mugger was running down the middle of West Newton Street. Gaining steadily on his man, Colin thought: I'm actually going to catch this guy! He could feel the smooth, round handle of the Slugger in his right hand. Raising the bat, he thought: Am I really going to hit this guy? Can I? Should I? Before he could deliberate further, he came abreast of his target and swung the Slugger in a short, powerful arc against the man's head.

27   As if he'd pulled some hidden trigger, the scene erupted in a clutter of disjointed images.

28   The mugger collapsed in a heap on the street.

29   Tripping over the body, Colin tumbled to his knees, sliding six feet along the ice.

30   The purse flew from the man's grasp, coming to rest in a puddle.

31   The Slugger broke in two, the barrel sailing onto a nearby stoop, the jagged handle still clenched in Colin's hand.

32   Struggling to his feet, Colin turned to confront his antagonist, who was hauling himself upright. For a moment, the two men stood in the middle of the street, staring at each other. The mugger shook his head slowly, as if to clear the mist before his eyes, and suddenly lurched forward.

33   My God, Colin thought, he must have a knife or a gun!

34   But either the man didn't see him or wanted nothing more to do with him, for he began staggering—half running, half walking—up the sidewalk.

35   Colin picked up the pocketbook. Once more he hesitated. He'd retrieved the woman's money, he'd given the guy a good thwack on the head—maybe he should just forget about him.

36   At that moment, Bobby Jacobs, the vacuum cleaner salesman, came steaming up the street, yelling, "What's going on?" Emboldened, Colin pushed the pocketbook into Jacobs' hands. "Hold this," he said. "I'm going after the guy."

37   Retrieving the Slugger's heavy barrel from the stoop, he ran up the sidewalk, nearly colliding with two black men dressed to the nines for an evening on the town. "Hey," yelled Colin. "Help me out, will you? See that guy down there? He just robbed a girl. Grabbed her pocketbook."

38   "Aw, man," said one of the men. "You *got* to be kidding."

39   "Come on," Colin said. "He smashed a black woman in the face."

"All right," said the second man. 40

Colin and his new ally resumed the chase. Just short of Shaw- 41
mut Avenue they corralled the mugger, who was too groggy to put
up much resistance. Colin grabbed him by one arm, the black guy
by the other, and together they propelled him onto Shawmut,
where a police car was advancing majestically up the avenue.
Colin jumped into the roadway and rushed directly into the squad
car's path, forcing it to a halt.

Alighting from his car in amazement, Patrolman Gerald Abban 42
asked, "What the hell's going on here?" Still out of breath from the
pursuit, Colin did his best to explain. Finally Abban took custody
of the mugger—who turned out to be Ruberto Caban, a thirty-
year-old Puerto Rican from nearby West Concord Street.

After other police came to the house to take his story, Colin was 43
left ruefully contemplating the evening's events. Only gradually
did the implications of what he'd done begin to sink in—he'd clob-
bered a guy over the head with a baseball bat. Not since boyhood
scuffles had he inflicted injury on another human being. It was one
thing to bluster, as many of his neighbors did, "If I ever get my
hands on one of those bastards . . ." It was something else to actually do it. And with a weapon as lethal as a baseball bat, there was
always the possibility of serious injury. Ruberto Caban had looked
a little wide-eyed out there, like a prizefighter who'd been hit once
too often. If anything was wrong with him, a zealous lawyer could
sue Colin for thousands in medical bills. For his own sake, as well
as Caban's, he hoped he hadn't inflicted any real damage.

The broader implications were even more disturbing. Nearly a 44
decade before, he'd moved into the city to help bring racial justice
to Boston. Now he was rushing out of his house to hit dark-
skinned people over the head. Before him on the kitchen table lay
his boyhood bat, splintered beyond all further use. Some of his
cherished assumptions were in smithereens as well.

Engaging the Text

1. One way the writer engages you, the reader, in his narrative
   is by using simple yet colorful adjectives as he moves you
   along with him on his chase after the mugger. He uses words
   such as assailant (1), deteriorated (2), majestically (41), ruefully
   (43), and zealous (43).

2. Diver also uses some proverbial phrases, almost clichés, to pinpoint the people in his sketch. The two black men are "dressed to the nines" (37) for an evening out. What does this mean?

3. The mugger, after being hit by Colin Diver's baseball bat, lumbers down the sidewalk "like a rogue elephant." Where does that phrase come from? Is it appropriate here?

4. Finally, the bat, Slugger, is "in smithereens" as are some of Diver's assumptions. Explain this—the phrase and the comparison.

5. This story is told in breathless fashion, a typical chase scene. How does the writer get this effect?

Engaging the Reader

1. Why did Colin and Joan Diver move into Boston's South End?

2. What happened after the first optimism of the young professionals' move into the city?

3. What feelings did Colin Diver have about using violence againts the mugger?

The Engaged Writer

1. Do you believe in using violence against muggers or intruders?

2. Would you like to live in a neighborhood such as South Boston? (Colin and Joan Diver and their children eventually gave up and moved to the suburbs.)

3. Look through your local papers for articles on some of these subjects: drug traffic in the "projects," gentrification of inner-city neighborhoods, and police success rate in prosecuting criminals such as muggers. Write an essay reporting on what you find.

4. In the book from which this story was taken, some American families discuss the decade of the 1970s and the changes it made in their lives. If there is a period in your life in which many changes occurred, write an autobiographical essay on that period of time and how it changed your life.

5. If you wrote an autobiographical account for the previous exercise, add to it a "frame story"—a trip back by plane, a letter in the mail, a leave-taking such as Annie John's ("A Walk to the Jetty")—that triggers a memory and sets off your story.

6. If you live in a city, write an account of how your city, your project, your neighborhood, or your street is dealing with the problems of crime, drugs, and vandalism.
7. Diver brings up another touchy problem in his account. Diver is white; he moved to South Boston with the idea of helping bring racial justice to Boston. Now he has "hit a dark-skinned" person over the head. Can white people help promote racial justice? Are Diver's worries as expressed in the last two paragraphs justified?

STEPHEN HAWKING

Public Attitudes Toward Science

Stephen Hawking is a British astrophysicist who has gone a long way to explain theories about black holes and other mysteries of the universe. His articles and books he says, "were written in the belief that the universe is governed by an order that we can perceive partially now and that we may understand fully in the not-too-distant future." Completely paralyzed and unable to speak, Hawking has nevertheless communicated his theories (with a computer and a voice synthesizer with an American accent) and written a best-seller, *A Brief History of Time* (1988). The following selection, originally a speech given in Spain in 1989 on receiving a prize award, has been updated and included in *Black Holes and Baby Universes* (1993).

Whether we like it or not, the world we live in has changed a great 1 deal in the last hundred years, and it is likely to change even more in the next hundred. Some people would like to stop these changes and go back to what they see as a purer and simpler age. But as history shows, the past was not that wonderful. It was not so bad for a privileged minority, though even they had to do without modern medicine, and childbirth was highly risky for women. But for the vast majority of the population, life was nasty, brutish, and short.

Anyway, even if one wanted to, one couldn't put the clock back 2 to an earlier age. Knowledge and techniques can't just be forgotten. Nor can one prevent further advances in the future. Even if all government money for research were cut off (and the present government is doing its best), the force of competition would still bring about advances in technology. Moreover, one cannot stop inquiring minds from thinking about basic science, whether or not they are paid for it. The only way to prevent further developments would be a global totalitarian state that suppressed anything new, and human initiative and ingenuity are such that even this wouldn't succeed. All it would do is slow down the rate of change.

3   If we accept that we cannot prevent science and technology from changing our world, we can at least try to ensure that the changes they make are in the right directions. In a democratic society, this means that the public needs to have a basic understanding of science, so that it can make informed decisions and not leave them in the hands of experts. At the moment, the public has a rather ambivalent attitude toward science. It has come to expect the steady increase in the standard of living that new developments in science and technology have brought to continue, but it also distrusts science because it doesn't understand it. This distrust is evident in the cartoon figure of the mad scientist working in his laboratory to produce a Frankenstein. It is also an important element behind support for the Green parties. But the public also has a great interest in science, particularly astronomy, as is shown by the large audiences for television series such as *Cosmos* and for science fiction.

4   What can be done to harness this interest and give the public the scientific background it needs to make informed decisions on subjects like acid rain, the greenhouse effect, nuclear weapons, and genetic engineering? Clearly, the basis must lie in what is taught in schools. But in schools science is often presented in a dry and uninteresting manner. Children learn it by rote to pass examinations, and they don't see its relevance to the world around them. Moreover, science is often taught in terms of equations. Although equations are a concise and accurate way of describing mathematical ideas, they frighten most people. When I wrote a popular book recently, I was advised that each equation I included would halve the sales. I included one equation, Einstein's famous equation, $E = mc^2$. Maybe I would have sold twice as many copies without it.

5   Scientists and engineers tend to express their ideas in the form of equations because they need to know the precise values of quantities. But for the rest of us, a qualitative grasp of scientific concepts

is sufficient, and this can be conveyed by words and diagrams, without the use of equations.

The science people learn in school can provide the basic frame- 6
work. But the rate of scientific progress is now so rapid that there are always new developments that have occurred since one was at school or university. I never learned about molecular biology or transistors at school, but genetic engineering and computers are two of the developments most likely to change the way we live in the future. Popular books and magazine articles about science can help to put across new developments, but even the most success-ful popular book is read by only a small proportion of the popu-lation. Only television can reach a truly mass audience. There are some very good science programs on TV, but others present sci-entific wonders simply as magic, without explaining them or showing how they fit into the framework of scientific ideas. Pro-ducers of television science programs should realize that they have a responsibility to educate the public, not just entertain it.

What are the science-related issues that the public will have to 7
make decisions on in the near future? By far the most urgent is that of nuclear weapons. Other global problems, such as food supply or the greenhouse effect, are relatively slow-acting, but a nuclear war could mean the end of all human life on earth within days. The relaxation of east-west tensions brought about by the ending of the cold war has meant that the fear of nuclear war has receded from public consciousness. But the danger is still there as long as there are enough weapons to kill the entire population of the world many times over. In former Soviet states and in America, nuclear weapons are still poised to strike all the major cities in the North-ern Hemisphere. It would only take a computer error or a mutiny by some of those manning the weapons to trigger a global war. It is even more worrying that relatively minor powers are now acquiring nuclear weapons. The major powers have behaved in a reasonably responsible way, but one cannot have such confidence in minor powers like Libya or Iraq, Pakistan, or even Azerbaijan. The danger is not so much in the actual nuclear weapons that such powers may soon possess, which would be fairly rudimentary, though they could still kill millions of people. Rather, the danger is that a nuclear war between two minor powers could draw in the major powers with their enormous arsenals.

It is very important that the public realize the danger and put 8
pressure on all governments to agree to large arms cuts. It proba-

bly is not practical to remove nuclear weapons entirely, but we can lessen the danger by reducing the number of weapons.

9   If we manage to avoid a nuclear war, there are still other dangers that could destroy us all. There's a sick joke that the reason we have not been contacted by an alien civilization is that civilizations tend to destroy themselves when they reach our stage. But I have sufficient faith in the good sense of the public to believe that we might prove this wrong.

Engaging the Text

1. Since this essay was originally a speech, its language is clear and simple, and at the same time persuasive. Look at other selections in *The Engaging Reader* that were written as speeches: Martin Luther King's "I Have a Dream" comes to mind. Find others and see how they compare in tone with this one.

2. Some words and phrases are crucial to understanding this piece: "a global totalitarian state" (2), "an ambivalent attitude toward science" (3), "Einstein's famous equation, $E = mc^2$" (4), and "genetic engineering" (6). Make sure you can fit these into the thesis of the piece. What is that thesis?

Engaging the Reader

1. Hawking makes several controversial statements here which need to be discussed. In your groups, see if you agree or disagree with the following:
    *   "Knowledge and techniques just can't be forgotten. Nor can one prevent further advances in the future."
    *   "Genetic engineering and computers are two of the developments most likely to change the way we live in the future."
    *   "Only television can reach a truly mass audience."
    *   "It is very important that the public realize the danger and put pressure on all governments to agree to large arms cuts."
    *   "As history shows, the past was not that wonderful."

2. What risks need to be taken to turn these ideas into action? Give some examples.

The Engaged Writer

1. From your responses to #1 in *Engaging the Reader,* write a persuasive paper incorporating the arguments you and your classmates drew up.
2. This speech mentions some of the most important issues of our time: medical advances (1), "Green" parties (3), acid rain, the greenhouse effect, nuclear weapons, and genetic engineering (4). For some of these, read Carl Sagan's "The Warming of the World" in Part Five: Controversies. These can be topics for longer documented papers that you may be assigned in this or another course.
3. Stephen Hawking himself demonstrates how a severely handicapped person can be productive, not to say brilliant. Research his life and how he overcame motor neurone disease to become a professor of astrophysics at Cambridge, married and a father, and the author of bestselling books. His life can be a subject of a paper, either on its own or as an example of risk-taking.

The Preamble and Bill of Rights of the Constitution of the United States

This document represents a response to a national risk of great dimensions. With the American Revolution of 1776, the former colonies were no longer dependent on any other country. For this new country to survive, it needed a code to base its rules on; this was the Constitution, adopted in 1789. Soon it was evident that individual rights needed protection; the first 10 amendments established these. A few changes occurred since then, notably the Thirteenth Amendment, abolishing slavery; the Fifteenth, guaranteeing that the right to vote shall not be denied or abridged on account of race, color, or previous condition of servitude; and the Nineteenth, granting women the right to vote.

Preamble

We, the people of the United States, in order to form a more per- 1
fect union, establish justice, insure domestic tranquility, provide for
the common defense, promote the general welfare, and secure the

blessings of liberty to ourselves and our posterity, do ordain and establish this Constitution for the United States of America.

Amendment I

2 Congress shall make no law respecting an establishment of religion, or prohibiting the free exercise thereof; or abridging the freedom of speech or of the press; or the right of the people peaceably to assemble, and to petition the government for a redress of grievances.

Amendment II

3 A well-regulated militia being necessary to the security of a free State, the right of the people to keep and bear arms shall not be infringed.

Amendment III

4 No soldier shall, in time of peace, be quartered in any house without the consent of the owner, nor in time of war, but in a manner to be prescribed by law.

Amendment IV

5 The right of the people to be secure in their persons, houses, papers, and effects, against unreasonable searches and seizures, shall not be violated, and no warrants shall issue but upon probable cause, supported by oath or affirmation, and particularly describing the place to be searched, and the persons or things to be seized.

Amendment V

6 No person shall be held to answer for a capital, or otherwise infamous crime, unless on a presentment or indictment of a grand jury, except in cases arising in the land or naval forces, or in the militia, when in actual service in time of war or public danger; nor shall any person be subject for the same offense to be twice put in jeopardy of life or limb; nor shall be compelled in any criminal case to be a witness against himself, nor be deprived of life, liberty or property, without due process of law; nor shall private property be taken for public use without just compensation.

Amendment VI

In all criminal prosecutions, the accused shall enjoy the right to a 7
speedy and public trial, by an impartial jury of the State and district wherein the crime shall have been committed, which district shall have been previously ascertained by law, and to be informed of the nature and cause of the accusation; to be confronted with the witnesses against him; to have compulsory process for obtaining witnesses in his favor, and to have the assistance of counsel for his defense.

Amendment VII

In suits at common law, where the value in controversy shall 8
exceed twenty dollars, the right of trial by jury shall be preserved, and no fact tried by a jury shall be otherwise re-examined in any court of the United States, than according to the rules of the common law.

Amendment VIII

Excessive bail shall not be required, nor excessive fines imposed, 9
nor cruel and unusual punishments inflicted.

Amendment IX

The enumeration in the Constitution of certain rights shall not be 10
construed to deny or disparage others retained by the people.

Amendment X

The powers not delegated to the United States by the Constitution, 11
nor prohibited by it to the States, are reserved to the States respectively, or to the people.

Engaging the Text

1. The language of the Preamble and Bill of Rights reflects the eighteenth-century style: clear, erudite, and elegant. Look up these words, indispensable for citizens: tranquility, ordain (Preamble), redress (1), grievances (1), militia (2), presentment (5), indictment (5), jeopardy (5), impartial (6), ascertained (6), construed (9), and disparage (9).

2. The language of the Constitution, though drafted two hundred years ago, remains clearer than some present-day government documents or insurance policies. How do you think this document managed to stay so relevant, in spite of the years? Were we just lucky or simply gifted with some good writers in Thomas Jefferson and his colleagues?
3. Summarize each of the amendments in your own words. Do you think you have made any improvement in the language?

Engaging the Reader

1. The first ten amendments of the Constitution are the backbone of our "rights" today. In the time since its drafting, many groups have tried, fought, demonstrated for, and finally succeeded in having their rights specified and included. These groups include blacks, women, those arrested for alleged crimes (the "Miranda" rights), the handicapped, homosexuals, and AIDS patients. Discuss what specific things have been done, or should be done, by society to guarantee these groups their rights.
2. Can you think of any other groups who need protection under the Bill of Rights?

The Engaged Writer

1. Give examples of incidents related to each of the first ten amendments to the Constitution and how the amendments apply today.
2. Take one of the incidents you listed in the first writing exercise and develop it into an essay. Some possible subjects include:

   — Should prayer be allowed in public schools?
   — Should newspaper reporters have to divulge their sources?
   — Should Nazi party members be allowed to have a rally?
   — Are gun control laws constitutional?
   — Can cars or people be searched for drugs without a warrant?
   — In a congressional hearing, does a government official have to respond to all questions?

— Should people with AIDS be in school or in the work-
place?
— Can the government take over one's property?
— Should the reading of "rights" to arrested criminals be
continued?
— Is freedom from sexual harassment a right under the
Constitution?

3. What constitutional issue did Colin Diver question by his
action against the mugger with his bat "Slugger" (J. Anthony
Lukas, "A Citizen Fights Back")?

The Seneca Falls Resolutions

The Seneca Falls Declaration of Sentiments and Resolutions in 1848
is the single most important document in the women's movement
of the nineteenth century. This struggle eventually resulted in the
Nineteenth Amendment to the Constitution in 1920, extending voting rights to women. In July 1848, a meeting in Seneca Falls, New
York, considered the social, civil, and religious condition and rights
of woman. Elizabeth Cady Stanton organized the conference, at
which the principal speaker was Lucretia Mott. Even here women
were in the background: Mott's husband chaired the convention,
and the resolution advocating voting rights for women passed only
when Frederick Douglass, the abolitionist and former slave,
defended it from the floor.

Whereas, The great precept of nature is conceded to be, that "man   1
shall pursue his own true and substantial happiness." Blackstone
in his Commentaries remarks, that this law of Nature being coeval
with mankind, and dictated by God himself, is of course superior
in obligation to any other. It is binding over all the globe, in all
countries and at all times; no human laws are of any validity if contrary to this, and such of them as are valid, derive all their force,
and all their validity, and all their authority, mediately and immediately, from this original; therefore,

   Resolved, That such laws as conflict, in any way, with the true   2
and substantial happiness of woman, are contrary to the great pre-

cept of nature and of no validity, for this is "superior in obligation to any other."

3   *Resolved,* That all laws which prevent woman from occupying such a station in society as her conscience shall dictate, or which place her in a position inferior to that of man, are contrary to the great precept of nature, and therefore of no force or authority.

4   *Resolved,* That woman is man's equal—was intended to be so by the Creator, and the highest good of the race demands that she should be recognized as such.

5   *Resolved,* That the women of this country ought to be enlightened in regard to the laws under which they live, that they may no longer publish their degradation by declaring themselves satisfied with their present position, nor their ignorance, by asserting that they have all the rights they want.

6   *Resolved,* That inasmuch as man, while claiming for himself intellectual superiority, does accord to woman moral superiority, it is pre-eminently his duty to encourage her to speak and teach, as she has an opportunity, in all religious assemblies.

7   *Resolved,* That the same amount of virtue, delicacy, and refinement of behavior that is required of woman in the social state, should also be required of man, and the same transgressions should be visited with equal severity on both man and woman.

8   *Resolved,* That the objection of indelicacy and impropriety, which is so often brought against woman when she addresses a public audience, comes with a very ill-grace from those who encourage, by their attendance, her appearance on the stage, in the concert, or in feats of the circus.

9   *Resolved,* That woman has too long rested satisfied in the circumscribed limits which corrupt customs and a perverted application of the Scriptures have marked out for her, and that it is time she should move in the enlarged sphere which her great Creator has assigned her.

10   *Resolved,* That it is the duty of the women of this country to secure to themselves their sacred right to the elective franchise.

11   *Resolved,* That the equality of human rights results necessarily from the fact of the identity of the race in capabilities and responsibilities.

12   *Resolved, therefore,* That, being invested by the Creator with the same capabilities, and the same consciousness of responsibility

for their exercise, it is demonstrably the right and duty of woman, equally with man, to promote every righteous cause by every righteous means; and especially in regard to the great subjects of morals and religion, it is self-evidently her right to participate with her brother in teaching them, both in private and in public, by writing and by speaking, by any instrumentalities proper to be used, and in any assemblies proper to be held; and this being a self-evident truth growing out of the divinely implanted principles of human nature, any custom or authority adverse to it, whether modern or wearing the hoary sanction of antiquity, is to be regarded as a self-evident falsehood, and at war with mankind.

[At the last session Lucretia Mott offered and spoke to the fol- 13 lowing resolution:]

Resolved, That the speedy success of our cause depends upon the zealous and untiring efforts of both men and women, for the overthrow of the monopoly of the pulpit, and for the securing to woman an equal participation with men in the various trades, professions, and commerce.

Engaging the Text

1. Find the following words in the Resolutions and check their meanings:

   — precept (Preamble)
   — coeval (Preamble)
   — degradation (5)
   — transgressions (7)
   — indelicacy (8)
   — impropriety (8)
   — instrumentalities (12)

2. Explain the meaning of the following phrase: "wearing the hoary sanction of antiquity" (12).
3. Compare the language of this document with that of the U.S. Constitution's Bill of Rights. Which is simpler and clearer?
4. Following the plan in "Writing a Summary of What You Read," summarize this document as if you were going to report it for a newspaper article.

Engaging the Reader

1. How have equity issues for women changed since 1848?
2. Could more progress be made in the realization of equal rights?
3. Which is more important, economic or social and political equality?
4. Compare the push for equal rights for women with the statements made by Washington and Du Bois on rights for blacks.

The Engaged Writer

1. Equality of men and women would, in our time, seem to be an established fact. Can you think of any areas where inequality still exists? Write about one of these.
2. Does the language used in these resolutions contain any ideas or concepts that seem strange to you today—issues important in 1848 that have ceased to be a problem? Write about one of these issues and why it may no longer be a problem.
3. What kind of risk was Frederick Douglass taking in supporting the women's movement? Look up Douglass's life and comment on his work for feminism as well as for abolition.
4. Compare the aims and goals for women expressed in the Seneca Falls Declaration with W. E. B. Du Bois's views on black civil rights.

EDITH WHARTON

A First Word

Edith Wharton (1862–1937) was a wealthy New Yorker who became a distinguished novelist, author of *Ethan Frome* and *The Age of Innocence*, among many others. After an unhappy marriage, she lived abroad, where she had many literary friends and a quiet life. Her autobiography, *A Backward Glance* published in 1933, from which this short passage is taken, sums up her philosophy of not being afraid of change.

1 Years ago I said to myself: "There's no such thing as old age; there is only sorrow."

I have learned with the passing of time that this, though true, is 2 not the whole truth. The other producer of old age is habit: the deathly process of doing the same thing in the same way at the same hour day after day, first from carelessness, then from inclination, at last from cowardice or inertia. Luckily the inconsequent life is not the only alternative; for caprice is as ruinous as routine. Habit is necessary; it is the habit of having habits, of turning a trail into a rut, that must be incessantly fought against if one is to remain alive.

In spite of illness, in spite even of the arch-enemy sorrow, one 3 *can* remain alive long past the usual date of disintegration if one is unafraid of change, insatiable in intellectual curiosity, interested in big things, and happy in small ways. In the course of sorting and setting down of my memories I have learned that these advantages are usually independent of one's merits, and that I probably owe my happy old age to the ancestor who accidentally endowed me with these qualities.

Engaging the Text

1. Comment on these statements that Wharton makes:

   — "... it is the habit of having habits, of turning a trail into a rut, that must be incessantly fought against if one is to remain alive" (2).
   — "... caprice is as ruinous as routine" (2).
   — "There's no such thing as old age; there is only sorrow" (1).
   — "One *can* remain alive ... if one is unafraid of change, insatiable in intellectual curiosity ..." (3)

The Engaged Writer

1. How does Wharton's resolve to "be unafraid of change" contrast with the views expressed in Rosenblatt's essay, "The Quality of Mercy Killing"?
2. Other topics that this essay might relate to include the celebrated "right to die" legal cases such as the Nancy Cruzan case, questions on ageing (Carolyn Heilbrun, "Naming a New Rite of Passage"), hospice care, or physician-assisted suicide. Use one of these as a topic for a documented paper.
3. Edith Wharton led a long and productive life as a writer. Her essay is essentially happy and upbeat. Comment on the philosophy of life that caused her to feel that way.

Writer's Guide

Writing a Summary of What You Read

Carl Sagan's essay, "The Warming of the World," (p. 229) lends itself well to summarizing. Writing a simple outline is the first step. To write a complete summary, take these steps:

1. Read through the essay once, quickly, to get the main thrust. Then write in your notebook a few phrases saying what the essay is about: "Climate changes—affect humans—atmosphere acts like greenhouse—too much CO_2 trapped will warm the atmosphere too much for life on earth. Global research, study needed—vital to solve this threat." This sketchy outline will help your understanding of the essay and provide a framework for its summary.

2. Either use the author and title of the piece you are summarizing as a title, or mention them clearly in your first paragraph. The reader needs to know what you are summarizing.

3. Then read through the essay again, carefully, with pen or highlighter in hand. Underline the most important sentence in each paragraph. This is sometimes, though not always, the topic sentence.

4. Avoid the temptation to underline everything. The figures Sagan gives are important, but they back up his general statements and are not statements themselves.

5. Go back to the beginning and start writing, putting the underlined statements in your own words. For example, for the first three paragraphs of Sagan's essay, you might say "In the beginning, humans depended absolutely on climate (para-

graph 1). The Ice Age forced our ancestors to develop skills to survive (2). The present, more temperate epoch has seen our species flourish and develop advanced technology to change our climate to support still more people. Yet we are still faced with dangers due to this changing of our climate (3)."

6. Read through your summary to be sure you have included all major points and not a lot of minor ones. Imagine that you are providing needed information for a person too busy to read the whole article.

7. Then, smooth out your summary paragraph. Be sure you have made adequate transitions between your sentences and that your summary makes sense. Fix up sentence structure and grammar so that it reads smoothly.

8. Be sure you have used your own words. Even two words together or a short phrase from the essay you are summarizing belongs to the author. Overborrowing of someone else's words or ideas means plagiarism. Place in quotation marks any of the author's exact words or combinations of words that you have used. See "Backing Up What You Say."

Summary of "The Warming of the World," by Carl Sagan

Human beings have survived many climate changes through thousands of years. We are warmed by the sun; if it were turned off, the Earth would freeze. The Earth's atmosphere modifies and changes the effects of the sun's heat. It prevents the infrared rays from reflecting back off the Earth. We owe our comfort to the balance of CO_2 and H_2O and heat in the atmosphere. The "greenhouse effect" is the ability of these gasses to absorb heat in the infrared and hence warm the Earth. We are upsetting this delicate balance by overproducing CO_2, which cannot be removed from the atmosphere and which increasingly heats it. Calculations show that this abundance of CO_2 will double by the year 2035, raising the Earth's temperature by possibly 4°C. Precipitation will change, ice caps will melt, and ocean levels will rise.

We need to deal with this problem globally, because we do not completely understand the severity of the results of this process; because the people living today may need to sacrifice for those who come later; and because the problem cannot be solved except by international agreement. Study, better understanding, and a "global consciousness" of its seriousness are essential to solve this problem that affects the whole planet.

GARRISON KEILLOR

How to Write a Personal Letter

It's surprising to find an advertisement in a collection of essays. But this essay was written as an ad for the International Paper Company in 1987 by Garrison Keillor. Keillor makes letter writing sound very attractive—intellectually and emotionally. He writes the kind of "how to" that Andrew Cain does in "Scribbling"—how we can make a simple art our own and bring it into our own lives.

We shy persons need to write a letter now and then, or else we'll 1
dry up and blow away. It's true. And I speak as one who loves to reach for the phone, dial the number, and talk. I say, "Big Bopper here—what's shakin', babes?" The telephone is to shyness what Hawaii is to February, it's a way out of the woods, *and yet:* a letter is better.

Such a Sweet Gift

Such a sweet gift—a piece of handmade writing, in an envelope 2
that is not a bill, sitting in our friend's path when she trudges home from a long day spent among wahoos and savages, a day our words will help repair. They don't need to be immortal, just sincere. She can read them twice and again tomorrow: *You're someone I care about, Corinne, and think of often and every time I do you make me smile.*

We need to write, otherwise nobody will know who we are. 3
They will have only a vague impression of us as A Nice Person, because frankly, we don't shine at conversation, we lack the confidence to thrust our faces forward and say, "Hi, I'm Heather Hooten, let me tell you about my week." Mostly we say "Uh-huh" and "Oh really." People smile and look over our shoulder, looking for someone else to talk to.

4   So a shy person sits down and writes a letter. To be known by another person—to meet and talk freely on the page—to be close despite distance. To escape from anonymity and be our own sweet selves and express the music of our souls.

5   Same thing that moves a giant rock star to sing his heart out in front of 123,000 people moves us to take ballpoint in hand and write a few lines to our dear Aunt Eleanor. *We want to be known.* We want her to know that we have fallen in love, that we quit our job, that we're moving to New York, and we want to say a few things that might not get said in casual conversation: *thank you for what you've meant to me, I am very happy right now.*

Skip the Guilt

6   The first step in writing letters is to get over the guilt of *not writing.* You don't "owe" anybody a letter. Letters are a gift. The burning shame you feel when you see unanswered mail makes it harder to pick up a pen and makes for a cheerless letter when you finally do. *I feel bad about not writing, but I've been so busy,* etc. Skip this. Few letters are obligatory, and they are *Thanks for the wonderful gift* and *I am terribly sorry to hear about George's death* and *Yes, you're welcome to stay with us next month,* and not many more than that. Write those promptly if you want to keep your friends. Don't worry about the others, except love letters, of course. When your true love writes *Dear Light of My Life, Joy of My Heart, O Lovely Pulsating Core of My Sensate Life,* some response is called for.

7   Some of the best letters are tossed off in a burst of inspiration, so keep your writing stuff in one place where you can sit down for a few minutes and *Dear Roy, I am in the middle of an essay for International Paper but thought I'd drop you a line. Hi to your sweetie too* dash off a note to a pal. Envelopes, stamps, address book, everything in a drawer so you can write fast when the pen is hot.

8   A blank white 8" x 11" sheet can look as big as Montana if the pen's not so hot—try a smaller page and write boldly. Or use a note card with a piece of fine art on the front; if your letter ain't good, at least they get the Matisse. Get a pen that makes a sensuous line, get a comfortable typewriter, a friendly word processor—whichever feels easy to the hand.

9   Sit for a few minutes with the blank sheet in front of you, and meditate on the person you will write to, let your friend come to

mind until you can almost see her or him in the room with you. Remember the last time you saw each other and how your friend looked and what you said and what perhaps was unsaid between you, and when your friend becomes real to you, start to write.

✂ Tell Us What You're Doing

Write the salutation—*Dear* You—and take a deep breath and   10
plunge in. A simple declarative sentence will do, followed by another and another and another. Tell us what you're doing and tell it like you were talking to us. Don't think about grammar, don't think about lit'ry style, don't try to write dramatically, just give us your news. Where did you go, who did you see, what did they say, what do you think?

If you don't know where to begin, start with the present   11
moment: *I'm sitting at the kitchen table on a rainy Saturday morning. Everyone is gone and the house is quiet.* Let your simple description of the present moment lead to something else, let the letter drift gently along.

✂ Take It Easy

The toughest letter to crank out is one that is meant to impress, as   12
we all know from writing job applications; if it's hard work to slip off a letter to a friend, maybe you're trying too hard to be terrific. A letter is only a report to someone who already likes you for reasons other than your brilliance. Take it easy.

Don't worry about form. It's not a term paper. When you come   13
to the end of one episode, just start a new paragraph. You can go from a few lines about the sad state of rock 'n roll to the fight with your mother to your fond memories of Mexico to your cat's urinary tract infection to a few thoughts on personal indebtedness to the kitchen sink and what's in it. The more you write, the easier it gets, and when you have a True True Friend to write to, a *compadre*, a soul sibling, then it's like driving a car down a country road, you just get behind the keyboard and press on the gas.

Don't tear up the page and start over when you write a bad   14
line—try to write your way out of it. Make mistakes and plunge on. Let the letter cook along and let yourself be bold. Outrage, confusion, love—whatever is in your mind, let it find a way to the page. Writing is a means of discovery, always, and when you come

to the end and write *Yours ever* or *Hugs and Kisses*, you'll know something you didn't when you wrote *Dear Pal*.

An Object of Art

15 Probably your friend will put your letter away, and it'll be read again a few years from now—and it will improve with age. And forty years from now, your friend's grandkids will dig it out of the attic and read it, a sweet and precious relic of the ancient Eighties that gives them a sudden clear glimpse of you and her and the world we old-timers knew. You will then have created an object of art. Your simple lines about where you went, who you saw, what they said, will speak to those children and they will feel in their hearts the humanity of our times.

16 You can't pick up a phone and call the future and tell them about our times. You have to pick up a piece of paper.

Engaging the Text

1. Keillor's work is very "down home"—funny and casual, like a friend writing you a letter. He uses words such as "wahoos" (paragraph 2), though, a reference to ugly, apelike yet human creatures in Jonathan Swift's *Gulliver's Travels*, that is meant to satirize the ugliness in humans.

2. Another word he uses in this deceptively simple "how to" essay is *compadre* (13), a Spanish word meaning godfather to the same child, hence, a person with close ties to you.

3. You are told that this essay is an advertisement for paper. Do you see any sign that it is so? No

4. Keillor uses some incomplete sentences (paragraph 2 and 4). Why do you think he uses them? Do they add to or subtract from, the essay? Or doesn't it matter? Because he is making a conversation

Engaging the Reader

1. Why does Keillor tell us he is a shy person? Do you agree that a shy person needs to write letters? Yes

2. List the steps Keillor advises us to take to get started on writing a letter. Skip the guilt, tells us what you are doing, that it easy object report

3. List the things he tells us not to worry about when writing this kind of letter. Why does he give this advice?

Grammar, orthographes, form

4. What are the advantages of a letter over a phone call? Which do you prefer? Why? *letters stayed for a long time keep memories, phone nothing stayed*

The Engaged Writer

1. Using specific examples, write a paper telling why you prefer a letter over a phone call or a phone call over a letter.
2. Keeping in mind Keillor's do's and don'ts, write a letter of the kind he describes to a friend you want to keep, and mail it.

SIGAL D'AVANZO

Dear Mom

Sigal D'Avanzo is a college student studying art in the United States, far from her native Israel and her parents. She wrote the following letter after reading Garrison Keillor's "How to Write a Personal Letter."

Dear Mom,

It's eight o'clock in the evening and I just woke up. I've been extremely busy at school and at work and I just had to rest or I would have collapsed. Recently life has become pretty hectic. I find myself always in a rush, hurrying from place to place in order to run the necessary errands, and trying to efficiently expend the twenty-four hours we have in a day.

How are you doing? The last time I heard from you was two weeks ago, when you gave me the terrible news of Zmira's sudden death. It's so awful to lose your best friend like this. It's weird how it works. People die every hour, but when it's somebody you know, you just can't digest it. The image is coming to you all the time. You remember your conversations and the things you did together and it seems almost illogical that it actually happened. It took me a couple of days to realize that she is gone. I hope you're feeling better now although there is nothing that can compensate for the loss of a dear friend.

4   Mom, I miss you so much. I miss everybody. Sometimes I wish I could "jump" for a visit, sit with you all in the living room, and have a talk or even an argument—anything! I didn't realize how tough it is to live in another country when you're so far away from your family and your old friends. You'll probably laugh, but each time I miss your food I cook my favorite dishes you used to make me. Chris says it's great but only I know what the original one tastes like!

5   About a week ago we celebrated the Jewish New Year. I made a traditional Israeli meal and I "Americanized" it. Chris and I have it all: we double-up and celebrate both Christian and Jewish holidays. What a fun life!

6   How is everybody? How is Dad doing in his work? How's Carmit doing in school? I hope she doesn't think only about boys and that she started to study for a change. It makes me angry to see a smart and talented girl wasting her time watching MTV everyday. If MTV was part of the curriculum, she probably would be the most successful student in the entire class.

7   A couple of days ago I started school at a community college near home. You won't believe me, but the thing I like the most is the gorgeous swimming pool they have. If the water was a little warmer it would be perfect! Besides the swimming pool, I also take some classes. I have Photography, Sculpture, Design and English. In January, I'm going to the Corcoran School of Art which is located right near the White House. What a strategic location!

8   I wish you could come here and I would show you around the area. I would like to take you downtown, show you the beautiful mall and the monuments, and take you to all the museums. I know Dad would love the Museum of Natural History because they have a magnificent collection of all these weird looking birds. I also would like you to come here just because I want you to actually see where I live and not only see it from a picture.

I remember when I first got here, one and a half years ago, I was overwhelmed. People seemed to talk too quickly and I could only catch the beginnings and the ends of their sentences. Everyone had a car and used it for everything. I didn't even have a driving license back then. Everything was so new and strange. I guess I understand things better now and I'm not as terrified driving on the highways as then. I used to clutch the steering wheel like it was the only floating piece on the entire sea, and I was drowning. Well, when looking back I can say that a little progress has been made since then. It's time to finish the letter now although it could continue forever. I have to go back to my hot chocolate! Say "hello" to everybody from me and send them my love. I hope to hear from you very soon.

Love,
Sigal

The Engaged Writer

1. Write a "personal letter" to Sigal D'Avanzo, welcoming her to this country and explaining some of the customs we have that seem strange to her (paragraph 8). If you can think of others that she might find odd, include them, too.
2. If you have lived in another country than the one in which you grew up, write about the customs you found strange when you first started living there. How did you adapt to the new life?
3. In your work, what kinds of communication media do you use? Memos? Phone calls? E-Mail? Internet? Faxes? Choose the one you use most, and draw up a set of recommendations like Keillor's for the most effective use of the media in your job.

Writing a Letter to the Editor

Most editors of magazines and newspapers set aside pages or columns for letters of comment on events of the day or on articles in the publication. In fact, editors have found that the "Letters" column is one of the most read and one that gives the widest audience to opinions. Metropolitan dailies sell a couple of million copies daily; those papers and weekly magazines circulate worldwide and are collected in libraries, where they are preserved on microfilm or microfiche and in services such as *Newsbank*. A letter to the editor, therefore, reaches a very large audience, a cross section of society. If you are concerned about a subject, this influential channel provides a way to express your ideas to many potential readers.

You can use the following list of tips when writing many other kinds of letters, such as letters to congressional representatives, senators, and state legislators, or to large companies or institutions about an important or controversial issue (such as the discussion on feeding the homeless in the article by Michael Satchell, "How People Survive on Leftovers").

1. Typewrite, double space, on one side of the paper. If this is not possible, write neatly in ink. The address of the newspaper or magazine appears on an inside front page, usually at the bottom, along with other information on editors, circulation, and policies.
2. Express your ideas as clearly and concisely as possible. You will notice that the *Time* letters (Letters Responding to "The Quality of Mercy Killing") are under 150 words. Editors may cut longer letters, printing those parts they consider most interesting to their readers.
3. Deal with only one topic in one letter. If you have another idea, write another letter!
4. Write clearly, simply, without flourishes. Your first sentence is most important. How many times have you read only the first sentence of a newspaper article?
5. If you are being critical, start with something positive, some praise or commendation. Avoid violent or crude language; you can be frank but calm.
6. If the newspaper is incorrect about something, give the true facts.
7. Always sign your name and give your address. You may request that your name not be used if the letter is published, but editors will never print an anonymous letter. Don't look for your letter the next day, and don't be disappointed if it never appears. Many letters may arrive on the same subject, and the editor selects only a few to print. *Time* probably received hundreds of letters on Roger Rosenblatt's article ("The Quality of Mercy Killing") but chose four representative views to print.
8. Mail your letter.

Looking Up Words in a Dictionary

A collegiate dictionary, usually with the word *college* or *collegiate* in its title, contains around 170,000 entries. An unabridged dictionary, heavy and large, contains over 2,500 pages and many thousands more words or "entries," along with other material, making it an almost complete small reference work. Libraries own various unabridged dictionaries. The copy on the book jacket or the blurb on the first pages of dictionaries you examine will tell you if the dictionary is abridged as well as the kinds of information included. To see if the dictionary will be really helpful to you, check a word you are familiar with. See if the entry includes these items:

Etymology key—traces the entry's derivation from foreign or ancient languages, with those languages listed in a pattern of development
Pronunciation key—stress and sound, spelled out as they sound
Definitions—one or more
Synonyms—words with the same meaning
Illustrations—visual, diagrams, pictures; or quotations, illustrating usage

A pocket dictionary may be good for a quick spelling check, but it won't have enough material to help you in really understanding the word or knowing how to use it yourself. Your dictionary should also have some of the following:

A guide to the dictionary and its use
Manual of style (punctuation, abbreviations, proofreaders' marks, capitalization rules, manuscript preparation)
Historical sketch of the English language

Sometimes you can figure out an unfamiliar word from its context—its place in the story or in the sentence or from the meaning of the rest of the sentence, even though you may never have seen the word before. After all, we first learned language by imitating those around us and guessing the meaning of their response. Our intuition can still help us figure out meanings. An example of finding a word's meaning this way is the huge word *hemidemisemi-*

quavers from an article reviewing a newly revised dictionary. So as not to interrupt your reading, you rapidly figure out that since the word occurs next to the mention of a symphony, it has something to do with music. You've heard the word "quaver," meaning a wobbly change of tone. The prefixes "hemi," "demi," and "semi" sound as if that quavering were somewhat more intense and prolonged than usual. So, for the moment, you forget the dictionary and file the word in your mind as "quavery part of a symphony," since you don't need to know the exact definition to understand what you're reading. On the other hand, perhaps it is essential to understand the word's exact meaning; then you use the dictionary.

Dictionary Exercise

Look back over one of the essays you have read, and choose a word or two that you cannot understand simply by looking at the rest of the sentence. Look it up in the dictionary, and see how much extra information you can find. Write the information down in the following blanks, and use it as a model for future dictionary exercises.

1. Copy the word in boldface, including the indications of syllables.

   _____

2. Copy down the most frequent (first) pronunciation indicated.

   _____

3. Add the stress mark where shown (').

4. Write down the abbreviation of the part of speech and the full words for it.

   _____

5. If the word is a verb, the dictionary shows its past tense and past and present participles. If it is a noun, unusual plurals are shown, as are the different comparative forms of adjectives. Though you may not need all this information right away, you should know it is there. Write down any important ones for the word you are looking up.

   _____

6. Copy down the definitions, beginning with the most frequent one.

_____

_____

7. Are there any restrictions (*Brit., Archaic, Obs., Physics, Informal, Slang*)? What do they mean?

_____

8. Are any derivations (etymologies) listed? These trace the word back to its roots, often in an ancient language, using the symbol "<" (meaning "derived from"). Copy these down.

_____

9. Copy down any run-on entries, synonyms, usage notes, that appear at the end of the definition.

_____

_____

10. Use the word in a sentence of your own.

_____

_____

WILLIAM J. BENNETT

Go Ahead, Major in the Liberal Arts

William J. Bennett is the man President Reagan chose to be Secretary of Education and whose conservative views worried professional educators. Previously, he'd served as Chairman of the National Endowment for the Humanities and showed himself an advocate for a humanistic education and for cultural literacy. Later, he served the Bush administration as "Drug Czar." The following newspaper column was written in 1985.

Late last year the National Endowment for the Humanities issued 1 a report recommending that the study of the humanities once again take its place at the heart of the college curriculum. Objections rose quickly from the doubters who long ago learned that the liberal arts, including the humanities, never put a scrap of gold or silver in anyone's pocket. Reading old stories and learning dead languages won't prepare people for jobs in the real world. Right?

2   Well, happily, the Career Center of the University of Texas has just performed a major public service for the nation, particularly for our college students and the future of their economic well-being. In the Oct. 10 issue of Career News, the center has demonstrated that the liberal arts do not in fact lead irrevocably to one of three choices: teaching, graduate school or the soup line.

3   The Career Center's survey of more than 1,300 recent University of Texas liberal arts graduates reveals that 80 percent are employed full-time, 12 percent are full-time students and 5 percent are voluntarily unemployed, while only 3 percent are unemployed and looking for work.

4   Those are encouraging numbers by any standard. Twenty-eight percent of those surveyed completed graduate degrees and now have careers in business, law, medicine, education and many other professional areas.

5   For those liberal arts majors who earned no graduate degree, 47 percent currently have jobs in the business world that require a college education. Another 24 percent have comparable jobs in non-business settings, such as human services, journalism and politics. And, surprise of surprises, only 8 percent hold teaching jobs.

6   I can hear the doubters asking: You mean our students can be students of the humanities and still find gainful employment? Seems that way. In fact, the U.T. Career Center survey concludes that liberal arts graduates have access to more sectors of the labor market than specialized graduates. They are entering a broad range of careers without training beyond the bachelor's degree, including banking, retailing, insurance, real estate, computer programming and systems analysis, radio-TV, public relations, advertising and market research.

7   So much for the myth that liberal arts majors have been magnanimously decreasing the surplus population of eligible candidates for paying careers. But that stubborn old story still lingers among students who watch in dismay as recruiters parade into campus placement offices to interview specialists, such as business majors or engineers.

At such a moment the competitive edge of a BBA seems large.   8
But the U.T. Career Center survey finds that it is an illusory advantage. Businesses are equally interested in liberal arts majors. The difference is that liberal arts majors often must generate first job opportunities on their own initiative without relying greatly on campus recruiters. But later, the Career Center finds, most of them succeed and become happily employed in the business world.

They may even have a distinct advantage in the end. The liberal   9
arts graduate often makes significant leaps of responsibility and advancement. A study of AT&T's management system for example, showed that 43 percent of the humanities and social science majors achieved at least the fourth level of the corporation's management hierarchy (a measure of considerable success), compared with only 32 percent for business majors and 23 percent for engineers.

Part of all this unsuspected success, says the U.T. Career Center,   10
ter, has to do with the fact that liberal arts graduates are likely to have developed certain skills that are indispensable to all areas of work, skills such as research, writing, speaking and analyzing. They can then easily develop more specialized "salable skills" in on-the-job training, internships or graduate schools.

More significant, however, are the indications that American   11
business leaders in all fields regard liberal arts education as a valuable economic resource. "A liberally educated person is still the type of individual needed at the highest levels of corporate life," says Robert Callander, president of Chemical Bank. "The technical skills are built upon this base. It is that peculiar mix of the behavioral sciences, natural sciences, mathematics, history and English that produces a mind capable, in later life, of bringing mature judgment to complex—and sometimes great—issues."

The humanities hold a central place in that peculiar mix. For it   12
is still required of every man, even in the late 20th century, that he should walk abroad among his fellow men, no matter what his chosen career. Even in the age of high technology and specialization, mankind is still our business. As the U.T. Career Center points out, every product or service still requires people to sell the product, people to distribute the product, people to work the product, talk with those who use the product and analyze future markets for similar products.

13   There are many things from which we may derive good by which we do not profit. The welcome message from the U.T. Career Center survey is that study of the humanities is not one of them. Their study does not—I repeat, does not—incapacitate a person for gainful employment. I hope that other schools around the country will follow U.T.'s lead and help get that message out. And I hope that the recognition of the humanities' value and profitability continues to grow among leaders of all fields and occupations.

14   Most of all, though, I hope that college students will pay attention to findings of this kind. Do not fear the world too much. Take the time to make mankind your business: read literature, study history, know philosophy, learn languages. You will find that the humanities and other liberal arts will help you succeed, and profit, in any career or endeavor.

Engaging the Text

1. In his discussion of the humanities, Bennett, in addition to citing many facts, frequently uses one part of speech, adverbs, to modify his verbs and lend color to the fact-filled argument. Some of these are irrevocably (2), happily (2, 8), voluntarily (3), greatly (8), and magnanimously (7). He uses adverbs also to modify adjectives, as in *liberally educated* (11). In your own writing, use some well-chosen adverbs to add depth to your verbs.

2. The second sentence in paragraph 12 brings up the subject of using "man" and "he" to include everyone. Rewrite that sentence to really include men and women. Hint: look at the last sentence in that same paragraph where Bennett avoids sexist language.

Engaging the Reader

1. Bennett appeals to students to major in the liberal arts, using a dollars-and-cents argument that might have a greater appeal to business majors. Do you think this approach is effective—or is Bennett confused about his audience?

2. The facts and studies that Bennett cites make this a kind of research paper. How convincing is it in its buildup of fact?

3. What did the University of Texas Career Center find about certain predicted outcomes of majoring in the liberal arts?

4. What facts does Bennett cite to prove his point that liberal arts graduates find employment?
5. What group of students seems to be interviewed first by campus recruiters? Do you think this is true on your campus? What do liberal arts majors have to do to counteract this, according to Bennett?
6. What skills do liberal arts graduates have to offer?

The Engaged Writer

1. Summarize Bennett's argument. (See "Writing a Summary of What You Read.")
2. Bennett summarizes several studies: data from the University of Texas Career Center, a study of AT&T's management system, and a speech by the president of Chemical Bank. Where would he find such information? Go to your library and look for the studies he mentions. To find them in the Library of Congress Subject Headings, look up some of the key words in these titles (liberal arts major, management systems, career centers). Look also in your library's magazine and newspaper indexes. Report on your findings in an essay or in class discussion. For information on the Library of Congress Subject Headings, see "Finding a Topic to Write On."
3. If your major is in a technical field, respond to Bennett's urging with a reasoned argument for majoring in your field.
4. If you are majoring in the liberal arts, find some other evidence to back up your choice, besides the studies Bennett cites in his article.

Finding a Topic to Write On

Throughout *The Engaging Reader* you are being given possible writing topics under the heading THE ENGAGED WRITER. The choice of writing topics remains undoubtedly the one big question for students, perhaps the one that concerns instructors like Robert Pirsig the most. Students still ask plaintively "What can I write *about?*" Do students ask how to write complete sentences? Or how to write coherent paragraphs? No! The universal plea is for a topic.

Often, though, in spite of instructors' lists of suggestions, study questions, or approaches, students still want to write on something they feel drawn to. Gun control, abortion, lowering the drinking age (or raising it, depending on point of view), history of witchcraft, and other gruesome topics are some of the worn-out subjects students think of when they choose topics for themselves. I call these topics "worn out" because little new can be written about them. Your paper should add something new, no matter how small, to the accumulated wisdom and comment on the subject you have chosen.

In addition, I would like to make a couple of specific suggestions or plans of action in searching for a topic. The first one: be interested! Let's say that the essay by William Bennett ("Go Ahead, Major in the Liberal Arts") makes you curious about career planning and career centers at colleges, and you would like to find out more about them. One good discovery would be the career center at your own college, which would have material to read and people to talk with.

Look over this book, especially the writing topics under "The Engaged Writer," some of which may suggest a topic for you. Newspaper accounts, TV news, and editorials, all suggest possible topics for the writer. Another technique to root out topics consists in freewriting. At a signal you start writing about anything at all, without taking your pen away from the paper. Don't worry about errors—just write! After a five- or ten-minute period, everyone stops, and re-reads the written material. Somewhere in there may be a germ of an idea for a topic.

Another method involves brainstorming. Each person in your peer group or writing group comes up with a possible topic, but the others do not pass judgment on it until each one has spoken. Then round after round of talk generates excitement until each one has been able to choose a topic.

Being curious is being on the right track, but your inquiry can even begin closer to home. Look at something so basic and simple as your own desk, workplace, dining or kitchen table. On mine, for example, is a calendar, a thermometer, a book of appliance instructions, a pair of glasses, a goose-necked desk lamp, a date book stuffed with slips of paper and receipts, a Bic pen, a credit card, a broken coffee mug filled with pencils and two unexplainable feathers, and a book called *Racism and Sexism*, along with my faithful computer.

Leaving out the title of the book (suggesting many good topics), on the desk sit several possible inspirations implied in the objects:

- How is pottery made? Where does the clay come from?
- Who invented the ball-point pen, and how is it made? What did people use before that for writing?
- Calendar reform—should we have 13 months in the year?
- Magnetic money—is it the cash of the future? What are the possibilities for credit card fraud?
- Computer fraud—how to cope with it?
- Who writes the instruction booklets for appliances? Is there any hope for finding readable ones?
- What kinds of birds did these feathers come from? Where can I find out about local birds, hunting laws? Should hunting laws be changed because of pressure from conservationists? Or from gun advocates?
- Who invented the paper clip? (There's always one of these somewhere in any workplace.)
- Can you think of a question for the thermometer? Perhaps: "I'd rather be at the beach!" This brings up a whole galaxy of questions: beach erosion; resort development; shifting college schedules to accommodate resort industries (where students often work).

Some of these need a little research; others need only some imagination to provide paper topics. Forget the *National Enquirer* type of topic. You have better ones right under your thumb.

The question you should always ask yourself when picking a topic for a paper is: "What about it?" What can I say about this topic? Is there any argument or shifting point of view connected with it? Would I want to read something about this topic? Every good topic begins with a question, with someone's curiosity. "Who did it?" "Shall we consider a candidate's small sins in electing her or him to office?" "Which of two good choices shall we make?" If your paper has extended knowledge by a jot, or pushed back ignorance by a bit, or put old things together in a new way, you have succeeded.

Library Search Techniques

Even more important for picking topics as well as finding information about them is your college library. Libraries and librarians remain an important natural resource. Lean heavily on them. For most of the assignments suitable for research in *The Engaging Read-*

er, a simple search strategy plan will help you get acquainted with the college library so that it no longer seems awesome and difficult. Following up on the Carl Sagan essay, I have prepared a TOPIC SEARCHER, adapted from several in use at the Prince George's College library. You can use this format for other topics, and with the help of your college librarians, prepare yourself for an assignment in any college course, or an on-the-job assignment.

The Greenhouse Effect—Topic Searcher

One of the library's best tools is a three-volume set of the *Library of Congress Subject Headings*. It contains all of the words or sets of words in which Library of Congress materials are indexed, but it is useful even if your library uses the Dewey Decimal System of organizing material. It acts both as a list of subjects to explore and a method of unearthing material from a library, since the headings are much the same as those in magazine and newspaper indexes. You may have an on-line catalog on your campus, a CD-ROM magazine and newspaper search program, or you may be able to use search services like DIALOG. Below is a typical entry from the *Library of Congress Subject Headings* with sub-entries giving cross-references to other related topics. One of these might be your working topic.

Greenhouse effect, Atmospheric
   (May Subd Geog)
     [QC912.3]
   UF   Atmospheric greenhouse effect
   BT   Atmospheric temperature
         Carbon dioxide
         Heat budget (Geophysics)
         Infrared albedo
         Solar radiation
   RT   Global warming

When you check the related term (RT), Global warming, you get more terms:

Global warming *(Not Subd Geog)*
     [QC981.8.G56]
   UF   Warming, Global
   BT   Global temperature changes

RT   Greenhouse effect, Atmospheric
—**Research** *(May Subd Geog)*
——**Law and legislation**
        (May Subd Geog)

To use *The Library of Congress Subject Headings,* try various combinations of key words until you find one, like "Greenhouse effect, Atmospheric" which explains what the terms include and directs you to other headings by abbreviations like UF ("Used For"), BT ("Broad Term"), or RT ("Refers To"). Checking up on this last, we find another list with more terms: "Global warming." These terms are the word combination you would use to look the subject up in an index, database, or search program.

Scope   The problem of the earth's warming stems from increasing difficulty with the delicately balanced ratio of gasses in the atmosphere. The recent increase in atmospheric CO_2 has caused temperatures to rise significantly in the last years. This could lead to drastic changes in the sea's level, in the water tables, and in air quality that could have serious effects on the earth's population. Carl Sagan, in "The Warming of the World," says that we do not fully understand the severity of the problem, that the next generations may be badly affected, and that the only solution is international cooperation.

Introductory Articles   Begin with good introductions and overviews, some of which can be found in the following sources: *Encyclopedia Americana, McGraw-Hill Encyclopedia of Science and Technology* and *Yearbooks,* and *Our Magnificent Earth: Rand McNally Atlas of Earth Resources.* Chicago: Rand McNally, 1979.

The following are also good sources:

Bernard, Harold W. *The Greenhouse Effect.* Cambridge: Ballinger, 1980.
Clark, Sarah L. *Fight Global Warming: 29 Things You Can Do.* Yonkers, N.Y.: Consumer Reports Books, 1991.
Fisher, David E. *Fire and Ice: The Greenhouse Effect, Ozone Depletion and Nuclear Winter.* N.Y.: Harper & Row, 1990.
Gribbin, John R. *Future Weather and the Greenhouse Effect.* NY: Delacort, 1982.
Kraljik, Matthew A. *The Greenhouse Effect.* N.Y. H. W. Wilson, 1992.
McCuen, Gary E. *Our Endangered Atmosphere: Global Warming and the Ozone Layer.* Hudson WI: McCuen, 1987.

Minger, Terrell J. *Greenhouse Glasnost: The Crisis of Global Warming: Essays.* Salt Lake City, Utah: Institute for Resource Management, 1990.

Titus, James G. *Potential Impacts of Sea Level Rise on the Beach at Ocean City Maryland.* United States Environmental Protection Agency, Office of Policy Planning and Evaluation, 1985.

Seidel, Stephen. *Can We Delay a Greenhouse Warning? The Effectiveness and Feasibility of Options to Slow a Build-Up of Carbon Dioxide in the Atmosphere.* Washington DC: Strategic Studies Staff, Office of Policy Analysis, 1983.

U.S. Congress. House of Representatives. Committee on Science and Technology; Subcommittee on Investigation and Oversight. *Carbon Dioxide and the Greenhouse Effect: Hearing Before the Subcommittee on Investigation and Oversight and the Subcommittee on Natural Resources, Agriculture Research and Environment of the Committee on Science and Technology.* 98th Congress, 2nd session (February 28, 1984).

U.S. Congress. Senate. Committee on Environment and Public Works, Subcommittee on Toxic Substances and Environmental Oversight. 99th Congress, 1st session (December 10, 1985). These and other government documents are on sale from the Superintendent of Documents, Washington DC.

Catalog   Your library's catalog may be on a database or on line. Consult it for books and audiovisual materials (audio cassettes, video tapes or laser disks and databases for periodicals.

You may find it advisable to narrow the subject down to one aspect: control, economic or political aspects, forecasts, or measurement of effects.

For other subjects, you might use some other CD-ROM indexes such as Ethnic Newswatch, the Cumulative Index to Nursing and Allied Health, or PsychLit.

Pamphlet File: Many libraries have a large number of general and technical publications filed (usually in folders) on these subjects. Look under the same headings as in the catalog.

Periodical Sources:

General Indexes

ProQuest (a CD-ROM search program that covers more than 1000 magazines and journals and often includes complete text of articles). Look under: Greenhouse Effect.

The Magazine Index (a machine index that covers approximately 400 popular magazines for the last five years). Look under: Greenhouse Effect, Atmospheric.

Reader's Guide to Periodical Literature (a printed index to about 200 popular magazines; also available on CD-ROM). Look under: Greenhouse Effect.

Specialized Indexes   *General Science Index* (an index to periodicals and journals specifically related to scientific fields; also on CD-ROM). Look under: Greenhouse Effect.

Newspaper Sources:

ProQuest, a CD-ROM search program that covers more than 1000 magazines and newspapers; often includes the complete text of articles.) Look under: Greenhouse Effect.

National Newspaper Index (a machine index to the "big five" newspapers: *New York Times, Washington Post, Christian Science Monitor, Wall Street Journal,* and *Los Angeles Times* for the last five years). Look under: Greenhouse Effect, Atmospheric.

Newsbank (an index to selected articles from newspapers all over the country). It provides the full text of the articles on microfiche or on CD-ROM; great for local opinion on issues. Look under: Air Pollution, Water Pollution, Climate and Weather.

General Questions for Longer Essays

1. Talk with the person who supervises or reviews the work that you do. Ask if some area needs improvement—or research, or a study to improve efficiency, especially in communicating. Make some recommendations, based on what you have learned in your writing classroom, that might help your office or your job to be more effective. Bring these recommendations to the next meeting of your Writers' Group, and add your classmates' input to your material. Organize these in a report to submit to your supervisor. It may gain you a promotion, or at least a kind word, in addition to some credit in your class!

2. Both the British and the American public radio have had for years a program called "Desert Island Disks." In this program, a celebrity interview contains a different slant: the person is asked to choose the records or disks he or she would like to take

along if cast away on a desert island. While playing these recordings over the air, the person is interviewed on other matters as well. The interviewer asks, for example, what book, what luxurious object, the interviewee would like to incorporate into that desert island scene. Choose a person from this book: Stephen Hawking, C. L. Rawlins, Marjory Stoneman Douglas, Endesha Ida Mae Holland are good suggestions, but you may choose another one if you wish. In teams of two, one as interviewer and the other as the "celebrity," organize a "Desert Island Treasury" of things, articles from *The Engaging Reader* or another book, movies, music, that you would take with you *if you were that person* (not yourself). Write it up as an interview (Q & A form).

3. Find a piece of writing that you have done previously, for this class as a diagnostic essay, for another class, or on the job. In your writing example, find a place where you could have added details about an inward, physical or emotional experience. Try adding these details to your writing example.

4. Do you have child care at your workplace or school? If so, describe it. If not, say why not. If you have children and work, what is your solution to the child care problem? How well does it work? Do a survey of people at your workplace. How many are parents? Do they want or need child care? You will think of more questions to answer in an essay.

5. Think about these serious problems connected with schools: sex education, prayer in school, drugs, AIDS incidence among children, violence in the classroom. Explore one of these problems in writing.

6. Here are some articles in *The Engaging Reader* which include issues to use as starting points for a documented paper on a current issue. Much material exists on your library's indexes and databases on the following: Sagan (global warming), Sobel (preservation of natural areas), Lukas (street violence), Cangialosi (the homeless), Smith (rural poverty), Kotlowitz (urban poverty).

McClintock, "Real Trouble Ahead," Question 4: Write a paper on the treatment of elderly or handicapped people today and their problems with their self-esteem.
Smith, "The Face of Rural Poverty," questions 1 and 2: the effects of poverty on children, or the causes, results, solutions, government reactions towards or another theme relating to poverty in America.

Heat-Moon, "South by Southeast," question 3, on the battle for civil rights.

Hubbell, "On the Road," question 5, on the problems of working women.

Sagan, "The Warming of the World," questions 3 or 4 on the problem of global warming.

Quinnett, "Enough of Roads," questions 4 or 5 on conservation of the wilderness.

Bloom, "Rock Music," questions 3 or 4 on the effects of rock music.

W.E.B. Du Bois, "Response to Mr. Washington," question 3 or 4 on the course of racial integration since 1964.

Bennett, "Go Ahead," questions 3 or 4 on career choices.

The Preamble and Bill of Rights, question 2 includes a whole list of controversial topics stemming from interpretation of the Bill of Rights.

ROBERT M. PIRSIG

How to Start

This selection discusses the writer's teaching experience when he tried to help students find topics for writing assignments. Pirsig is also a storyteller. He wrote a book that he confesses has little to do with orthodox Zen Buddhist practice and actually is not very factual on motorcycles, either. In the book, Pirsig describes a trip across country on a cycle with his son, Chris. Taking on the character of Phaedrus, speaker in one of Plato's dialogues, he searches for the truth, for the meaning of life, as Plato's dialogues do. The resulting book, *Zen and the Art of Motorcycle Maintenance*, written in 1974, is a moving tale of one man's search, told with originality. The following selection is from Chapter 16 of *Zen and the Art of Motorcycle Maintenance*.

He'd been innovating extensively. He'd been having trouble with   1
students who had nothing to say. At first he thought it was laziness but later it became apparent that it wasn't. They just couldn't think of anything to say.

2   One of them, a girl with strong-lensed glasses, wanted to write a five-hundred-word essay about the United States. He was used to the sinking feeling that comes from statements like this, and suggested without disparagement that she narrow it down to just Bozeman.

3   When the paper came due she didn't have it and was quite upset. She had tried and tried but she just couldn't think of anything to say.

4   He had already discussed her with her previous instructors and they'd confirmed his impressions of her. She was very serious, disciplined and hardworking, but extremely dull. Not a spark of creativity in her anywhere. Her eyes, behind the thick-lensed glasses, were the eyes of a drudge. She wasn't bluffing him, she really couldn't think of anything to say, and was upset by her inability to do as she was told.

5   It just stumped him. Now *he* couldn't think of anything to say. A silence occurred, and then a peculiar answer: "Narrow it down to the *main street* of Bozeman." It was a stroke of insight.

6   She nodded dutifully and went out. But just before her next class she came back in real distress, tears this time, distress that had obviously been there for a long time. She still couldn't think of anything to say, and couldn't understand why, if she couldn't think of anything about all of Bozeman, she should be able to think of something about just one street.

7   He was furious. "You're not *looking!*" he said. A memory came back of his own dismissal from the University for having *too much* to say. For every fact there is an *infinity* of hypotheses. The more you *look* the more you *see*. She really wasn't looking and yet somehow didn't understand this.

8   He told her angrily, "Narrow it down to the *front* of *one* building on the main street of Bozeman. The Opera House. Start with the upper left-hand brick."

9   Her eyes, behind the thick-lensed glasses, opened wide.

10   She came in the next class with a puzzled look and handed him a five-thousand-word essay on the front of the Opera House on the main street of Bozeman, Montana. "I sat in the hamburger stand across the street," she said, "and started writing about the first brick, and the second brick, and then by the third brick it all started to come and I couldn't stop. They thought I was crazy, and they kept kidding me, but here it all is. I don't understand it."

Neither did he, but on long walks through the streets of town   11
he thought about it and concluded she was evidently stopped with
the same kind of blockage that had paralyzed him on his first day
of teaching. She was blocked because she was trying to repeat, in
her writing, things she had already heard, just as on the first day
he had tried to repeat things he had already decided to say. She
couldn't think of anything to write about Bozeman because she
couldn't recall anything she had heard worth repeating. She was
strangely unaware that she could look and see freshly for herself,
as she wrote, without primary regard for what had been said
before. The narrowing down to one brick destroyed the blockage
because it was so obvious she *had* to do some original and direct
seeing.

He experimented further. In one class he had everyone write all   12
hour about the back of his thumb. Everyone gave him funny looks
at the beginning of the hour, but everyone did it, and there wasn't
a single complaint about "nothing to say."

In another class he changed the subject from the thumb to a coin,   13
and got a full hour's writing from every student. In other classes it
was the same. Some asked, "Do you have to write about both
sides?" Once they got into the idea of seeing directly for themselves
they also saw there was no limit to the amount they could say. It
was a confidence-building assignment too, because what they
wrote, even though seemingly trivial, was nevertheless their own
thing, not a mimicking of someone else's. Classes where he used
that coin exercise were always less balky and more interested.

As a result of his experiments he concluded that imitation was   14
a real evil that had to be broken before real rhetoric teaching could
begin. This imitation seemed to be an external compulsion. Little
children didn't have it. It seemed to come later on, possibly as a
result of school itself.

That sounded right, and the more he thought about it the more   15
right it sounded. Schools teach you to imitate. If you don't imitate
what the teacher wants you get a bad grade. Here, in college, it was
more sophisticated, of course; you were supposed to imitate the
teacher in such a way as to convince the teacher you were not imitating, but taking the essence of the instruction and going ahead
with it on your own. That got you A's. Originality on the other
hand could get you anything—from A to F. The whole grading system cautioned against it.

16   He discussed this with a professor of psychology who lived next door to him, an extremely imaginative teacher, who said, "Right. Eliminate the whole degree-and-grading system and then you'll get real education."

Engaging the Text

1. The following are some key words from Pirsig's text. In checking their meanings, jot down how they are important to the philosophy of education Pirsig "innovates" (paragraph 1).

    — disparagement (2)
    — creativity (4)
    — drudge (4)
    — insight (5)
    — dutifully (6)
    — hypotheses (7)

2. Though this writing makes us think it is autobiographical, the writer continually refers to himself as "he." We call this writing in the third person. Do you think this technique is effective in this selection? Why or why not?
3. Look through the essay, and note how the paragraphs begin. Each one has some kind of link with the preceding paragraph. Underline the transition words that link the paragraphs. Try to use such links in your own writing.

Engaging the Reader

1. What was the trouble with Phaedrus's students? Were they lazy? Or couldn't they find anything to say?
2. What subject did the "girl with strong-lensed glasses" first choose? Why do you think it wasn't a good topic for a student essay?
3. What suggestions did the teacher make? Were they good ones?
4. What conclusions did the teacher come to about his own writing and teaching methods as a result of this experience?
5. Do you agree with the conclusion expressed in the last line?

The Engaged Writer

1. Write about the front of one building on your college campus.
2. Write about the back of your own thumb.

3. Write about one side of a coin.
4. Explain the idea Pirsig expresses here, that the student was "blocked because she was trying to repeat, in her writing, things she had already heard. . . ." He says that once students "got into the idea of seeing directly for themselves they also saw there was no limit to what they could say. It was a confidence-building assignment too, because what they wrote, even though seemingly trivial, was nevertheless their own thing, not a mimicking of someone else's."

Getting Started

Getting started is perhaps the most difficult part of any paper. If you can get that first paragraph written, you've taken off on the project, and you're on your way.

Your first paragraph should both announce your topic and stimulate your readers' interest. To accomplish these goals consider trying one of the following approaches:

1. Take a firm stand. Put your thesis statement in the first paragraph. Hide nothing; be positive! Example: "Close at hand Kaidab Trading Post showed striking aspects of life and activity" (Zane Grey, "At Kaidab Trading Post"). This calls on the writer to develop the two subtopics, "life" and "activity," and that is what Grey does.
2. Stand back and look at the subject with a brief narration or description to tell a story or set the scene. Example: Gail Godwin's snippets of gossip about famous people who kept diaries (Gail Godwin, "A Diarist on Diarists").
3. Tell an anecdote or a bit of someone's life. Example: Jack McClintock, "Real Trouble Ahead."
4. Explain your own involvement with the subject. Here's where you can bring in your own experience, so you show where you stand and how you got interested in the subject yourself. For example:

   Maybe it's because I, too, was born and raised in a small south Georgia town, but I found sitting down to talk to Rosalynn and Jimmy Carter as comfortable as lazing in a porch swing on a summer afternoon, sipping minty iced tea (Sara Pacher, "The Restoration of Jimmy Carter").

5. Give a startling fact, like "Six months in America and already I was a jailbird" (George and Helen Waite Papashvily, "Yes, Your Honesty").
6. Define terms, or how you, the writer, intend to define them in this paper, especially ideas central to your paper. Example: "Book scribbling . . . is its own art form, a hybrid of two other pleasurable pastimes—reading and writing" (Andrew Cain, "Scribbling").
7. Give some statistics. These won't be dry if they are vitally linked with the subject. Example: "One-third of the population of the South is of the Negro race" (Booker T. Washington, "Cast Down Your Bucket Where You Are").
8. Give two strong before-and-after descriptions for a vivid contrast. Example: "Martin Luther King, Jr., Drive used to be Sylvan Street" (William Least Heat-Moon, "South by Southeast").
9. Give background information or biographical facts on a person featured in the story or essay. Example: N. Scott Momaday, "The End of My Childhood."
10. Ask a question: "What would you do if crime went out of control in your neighborhood and the police proved ineffective?" (The narrative by J. Anthony Lukas, "When a Citizen Fights Back," indirectly poses this question.)
11. Start with a quotation, something really splendid written by someone famous to kick your paper off to a good start. This is not an imitation but a decoration. Example: William Least Heat-Moon quotes Walt Whitman in paragraph 1 of "South by Southeast."
12. Give vivid historical detail: "It is one of those coincidences of history that Alice Roosevelt Longworth, daughter of the grand and unforgettable Teddy and wife of the totally forgettable Nicholas, died the very same week two more books were published about her cousin, Eleanor" (Richard Cohen, "Glittering Alice and Sad Eleanor").
13. Start with humor. It does have a place in many kinds of writing. Example: "Inside a local eatery on a recent night, I noticed a fat brown dot walking along the counter top" (Courtland Milloy, "Those Cocky Roaches").

NOTE: Also try one of these ideas as a conclusion. You don't want a deafening conclusion; a graceful closing is all that is necessary.

Backing Up What You Say

All of us do research every day of our lives. Something as simple as looking up someone's number in the phone book, checking the price of an item in several stores, looking in the regulations to respond to some question on the job, finding out the postage rate for Australia—all of these involve looking for backup to what we say.

1. Support your ideas with facts and reasonable explanations. When you state, as Allan Bloom does, that rock music "provides premature ecstasy," you must develop and explain this idea as he does. You are obliged to explain how rock music does this and why it is so debilitating (if you think so!).
2. Support your ideas by quotations from appropriate sources. But when you quote, keep the following in mind: Writers are possessive about their words. Particularly if they think their writing contains original ideas, writers insist that others credit them whenever using their words or ideas. Failure to do so constitutes plagiarism, which must be strictly avoided.

Documentation guides, or style manuals, have been developed to aid the researcher in this type of writing. An important part of research is using quotations from other writers properly. Following are some simple rules for using a quotation:

Whenever you quote someone, first explain that you are about to do so by saying something like "As Richard Cohen says . . ." or "According to Allan Bloom . . ." You are safe if you never start a sentence of your own with a quotation. Keeping that simple precaution in mind will save you from the temptation of letting your quotations tell the story. Your paper is not a patchwork quilt, snipped together from others' work, but a cake with a few raisins and maybe a few nuts in it. The cake is yours!

After you use the quotation, explain what it means or why it is important to your writing. Say something like, "Cohen means that most people were not affected by the stock market crash; they were always poor."

Every idea borrowed from another writer should be acknowledged. The simplest way to do this is to cite the page numbers where you found the information in parentheses right after you either quote the author or state the idea in your own words:

Quoting: Allan Bloom, in *The Closing of the American Mind,* says that students' "meaningful inner life is with the music" (75).
In Your Words: Students hear a message from Allan Bloom on the pervasiveness of rock music (*The Closing of the American Mind* 75).

Use quotations and ideas from others' work only to back up your own ideas. Otherwise, your essay becomes a cut-and-paste job that often makes no sense. Tell the story yourself.
Use quotations only if the message is extraordinary and told better than you could do it.

We, the people of the United States, in order to form a more perfect union, establish justice, insure domestic tranquillity, provide for the common defense, promote the general welfare, and secure the blessings of liberty to ourselves and our posterity, do ordain and establish this Constitution for the United States of America.

Could you say it any better?
Indent a long quotation (over four lines like the one preceding) without quotation marks. But always introduce every quotation in your own words, like this:

As Thomas Jefferson wrote in the Declaration of Independence "we mutually pledge to each other our Lives, our Fortunes, and our sacred Honor."

At the end of your essay, list any books or articles you used to help you write it. Consult any good handbook for the information you need to include in this list and how to organize it.

Own a college handbook for writers and use it. If you have to do research on the job or in a college class, find out what system or style manual is being used and stick to it. Use punctuation, placement on the page, and other required details carefully and accurately. In these small things, originality is not advised. Save your innovations for your writing and other creative work.
Finally, avoid saying "In my opinion . . ." Make a judgment, not an opinion (often a gut reaction without evidence) on the ideas you have gathered. Don't tell people how to think; instead show them,

as the essays in the Controversies section of this book do. Let the evidence speak.

From Source to Paper with a Sample Documented Essay

A miniresearch paper explains why one student, Maribel Etudiante, chose a topic and how she intends to develop it.

First Steps

1. *Locate your source.* "Funding our Heritage" is part of a paper quoting from the two *Washington Post* letters on pp. 368–369. Be sure you include the complete information on your Xerox copy: author, title of publication, date, and page number.
2. *Prepare bibliography cards.* Note all necessary information as on the sample bibliography cards on p. 367.
3. *Make note cards.* (See examples on p. 369.)
   a. Make as many note cards as needed from each source.
   b. Make notes brief, on one side of card *only*.
   c. Be sure to identify author and page.
   d. Mark all quoted material correctly with quotation marks.

Bibliography Cards:

```
Gingell, Mary.

"Letters to the Editor,"

Washington Post 11 Oct. 1990: A10.
```

```
Korn, Randi and J. Daniel Rogers.

"What Americans Hold Dearest."

"Letters to the Editor," Washington Post 21 Oct.
1990: C6.
```

Letters to the Editor
Reflections on the Federal Deficit

I read with interest your list of federal closings resulting from the budget deadlock [news story, Oct. 8]. The obvious question to me was why the federal government is even in the museum business (Smithsonian Institution, National Gallery of Art), the library business (Library of Congress), the entertainment business (Ford's Theatre, Wolf Trap Farm Park), the road-maintenance business (picnic areas along GW Parkway) and the park business (Rock Creek Park Nature Center, Great Falls Park, Assateague Island National Seashore)?

The services provided to patrons of these and many other federal recreational facili-

ties should be paid for by user fees and contributions, or the facility in question should be shut down. There is nothing so essential about these services that taxpayers should be forced to pay for them.

Better still, why doesn't the federal government sell off these and other business that could be handled just as well, if not better, by the private sector, and stick to its primary function, protecting the lives, liberty and property of American citizens on American soil?

MARY GINGELL
ANNANDALE

Washington Post
11 Oct. 1990: A10.

'What Americans Hold Dearest'

Mary Gingell of Annandale questioned the role of the federal government in funding museums, libraries, national parks and performing arts centers [letter, Oct. 11].

She attacked what Americans hold dearest without realizing the consequences. If the preservation of our heritage and environment is not the responsibility of the federal government and every Ameri-

can, whose responsibility is it? If the cost of maintaining the Smithsonian, Library of Congress or the national parks were not shared by all Americans, not all would be able to afford to visit and use them. Whether you earn $10,000 or $10 million, you can see the Grand Canyon, Old Faithful and any of the museums and parks and know that these American treasures belong to you. These monuments and institutions hold in trust the natural and cultural heritage of all Americans.

Mary Gingell is plotting the demise of our national heritage. By supporting parks and cultural institutions we are committed to ensuring that this national wealth will be there for our generation and the next. They are part of our national spirit and life. Mary Gingell says that these institutions should be sold so that government can adhere to its main task of "protecting the lives, liberty and property of American citizens." Isn't that what the Smithsonian, national parks, National Gallery of Art and the Library of Congress are doing?

RANDI KORN
J. DANIEL ROGERS
ALEXANDRIA

Washington Post
21 Oct. 1990: C6.

Note Cards:

Gingell

She says parks, etc. should be sold so that government can do its main task of "protecting the lives, liberty and property of American citizens." (A10)

Korn

"Mary Gingell is plotting the demise of our national heritage. By supporting parks and cultural institutions we are committed to ensuring that this national wealth will be there for our generation and the next." (C6)

Korn & Rogers call these "American treasures." (C6)

---

4. *Use sources to back up your statements.*
    Several ways of integrating quotations from the articles are illustrated in the sample paper on pp. 370–372.

    a. *Quoting key words*
        In paragraph 1, only two words are quoted as a part of Maribel's own sentence (with citation at the end).

    b. *Using a long quotation*
        In paragraph 2, a long quotation (more than four lines) is indented, without quotation marks, but with page number at the end.

    c. *Using a signal phrase*
        Paragraph 2 includes a quotation as part of Maribel's own sentence with page number in parentheses at the end. In general, you must say you are going to quote something, quote it, and then explain it. Never start a sentence with a quotation unless within it you have an adequate "signal phrase" such as "according to _____," or "as _____ says."

    d. *Using paraphrases and summaries*
        In paragraph 3, Maribel paraphrased her source, putting Gingell's argument in her own words. When you paraphrase or summarize material, be sure to include a citation.

    e. *Using correct punctuation*
        Put a period at the end of a complete sentence, which includes the citation as well, as in paragraph 2. Note that punctuation is handled differently for a long quotation; see the end of paragraph 2 where the citation is *after* the period at the end of the sentence.

[title page]

FUNDING OUR HERITAGE
by Maribel Etudiante

English 101-9331
Dr. King
April 1, 1995

[1] The Washington Post "Letters to the Editor" columns often hold clues to what local citizens think about important topics. One of these issues arises around an interchange of ideas about funding our public areas such as parks, libraries, and museums. Letter writers to the *Post* disagree on who should pay for these "American treasures" as Randi Korn and J. Daniel Rogers put it (C6).

[2] The controversy began in a letter to the *Post* on October 11, 1990, in which Mary Gingell "questioned the role of the federal government in funding museums, libraries, national parks, and performing arts centers" (C6). Korn and Rogers replied to this letter in the October 21 issue by stating:

> Mary Gingell is plotting the demise of our national heritage. By supporting parks and cultural institutions we are committed to ensuring that this national wealth will be there for our generation and the next. (C6)

[3]

Gingell seems to think that museums and parks are lux-
uries that have nothing to do with American life. She
feels that "property" of individual citizens is more
important (A10). This topic intrigued me to the point of
wanting to write my documented paper for this class on
the question of whether, as Gingell indicated, the museums should be sold so the government can accomplish
its main job of "protecting the lives, liberty and property
of American citizens" (A10).   [4]

I plan to investigate how much these facilities cost, and
collect facts from the experts as to their value as cultural heritage. I would also try to find out how many
people visit the national facilities each year and what
their views might be. Though this would greatly enlarge
the topic, I think I should find some information on the
legal and moral justification for the government's role
in funding cultural enterprises such as those listed. The
Preamble of the United States Constitution should provide some backup information.

Works Cited

Gingell, Mary. "Letters to the Editor." <u>Washington Post</u> 11 Oct.

1990: A10.

Korn, Randi and J. Daniel Rogers. "What Americans Hold

Dearest." "Letters to the Editor." <u>Washington Post</u> 21 Oct.

1990: C6.

Notes on Writing Your Documented Paper

1. Write your paper in your own voice. You are in control of your paper; the words should be yours with accurate quotations *within* your sentences.
2. When you read your sources, make sure you are summarizing accurately. In one paper, a student used an article about teenage parental consent for abortions that clearly stated just the opposite from the thesis he held. Read your sources clearly and summarize them accurately.
3. Avoid following the words of the article too closely. A good rule is: if you use more than a single word, put the words in quotation marks. Figures and statistics don't need to be quoted, but they do need to be cited.
4. Each paragraph that contains paraphrases or quotations or statistics should have at least one citation of their source, usually at the end.
5. Each quotation should be introduced by a signal word or phrase. A list of a few of these follows:

   — According to Mary Beard, " . . ."
   — In the words of Ida Mae Holland, " . . ."
   — As scientist Carl Sagan points out, " . . ."
   — W.E.B. Du Bois argues that " . . ."
   — William Least Heat-Moon admits that " . . ."
   — Paul Quinnett reports that " . . ."
   — Marjory Stoneman Douglas stated in an interview that " . . ."

— Richard Cohen offered a challenging argument for this view: " . . ."

6. Do not drop a quotation in a paragraph without introducing it.
7. Avoid paraphrases too close to the original text.
8. Be sure to acknowledge any borrowed ideas.

Checklist

author in signal phrase, page number in parentheses
author and page number in parentheses
include title if not mentioned in signal phrase

RICHARD J. SMITH AND MARK GIBBS

The Internet: Past, Present, and Future

As the introduction to the book *Navigating the Internet* (1994), this chapter defines the term Internet and gives some history. It appears in one of the large number of instruction books spawned by the new communications industry (thus exploding the myth that electronic media will drive out books).

"One does not discover new lands without consenting to lose sight of the shore for a very long time."

ANDRÉ GIDE

What Is the Internet?

Ask for a definition of the Internet and depending on whom you ask, you'll get either a simplistic answer or one that is long, detailed, and mainly incomprehensible.   1

Librarians who use the Internet for researching library catalogs will probably access it through *Gopher*. They see a simple menu-driven interface and they probably rate it all as pretty easy.   2

3   An engineer might talk about *telneting* to this site or *ftping* to that site, neither of which probably makes much sense without demos and some experimentation.

4   You could also ask a technical guru who writes programs for the Internet, but you'd better take two aspirins and lie down afterward.

5   The Internet is hard to sum up, except in generalities, because so many different services and facilities are available. The simplest way to describe the Internet is with one word—communication. To some people, it's just a way to send electronic mail to other people—a pipeline from here to there. To others, the Internet is where they meet their friends, play games, argue, do work, and travel the world.

The Cyberspace of the Internet

6   If you've read William Gibson's excellent science fiction novels, you probably remember his vision of "Cyberspace" and the global computer network called "The Matrix."

7   Cyberspace was the environment where computers and people lived and worked. It was a place with a reality every bit as valid as the everyday, real world. Indeed, for many of its users, Cyberspace *was* the real world!

Navigator's Note: William Gibson's books are dark visions of a wild and dangerous future society suffering from too many people and too much technology. His first book, *Neuromancer*, created a whole new subgenre of science fiction writing that is now called "Cyberpunk." Highly recommended.

---

8   The Internet may well become Gibson's Matrix. Already, the Cyberspace of the Internet is a huge place. Much like the high seas, the Internet physically covers the globe, going from America to Europe, the Near East, the Far East, the Orient, Australia, South America, and back again.

9   It is divided into oceans (subnetworks), with channels (connections between networks), continents (the supercomputers),

big islands (the mainframes and minicomputers), and what the uncharitable might see as floating logs (personal computers). Bobbing around between these landfalls are people, whose software takes them thousands of virtual miles from one port to another.

A big difference between navigating the seas and navigating the 10 Internet is the speed of the journey (though I guess the lack of actual water might also be an issue, but work with me on this).

Around the World in Seconds

Netfarers differ from seafarers in that they travel at thousands of 11 miles per second without leaving their chairs! You can go from California to Australia, pick up a file, copy it to London and Frankfurt, and do it all before your coffee gets cold.

The speed at which you can do things on the Internet is remark- 12 able, not because the Internet is particularly speedy (local area network users will notice that it's not fast in comparison to, say, an Ethernet system), but because it enables you to travel around the world in seconds. It is a technical achievement of incredible dimensions.

The Internet is built from hundreds of smaller networks. It con- 13 nects about a million computers and tens of millions of users. Beyond its components and statistics, how it's used, and which directions it's taking, the really striking thing about the Internet is its constant growth. Today there are 13 systems that help you find files in a catalog of over two million. Next month there may be 30; the month after, 300. The Internet is expanding at an incredible pace.

Marriage, Fame, and Fortune

People have met and married, found fame and fortune, and con- 14 ducted scientific research on the Internet (although usually not at the same time). The Internet was used by Iraq to support their command and control system during the Gulf War (much to the U.S.'s irritation) and has been used for espionage by hackers in the pay of the KGB.

As you start to explore the vast ocean of the Internet, you'll be 15 staggered by what's available. Do you want to find the definitive reference to the genome of the mouse? The Jackson Laboratory at merlot.welch.jhn.edu (don't worry, we'll cover Internet addresses later) has that information in a huge work called *The Encyclopedia of the Mouse Genome.*

16   Do you want to find the locations in Australia where the plant commonly called *aalii (Dodoneae viscosa)*, a native of Hawaii, has been found? Check out the botanical database available through Australian National Botanic Gardens in Australia.

17   The Internet holds data riches beyond your wildest imaginings (unless you have a particularly fertile imagination). It contains only a fraction of the vast mountains of human knowledge, yet it will overwhelm you.

What's Connected to the Internet?

18   So, what's connected to the Internet? In hardware terms, computers of every kind. There are PCs, Macintoshes, UNIX machines, various minicomputers, IBM mainframes, exotic systems not found outside artificial intelligence laboratories, and supercomputers.

19   Working on those computers are programs that handle communications, manage databases, play games, and support electronic mail, along with thousands of other applications.

20   In terms of available services, news feeds provide coverage of the very latest international and national events, daily updates from NASA, weather forecasts, and satellite photographs only 45 minutes old. Library catalogs and databases on botany and particle physics are among the thousands of data collections. Millions of files are available—files of useful data and files of obscure data that someone, somewhere, thinks are important. Programs of every sort, for most types of computers, can be found. Many are free, and many come with source code.

21   Finally, there are people—tens of millions of them, many of whom use the Internet every day. Some never seem to be anywhere else but on the Internet!

Who Uses the Internet?

22   Who are these people on the Internet? People of all types: librarians, teachers, scientists, engineers, students (as young as five), along with commercial organizations, universities, and governments. At one time there was even a Coca-Cola machine.

The lure of the Internet is communication and access. If you 23
want to exchange ideas and develop knowledge, the Internet is the
place to do it.

For example, when the discovery of cold fusion (now dis- 24
proved) was announced in 1991, scientists couldn't wait for the
normal process of peer review and validation to explore the idea.
Their solution? Conferences on the Internet. What was, in effect,
an around-the-clock discussion developed; as new information
became available, the participants analyzed it. This was a completely new way of interacting, and those involved found it to be
invaluable.

Access to knowledge is the other great lure. Librarians—whose 25
job it is to find documents, books, and other materials—share their
catalogs through the Internet. Indeed, some of the Internet's most
enthusiastic users are librarians. Catalogs for the French National
Institute for Electronic Research, the Library of Congress, and classical Chinese literature can all be found on the Internet.

Engaging the Text

1. Notice the short, one-or-two sentence paragraphs, the explana- [13]
   tory subheadings—all designed to make the explanation clear.
2. Smith and Gibbs make a traditional beginning of their chapter—employ an epigraph, a quotation from another writer to
   start their own discussion. Explain the quotation from André
   Gide; how does it apply to a discussion of the Internet?

Engaging the Reader

1. True to the pop-up menu familiar to computer users, Smith
   and Gibbs insert a box: Navigator's Note. Is this useful to you?
2. Though this is a technical manual, Smith and Gibbs also use a [14]
   device familiar to readers of literature: metaphors. Throughout, they
   compare space, or "cyberspace" to an ocean and traveling around
   it as "navigating." Find examples of their use of metaphor in the
   text. Is this a useful device for understanding the technology?

The Engaged Writer

[15]

1. Explain a complex process or system which is a part of your
   work, art, recreation, or other sets of knowledge in the same
   kinds of terms Smith and Gibbs do.

2. Students in medical fields have already stopped buying hard copies of textbooks. Their readings are downloaded off Internet and CD-ROMs. Write a paper on what use you would make of the Internet; or if you already do use it, how you use it in your work, your studies, or your leisure.

3. Are you on Internet? My E-Mail address is ak93@umail.umd.edu or ak1@pgstumail.pg.cc.md.us. If you get this message, send me one telling me how you have used this book and what you like or want changed about it in a future edition.

WordPerfect®, Novell Applications Group: Grammatik®

WordPerfect® is a popular word processing software that, among other things, lets the writer check spelling and grammar, and check for stylistic flaws in writing, in a program called "Grammatik®." This is a great boon for writers, liberating them from many low order concerns in writing and allowing them to concentrate on organization, content, and style. The enclosed portion of the Reference Manual for *WordPerfect Version 6.1 (Windows) with Grammatik 6.0a* uses a different style of writing from the paragraphs and essay form of the other selections in *The Engaging Reader*; it uses lists, bullets, and diagrams to make each step clear. Updates appear often for this and other word processing software. This one is the latest as we go to press, though a new version is in the works. This present version, besides proofreading your writing for grammar and style errors and enabling you to choose a checking style, continues with more helps not included here: checking parts of speech and giving statistics on sentence length, complexity, readability, and use of passive voice. It also allows you to add a supplementary dictionary with lists of words you often misspell and words you want to skip.

Grammatik

Use Grammatik to proofread documents, parts of documents, and text entry boxes for grammar and style errors. You can choose the checking style that's best for your writing or create a customized checking style. You can view statistics that can help you make your writing easier to understand.

Starting Grammatik

1. Open a document, then choose **Grammatik** from the **Tools** menu.

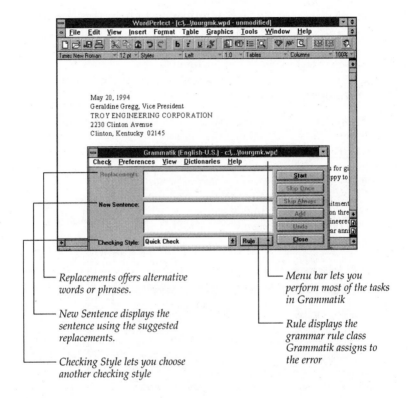

Replacements offers alternative words or phrases.

New Sentence displays the sentence using the suggested replacements.

Checking Style lets you choose another checking style

Menu bar lets you perform most of the tasks in Grammatik

Rule displays the grammar rule class Grammatik assigns to the error

2. If you want, choose one of the following menus, then select the menu item you want to use.

Menu	Lets you
Check	Check a sentence, a paragraph, a document, or a selected portion of a document.
Preferences	Edit a checking style or set environment preferences.

Menu	Lets you
View	Display parts of speech, the parse tree, or statistics.
Dictionaries	Select, add, and modify supplementary dictionaries.
Help	Get information to help you use Grammatik and improve your writing.

3. Choose **Start** to check the document.

Proofreading a Document

When you start checking a document, Grammatik searches for, then highlights, the first error it finds.

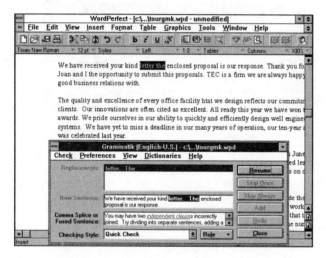

Replacing Incorrect Words

Some writing problems can be corrected instantly by using a replacement word or phrase in the Replacements text box.

1. Select the replacement word or phrase you want, then choose **Replace**.

If none of the suggested replacements are appropriate, you can edit the text manually.

To edit text manually,

1. Place the insertion point in the document window, then click once.
2. Type the new text.

Rechecking Text
Grammatik automatically rechecks from the beginning of any sentence in which errors were detected. If you edit text manually, you can recheck from where you place the insertion point in the document window, including new sentences you've added.

1. Place the insertion point in the text, then choose **Resume**.

Ignoring a Problem
In some cases, you may want to ignore the Grammatik advice. Perhaps a false error was reported, or you don't agree with the advice. Choose one of the following options to override the Grammatik advice.

Option	*Lets you*
Skip Once	Ignore the highlighted phrase for this occurrence only.
Skip Always	Ignore the highlighted phrase for the rest of the proofreading.

Using the Rule Pop-up Menu
While you are proofreading, you can turn rules on or off, mark a problem, write an error to a file, and get grammar help from the Rule pop-up menu.
To use the Rule pop-up menu,

1. Open a document and start proofreading.
2. Click the **Rule** pop-up menu, then select the option you need. The following table describes each option.

Option	*Lets you*
Turn Off	Ignore all errors associated with a specific rule class for this proofreading session.

Option	*Lets you*
Turn On	If you've turned off rules during the proof-reading session, you can turn them back on. Select the rule to turn on from the list box.
Save Rules	Save the rules you've turned off as a new checking style.
Mark	Mark a problem you want to return to later.
Help	See the online Grammar and Writing Help for the current rule class.
Write Error	Write the current error to a file. Grammatik uses the current filename with a .ERR extension.

Choosing a Checking Style

Grammatik uses different sets of proofreading criteria based on different kinds of writing.
To choose a checking style for the current document,

1   Choose a style from the Checking Style drop-down list.

To choose a checking style for all documents,

1. Choose **Checking Styles** from the **Preferences** menu, select the style you want, then choose **Select**.

Editing a Checking Style

If your work requires a special checking style that is not covered by the Grammatik predefined styles, you can create your own style by changing the default settings for rule classes, thresholds, and formality level.

1. Choose **Checking Styles** from the **Preferences** menu.
2. Choose the checking style closest to your planned custom style, then choose **Edit**.
3. Select or deselect the rules you want to turn on or off.
   If you need information about a rule class, click the question mark (?) button.
4. Type new values in the Maximum Allowed text boxes, if you want. See *Changing the Maximum Allowed Values* later in this section for more information.

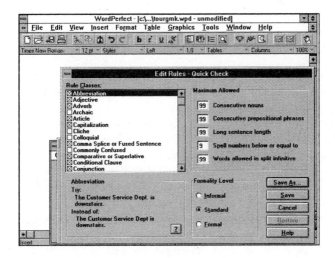

5. If you want to change the formality level, select a new level. See *Changing the Formality Level* later in this section for more information.

6. Choose **Save**. An asterisk (*) appears beside the modified checking style name.

   or

   Choose **Save As**, then type a new name for your checking style.

Restoring Checking Style Settings

When you choose Save after editing a checking style, the original settings for the checking style are altered for your custom style. If you decide later that you want to return to the original settings, use Restore.

1. Choose **Checking Styles** from the **Preferences** menu.
2. Select a checking style with an asterisk (*), then choose **Edit**.
3. Choose **Restore**, then choose **Save**. The asterisk disappears.

Changing the Maximum Allowed Values

Changing the maximum allowed values is another way to customize a checking style. The table below describes the different values.

Set this value	*To do this*
Consecutive nouns	Grammatik flags this many or more successive nouns.
Consecutive prepositional phrases	Grammatik flags this many or more successive prepositional phrases.
Long sentence length	Grammatik flags sentences containing this many or more words.
Spell numbers below or equal to	Grammatik flags numbers below or equal to this number that are not spelled out (e.g., nine instead of 9).
Words allowed in split infinitive	Grammatik flags this many or more words coming between "to" and its verb (e.g., "to go" versus "to boldly go").

To change a maximum allowed setting,

1. Choose **Checking Styles** from the **Preferences** menu.
2. Select a checking style, then choose **Edit**.
3. Type new values in the Maximum Allowed text boxes.
4. Choose **Save** to use the original checking style name. An asterisk (*) appears.
   or
   Choose **Save As**, then type a new name for the checking style.

Changing the Formality Level
Because there are no hard and fast rules about levels of formality, you can adjust this setting for your specific audience and style.

If you plan to use many colloquial expressions in your document, choose *Informal*. If you plan to write in moderate, everyday language, choose **Standard**. If you want your writing to be as polished as possible, choose **Formal.**

To change formality.

1. Choose **Checking Styles** from the **Preferences** menu.
2. Select a checking style, then choose **Edit**.
3. Select the formality level you want.

4. Choose **Save** to use the original checking style name. An asterisk (*) appears.
   or
   Choose **Save As**, then type a new name for the checking style.

Changing Preferences
You can customize the way Grammatik works through the Preferences menu.

1. Choose **Environment** from the **Preferences** menu.
2. Select the options you want.

Engaging the Text

1. Notice the clear explanations, the diagrams of the way the material appears on the computer screen, and the ways the method can be made more flexible (changing the checking style or creating a customized writing style).
2. If you or your classmates have used similar grammar checkers, talk over with them whether these programs have helped improved your writing. If you have not used them, do you think they would help?

The Engaged Writer

1. If you have this program available, apply it to a piece of your writing, perhaps something you have done for this class. When Grammatik has finished proofreading your document, study the results. Does it show a pattern, for example of overuse of passive voice? Especially persistent spelling errors? Subject/verb agreement? If it does, write an analysis of your writing in paragraph form, including the information Grammatik gives you. Conclude with an appraisal of how useful this information will be for you.
2. After you do topic 1, decide how you would like to change Grammatik to meet your needs for the following writing situations:

   A letter to your best friend
   A paper for the class you are now in
   An instruction booklet for a piece of equipment you use on your job
   A news article for your college paper

An invitation to a gathering to mark a holiday
A speech for a political gathering—rally, caucus, or fund-raiser
An application letter for a prestigious job or promotion '

3. Write an instruction booklet for a piece of equipment or a process you use on your job, in the style of the Grammatik section above. You may use diagrams as well as lists and process steps, if that is appropriate.

A Guide for Composition Revision

Most writing assignments start with the assumption that you attend class to improve reading comprehension and writing skills rather than to show off what you already know. Therefore all students, of whatever level of skill, can improve and should not expect to do finished work in a first draft. The paper hardly exists (including this one) that hits perfection immediately—or ever! In this section, I would like to list a few strategies to help you rewrite or revise papers—even work that "passes" or meets requirements. So, with draft paper in hand, follow these steps toward a better paper:

1. List all the subjects in each paragraph on a piece of paper. If any of the subjects in one paragraph stray from the main idea or topic sentence of that paragraph, eliminate them or create a separate paragraph for them.
2. Underline all the verbs in the piece of writing. If more than half of them are forms of the verb "to be" ("is," "was," "are" or passive voice: "my mother was kissed by me"), search for more active verbs for as many of them as you can. Revise whole sentences if you need to. Lively verbs make papers vibrate and people move! Say it positively: "I kissed my mother."
3. Count the words in each sentence. Variety being the spice of many activities, sentence length should not be uniform. Decide what the effect of the sentence should be. If your tone is terse and tough, short sentences do well. If that is not the case, and you have too many short or "kernel" sentences (subject—verb—object), try combining them, subordinating the least important parts to the important ideas (as this sentence does).

4. Check transitions between paragraphs and between sentences within paragraphs. Each sentence should somehow link to the following sentence, as each paragraph should flow smoothly into the one following it. The object of writing an essay is to move the reader along by smooth stages so that she ends up agreeing with you at the end of the essay, or a least accepting what you say because she can follow all your steps. Nothing is more boring to the reader, though, than a listing of "First . . . second . . .in conclusion." Instead, use variety in linking sentences and paragraphs by repeating key words or a variation of them or by using transitional words and phrases.

5. Look through your paper and see if you have used many abstract nouns. For example, a convicted rapist, imprisoned on his second offense because he failed to appear for trial in a previous arrest, wrote to the judge asking to be freed: "As for my being considered a risk, well, your honor, there's no threat to this extent, for I am a God-fearing man and my ultimate values are spiritual, which includes human dignity, liberty, opportunity and equal rights as well as justice." The judge, unmoved, did not release him. Could it have been all those empty abstractions?

6. Finally, read through your paper as if for the first time. Find some spots where detail seems thin and add some to make the picture more vivid to your readers. You might want to add an incident or a concrete example (as I just did with the letter from the rapist) to illustrate your point.

Writing "Re-Vision"

These ideas will certainly improve your paper and make it look more like a finished product. But there is more to come. You really need to look at your paper from a different angle. In addition to these mechanical ways of finetuning your paper into a smooth production, comes true re-visioning—looking at your paper through new eyes.

Possibly this different angle will be through the eyes of your writing group. Ask the members of your writing group specific questions such as:

What do you see as my strongest argument?
Have I placed it in the right spot to give it full advantage?
What seems to be my thesis?

The keys to unlock the deadness or dullness of a paper often are in its structure: make an outline of what you have written and see if the outline makes sense.

> Does it have a particular organization such as chronological (according to time), spacial (where it is placed), logical (according to its importance, ascending or descending)?
> Does it skip around from point to point or does it move smoothly along its logical path?
> Does it avoid illogical appeals to the emotions?
> Are you vacillating—arguing for the other side so that it's not clear where you stand?
> Does it develop ideas—show rather than tell?

Then again, your revision, instead of occurring in your writing group, might be done alone. Ask yourself such questions as:

> How do I feel about this today, as opposed to yesterday, or last week, when I wrote the first draft?
> Have I read or heard something that gives me a new angle on this subject: a newspaper article, a television program, a conversation with a friend, an idea from another class?

Rough up your paper a little, turn it inside out like a glove, and see if you still like it. Bring it to your college Writing Center for some expert vetting. Your Writing Center won't write it for you, but it can give advice on how to improve it.

Concluding: How to End What You Write

Too many writers become anxious about concluding what they are writing. They feel that they must beat the drum, stand at the barricades, and play "Taps" over a solemn conclusion to their work. Or they begin with the deadly words, "In conclusion, it is my opinion . . ." to which the silent response of the reader is "So what?"

In your paper you may have been making a point and leading up to a certain interpretation of the facts you present. You may rightly think, as you reach the end, that repeating these points once more will bore your reader. In that case, don't. Here are some good ways to make a graceful ending to a paper after you've stated the main points:

1. Select another event illustrating the main point you have made, and end with that in a brief story (see Roger Rosenblatt, "The Quality of Mercy Killing").
2. Put your paper aside for some hours or days (if the deadline has not yet arrived—and it's a good idea to write ahead of deadlines). Then reread it as if someone else had written it. You will then see, as if inspired, which important idea you should stress in your summary.
3. Make your ending short and brisk; do not dwell on it. Leave your reader, as at a good meal, wanting more (see Jeff Lowe, "On the Edge").
4. The thunderously grand ending will turn off most readers. Only promise what you can deliver. You are not an expert—yet—on your subject, and pretending to be one loses the reader's interest.
5. Preaching to the reader also risks losing your credibility and the reader's interest. You will turn off otherwise interested readers if you insult them by telling them what they ought to think.
6. This paper is just one of many you are going to write so you don't need to say it all in one paper. Be graceful in your language and moderate in your thought. An example of a good conclusion is shown in the last two sentences of Carl Sagan's essay "The Warming of the World": "The solution to these problems requires a perspective that embraces the planet and the future. We are all in this greenhouse together."
7. Also try one of the ideas from the list of ways of "Getting Started" as a conclusion. You don't want a deafening conclusion to your essay; a graceful closing is all that is necessary.

8. Try to have your last sentence sound like music. This perhaps is a strange way to put it, but during the eighteenth century, English writers used rhythmic devices, much like those in poetry, for particularly important sentences, like the first one or the final one. Look at the stirring rhythm of the Preamble to the Constitution of the United States for an example of prose with rhythm and dignity. Try to put that rhythm and dignity into your best, most important work.

Glossary of Terms

Alliteration   Several words beginning with the same sound, in poetry or sometimes in prose. Example: Ray Bradbury, in "The Impulse to Write" says "he might as well be out picking peaches or digging ditches."

Allusion   Referring to something familiar to most readers to make the discussion richer. Literary allusions are often to the Bible or to Shakespeare. Example: Roger Rosenblatt's, "The Quality of Mercy Killing" alludes to a speech in Shakespeare's *The Merchant of Venice.*

Argumentative Writing   Writing to persuade the reader to adopt the writer's view or judgment. See Part Five, "Controversies," for examples.

Autobiography   A life story written by the person who has lived it. Examples are the essays by Russell Baker (*Growing Up*), Edith Wharton ("A First Word"), and Amiri Baraka (*The Autobiography of LeRoi Jones*).

Classification   Dividing ideas or items in categories or types so you can discuss or write about each larger classification rather than each item separately. An assignment on this follows Courtland Milloy's "Those Cocky Roaches."

Clichés   Phrases or sayings that were once clever and new but are now old as the hills and to be avoided like the plague.

Documentation   Backing up facts and ideas that you could not know without reading about them in another source; crediting that source. See "Backing Up What You Say."

Ecology   Science dealing with the relationships of organisms and their environment; it has been extended to the study of people and the effects of their crowding on this planet. See Carl Sagan, "The Warming of the World."

Etymology   Derivation of words; what languages they originally came from. See "Looking Up Words in a Dictionary."

Expository   Writing that shows or tells something; information and fact rather than imagination and fiction. This glossary is expository.

Gerund   A noun made from a verb, out of the present participle form (running, jumping, dancing) and used as a subject or object of a sentence: "Scribbling is fun."

Image   Words that form a picture in the reader's mind; an image appeals to the senses of sight, taste, touch, even smell. Poetry is full of these images.

Inflected Forms   The different spellings of words to indicate a different use, for example: degree (big, bigger, biggest); number (beef, beeves), time (is, was). The dictionary lists these.

Interview   A planned conversation between two people with the aim of finding out information or discussing an event, or learning more about that person's ideas, history, or background. An interview may often be taped; the interviewer needs to prepare questions carefully. Examples: Endesha Ida Mae Holland ("Granny Midwives"), and Sara Pacher, "The Restoration of Jimmy Carter."

Journal   A chronicle of events (from French, *jour* = day) written in daily; not the intimate details of a diary but reflections on events, reading, travel, and ideas. Students often keep journals of their reading assignments and reactions to them as a source for future writing assignments.

Metaphor   A specific object compared to another thing, usually an idea or concept, without using the words "like" or "as." Booker T. Washington compares the relationship of blacks and whites to the fingers on the hand ("Cast Down Your Bucket Where You Are").

Narrator   The person telling the story, the "I." In a fiction story, the narrator might be, but is not necessarily, the writer. For example, Amy Tan's story "Scar" is told from the point of view of one of the women in the book.

Parable   A simple story, often dealing with basic agricultural life-styles, that has broader implications. Each element of the story illustrates an ethical or religious principle. Booker T. Washington uses the parable of the water bucket to explain his attitude toward future black development ("Cast Down Your Bucket Where You Are").

Paradox   An apparent contradiction understandable by intuition; for example, "people talking without speaking, people hearing without listening" (Paul Simon, "The Sound of Silence").

Paragraph Coherence   Making a paragraph hang together and discussing one subject without wandering off the point.

Participles parts of a verb used with auxiliaries (*have, had, is, was*); listed in the dictionary after the derivation, generally ending in -*ing* (present), -*ed* (past).

Personification Giving human qualities to a nonhuman object. Carl Sandburg personifies aspects of his city in the poem *Chicago.*

Plagiarism Using someone else's words or ideas without credit; more seriously, passing off an entire piece of work by someone else as one's own. See the discussion in "Backing Up What You Say."

Point of View Referring to the vantage point of the writer, not to the life of the author or the opinion of the reader. A first person narrative uses the first person "I" as Elinore Pruitt Stewart did in her *Letters of a Woman Homesteader.* Usually in essays, editorials, and reports, writers use the impersonal third person (he, she, they). Writers need to be consistent in point of view throughout a piece of writing.

Pun A play on words, so that words have a double meaning. The title of Sara Pacher's "The Restoration of Jimmy Carter" plays with the idea that both the ex-president and the old houses are being restored.

Realism Everyday speech, ordinary people, simple emotions in fiction, rather than fantastic imaginings. A good example is George Moore's "A Kitchen Maid"—an ordinary girl in an ordinary job and in a common predicament.

Satire Making fun of something with the idea of improving it, or sometimes just for the fun of it. Some of the items in Michael Dobbs's "The ABCs of the USA" use satire.

Sexist Language Excluding one gender. Examples: using separate words for female roles ("poetess"); using "he" or "him" to include women; generally casting one sex in an inferior role (making the nurse always female and the doctor male). Solution: use gender-neutral words ("police officer," "poet"); alternate gender roles.

Signal Phrase A phrase used to introduce a quotation by someone else. It should always be used to signal the reader that you are about to use someone else's words.

Summary Condensing the words of another into a short account that includes all the important ideas without copying the writer's exact words (for further information, see "Writing a Summary of What You Read")

Symbolism Using a specific object to represent an idea or concept: for example, the flag stands for America; a swastika for Nazism; an arrow for a direction; a gravestone for death. The object, though, also exists as itself. Example: the parade float covered with flags and graves on which the helpless, crippled Russell is placed in "Most-Decorated Hero," Louise Erdrich.

Synonym   A word that means the same as another word. A list of these often appears at the end of the definitions in the dictionary.

Tense   The time sense of a verb: past, present, or future: "I am, I was, I will be, I have been, I will have been, I would have been."

Thesis   The subject of a piece of writing plus an attitude toward that subject for example,

"Prayer   should (or should not) be allowed in schools."
(subject)   (attitude)

Topic Sentence   The main idea of a paragraph, supported by subtopics within that paragraph.

Transitions   Ways to link ideas, sentences, or paragraphs. Needed for smooth and effective writing (see list of transitional words and other ways of making smooth transitions following Paul Quinnett's "Enough of Roads").

Values   Basic worth, the ideas we live by and think worthwhile. Many essays in this book talk about values.

Acknowledgments

Andrew, Cain, "Scribbling," *Page News & Courier* (Luray, VA) 17 Jan. 1985: 2. Reprinted by permission.

Ray Bradbury, "The Impulse to Write." From *Zen and the Art of Writing* by Ray Bradbury. Reprinted by permission of Don Congdon Associates, Inc. Copyright © 1989 by Ray Bradbury.

Gail Godwin, "A Diarist on Diarists," *Antaeus* magazine. Reprinted by permission of the author.

Patricia Cornwell, "In Cold Blood," *Washington Post Book World*, 31 July 1994. Copyright © 1994, Washington Post Writers Group. Reprinted with permission.

From Walt Whitman, "Song of Myself," *Leaves of Grass*, Comprehensive Reader's Edition, ed. Harold W. Blodgett and Sculley Bradley (New York: New York University Press, 1965).

Robert Grudin, "A Dog." Reprinted by permission of Random House, Inc. from *BOOK: A Novel* by Robert Grudin. Copyright 1992 by Robert Grudin.

Amy Tan, "Scar." Reprinted by permission of The Putnam Publishing Group from *The Joy Luck Club* by Amy Tan. Copyright © 1989 by Amy Tan.

Jack McClintock, "Real Trouble Ahead," *New York Times Magazine* (About Men column), 9 Aug. 1987. Copyright © 1987 by The New York Times Company. Reprinted by permission.

George Moore, "A Kitchen Maid," *Esther Waters* (London: Walter Scott, 1894).

From Russell Baker, *Growing Up* (New York: Congdon & Weed, 1982): 151–157. Reprinted by permission.

Richard Rodriguez, "The Achievement of Desire." From *Hunger of Mem-*

ory by Richard Rodriguez. Copyright © 1982 by Richard Rodriguez. Reprinted by permission of David R. Godine, Publisher.

From *There Are No Children Here: The Story of Two . . .* by Alex Kotlowitz. Copyright © 1991 by Alex Kotlowitz; Photographs © 1991 by Kevin Horan. Used by permission of Doubleday, a division of Bantam Doubleday Dell Publishing Group, Inc.

Julia Flynn Siler, "Growing Up Poor—and Scared to Death." Reprinted from April 22, 1991 issue of *Business Week* by special permission, copyright © 1991 by McGraw-Hill, Inc.

Michael Dobbs, "The ABCs of the U.S.A.: Americana, Seen with European Eyes," *Washington Post* 21 June 1987: F1. Reprinted by permission.

Richard Cohen, "Glittering Alice and Sad Eleanor," *Washington Post* 4 Feb. 1980: C1–3. Copyright © 1980, Washington Post Writers Group. Reprinted by permission.

Louise Erdrich, "Most-Decorated Hero." From *The Beet Queen* by Louise Erdrich. Copyright © 1986 by Louise Erdrich. Reprinted by permission of Henry Holt and Company, Inc.

From "South by Southeast," Chapter 4 (pp. 97–99), from *Blue Highways: A Journey Into America* by William Least Heat-Moon. Copyright © 1982 by William Least Heat-Moon. By Permission of Little, Brown, and Company.

Sue Hubbell, "On the Road: A City of the Mind." *Time* 3 June 1985: 12–13. Copyright 1985 Time Warner Inc. Reprinted by permission.

Donald P. Baker, "Graduation in the Mountains," *Washington Post* 15 June 1986: C8. Reprinted by permission.

Excerpt from Amiri Baraka, *The Autobiography of LeRoi Jones* (New York: Freundlich Books, 1984). Reprinted by permission of Sterling Lord Literistic, Inc. Copyright © 1984 by Amiri Baraka.

Aldo Leopold, "Red Lanterns." From *A Sand County Almanac: And Sketches Here and There* by Aldo Leopold. Copyright © 1949, 1977 by Oxford University Press, Inc. Reprinted by permission.

C. L. Rawlins, "Deep in Truth's Country." Reprinted by permission from the Sept.–Oct. 1991 issue of *Sierra* magazine.

Courtland Milloy, "Those Cocky Roaches," *Washington Post* 31 March 1985: B3. Reprinted by permission.

"The Fish" from *The Complete Poems 1927–1979* by Elizabeth Bishop. Copyright © 1979, 1983 by Alice Helen Methfessel. Reprinted by permission of Farrar, Straus and Giroux, Inc.

Joan Ackermann-Blount, "In New Mexico: A Family Lives in Its Own World," *Time* 5 Oct. 1987: 12–13. Copyright 1987 Time Warner Inc. Reprinted by permission.

Claudia Tate, "Audre Lorde." *Black Women Writers at Work* edited by Claudia Tate. Copyright © 1983 by Claudia Tate. Reprinted by permission of The Continuum Publishing Company.

George and Helen Waite Papashvily, "Yes, Your Honesty," *Anything Can Happen* (New York: Harper & Row, 1945). Copyright © Helen Waite Papashvily. Reprinted by permission.

Zora Neale Hurston, "Work." Excerpt from *Mules and Men* by Zora Neale Hurston. Copyright 1935 by Zora Neale Hurston. Copyright renewed 1963 by John C. Hurston and Joel Hurston. Reprinted by permission of HarperCollins Publishers.

Lee Smith, "The Face of Rural Poverty." Reprinted by permission from *Fortune* magazine; © 1990 The Time Inc. Magazine Company. All rights reserved.

Claire Safran, "Hidden Lessons: Do Little Boys Get a Better Education Than Little Girls?" Reprinted with permission from *Parade*, copyright © 1983, and with permission of the author.

From Sara Pacher, "The Restoration of Jimmy Carter: From President to Chairman of the Boards." Reprinted with permission from *Mother Earth News* magazine. Copyright © 1987 (Sussex Publishers, Inc.).

Carolyn Heilbrun, "Naming a New Rite of Passage." Reprinted by permission of Carolyn Heilbrun. Copyright © 1991 by Carolyn Heilbrun. Originally appeared in the summer 1991 issue of *Smith Alumnae Quarterly*.

Leslie Marmon Silko, "The Man to Send Rain Clouds" Copyright © 1981 by Leslie Marmon Silko. Reprinted from *Storyteller* by Leslie Marmon Silko, published by Seaver Books, New York, NY.

The Jicarilla Apache, "How the Apaches Got Clay." Reproduced by permission of American Folklore Society from *Memoirs of the American Folklore Society* 31, 1938. Not for further reproduction.

Endesha Ida Mae Holland, "Granny Midwives." *MS.* June 1987: 48–51. Reprinted by permission.

Margaret Spillane, "From the Mississippi Delta." This article is reprinted from *The Nation* magazine/The Nation Company, Inc., © 1991.

Mark Holston, "Rhythm Four Strings," *Américas*, Volume 43, Number 1 (1991). Reprinted from *Américas*, a bimonthly magazine published by the General Secretariat of the Organization of American States in English and Spanish.

Portia K. Maultsby, "African Cultural Traditions in the Blues," *Maryland Humanities*, February, 1994. Reprinted by permission of the author.

Allan Bloom, "Is Rock Music Rotting Our Kids' Minds?" From *The Closing of the American Mind*. Copyright © 1987 by Allan Bloom. Reprinted by permission of Simon & Schuster.

From Polingaysi Qoyawayma. *No Turning Back* (Albuquerque, NM: University of New Mexico Press, 1964). Reprinted by permission.

From *Zlata's Diary* by Zlata Filipović. Translation copyright © 1994 Editions Robert Laffont/Fixot. Used by permission of Viking Penguin, a division of Penguin Books USA Inc.

From Zane Grey, "At Kaidab Trading Post," *The Vanishing American* (New York: Harper & Row, 1922) 37–42. Copyright © by Loren Grey. Reprinted by permission.

"Chicago" from *Chicago Poems* by Carl Sandburg, copyright 1916 by Holt, Rinehart and Winston, Inc. and renewed 1944 by Carl Sandburg, reprinted by permission of Harcourt Brace Jovanovich, Inc.

From Grace Cangialosi, "Wild Willie," from *A Kairos Winter* (The Servant Leadership School 1994). Copyright 1994 by Grace Cangialosi. Reprinted by permission of the author.

Michael Satchell, "How People Survive on Leftovers," *Parade* 10 Feb. 1985. Reprinted with permission from *Parade*, copyright © 1985.

Sara Rimer, "At a Welfare Hotel, Mothers Find Support in Weekly Talks," *New York Times* 3 Feb. 1986. Copyright © 1986 by The New York Times Company. Reprinted by permission.

Carl Sagan, "The Warming of the World." First published in *Parade*. Copyright © 1985 by Carl Sagan. All rights reserved. Reprinted by permission of the author.

Paul Quinnett, "Enough of Roads," *Audubon* 4 July 1985: 18–21. Reprinted from *Audubon*, the magazine of the National Audubon Society, copyright © 1985.

Melody Ermachild Chavis, "Street Trees." Reprinted with permission from the July/August 1994 issue of *Sierra* magazine and the author.

Ed Malles, "Hallowed Ground," *Southern Living*, June 1994. Copyright © 1994 Southern Living, Inc. Reprinted by permission.

Booker T. Washington, "Cast Down Your Bucket Where You Are: The Atlanta Exposition Address," *Up From Slavery* (New York: Doubleday, Page and Company, 1901).

W. E. B. Du Bois, "Response to Mr. Washington," *The Souls of Black Folk: Essays and Sketches* (1903). Reprints WSP, 1970.

Martin Luther King, Jr. "I Have a Dream," *Negro History Bulletin* 21, May 1968. Reprinted by arrangement with The Heirs to the Estate of Martin Luther King, Jr., c/o Joan Daves Agency as agent for the proprietor. Copyright © 1963 by Martin Luther King, Jr., copyright renewed 1991 by Coretta Scott King.

Henry Louis Gates, Jr. "The Last Mill Picnic." From *Colored People* by Henry Louis Gates, Jr. Copyright © 1994 by Henry Louis Gates, Jr. Reprinted by permission of Alfred A. Knopf Inc.

Roger Rosenblatt, "The Quality of Mercy Killing" *Time* 26 Aug. 1985: 74. Copyright 1985 Time Warner Inc. Reprinted by permission.

Letters Responding to "The Quality of Mercy Killing," *Time* 16 Sept. 1985: 15. Copyright 1985 Time Warner Inc. Reprinted by permission.

N. Scott Momaday, "The End of My Childhood," *The Names* (New York: Harper & Row, 1976). Reprinted by permission.

Index